C0-AVI-868

JOHN MILTON
AMONG THE POLYGAMOPHILES

JOHN MILTON AMONG THE POLYGAMOPHILES

Leo Miller

LOEWENTHAL PRESS
NEW YORK

LIBRARY OF CONGRESS CATALOG CARD NUMBER: 73-89792

ISBN 0-914382-00-4

Printed in the United States of America

LOEWENTHAL PRESS

P.O. Box 1107

New York, N. Y. 10009

To my dear darling beloved wife Diana
to whom I am married twice most monogamously
who patiently accompanied me
through all the rare book collections
although she thoroughly disagrees
with everyone in the book except Kathy Luther

Contents

Foreword

Dear Reader:

This book was originally begun, long ago, as a short footnote aiming to clarify the case for the legality of polygamy composed by John Milton. Like many other studies beginning in Milton's works, it refused to stay put in one pigeonhole.

Inevitably, therefore, this book elects to ignore the taboos which restrict scholarly studies done only by paid specialists for the attention only of other paid specialists. Let those who so choose zealously guard their private patches, along with the privilege to ignore any other field of knowledge. Laymen, amateurs, and professionals, all and sundry, are invited to join in exploring these underground streams in the dark and winding caverns of the human mind, pushing aside all academic barriers, those departmental divisions into fragmented "subjects" which have replaced a full and generous education for our culturally deprived university graduates.

So please do not be disturbed if the book seems to wander from "English Literature, Seventeenth Century" into "Social History of Germany," or meander into "Law of Marriage in Principle and Practice," grazing past "Reformation Dogmatics" and "Catholic Theology," straying into "Sociology of the Family," making side excursions into "Bibliography and Library Science," with divers adventures along the way.

So be it. So this book is not a morose monograph. It is a story, or an interconnected series of stories, of passions and of politics, of sublime poets and of powerful princes and of common people, and of famous preachers who counselled them or condemned them, and sometimes married them, with one eye on the Holy Book and one eye on the main chance.

So we find ourselves recalling from the dead a legion of poor forgotten souls, quixotic anti-heroes like Johan Leyser and Lorenz Beger, and their frantic opponents. Illustrious names, Leibnitz, Pufendorf, here turn up in unfamiliar circumstances, and so do old friends, Jonathan Swift, Cyrano de Bergerac, William Blake, Lucas Cranach, many more. The history of ideas, usually approached from the viewpoint of great orthodox, liberating or progressive thought, is here taken into strange waters; but good navigators need to know not only the deep channels but the mud flats, the quicksands and the shoals as well.

So come along; and please be amused. Please smile at these follies of men fumbling with their fates in a world beyond their control, smile with compassion, and with indulgence. Let not scholarship in the humanities forget humanity.

And please do not be alarmed by the inclusion of passages in several languages. Every one is translated into English or explained immediately. The original texts are included so that the evidence is readily available to you, for you should not believe anything until you have the proof. These translations have all been done fresh or revised for this book, for uniformity in style, and with preference for precision, a quality not always found in translation. In rendering some doggerel verse, I have taken more liberties.

For smoother reading, a great deal of matter is reserved into notes at the end. Footnotes, like attics, are out of style, but like well kept attics in older houses, they can provide a deal of worthwhile rummaging.

I have spent four years tracking down the originals of forgotten books by forgotten authors, acquiring microfilms and photocopies at great expense unaided by any foundations or grants, having to rely heavily on correspondence with libraries and archives in Europe and America. Their staffs have been most cooperative. Yet, whenever it became possible to make a visit in person, from Columbia to Copenhagen, from Harvard to Halle, invariably I found on their shelves pertinent and essential books and documents which had been reported non-existent, not listed in the catalogues, or totally unknown to any one living. No matter how exhaustively I searched, whenever I looked again, new editions and new issues turned up. Where I have finally been forced to leave some gaps, I hope at least to have opened the way for others to fill them in. As our friend Milton says in his *Areopagitica,* to be still searching what we know not, by what we know, still closing up truth to truth, as we find it, that is the golden rule.

For reader-friends who are professional Milton students:

impatient (even as I would be) to know what may be found herein by way of addenda to the life records of John Milton, and to his early reputation, please look for:

Milton's visitors: Vlitius and the Ambassador's son; Lassenius; the Roos case.

His divorce doctrine on the Continent: Boeckelmann, Horn, Diecmann, Arnold, Pufendorf, Finck, Thomasius, von Mastricht, Juncker.

His fame as polygamophile: Kempe, Leyser, Feltmann, Bayle, Möller.

His polygamophile writings expounded: *Christian Doctrine, History of Britain.*

His knowledge of Philip of Hesse, of Ochino.

His State Letter on Königsmarck.

His *Commonplace Book* comments rescued from a recent commentator, on Justin Martyr, Girard, Thuanus, Castalio, Valentinian, Gildas.

Questions still open: The 1657 (London) Dialogue of Polygamy

Questions still open: Why were the ideas summarized by Velthusius attributed to Milton?

New European bibliographical resources hardly tapped as yet.

An exhaustive anthology of polygamophiles by which to assess Milton's thought, with a minor note on William Blake.

Acknowledgments

To the very many libraries and scholars who have helped me I have tried to do justice each in his proper place. Without my good neighbors, the New York Public Library, Columbia University, Union Theological Seminary and General Theological Seminary, none of this work would have been possible: my debt to them is too great to credit at every point; as it also is to dozens of other libraries and scholars in the United States, England, the Netherlands, France, Belgium, Sweden, Denmark, Poland, Germany, Norway, Finland, and elsewhere, not named herein, who cooperatively sought for materials I requested and reported negative results.

JOHN MILTON
AMONG THE POLYGAMOPHILES

1

Milton, Unable to Divorce His Wife, Seeks a Solution in Polygamy

That John Milton was a great poet, some people have heard. A few people also know that he wrote political pamphlets, in prose, favoring republican government against monarchy, advocating separation of church from state, and defending freedom of the press from pre-censoring licensers. Only a very few specialists know that he also wrote on theology, so very few indeed know that in his *Treatise on Christian Doctrine* he devoted considerable effort to argument in favor of the "lawfulness" of polygamy.

Why did Milton choose to formulate a case for the right of a man to marry more than one woman? One reason was his own personal history. Soon after his first marriage, which took place about May 1642, his wife Mary left him and went home to mother with a definiteness that amounted to desertion. As the laws of England then stood, he was unable to get a legal divorce which would free him to marry another. During the next three years he published a series of books urging that the law be reformed so as to permit divorce not only for gross breaches of matrimony, such as adultery or frigidity, but for the most fundamental breach possible, personal incompatibility. Since Milton's thought in this respect was far ahead of his time, his eloquence did not lead to any change in divorce law. Even though—in that time of intense religious reformation—he cited in favor of his argument the authority of eminent Protestant reformers (particularly Martin Bucer, colleague and close associate of Martin Luther), Milton mainly achieved a great deal of personal abuse for himself.

Presently in his deserted loneliness, Milton was attracted to a nubile female who is known to history only as the handsome and witty daughter of some Dr. Davis. Undaunted by his failure to move Parliament to alter the ban on divorce, he turned to the rather more difficult task of trying to convince Miss Davis, first of all, and the ruling authorities second, that bigamy should be lawful.

If Miss Davis had been more amenable, it is quite possible that Milton might have followed up his dissertations on divorce with polemics for polygamy. That same Martin Bucer, in whom he found a collateral teacher on the liberty of divorce, stood ready also to justify plural marriage. Milton's *Commonplace Book,* into which he copied significant items from his reading, shows him making notes from other authorities tending to the same conclusion. In the first edition of his *Doctrine and Discipline of Divorce* (1643) he dropped a hint of such intentions: St. Paul, he recalls, had suggested (I Corinthians, vii, 15) that "a person deserted, which is something lesse then divorc't, may lawfully marry again." But circumstances changed. Miss Davis was averse to his motion; Milton's presently contrite wife returned to him; and their reconciliation closed the issue from a practical point of view.

However, Milton was fully convinced, and in the Latin text of his *Treatise on Christian Doctrine,* Book I, Chapter X, he set forth his honest opinion. He died before this work was finally revised. When his acquaintance Daniel Skinner tried to have it printed, the manuscript was seized and suppressed by the regime in power, so that it was unknown until it was rediscovered a hundred and fifty years later in the musty bins of the State Paper Office. Aside from some passing comments in his *History of Britain* (begun about 1647, finished about 1670) so far as is now known he never published anything overtly on polygamy in his lifetime. A few contemporaries knew Milton's private opinion (and, as we shall see, mentioned it in print), but the memory was soon forgotten so thoroughly that for three hundred years Milton devotees read and reread Milton's hymn to wedded love in *Paradise Lost,* "Whose bed is undefil'd and chaste pronounc't/Present or past, as Saints and Patriarchs us'd" (IV, 761-762), and never guessed its polygamophile content.[1]

Some years before his own marital problem developed, in the course of his studious reading, Milton jotted three pertinent notes into his private *Commonplace Book.*[2] On page 109, about 1635-1637 he observed

> Polygamiã veterũ Judaeorũ propter varia mysteria sub ea latentia haud inconcessam fuisse ait Justin mart: Tryph: p. 364. et 371.
>
> Polygamy was not forbidden among the ancient Jews, because of the various mysteries secreted therein, says Justin Martyr in his dialogue with Trypho, pages 364 and 371.

The significant thought which Milton culled here was not the obvious fact that plural marriage was socially legitimate in Old Testament times, but rather that it was to be interpreted in theological terms as a "typological mystery," in which the events narrated in the Old Testament were to be understood as symbolical, foreshadowing events that would come to pass under the New Dispensation. According to Justin Martyr, who was a writer of Christian propaganda in the second century A.D., the bigamous marriages of the patriarch Jacob with the sisters Leah and Rachel were to be understood as prefiguring the two relationships of the Christ to the older synagogue (Leah) and the newer church (Rachel).[3]

Further down on the same page in that *Commonplace Book,* though perhaps entered at an earlier date, there is a notation rather more pertinent to the issue:

> Digamiam lege sanxit Valentinianus. Socrat: 1. 4. c. 30. grec:
>
> Valentinian sanctioned bigamy by a law. Socrates Scholasticus, book 4, chapter 30, Greek text.

Here Milton has been reading in the *Ecclesiastical History* of Socrates Scholasticus (about 440 A.D.) and he has come across the droll story of the Christian Emperor of Rome, Valentinian I, whose Queen Severa bubbled to him about the beauties displayed at the bathhouse by her friend Justina, so that he was led to investigate for himself, and then to take Justina also to wife, bigamously, using his imperial power to decree a law whereby any man could have two wives at the same time. To the sixteenth and seventeenth century mind in western Europe, the decree of a Christian emperor was "authority" for the lawfulness of plural marriage. The story had been challenged by some scholars as fabulous, and lacking confirmation from other sources, but Melanchthon the Protestant and Bellarmine the Catholic both believed such a law had been enacted, and so did many others.[4]

The third note on polygamy in the *Commonplace Book,* among those which Milton presumably entered before his marriage, was about King Henry II, under the heading *Concubinatus,* on page 110, copied probably about 1639-1641. In Raphael Holinshed's *Chronicles* of England, Milton has read of Henry II that "He was out of measure given to fleshlie lust, and satisfieing of his inordinate concupiscence. For not contented with the use of his wife, he kept manie concubines . . ." Milton's notation is his editorial comment that concubinage was

> the cause of household disquiet as it turn'd both wife & children against our Hen. 2. Holinsh. p. 87.

This comment implies a certain doubt, which Milton must later have resolved. In sixteenth and seventeenth century debate, as often as it was alleged that polygamy ensured a quarreling household, so often could it have been affirmed that monogamy was no guarantee of domestic tranquillity.

It was during his years of the great heartache that Milton formulated his thought on polygamy, the years 1643-1645 when he was most heavily engaged in composing and revising his four published books on the right to divorce as the necessary safeguard of true love and true marriage. During these years his *Commonplace Book* shows a dozen random jottings on plural marriage, as if picked up by chance in the course of his perpetual readings in history. Perhaps if we had his (now lost) *Index Theologicus,* it might show something more systematic, more in line with what we find when we turn to his major discussion in his *Treatise on Christian Doctrine.*

There, in his compilation of theology, his argument is entirely and only: what does the Bible say? There is no consideration of practical problems or of practical consequences, and no intention of any such consideration. There is no argument and no intention of any argument from personal observation, nor from the reports of far travellers in Moslem lands; no citations from court cases or from law codes, not from literature and not from life.

Only one thing counts for him: the Holy Scriptures and their testimony that the patriarchs of the Old Testament were polygamous without a doubt. For really strict and consistent believers in the moral authority of the Bible, whatever may be their attitudes on polygamy in practice, it is simply not possible to condemn these patriarchs. As for the New Testament, nowhere is there any explicit condemnation of plural marriage, any more than in the Old.

Those Christian theologians who took the trouble to deny the "lawfulness" of polygamy had to derive their opinions by exegesis, that is to say, by quoting Bible verses out of context and stretching them to fit. By this method anything can be argued, even if nothing can be proved.

One of the texts most often abused in this connection was in Paul's epistle, I Timothy iii, 2, "A bishop must be blameless, the husband of one wife." Many commentators who cited this verse drew the inference that thereby bigamy was banned not only to bishops but to all persons. That reading did not hinder others, a few at least, who inferred the exact opposite,

When Cajus was accused of Bigamy,
Confessing, he professing did reply,
A Bishop Husband of one wife may be:
May not a Lay-man have two or three?

(*John Owen's Latin Epigrams Englished by Thomas Harvey, Gent.*, London, 1677, from the Latin of Owen's Epigram 134 in his Book I,

> Accusaretur cum coram praesule Cajus
> Confessus bigamus; seque professus ait:
> Unius uxoris vir Episcopus esse jubetur,
> Ergo licet laico nunquid habere duas?)[5]

In this petty chopping of legalistic technicalities, in which the Holy Scripture is the Constitution and the Statute, Milton's discussion in his *Treatise on Christian Doctrine* at least has the merit of being extremely literal and hewing close to the precise meaning (although elsewhere, on the issue of divorce, his merit lies in his being the exponent of charity and the enemy of narrow literalism). In this present context, Milton secures his case deftly by hanging it at once on the bosom of Abraham and other holiest pillars of the Christian faith. By the same precedents he at the same time resolves the vital question whether the children of bigamous marriages were "legitimate" or "bastards" (in social standing and in property inheritance, implied, though not expressed): the holy offspring of the holy patriarchs, by definition, could not be "illegitimate."

Having first entrenched himself in this strong position of defense, Milton sallies out in rebuttal against those who deny the lawfulness of polygamy; regrettably, not naming any. The particular texts which he chose to deflate were the customary verses invoked by "orthodox" theologians and by them dragged out or squeezed together to suit: Genesis ii, 24; Leviticus xviii, 18; Deuteronomy xvii, 17; Malachi ii, 15; Matthew v, 32 and xix, 5; I Corinthians vii, 2, 4, and somewhat apart, I Timothy iii, 2. These pages of skillful interpretation and confutation offer a good sample of Milton's own rules for the right way to read Holy Writ: pay close attention to the language, examine the context, distinguish literal from figurative expression, consider what has gone before and what comes after, compare one text with another, and, (to differentiate the doctrine of God from the fallacies of human reasoning) to admit no inferences but such as follow necessarily and plainly from the words themselves (*Christian Doctrine,* Book I, Chapter XXX, Columbia edition, XVI, 264).

The texts he selects as positive support for his own case are effective, because they do reflect the facts of polygamy as it actually did exist in Bible times. (There is one tactically questionable selection: he includes the twenty-third chapter of Ezekiel, with its purple passages about the two whores Aholah and Aholibah, a chapter which ancient rabbis would not let their pupils read until they reached the age of thirty. Possibly Milton felt it was strong evidence because it was so extreme: if God Himself says that He took those two women as his wives, even though it is a parable, it shows that bigamy could not have been considered dishonorable or shameful.)[6]

These pages also furnish a good illustration of Milton's practice in the use of his own Aristotelian-Ramist-Miltonic brand of formal logic. He likes to formulate an issue into an either-or two horned dilemma, in which one alternative is considered "proved" as soon as the other choice has been reduced to absurdity. Each point at issue, and each Bible phrase, is made to yield its conclusion by invoking the laws of the various logical pigeonholes or categories into which it can be classified: "relation," "species" in contrast to "number," "diverses" and "disjuncts," the theoretical requirements of a precise definition. These pages, like the pages discussing divorce in the *Treatise on Christian Doctrine*, resemble Milton's *Tetrachordon* (1645) in respect to frequent traces of his kind of formal logic, suggesting that they, with his *Artis Logicae Plenior Institutio* (first published in 1672) were all originally drafted about the same time.

Here too Milton insists that "it is the [divine] precepts themselves that are obligatory, not the consequences deduced from them by human reasoning; for what appears a reasonable inference to one person, may not be equally obvious to another intelligent person," (Columbia edition, XV, 134).

In keeping with the general pattern of his *Treatise on Christian Doctrine,* references to Scripture commentators are few, although pages could be filled with extracts from theologians from whose expositions he had absorbed formulations even in their own words. Twice there are citations to the Junius-Tremellius (= Protestant, Latin) translation of the Bible. In the first of these he criticizes: "Here Junius turns the passage *mulierem ad sororem suam* into *mulierem unam ad alteram,* 'a woman to her sister' into 'one woman to another' that he may have whence to prove polygamy illicit by a clearly forced and inadmissible interpretation" (Columbia edition, XV, 126). Milton is here calling attention quite specifically to Junius' own marginal note, which admits what Milton here alleges, that Junius doctored the translation to help remedy the absence of Scripture prohibitions against polygamy.[7] Another allusion is to a book by Theodore Beza, associate of John Calvin, of which more to come hereafter.

Having concluded his "artificial" argument (to use Milton's term for inference from logical constructs), he proceeds to "inartificial" argument, or testimony by documented cases from the Bible:

—Abraham, whose barren wife Sarah gave him permission to use her maid Hagar to bear him children, Genesis xvi.

—Jacob, who was married to two sisters at the same time, and who also accepted their offer for him to use their personal maids as breeders and concubines, Genesis xxx.

—Moses, by a rather unusual and special (exclusively Miltonic?) interpretation of Numbers xii, 1.[8]

—Gideon, "a man most outstanding in faith and religion," *fide ac religione praestantissimum* (Columbia edition, XV, 148) says Milton, directing us to Judges viii, 30, 31, where it is written "And Gideon had threescore and ten sons of his body begotten: for he had many wives."

—Elkanah, every year bringing his two wives along with him to the sacred shrine of Shiloh into the immediate presence of God, who blessed him with the son Samuel who became the great prophet and king-maker, I Samuel, i, ii.[9]

—Caleb, in one of the many muddled genealogies that torment Bible scholars, enrolled in I Chronicles ii, 46, 48, with two concubines, Ephah and Maachah.

—Manasseh, son of Joseph, whose previously unmentioned Aramitic concubine is suddenly remembered in passing, I Chronicles vii, 14.

This brings Milton up to King David, here designated as a prophet, "no mortal more dear to God," who took Abigail and Ahinoam to wife, in addition to Michal, in a time "when he was entirely occupied in the study of the law of God and in the right regulation of his life;" and afterwards, when "David perceived that Jehovah had established him king over Israel . . . and David took himself more concubines and wives," I Samuel xxv, 42, 43, and II Samuel v, 12, 13 (Columbia edition, XV, 148).

Milton continues with his Bible collection of oft-wedded worthies, murmuring "I pass over Solomon, though he was the wisest [of men], because he seems to have exceeded due bounds, although it was not objected to him that he had taken many wives, but that they were alien born" (I Kings xi, 1; Nehemiah xiii, 26). Solomon's son and heir, King Rehoboam, had eighteen wives and threescore concubines; says Milton, not in the time of his iniquity, but "during the three years in which he is said to have walked in the ways of David," II Chronicles xi, 17, 21, 23. Last he lists the reforming King Joash, who took two wives by the advice of the most holy and wise priest Jehoiada.

Satisfied with the conclusive weight of this tabulation, Milton winds up with the theological rule *Praxis sanctorum est interpres praeceptorum,* "the practice of the saints is the interpretation of the commandments."

Hence the opinion of the famous American anti-slavery agitator and Unitarian minister William Ellery Channing, who was one of the first to read Milton's *Treatise on Christian Doctrine* when it was published in 1825. Channing affirmed that if Milton's "error" in defense of polygamy is judged by Scripture, "nowhere is he less liable to reproach." (*Remarks on the Character and Writings of John Milton, occasioned by the publication of his lately discovered "Treatise on Christian Doctrine,"* London, 1826, page 37.)[10]

Hilaire Belloc, who wrote from a rather right-wing conservative viewpoint, and as a Catholic publicist was doubly hostile to

Milton on ideological grounds, seized on these polygamist views to poke fun. Yet in his *Milton* (London, 1935, page 298) he renders the same verdict as Channing:

> And again he was—on Old Testament premises—perfectly right. Those to whom he was addressing his arguments, and who were for him "The Churches of Christ," that is the reformed bodies up and down Europe, with all their infinity of vagary, at least agreed on this—that Scripture was the only authority, and certainly if you make Scripture the only authority and rely especially on the Old Testament, polygamy is not only obviously but enthusiastically taken for granted.

The fact is that, while Milton's extended argument is unusual, the concept of polygamy, or legal bigamy, was not so finally rejected in the sixteenth and seventeenth centuries as it is in our time: in the context of his West European intellectual milieu, that is, for it is proper to distinguish that from the vast regions of our world where polygamy was legal then and has remained legal into our twentieth century. It is also proper, in weighing Milton's thought on this matter, to exclude from consideration all cases of bigamy by stealth, where a man deceives one or both wives; or bigamy from passion, knowingly in violation of the community's moral code and with no intention of changing the community's opinion; or by erratic ideologists such as the Attaways and Jenneys of Milton's day, who cast off their "unbelieving" mates and took new "sanctified" spouses; and extra-matrimonial liaisons, which throughout recorded history have existed side by side with formally and institutionally sanctioned marital unions.[11]

The truth is that Milton's case for legally and socially approved polygamy was not just another aberration of a cantankerous and crotchety character. Other prominent persons faced with predicament sometimes like his, sometimes not like his, considered the same kind of proposals. Actually foremost theologians saw the issues very much as he did, and foremost legal authorities wavered in doubt.

2

The Protestant Reformers, Challenged by the Lust of Temporal Lords, Suggest Polygamy

Foremost among those who also believed in the acceptability of polygamy, under Bible law, at least in special and extenuating circumstances, were those prime leaders of the Protestant Reformation, Martin Luther, Philip Melanchthon, Martin Bucer.

Milton was acquainted, at least to some extent, with their participation in the bigamy of Landgrave Philip of Hesse, as we can read in his *Commonplace Book,* page 110,

> concubinam uxori inducere, negotio cum pastoribus communicato, haud se indignum existimabit Philippus ille Hassiae princeps protestantium dux Thuan: hist. 1. 41. p. 447

> Philip, Prince of Hesse, that leader of the Protestants, did not think it improper for himself to add a concubine to his wife, after taking the matter up with his pastors. (Thuanus, History, Book 41, page 447).

Philip of Hesse was ruler over one of the first states in Germany to become Lutheran, and organizer of their political and military alliance. As a young man he was subjected to the customary princely-dynastic marriage with Christina of Saxony. Although they did have seven children together in their sixteen years of married life, somehow Philip felt he never found a fit mate in Christina. In 1526, not quite three years after his marriage, he asked Luther if he might follow the example of the Bible patriarchs and take himself a second wife.

Luther replied quite cautiously, in a long series of guarded negatives which left the door open (letter of November 28, 1526):

> Der ander sache halben ist meine trewliche warnung und radt, das (die Christen sonderlich) nicht mehr denn ein eheweyb ymand haben solle, Nicht allein darumb, das es ergerlich ist und kein Christen on not ergernis geben, sondern auffs vleyssigst meiden solle, Sondern auch darumb, das hie kein gotts wort furhanden ist, darauff man sich lassen muge, das gott von den Christen wol gefalle. Heyden und turcken mugen thun, was sie wollen. Die alten veter haben ettliche viel weyber gehabt, aber dazu sind sie mitt not gedrungen, als Abraham und Jacob und hernach viel konige, welchen die weyber ihrer freunde wie ein erbe heymsterben nach Mosis gesetze. Nu ist nicht genug eym Christen, der veter werck anzusehen, Er mus auch ein gottlich wort fur sich haben, das yhn gewis mache, gleich wie sie gehabt haben. Denn wo die not und ursach nicht gewesen ist, haben die alten veter auch nicht mehr denn ein eheweib gehabt, als Isaak, Joseph, Mose, und der viel. Derhalben ich hiezu nicht zu raten weis, sonder widder raten muss, sonderlich den Christen, Es were denn die hohe not da, als, das weyb aussetzig odder sonst entwendet wurde.[12]

> About that other matter, it is my faithful warning and advice that Christians especially should not have more than one wife, not only because it is a scandal, which no Christian ought to offer without necessity, but rather most diligently should avoid, but also because there is no word of God here on which one can rely, that it would be agreeable to God on the part of a Christian. Heathen and Turks may do what they will. Some among the old patriarchs had many wives, but they were impelled to it under necessity, as Abraham and Jacob and afterward many kings, who inherited the wives of their friends under Moses' law. It is not enough for a Christian to appeal to the conduct of the patriarchs, he must also have a divine word for himself to make him certain, just as

they had. There where no necessity or cause existed, the old patriarchs also had no more than one wife, as Isaac, Joseph, Moses and many others. Therefore I am not able to advise this, rather must advise against, especially for Christians, unless there be the highest need, as for example, if the wife have leprosy or is taken away from the husband in some other way.[13]

This politic view had earlier been formulated by Luther in a letter to Gregory Brück, Chancellor of Saxony, January 13, 1524. It had been reported that the idea of polygamy among other social changes was being accepted by Andreas Bodenstein von Carlstadt, a Reformer sometime previously associated with Luther and presently dissident from him. Luther commented:

> Ego sane fateor, me non posse prohibere, si quis plures velit uxores ducere, nec repugnat sacris literis; verum tamen apud christianos id exempli nollem primo introduci, apud quos decet etiam ea intermittere, quae licita sunt, pro vitando scandalo et pro honestate vitae, quam ubique Paulus exigit.[14]
>
> I confess, indeed, I cannot forbid anyone who wishes to marry several wives, nor is that against Holy Scripture; however, I do not want that custom introduced among Christians, among whom it is proper to pass up even things which are permissible, to avoid scandal and to live respectably, which Paul everywhere enjoins.

Still earlier, in his *Prelude on the Babylonian Captivity of the Church* (1520) Luther had boldly published other alternatives to a bad marriage:

> Quaero casum eiusmodi: Si mulier impotenti nupta viro nec possit nec velit forte tot testimoniis et strepitibus, quot iura exigunt, iudicialiter impotentiam vir probare, velit tamen prolem habere aut non possit continere, Et ego consuluissem, ut divortium viro impetret ad nubendum alteri, contenta, quod ipsius et mariti conscientia et experientia abunda testes

sunt impotentiae illius, vir autem nolit, tum ego ultra consulam, ut cum concessu viri, cum iam non sit maritus sed simplex et solutus cohabitator, misceatur alteri vel fratri mariti, occulto tamen matrimonio, et proles imputetur putativo, ut dicunt, patri. An haec mulier salva sit et in statu salutis? Respondeo ego, quod sic, Quia error et ignorantia virilis impotentiae hic impedit matrimonium, et tyrannis legum non admittet divortium, et mulier libera est per legem divinam, nec cogi potest ad continentiam. Quare vir debet concedere eius iuri et alteri permittere uxorem, quam specietenus habet.

Ulterius, si vir nollet consentire nec dividi vellet, antequam permitterem eam uri aut adulterari, consuleram, ut contracto cum alio matrimonio aufugeret in locum ignotum et remotum.[15]

Consider a case of this kind: If a woman, married to an impotent man, cannot or does not want to prove her husband's impotence in court with all the evidence and clatter which the law demands, yet she wants to have children, or is not able to be continent: and if I were to have counselled her to obtain a divorce from her husband in order to marry another, satisfied that her own and her husband's conscience and their experiences are ample testimony of his impotence; but the husband refused his consent; then I would further counsel her, that, with the consent of the man, who is not really a husband, but a simple and unbound fellow-lodger, to be married with another, say her husband's brother, by secret matrimony however, and to ascribe the children to the so-called putative father. May such a woman be saved and in a state of salvation? I answer that yes, because an error and ignorance of the man's impotence impedes the marriage, and the tyranny of the law does not permit divorce, and the woman is free by divine law, nor can she be compelled to continence. Wherefore the man ought to concede her right and give up to someone else the wife who is his only in appearance.

Further, if the man will not consent and does not want

to be separated, before I would permit her to burn or to commit adultery, I would counsel her to contract a marriage with another and flee to a distant and unknown place.

At this early date Luther still had his doubts, despite his readiness to help that poor woman out of her predicament:

> Ego quidem ita detestor divortium, ut digamiam malim quam divortium, sed an liceat, ipse non audeo definire.[16]

> Indeed I detest divorce so much, that I prefer bigamy rather than divorce, but whether it may be permitted, I do not dare to determine by myself.

Whatever he thought of Luther's answers, Philip of Hesse managed somehow, in the manner of great lords, for fourteen years. Meanwhile another ruling prince consulted the Reformers about the lawfulness of bigamy, this time the often-to-be-wived Henry VIII of England.

This happened before Henry VIII worked out his divorce from Catherine of Aragon so that he could legalize his already sometime consummated union with Ann Boleyn. Several times between 1528 and 1530 his envoys spoke with Pope Clement VII about the possibility of papal approval for bigamy. Clement liked this idea as little as he liked the idea of a divorce, from both political and religious considerations, but he did have to give serious attention to the king's suggestion. At least one eminent Catholic divine among Clement's advisers, perhaps Cardinal Cajetan, may have spoken in favor of a papal dispensation to permit bigamy.[17]

Henry VIII also sounded out the Protestant Reformers. Their reply was formulated in a memorandum *De Digamia Regis Angliae* ("On Bigamy for the King of England"), August, 1531, written by Philip Melanchthon, whom Milton ranked after Wyclif and Luther as the "third great luminary of reformation" (in his *Tetrachordon*):

Quid autem, si utilitas publica propter successionem haeredis suadet coniugium novum, ut accidit in casu regis Angliae, ubi publica utilitas totius regni suadet novum coniugium? Hic respondeo: si vult rex successioni prospicere, quanto satius est, id facere sine infamia prioris coniugii. Ac potest id fieri sine ullo periculo conscientiae cuiuscunque aut famae per polygamiam. Etsi non velim concedere polygamiam vulgo, dixi enim supra, nos non ferre leges, tamen in hoc casu propter magnam utilitatem regni, fortassis etiam propter conscientiam regis, ita pronuncio: tutissimum esse regi, si ducat secundam uxorem, priore non abiecta, quia certum est, polygamiam non esse prohibitam iure divino, nec res est omnino inusitata. Habuerunt multas coniuges Abraham, David, et alii sancti viri, unde apparet, polygamiam non esse contra ius divinum. Ac leguntur exempla recentia. Nam Valentinianus imperator legem tulit, ut liceret, duas coniuges habere simul, duxitque ipse Iustinam, priore coniuge Severa non abiecta, et successit, in imperio filius ex posteriori natus. Et Theodosius filiam ex illo natam in matrimonio habuit. Ita mansit imperium aliquam diu apud eos, qui ex eo coniugio procreati erant.

Proderit autem ad vitandas quasdam offensiones peteri dispensationem pontificiam ut permittatur regi polygamia, idque credo Romae impetrari posse. Nam divinum ius non repugnat, et Pontifices ante concesserunt aliis, ut Georgio cuidam in Anglia. Sin vero Papa non volet dispensare, rex Angliae tamen potest ducere, quia Pontifex non potest recusare, quo minus dispensat rex in tali necessitate, ubi postulat caritas dispensationem, vel propter conscientiae periculum, vel propter regni periculum.[18]

What, however, if public utility advises a new marriage for the sake of an heir to the succession, as happens in the case of the king of England, where the public weal of the entire kingdom advises a new marriage? To this I answer: if the king wants to look out for the succession, how much more satisfactory it would be to do it without disgrace to his first wife. And it can be done without any danger whatever to his conscience or reputation, through polygamy. Although I would not like to concede polygamy to the common people, for I have said above, we do not propose laws, however in this case because of the great utility to the realm, also perhaps for the sake of the king's conscience, I decide thus: it would be safest for the king if he marries a second wife, not divorcing the first, because it is certain that polygamy is not prohibited by divine law, nor is the practice entirely uncommon. Abraham, David and other holy men have had many wives, whence it is clear that polygamy is not against divine law. And more recent examples may be cited. For Emperor Valentinian proclaimed a law that it was permissible to have two wives at once, and himself married Justina, without having divorced his first wife Severa, and his son by the later marriage succeeded to the Empire. And Theodosius took to wife the daughter born from that latter marriage. Thus the Empire remained a long time in that line which was procreated by that marriage.

It may be advantageous, besides, to avoid certain difficulties, to seek a papal dispensation that would permit polygamy to the king, and I believe it can be asked of Rome. For it is not against divine law, and Popes have formerly conceded it to others, as in the case of a certain George in England. Even if the Pope does not want to dispense, the king of England can however, marry because the Pope cannot take exception to the king dispensing in a case of such necessity, where charity demands a dispensation, whether because of danger to conscience or danger to the kingdom.

In the matter of King Henry VIII, whose playboy amours were automatically political imbroglios, Melanchthon emphasizes the example of the Christian Emperor Valentinian I as assurance not only of the legitimacy of the children born in a bigamous marriage, but also of their incontestable claim to inherit the throne. (Milton also asserted the legitimacy of such children, though without reference to the succession of kings, in his *Treatise of Christian*

Doctrine; and in his *Commonplace Book* he recorded four historical instances in France and Italy where sons of concubines succeeded to the throne.[19])

Melanchthon, it will have been noticed, suggested that it might be possible to apply to the Pope for a dispensation. He cites as precedent "a certain George in England": this allusion is regrettably obscure. It has been suggested that Melanchthon meant not "Georgio" but "Gregorio," with reference to Gregory II's letter of 726 A.D. to his missionary St. Boniface (born as Winfrid in England). Boniface, trying to convert the heathen in Germany, asked what he should do about their habit of taking more than one wife. Gregory II, concerned with the main objective, advised him not to be over-rigid about their irregular forms of marriage, and to wink at their customary unions. If, however, the emendation of "Georgio" to "Gregorio" be indeed acceptable (which I entirely doubt) it might be better applied to the earlier Gregory I, who as the historian Beda relates, gave rather similar counsel to Augustine, his missionary to England, about 596 A.D., not to be too fastidious in such situations.[20]

A "precedent" for papal permission for polygamy not cited by Melanchthon, but later included in the memorandum prepared by Philip of Hesse and his aides for Bucer to bring to Luther, was the dispensation for the bigamy of Graf von Gleichen, which is often mentioned in sixteenth and seventeenth century writings. During the crusade of Frederick II, about 1228, Graf von Gleichen was taken captive by a Turkish sultan, and was compelled to serve as a slave. The sultan's daughter saw him, became enamoured of the handsome Count, and offered him freedom if he would marry her. Von Gleichen demurred, having a wife and children back home in Thuringia. The Turkish princess pointed out that they were then subject to Islamic law, where prior marriage was no bar, and soon prevailed on him to accept liberation with her love. So they were married, and sailed away to Venice, where he made application to Rome for his dispensation. According to the story, it was granted, and equally remarkable, on his return to Thuringia, Wife Number One was so happy to recover her husband that she willingly accepted the Turkish princess as co-wife; especially since the latter proved childless. (The tradition is now regarded as a romantic fiction, possibly grounded on some actual incidents; it has often been adapted in German literature.)[21]

Some weeks after Melanchthon's memorandum, on September 3, 1531, Luther gave a similar answer to Henry VIII's problems in a letter to Robert Barnes, an Englishman early adhering to Lutheranism. Luther advised that (in his opinion) divine law was against divorce, but

> Potius id permittat ut rex et alteram reginam ducat, exemplo patrum, qui multas uxores habuerunt etiam ante legem, sed se ipsam non probet a regio coniugio et nomine Anglicae reginae excludi.[22]

> Rather it permits the king to marry a second queen, by the example of the patriarchs, who had many wives even before the Law, but it does not approve that the first be excluded from her royal marriage and the name of English Queen.

Henry VIII did not follow this advice, but some eight years later it was quoted back at Luther by Philip of Hesse. At this time Philip had taken a fancy to seventeen year old Margaretha von der Saal, and for a change he wanted to marry his fancy. It appears that an attack of conscience coincided with an attack of venereal disease. It also appears that Margaretha's strong-willed mother demanded that someone with rather more moral standing than Philip should decide whether bigamy was lawful.

Philip discussed his desires with Martin Bucer, and secured his help, in November, 1539. Bucer next took the proposition to Luther and Melanchthon. On December 10, 1539 they joined with other prominent Protestant pastors in a written statement giving their consent. This document was signed by Martin Luther, Philip Melanchthon, Martin Bucer, Antonius Corvinus, Adam Fulda, Johan Lenning, Justus Winther and Dionysius Melander; and witnessed by the notary public Balthasar Raid. Philip's first wife, Christina, was somehow also induced to give her consent in writing. The bigamous wedding ceremony was performed on March 4, 1540 by Philip's court preacher, Dionysius Melander, Bucer and Melanchthon being present.[23]

Luther, and Melanchthon even more, wanted to keep the bigamy secret, but inevitably there was gossip afloat. The rumor served as a ready-made taunt for their opponents to use, but even more embarrassing to them was the eagerness of several Protestant ministers close to Philip of Hesse to expatiate further from the pulpit in favor of the principle of polygamy, which led to the publication of some ephemeral writings pro and con.

Most prominent "pro" was the *Dialogus, das ist, ein freundtlich Gesprech Zweyer personen, Da von, Ob es Göttlichem, Natürlichen, Keyserlichem, und Geystlichem Rechte gemesse oder entgegen sei, mehr dann eyn Eeweib zugleich zuhaben. Uund wo yemant zu diser zeit solchs fürnehme, ob er als eyn unchrist zuuerwerffen und zuuerdammen sei, oder nit* ("Dialogue, or a friendly conversation between two persons, whether it is in accord with or against Divine, Natural, Imperial and Canon Law to have more than one married wife at the same time. And if anyone in this age should take such a wife, whether he should be cast out and damned as unchristian, or not").

This *Dialogus* came out in 1541 under the pseudonym Hulderichus Neobulus: *Hulderich* being German for *full of grace,* and *Neobulus* might be quasi-Greek for *new counsellor.* It is now attributed to Johan Lenning, although in its day, and since, Bucer was often believed to be the author.[24] To Luther, the *Dialogus* was most disturbing.

Fundamentally Luther had little difficulty squaring the demands of his conscience with his political need to keep the favor of Philip of Hesse, since he did accept the dogma of lawful polygamy, although he had some twinges when he learned, after the bigamous marriage, that Philip was keeping still another concubine on the side. He was not, however, prepared to extend the privilege generally; and he resented the way Neobulus had been less than discreet in using the Lutheran name. The *Dialogus* introduces the issue with this exchange between its characters Eucharius and Parzasius, seated secluded in a garden:

Eu. Hastu nit gehört, was jetz für eyn geschrey uberal gehe?
Pa. Was geschreys?
Eu. Was? das man sagt, ir Lutherische wöllet Türckisch und Mönsterisch werden.[25]

Eu. Haven't you heard the hullaboo that's going around everywhere?
Pa. What hullabaloo?
Eu. What? everyone is saying that you Lutherans want to carry on like the Turks and the Münsterites.

Luther began to draft a reply to Neobulus, parodying that pseudonym into *Nebulo,* "villain", but Melanchthon, who was more sensitive and unhappy about any publicity in this matter, talked him out of it. Luther contented himself with a blast that anyone following Neobulus' counsel to take more than one wife could expect the Devil would have a welcoming bath ready for him in hell.

In the privacy of his home, where Luther might be thought to have some wider latitude in the expression of his ideas, his opinions on plural marriage did not at all meet with enthusiastic reception. We are told by Johan Schlaginhaufen, who was a frequent visitor at the home of the Herr Doktor and Frau Luther, of a conversation there in the spring of 1532, when Luther, the doctor of theology, remarked,

> "The time will come when a man will take more than one wife."
>
> The Doctor's wife responded: "The devil believe that!"
>
> Said the Doctor: "The reason, Ketha, is that a woman can bear only one child a year, while her husband can beget many."
>
> Ketha responded: "Paul says 'let each have his own wife'."
>
> The Doctor then replied: "His own, but not one alone. That is not in Paul."
>
> So he kept on joking for a long time, till the Doctor's wife said: "Before I put up with that, I would rather go back into the convent, and leave you and all your children."[26]

3

Castalio and Ochino, Reading the Same Bible, Consider the Values of Bigamy

There was a second group of Reformation leaders among whom an inclination to justify polygamy was observed by Milton. Into his *Commonplace Book* he copied on page 114 another note from Thuanus' *History of His Own Times*:

> Sebastianus Castalio Allobrox Bernardinũ Ochinum secutus, cujus dialogos Latinos fecit, polygamiam adstruere videtr. Thuan. Hist. l. 35. ad finem. p. 271.

> Sebastian Castalio, the Swiss, following Bernardino Ochino, whose dialogues he made Latin, appears to support polygamy. Thuanus, History, Book 35, near the end, page 271.

Bernardino Ochino (1487-1564) and Sebastian Castalio (= Castellio, Châteillon, 1515-1563) were Radical Reformers, radical in contrast to Luther and Calvin. They were "unitarians" who did not believe dogmas like the Trinity of God and the depravity of man; liberals who did believe in religious toleration. Ochino, born in Siena, Italy, had been vicar-general of the Capuchin Order of Franciscan friars before joining the Protestant revolt against Rome. He had been welcomed in England 1547-1549 as an outstanding spokesman of the Reformed persuasion. Castalio was known in his time throughout western Europe for speaking out against persecution of "heretics" whether by Catholics or by Calvinists, and in our time has been celebrated for this role by Stefan Zweig, *The Right to Heresy* (1936). Both men were bold spirits.

As Milton noted, Castalio had the reputation of being tolerant towards polygamy. In the index to Castalio's Latin translation of the Bible there may be noticed a focus on such items as these:

> Uxores Abiae quot 462.60 Davidis quot 311.60 recensetur 320.15 duas habuit Elcana 280.36

> Wives, How many Abia had 462.60. How many David 311.60 recounted 320.15 Elcana had two 280.36

Ochino, his friend, had a particularly restless and inquiring mind, which led him late in life to compose *Thirty Dialogues* debating many issues: arguments for and against the tenet of the Trinity; arguments for and against the right to divorce in such special cases as adultery, or profound disagreement in religion; and also the issue of polygamy. Above all, by offering both sides in each discussion, Ochino in effect upheld the right of each individual person to independent free thought. Ochino was eloquent in Italian, much less so in Latin. Therefore his friend Castalio did him the service of rendering his bulky Italian text into Latin, as Milton tells us.[27]

The twenty-first among these dialogues introduces Ochino opposing polygamy against the cogent arguments of his friend Telipolygamus, who is miserable with a sickly and sterile wife, but who does not want to resort to a perjured divorce, or adultery, or poison. The two friends retrace precedents in the Bible, in the practice of different nations, instances from history; they argue the inconsistency of prohibiting a stable legalized bigamy while permitting prostitution and promiscuity, and so on. At the end Ochino allows the issue to remain unresolved.

This particular dialogue afforded the Zurich authorities an excuse to banish Ochino without a hearing, and he spent his last months an outcast wanderer in exile. Castalio was in danger of an even more summary penalty, but death from common mortality removed him from the reach of persecution.

Why did Ochino compose this dialogue? There is nothing known from his personal life to suggest a personal motivation. It must be judged that Ochino, then a man past seventy-five in age, wrote as a thoughtful clergyman seeking solutions to social questions at a time when divorce and remarriage were not widely accepted procedures. A parallel reading of the *Dialogue* of Neobulus (1541) with the *Dialogues* of Ochino (1563), published only twenty-two years apart, quickly establishes a kinship. Ochino freely borrowed arguments and examples.[28] Ochino is clearly in the mainstream of that discussion which we encountered in Luther even before he had to deal with the passions of Henry VIII and Philip of Hesse.

Did Milton ever follow up his note from Thuanus and read Ochino's works at first hand? From the general pattern of his behavior in such matters, one would expect that he would have sought them out. Investigation reveals a seeming paradox. Nowhere else in all his writings is there a mention of Ochino, yet it can be definitely shown that not less than six times did Milton read a specific discussion of Ochino's opinions on polygamy.

Without question Milton knew the major Calvinist polemic composed in opposition to Ochino: Theodore Beza's *Tractatio de Polygamia in qua et Ochini Apostatae pro Polygamia et Montanistarum ac aliorum adversus repetitas nuptias argumenta refutantur,* etc. ("Treatise of Polygamy, in which are refuted the arguments of the apostate Ochino for polygamy, and of the Montanists and others who oppose repeated marriages"). In Beza's point by point rebuttal, he charges that Ochino's argument defended incest rather than polygamy in the case of King David, II Samuel xii, 8. Milton does not name Ochino, but he mentions Beza in his specific surrebuttal to this charge (*Treatise on Christian Doctrine,* Columbia edition, XV, 140).[29]

Milton definitely came across Ochino's name and ideas not less than five times in his readings during the years of his divorce essays. At various points in his *Doctrine and Discipline of Divorce,* his *Tetrachordon* and his *Colasterion,* he quotes from the following five authors:

Johannes Gerhard, *Locorum Theologicorum . . . Tomus Septimus, De Coniugio* ("Seventh Book of Theological Texts, of Marriage"; several editions appeared before Geneva, 1639), gives copious attention to Ochino in a full chapter on polygamy.

David Pareus, *Operum Theologicorum Tomi II,* ("Two Volumes of Theological Works"), Frankfurt, 1628, discusses polygamy pro and con several times, in regard to Abraham, Jacob and others, with repeated reference to Ochino.

André Rivet treats Ochino with hostility in Exercitatio XXVI, pages 129-134 in his *Theologicae & Scholasticae Exercitationes CXC in Genesin,* "190 Theological and Scholastical Studies in Genesis," 1633 edition by Bonaventura and Abraham Elzevir, Leyden, (printed as *CXCI,* "191" Studies in later editions).

Henning Arnisaeus of Halberstadt, *De Jure Connubiorum Commentarius* ("Commentary on the Law of Marriages") Frankfurt, 1613, and Strassbourg, 1636, in additional to practical matters of dowries, physical inspection of brides, divorce, etc., devotes Chapter 4, pages 184 to 211, to polygamy, with specific attention to Ochino.

Frederick Spanheim, *Dubiorum Evangelicorum Pars Tertia* ("Third Part of the Evangelic Doubts," Geneva, 1639 and other editions) discusses divorce in "Doubts" 120 and 121, polygamy and concubinage in number 122, reviewing Ochino and Beza-on-Ochino.

Milton could not possibly have missed any of these references. His silence suggests a discretion rare in his career, perhaps matched only by his holding off overt publication of his unitarianism (which he also shared with Ochino) until after his death.

4

Several of Milton's English Contemporaries Do Not Disagree

In 1657 there appeared in London a little booklet entitled *A Dialogue of Polygamy, Written Originally in Italian: Rendred into English by a Person of Quality; and Dedicated to the Author of that well-known Treatise call'd Advice to a Son. London, Printed for John Garfeild, at the Rolling Press for Pictures, near the Royal Exchange in Cornhill, over against Popes-head Alley, 1657.*

It includes a translation of Ochino's dialogue on plural marriage, pages 1-89; with a separate title page and separate pagination, pages 1-61, a translation of Ochino's *A Dialogue of Divorce,* in which he and his companion Meschinus consider adultery as a ground for divorce, with a final hint that "infidelity" (that is, ideological disagreement) may also be a valid ground for divorce; both preceded by a short essay on Ochino, promising further extracts if these first receive a good reception; a preface by John Garfeild defending the propriety of this publication; and a dedicatory foreword addressed by the anonymous translator "To that ingenious, judicious, free-spirited Gentleman, the Author of that well-known Book, lately published under the Title of, *Advice to a Son.*"

Who in England of 1657 picked these two dialogues out of thirty by Ochino to revive and popularize? and why?

There are two men to whom this translation has been ascribed, and in each instance the ascription has special interest.

Anthony à Wood, chronicler of Oxford University, in his *Athenae Oxonienses* (1692) article on Henry Cuff, recorded the opinion of Dr. Thomas Barlow, sometime keeper of the Bodleian Library:

> Dr. Barlow saith, that it was suspected that Francis Osborne, author of *Advice to a Son,* an old atheistical courtier then living in Oxon, did translate the said book into English, and dedicate it to himself.

Francis Osborne is now another all but forgotten name, but in its time his *Advice to a Son* was a best seller that went through five editions in its first year (1655-1656). Samuel Pepys read it and reread it. William Petty thought that its clever paradoxes would not stand up under close examination, but he agreed that in popular esteem it was ranked with *Religio Medici* and *Hudibras.* In that same article on Cuff, Anthony à Wood tells us that the Oxford authorities felt that this book "did instill principles of atheism" among the young scholars, so in July 1658 they ordered "that no booksellers, or any other persons should sell the books; which afterwards made them sell the better."

One reason why the 1657 *Dialogue of Polygamy* may have been attributed to Osborne was his misogynous attitude to women and wedlock, climaxed by this paragraph under "Love and Marriage" in his *Advice to a Son*:

> Whence it may be strongly presumed, that the Hand of policy, (which first or last brings all things, expedient to Human Society, under the imperious Notion of Religion) hung this Padlock upon the Liberty of Men, and after Custom had lost the Key, the Church, according to her wonted Subtility took upon her to protect it; delivering in her Charge to the people, that *single Wedlock* was by divine Right, making the contrary, in diverse places, Death; and where she proceeded with the greatest moderation, Excommunication: condemning thereby (besides four fifth parts of the world) the holy Patriarchs, who among their so frequent Dialogues held with their Maker, were never reproved for multiplying *Wives* and *Con-*

cubines, reckoned to David as a Blessing, and to Solomon for a Mark of Magnificence.[30]

Osborne was clearly the kind of person to be interested in Ochino, but he was hardly the kind of person to write an address to himself proclaiming himself as an ingenious, judicious and free-spirited gentleman. So the 1657 *Dialogue* is more likely to be by someone else, and someone else is indeed suggested.

It happened that Osborne's popular best seller evoked a pamphlet in protest written by an astrologer and rosicrucian named John Heydon, using the pen name Eugenius Theodidactus, *Advice to a Daughter, in Opposition to the Advice to a Son.* A young law student sprang to the counter-attack, in defense of Osborne, with a pamphlet *Advice to Balam's Ass; or Momus Catechised. In Answer to a certaine Scurrilous and Abusive Scribler, one JOHN HEYDON, author of Advice to a Daughter. By T. P. Gent.* (1658). Thereupon Heydon issued a second edition of his *Advice to a Daughter* (1659), now embellished "With a Word of Advice to T. P." Addressing Osborne, Heydon wrote in his preface,

> And your pragmatical man T.P., I doubt not but the Boyes will hoot at him when they are acquainted with his tricks, and what a sawcy unmannerly rude fellow he is. He it is said writ a Dialogue of Polygamy: and his Master cast a paper full of durt against the Book of the late incomparable King Charls.

T. P. is Thomas Pecke, born 1637 in Wymondham; studied there at the Free School of Thomas Lovering; put in a year or so at Gonville and Caius College, Cambridge; switched to law studies at the Inner Temple in June, 1657, being called to the bar 12 February 1664. In 1658 he published in broadside *An Elegie upon the Never Satisfactorily deplored Death of that Rare Column of Parnassus, Mr. John Cleeveland;* and the following year a book of verses, of which most were translations of Latin and neo-Latin epigrams, *Parnassi Puerperium: or, Some Well-wishes to Ingenuity, in the Translation of Six Hundred, of Owen's Epigrams; Martial de Spectaculis, or of Rarities to be seen in Rome; and the most Select, in Sir Tho. More. To which is annext A Century of Heroick Epigrams, (Sixty whereof concern the Twelve Caesars; and the Forty remaining, several deserving Persons.) By the author of that celebrated Elegie upon Cleeveland: Tho. Pecke of the Inner Temple, Gent . . . Printed at London, by J. Cottrel, for Tho. Bassett in St. Dunstans Church Yard in Fleet-Street. 1659.*

In his *Parnassi Puerperium* ("Parnassus' Giving Birth"), Pecke identifies himself as author of *Advice to Balam's Ass,* but he does not seem ever to have claimed the *Dialogue of Polygamy*: if it was indeed his, possibly for reasons of discretion, hardly of modesty. What renders Heydon's assertion plausible, though not at all proved, is that Pecke did so much other translation from Latin; and that enthusiasm for Osborne is a common trait in the anonymous *Dialogue of Polygamy* and Pecke's *Advice to Balam's Ass.*[31]

But Heydon's book is a tangle of obscurities, of which Samuel Pepys wrote in his diary, December 22, 1662: "Six or seven o'clock and so up, and by the fireside read a good part of *The Advice to a Daughter* which a simple coxcombe has wrote against Osborne, but in all my life I never did nor can expect to see so much nonsense in print."[32]

In this context Heydon's clause "his Master cast a paper full of durt against the Book of the late incomparable King Charles" is tantalizing. It immediately suggests John Milton, whose *Eikonoklastes* was the outstanding book written against *Eikon Basilike,* the so-called Book of King Charles' last meditations. In that age John Milton was also the notorious *Divorcer,* the lonely advocate of freedom to divorce. Since the 1657 *Dialogue of Polygamy* also printed Ochino's dialogue on divorce, Milton could have been considered Thomas Pecke's master on that account.

Unhappily Heydon was indeed a coxcombe given to unclarity. Elsewhere in the same publication he baits Pecke "with thy master Francis Osborne," which leaves us with a compound dilemma. If Heydon always meant "Osborne" when he said "master", which would be the simplest interpretation, then the "paper full of durt" must refer to some writings against the King's Book: but no such writing can be identified among the known works of Francis Osborne. Osborne did write pamphlets in support of the Commonwealth, urging both royalists and Levellers to accept the republic of Cromwell, but nothing like an attack on *Eikon Basilike.* The one other notable book directed against the *Eikon Basilike,* the *Eikon Alethine* (1649, author unknown) is stamped throughout with a distinctive style which differs materially from the style of Osborne's known works.

So we are turned back again to Milton as the man whom Heydon (probably) meant: but still there is nothing anywhere in Milton's writings, or the surviving Milton documents, or the memoirs of his early first-hand biographers, to connect him with Osborne or with Pecke. Pecke is not even mentioned among the versifiers catalogued by Milton's nephew Edward Phillips in his *Theatrum Poetarum* (1675). There remains the possibility of more indirect evidence of some link between Pecke and Milton. There was in those years a young man in London, Payne Fisher (1634-1693), who wrote verses in Latin and fancied himself poet laureate to Cromwell. Using Paganus Piscator as a somewhat Latinized form of his name, he wrote verses for Pecke's marriage to Lucy Ball, and some lines for inclusion in Pecke's *Parnassi Puerperium;* while Pecke included a quatrain *To his loving friend Mr. Payn Fisher* in that little volume. In the 1656 *Piscatoris Poemata* ("Fisher's Poems"), interspersed with odes to Cromwell are complimentary verses by more than a dozen friends of Fisher's, of which most important for us are the Latin hendecasyllabics addressed to Fisher by Marchamont Nedham, Milton's friend, whose newsweekly *Mercurius Politicus* Milton had to approve each week from March 1651 to January 1652 on behalf of Cromwell's government whose organ it was. Once again we meet verses by Paganus Piscator in 1660 prefixed to the *Montelion* of John Phillips, Milton's somewhat alienated nephew.[33] There are other names among Pecke's acquaintance, and Fisher's, of men who may also have figured among Milton's acquaintance, but none very close.

In the absence of a definitive ascription of the 1657 translation, other candidates for authorship may be considered. One nominee, who could have written that fulsome praise of Francis Osborne in the preface, was his son John Osborne, for whom he wrote the *Advice*. John Osborne matriculated at Magdalen College, Oxford, 1648 (so he might presently have met Edward Phillips there); became fellow of All Souls, 1650; Bachelor of Civil Law, 1654; and entered the Inner Temple, 1657, the same year as Pecke.

I am sorry to leave the authorship of that 1657 *Dialogue of Polygamy* an unsolved question, but barring some lucky find that is where the matter rests.[34] In any case, the booklet did not draw very much attention. It does not appear in the catalogue of the great collection of contemporary pamphlets assembled by Milton's friend George Thomason, nor in the 1681 auction catalogue of the library of Milton's physician friend Nathan Paget. Neither is it mentioned by any of the many continental writers on polygamy. On June 22, 1658 it seems to have come in for passing mention at a session of the Council of State. In the midst of weightier matters of concern, that body took notice of several other recent books which displeased one member or another, took steps to enforce the laws against unlicensed books, and to select additional licensers of the press.[35] Whether Garfeild the publisher, or the anonymous translator, of the 1657 version, heard from any of the authorities on its account, does not appear on record, and the little booklet disappears from view until 1732; which is another story.[36]

5

Some Better Known Great Minds Do Not Disagree

Among the learned laity in Milton's century there were men far more important than Osborne or Pecke who studied society at first hand, and gave thought to its laws, and who, in consequence, were far from condemning polygamy.

Sir Walter Raleigh (1552-1618) was one. Among his many more spectacular activities, he wrote *A History of the World.* John Milton read it, and under *De Matrimonio* in his *Commonplace Book,* page 114, wrote:

> To forbidd Polygamy to all hath more obstinat rigor in it then wisdom. Hence Sir Walter Raughleigh well observes that by such rigor the kingdom of Congo was unhappily diverted from the Christian religion, wch it willingly at first embrac'd, but after with great fury rejected, because pluralitie of wives was deny'd them; I know not, saith he, how necessarily, but more contentiously then seasonably. Hist. of ye World: L. 2. c. 4. sect. 16.[37]

Sir Thomas Browne (1605-1682), the great prose stylist of that era, wrote in his *Religio Medici,* 1642, Part II, section 9,

> I was never yet once, and commend their resolutions who never marry twice: not that I disallow of second marriage; as neither, in all cases, of polygamy, which considering some times, and the unequal number of both sexes, may also be necessary.[38]

Hugo Grotius (1583-1645) taught in his *De Jure Belli ac Pacis* ("On the Law of War and Peace," 1625) that polygamy was permitted by the law of nature, although he felt that it was banned by the New Testament (Book I, chapter 2, section 6; Book II, chapter 5, section 9).

Samuel Pufendorf (1632-1694), second only to Grotius as a legal authority in that century, knew Milton's theory of divorce, and argued against it in detail in his *De Jure Naturae et Gentium* ("On the Law of Nature and Nations", 1672). In his comments on polygamy he does not mention Milton; but, says Pufendorf, Book VI, chapter 1, section 16,

> Haec species polygamiae utrum juri naturali repugnet, nec ne, inter eruditos non satis convenit. Nos quae in utramque partem jactantur argumenta proponemus, judicio penes lectorem relicto.

> Whether or not this form of polygamy is repugnant to the law of nature is a question upon which the learned are not in entire agreement. We for our part will set forth the arguments for both sides leaving the decision to the reader.

As an instance of this uncertainty among the learned, Pufendorf cited Thomas Hobbes, who observed that while adultery may be forbidden by natural law, it is defined only by civil law, and therefore what is considered matrimony, or adultery, varies from place to place (Hobbes, *De Cive,* "Philosophical Elements of a True Citizen" Chapter VI, 16, and Chapter XIV, 9). In his *Leviathan,* practical Hobbes shrugs an indifferent shoulder (Chapter 21),

> in some places of the world, men have the Liberty of many wives; in other places such Liberty is not allowed.

6

Some Catholic Spokesmen Do Not Disagree

The foregoing voices were all Protestant. The issue of polygamy was for a long time also far from settled among Catholic theologians. Not until the Council of Trent was there a definitive decision against plural marriage; and that, Bellarmine tells us, was to a considerable degree motivated as a direct shaft against Luther.[39] The Jesuit writer Thomas Sanchez (1550-1610) catalogued among those mentors of the Roman church who did not deny the lawfulness of polygamy under the law of nature the names of Duns Scotus, Gabriel Biel, Durandus de St. Portian, John Gerson, Alphonsus Tostatus of Avila, Miguel de Medina, Miguel de Palacios, Alphonsus of Vera Cruz, and Thoma de Vio Cardinal Cajetan.[40]

Cardinal Cajetan (1470-1534) is commonly considered to have been that unnamed eminent divine whom Pope Clement cited to Henry VIII's envoys as favoring the solution by bigamy. In his *Commentaries on the Five Mosaic Books,* Cajetan repeatedly took a stand permitting polygamy. On Lamech, first bigamist so mentioned in the Bible, Cajetan offered:

> De stirpe Cain quinta generatio introduxit pluritatem uxorum, quae Augustino teste, quando mos erat, peccatum non erat.

> The fifth generation from the stock of Cain introduced plurality of wives, which, as Augustine witnesses, was not a sin when it was the custom.

Cajetan is here invoking the epigram which Augustine of Hippo quipped at Faustus the Manichean who had teased him with the polygamy of the Bible patriarchs: When it was the custom, it was no sin; when it was sin, it was no longer the custom. Cajetan omitted no opportunity to press the point home, even if (as here) deliberately omitting the negative second half of Augustine's epigram. When he comes to Jacob's marriage with Leah and Rachel, Cajetan emphasizes

> non est igitur contra naturale ius connubium cum duabus sororibus vivis.

> It is therefore not against the natural law to marry two living sisters.

Cardinal Cajetan was equally explicit and emphatic with regard to Abraham, who was urged by his childless wife Sarah to use her own maid as his concubine:

> Nihil hic de divina dicitur dispensatione, nihil reprehensibile insinuatur. Et quia hic primum sacra Scriptura pluralitatem uxorum apud viros iustos aperit, annotabis, prudens lector, & quae diximus, & consequenter, non esse contra ius naturae, pluralitatem uxorum. Non est fas credere, quod Abram contra ius naturae alteram duxerit uxorem.[41]

> Nothing is here spoken of divine dispensation, nothing insinuated as reprehensible. And since here the Sacred Scriptures show the first time plurality of wives among just men, you will observe, prudent reader, both as we have said, and consequently, a plurality of wives is not against the law of nature. It is not right to believe that Abraham took a second wife against the law of nature.

Cardinal Robert Bellarmine (1542-1621) wrote against Luther's heresy on this point as well as on others, and was bound to preach the doctrine of the Council of Trent which anathematized defenders of polygamy, but even he conceded,

Quod vero ad polygamiam illam attinet, qua unus vir multas uxores habet, non est omnino extra controversiam an talis polygamia juri naturali repugnet.[42]

As far as that kind of polygamy goes, by which one man has many wives, it is not entirely out of controversy whether such polygamy is against the law of nature.

In the seventeenth century, even after the Council of Trent, the eminent scholar Marinus Mersenne (1588-1648) still regarded polygamy as a debatable issue. In his *Quaestiones Celeberrimae in Genesim* ("Outstanding Questions in Genesis", 1623), a book approved by the Faculty of Theology of Paris, he expressed his preference for monogamy, but citing Lamech before the Flood and the Patriarchs after, he agreed that polygamy was not specifically forbidden. He cited as a positive argument for polygamy its possible value in meeting the need to increase population more rapidly in earlier times (Quaestio LIV, columns 1473-1476).

7

Polygamy and Population: Paracelsus to Petty

It was well known that the Earth was largely uninhabited in early times. Speculative theologians remembered God's injunction to Adam and Eve to be fruitful and multiply, and speculating scientists sought a connection between many wives and many children.

Theophrastus Paracelsus (pseudonym of Philip von Hohenheim, 1493-1541, he who helped to make the turn from the magic of medieval alchemy to the greater marvels of modern chemistry) was among those who speculated that there was a large excess of women born and maturing, for which polygamy might be a specific remedy,

> so doch got êlich geboten hat die ding zu halten, und hat kein zal gesetzt, vil oder wenig.
> und so ein solcher uberfluss do wer, in die ê die ding zu ordnen, und das gebot gottes zu halten.
> so es doch mit einer frauen nit beschehen mag, beschech mit zweien, so die zeit erfordert und das in gleichem weg, nit mit parteischen hendeln, sonder als du wilt das (man dir tue), also tue mir auch,[43]

> So therefore God ordained that it should be handled by matrimony, and has set no number, many or few.
> and if there be such a surplus, let it be taken care of by marriage, and let God's commandment be kept.
> so then if this cannot be done with one wife, let it be done by two, as the time requires, and let it be done on the level, not with one-sided behavior, but rather as you would have done to you, so you do also to me.

This problem also enters into one of Milton's rare references to real life in his *Treatise of Christian Doctrine.* He cites

> *Issacharis posteros ad tricies sexies mille, qui multas habuerunt uxores et liberos,* cap. vii, 1, 4; contra atque nostri hodie Europaei, qui desertos potius agros esse multis in locis sobolis inopia patiuntur.[44]

> *the sons of Issachar, six and thirty thousand,* [*for*] *they had many wives and children,* [I Chronicles] chapter vii, 1, 4, contrary to our present day Europeans, who rather permit fields to remain uncultivated in many places for lack of population.

Actually, in rural England, depopulation was as much a result of, as a cause of, decultivation, and was a widespread concomitant of "enclosures." Which parts of Europe Milton meant, he did not indicate. However, Germany had suffered most severely from depopulation during the Thirty Years War (1618-1648), and that depopulation is sometimes cited in histories of marriage as the reason for a decree said to have been enacted by the Franconian district council (Kreistag) at Nuremberg, February 14, 1650, legally permitting two wives to every man. This peculiar proposal, part of a package discouraging monasticism and other bars to marriage, may conceivably have been considered, but it can hardly ever have gone into effect; certainly it appears to be unknown to all seventeenth century writers on polygamy.[45]

These speculations on population led the more sceptical savants of the seventeenth century into serious inquiries about the demographic facts of the Ottoman Empire and other realms where polygamy was permitted. More accurate information tended to prove that polygamy was no greater producer of population than monogamy. At the same time the statistical studies of William Petty and John Graunt (*Natural and Political Observations Made upon the Bills of Mortality,* various editions 1661-1676) showed that the disparity of males and females was much less than had been supposed. Petty and Graunt also discarded myths based on farmers' experiences with horses and geldings, bulls and oxen, rams and wethers, in deciding in principle against Mohammedan polygamy.[46]

8

The Radical Reformation and the Platonic Idea of Community of Women

So far the pundits we have cited as favoring or tolerating polygamy have all been accepted in historical writing as "respectable," although some were "heretical" in one context or another. In every instance their own testimony confirms their tenets.

In a different setting are the many diverse sects loosely grouped under the name *Anabaptist,* who are known to a very large degree not from their own writings but from the writings of their most hostile and prejudiced enemies.

Most of these sects appear to have been austere in behavior, and stern in condemnation of adultery and prostitution, in their own midst or among their neighbors. (Whether loose sexual behavior was more widespread then than in other eras, who can say, but the sixteenth century had its full share of scandals among a clergy pledged to celibacy; and the shire records of England in the seventeenth century show the justices of the peace constantly occupied with making provision for unwed mothers and their hapless offspring.)[47]

These sects of the Radical Reformation arose among people who did not have political power, side by side with the Lutheran Reformation (and later, the Calvinist) which was supported by powerful princes and magistrates in office. The radical sects reacted against those ills of the church and against those ills of the economic order which bore heaviest on the great majority of the common people. They reacted against the inherited medieval concept of marriage as a priestly sacrament draped over courtly adultery. For deeply religious people seeking salvation through a new covenant between God and the true believers, marriage was also a godly covenant of a particular kind between two true believers. For such humble folk this was a bond of union far more powerful than the traditional church ceremony.

On occasion this kind of conviction could lead to the conclusion that living with an unbelieving wife (given the usual conflicts and maladjustments in married life) was unholy, a union to be broken off by one bent on following Christ; and given the common everyday attractiveness of "another" woman, the complaisance of another woman who shared the new faith could lead to the conclusion that the second union was the holy one in the sight of God. Legal divorce was all but impossible. Bigamy was Biblical. So there were pious men like Nicholas Frey in Strassbourg in the 1530's who accepted a martyr's death by drowning rather than repudiate such a religious bigamy.

If sincere and devout men could believe so, men who would undergo torture and death in flames at the stake, there were bound to be some others who could find in these concepts convenient excuses for the kind of conduct for which they formerly found absolution at the hands of the compliant clergy of the old faith. There were not lacking opponents who claimed that some Anabaptists had persuaded credulous women that to follow Christ they must sacrifice all that they had been taught to hold dear; that publicans and harlots had priority on admissions to the kingdom of heaven; that intercourse with a "heathen" husband was sin, but with regenerate brethren was sanctified: but strictly speaking, if there were such, these occasional charlatans were not advocates of plural marriages or polygamy.

Some of the earliest Anabaptist sects, seeking to build an ideal society, preached "community of goods" of a sort, which lent color to the charge thrown at them that they preached "community of women": which is also not at all the same concept as polygamy. Such charges were made often in the polemical literature of the sixteenth and seventeenth centuries, and remain in the category of politicians' propaganda, unverified and unverifiable.

The fact is that one sect which most emphatically endorsed "community of goods," the Hutterites, as emphatically reaffirmed monogamy. In their preaching they looked to the so-called "Epistle of Clement of Rome" as an Apostolic blessing on the communal sharing of wealth, but they specifically rejected its one phrase recommending a concomitant community of wives. In those years this "Epistle" was (erroneously) attributed to that Clement who was the Apostle Peter's immediate successor at Rome, and it was believed that he had indeed said that the wisest of the Greeks had taught that among brethren all goods should be in common, including wives. The Hutterites accepted the principle on worldly goods, but not as to women.[48]

This "Epistle of Clement of Rome," as well as Plato, was cited in favor of "community of women" (not *polygamy*) by the Italian philosopher Tommaso Campanella (1538-1639) in his quasi-Utopia *City of the Sun* (1623). Samuel Pufendorf, in his *De Jure Naturae et Gentium* ("On the Law of Nature and Nations," 1672) Book VI, Chapter 1, section 15, rehearses these notions from Plato's *Republic,* Marsilius Ficinus on Plato, and Campanella; he rejects their "community of women" outright, while he leaves the decision on polygamy open.[49]

In the cultured courtly salons of those centuries, "Platonic love" was a parlor game, and "Plato's community of women" was often good for a tickling conversation. It is significant to contrast in this respect the cavalier Thomas Randolph (1605-1635) and the puritan revolutionary John Milton. Randolph wrote, in the spirit of the Stuart courtiers who played with Plato's name when they flirted with other men's wives, *Upon Love fondly refused for conscience's sake,*

> It was not love, but love transform'd to vice
> Ravished by envious avarice,
> Made women first impropriate; all were free;
> Enclosures men's inventions be.

Milton was a poet who sang hymns to married love whose chaste bed was a "perpetual fountain of domestic sweets" (albeit with the possibility of having more than one woman in his private stock). He would agree that under the original law of nature established by God in Eden there was no private property ("proprietie" is his seventeenth century form of that word); all things were intended to be shared in common *except* wedded love, the

> sole proprietie
> In Paradise of all things common else.
> (*Paradise Lost* 4:751-752, 760)

9

John of Leyden and His Polygamous Kingdom of Münster

There was one conspicuous case during the era of the Protestant Reformation when Bible authority for polygamy was invoked in practice: Münster, in Westphalia, Germany, in 1534. Among the many dramatic episodes in many communities where radical sects took root and flourished and were suppressed in their own blood, the most theatrical was the conversion of Münster, first to a Lutheran town (1533) and then for a little more than a year into a New Jerusalem where petty and passionate mortals struggled to create a utopian fantasy they misread from the Old Testament and the New, while suffering the agonies of siege without, and recurrent rebellion within. At the beginning of their melodrama, Münster was a town of perhaps 15,000; soon depleted, as thousands left: professing Catholics, orthodox Lutherans, or simply burghers seeking security from social change; some fleeing, some ordered to leave; mostly men leaving. At the same time an immigration of religious enthusiasts, male and female, further upset the normal balance of population. By mid 1534 it was estimated that there were in Münster three times as many women as men.

So the revolutionary authorities who wanted to be reforming saints found themselves straining to maintain civil order under conditions of total disorder; seeking to live by the Book, they were desperately tormented by the continued and inescapable guilt of adultery rampant in their midst; fanatical believers in male supremacy, they faced a daily multiplication of households devoid of adult male members; all the time confronted with a city to feed, a thoroughly disorganized economic life to manage.

In this swirling whirlpool the men at the helm in Münster decreed that every woman had to choose a male protector and guardian; and to make this possible, they declared all previous marriages invalid, so that the women of Münster were relieved of any responsibility to their absent husbands. In effect this procedure established general polygamy for the men who remained (July, 1534). A few months later this decree was relaxed to permit any woman to terminate her status in these multiple unions. John of Leyden (John Beukels or Bockelson), who acted the starring role of King David in this often gruesome charade, was said to have had fifteen of these wives at one time, but when the siege became critical, fourteen were permitted to leave him, and Münster, only Divara his Queen remaining with him.

How this polygamy really worked in practice is now impossible to know. In the writings of their opponents, the leaders of the Münster "kingdom" were portrayed as monsters of unbridled licentiousness; which does not agree with other reports of their personal rectitude. Traditions vary. Heinrich Heine, the great German poet and freedom-fighter, worshipped the memory of John of Leyden as a martyr in the cause of human liberation, and passionately kissed as holy relics his torture chains preserved at Münster city hall.

Since the polygamy of Münster was incidental to a more fundamental program of social transformation, it was discussed by its protagonists only in connection with their whole system, in the one major theoretical work published in their justification. Bernard Rothman (1495-1535), their chief preacher, who was reported to have taken nine wives or protected women, set forth a pamphlet in October 1534, *Restitution, or the Setting Up Anew of Just and Wholesome Christian Doctrine, Faith and Life* in which he propounded their ideas on restoring the imagined rule of saints. Chapters dealt with Holy Scripture, Christ, Baptism, the Church, Free Will, as well as with marriage and male domination, in the course of which Rothman wrote, in their local dialect,

> Item, dat eth einem man fry ys, mer dan eine frouwe tho gelick in der Ehe tho hebben, betügen noch de exempel der

> hilligen Oltueder, als van anfanck des menschliken geslechtes an wo dan völe in der schryfft uhtgedrücket steit. Nemptlick, van Lamech, Abraham, Jacob, David, Helkanah, etce. biss tho der Apostelen tydt tho.[50]
>
> Item, that a man is free to have more than one woman properly in marriage, according to the example of the holy Patriarchs, from the beginning of the human race and as often is expressly stated in Scripture. Namely, of Lamech, Abraham, Jacob, David, Elkanah, etc. up to the time of the Apostles.

The Münster community, with its ideals and its idiocies, was foredoomed to destruction. Its inhabitants were slaughtered, their leaders tortured to death, their writings burned, leaving only a few wretched mourners to wonder what might have happened if fate had not precluded any further evolution of their efforts. The one lasting residue of the Münster episode was a handy label with which all radical sectaries could be slandered as polygamophiles regardless of their actual beliefs or practices.

For example, in Milton's day, William Walwyn was one of the most high-minded spokesmen of the Levellers' movement (which is still called by that misnomer applied to them by the enemies of their democratic principles). He had occasion to complain unhappily that

> Another new thing I am asperst withall, is that I hold Polygamie, that is, that it is lawfull to have more wives than one.

Walwyn protested that he had lived faithfully with one wife for twenty-one years and had nearly twenty children as witness thereof (*The Fountain of Slander Discovered,* 1649, page 7).

10

A Century of Discussion: Exactly What Were They Talking About—and Why?

Between the 1563 Latin and the 1657 English translations of Ochino's dialogue, no West European writer is known who argued publicly in favor of polygamy. Yet in a great number of published studies in law or theology, pundits felt it necessary to take a stand against polygamy, many more than it would be worth enumerating. These commentators were scattered through several countries over a span of several lifetimes; some in close contact with each other, some separated by religious hostilities, or national barriers, or simply by ignorance of one another, so that any account becomes a hop, skip and jump kind of story.

What they understood by polygamy was fairly uniform. In the theological and juristic manuals of the sixteenth and seventeenth centuries, there is often found a discussion of definitions and concepts ritualistically repeated from one writer to another, along the following lines.

"Polygamy may be of two kinds, in relation to time, successive polygamy and simultaneous polygamy. By successive polygamy is meant the marrying of a second, third or *n*th spouse, when the preceding union has been dissolved by death, annulment or divorce." This kind is almost always regarded as "lawful." St. Jerome is quoted on this kind of plural marriage, "I do not condemn the twice-married, the thrice-married, or the eight-times-married octogamists, if they may be so called."[51] Those rare opponents of marriage by widows, or by the divorced (to whatever degree divorce was permitted) were considered heretics, like the ancient Montanists; or freaks, like Rev. Primrose, whose idiosyncrasy was satirized by Oliver Goldsmith in his Vicar of Wakefield, and similar strait-laced divines.

"Simultaneous polygamy means the cohabiting with more than one woman, wives or concubines, where the relationship is sanctified by religious ceremony, or legalized by civil law"—as among the Moslems of that time, or among the Bible patriarchs. This is the kind which was the subject of most discussion, and at times, debate pro and con.

"Polygamy may be of two kinds with respect to the ratio of the sexes: one woman having several husbands, or one man having several wives." The former kind, one-woman-several-men, was reputed to have existed in some bygone times, and to be still extant in some remote regions. In every instance, without exception, the writer on polygamy was a man, and in every instance, without exception, this form was repudiated as absurd, as against the law of nature and the laws of God.[52]

The other kind, one-man-several-women, was the subject matter of discussion, and at times of debate. It was usually called *polygamy;* sometimes, very rarely, more precisely, *polygyny.* Towards the end of this period of discussion, Christian Thomasius in Germany tried to shift the topic into the variant framework of *bigamy* and *concubinage,* on which more anon.

The terms of the debate—What does Scripture and Christian precedent say?—put the issue almost always in terms of the man's right to marry many wives, or an unlimited number of wives at any time. In the real life cases of Henry VIII, Philip of Hesse, Charles Louis of the Palatinate and John Milton of 1643-1645, the aim was actually more limited. The second wedding, in spite of the rhetoric, was intended only to legitimatize the use of a single spouse, though she was second in point of time and sequence of ceremony. The prior wife was to remain a wife in name and title and right to maintenance, though not in cohabitation. In these four instances the dual marriage was proposed as a substitute for divorce.

So much for what was being discussed. Considering, however, that from 1563 to 1657 no one publicly argued for polygamy, why did so many feel obligated to take a stand against polygamy? Intensive digging into the times yields no one answer, but rather suggests a situation of multiple determination, in which a variety of diverse factors operated, impinging on those men whose trade was the custody and transmission of social rules and regulations.

It was a time when an Age of Individual Inquiry was openly displacing to some degree the Age of Blind Faith. Even theologians steeped in rigid dogma could not simply ignore the facts of Old Testament polygamy. So Balthasar Meisner, in a work cited among Lutheran theologians for a hundred years, *Philosophia Sobria* (1611), gravely posed the question pro and con, as to whether the Patriarchs sinned in plural marriage, or whether Jacob did wrong in marrying two sisters.

Particularly in regions where the various Protestant Reformations left their mark, matters of matrimony were an acute issue. When Luther upset churchmen's celibacy and broke his monastic vows, when Henry VIII seceded from the Papacy to effect a divorce, they called all other marital traditions into question. These questions had to be raised at a time when monogamy-preaching Europe was suddenly conscious of being a small enclave surrounded by a polygamy-permitting world. In Europe itself the Ottoman Empire then reached up to the outskirts of Vienna. Explorers and missionaries invariably reported on ruling élites in Asia, Africa and the Americas for whom monogamy was no principle at all.

These challenges likewise affected lawyers in an age when law was still not emancipated from theology. As a matter of fact, in their changing manners of discussion of polygamy may be traced some facets of their liberation from theology. The earlier legal writers in this period wrote in the fashion of the theologians, like Alberico Gentili (1552-1608), a Protestant refugee from Italy, friend to the notables of the Elizabethan era, whose writings were also cited on the continent for more than a hundred years, *Alberici Gentilis, I. C. Professoris Regii. Disputationum de Nuptiis Libri VII, ad Illustrissimum D. Thomam Egertonum custodem magni sigilli Angliae . . . Hanoviae. Apud Gulielmum Antonium, MDCI,* "Alberico Gentili, Regius Professor of Law, His Seven Books of Disputations on Marriage, to the Most Illustrious

Thomas Egerton, Keeper of the Great Seal of England, Hanau, at Wilhelm Antonius', 1601." But it was precisely in this connection that Gentili commented: "Neither our most learned nor our most subtle theologians satisfy me" (in his *De Iure Belli Libri Tres,* "Three Books on the Law of War", Book III, Chapter xv). In the middle of the seventeenth century, John Selden's *Hebrew Wife* (*Uxor Ebraica,* 1646) supplied a definitive compilation of Biblical, Talmudic and Rabbinical tradition, to be cited by every continental writer with any pretensions to skill in these matters. When Grotius and Pufendorf offered their judgments, the discussion of marriage became involved in new formulations of natural law and the law of nations.

Lawyers as well as theologians from time to time came up against practical problems, cases of bigamy, in which statutory law made by kings and magistrates applied, rather than what the preachers might say about divine law or church law. Whether instances were rather rare, or the records are sparse, we have little to go on; but a few cases seem to have made for a lot of discussion. There was a case of an Amsterdam burgher, or mariner, cited in 1644 by Antonius Matthaeus of Utrecht, in his *Commentarius ad Lib. XLVII & XLVIII Dig. de Criminibus* ("Commentary on Books 47 and 48 of the Digest, on Crimes"), a bigamy which was winked at by the municipal authorities: his book also was reprinted for a hundred years, and this one instance, with no specifics added, was cited many times by other writers. Matthaeus in 1644 also mentions one Heinrich Cannemaker of Gorikum, who was beheaded for fraudulent and clandestine deceits practiced in marrying widows and virgins, no date given, as if it were current news; but it really had happened in 1305.

This double standard seems to have obtained in other instances. Another widely cited legal text, Henricus Brouwer, *De Jure Connubiorum* ("On the Law of Marriages," 1665) complained that no one had been recently punished by death for bigamy, though it was perjurious, robbery of dowry, destructive of matrimony, etc. Brouwer observed that whipping or banishment were more likely to be the penalties and ascribed it to the "lenitas" (gentleness, mildness) of his Dutch people.[53] During the same period Michael Siricius, in his *Uxor Una* ("One Wife", 1669, page 139) mentions seeing an execution for bigamy carried out in Giessen, Hesse, and Christian Kortholt's *Sendschreiben* ("Circular Letter", 1682, page 22) also says he had seen such an execution, —which may be the same one; of Siricius and Kortholt, more presently.

One other reason for the frequent recurrence of the polygamy issue must be considered, the likelihood that it was an overt expression of unconscious desires, of repressed temptations, of daydreams turned upside down. No doubt the topic was always titillating to touch upon.

In that age of exploration into new worlds, and dreams of a better world, Thomas More had banned polygamy from his Utopia and Francis Bacon from his New Atlantis. In romances of travel less dedicated to ideals, fiction often spoke more frankly the covert follies of men. Cyrano de Bergerac knew Campanella's *City of the Sun,* with its Platonic community-of-women, but in his own *Voyage to the Sun* he fantasied instead a poly-polygamous "kingdom of lovers", a *Royaume des Amoureux,*

> Au Païs d'où je viens, à l'âge de seize ans, on met les Garçons au Novitiat d'Amour; c'est un Palais fort somptueux, qui contient presque le quart de la Cité. Pour les Filles, elles n'y entrent qu'à treize. Ils font là les uns & les autres leur année de probation, pendant laquelle les Garçons ne s'occupent qu'à mériter l'affection des Filles, & les Filles à se rendre dignes de l'amitié des Garçons. Les douze mois expirez, la Faculté de Médicine va visiter en corps ce Seminaire d'Amans: Elle les tâte tous l'un après l'autre, jusqu'aux parties de leurs personnes les plus secrètes; les fait coupler à ses yeux; & puis selon que le mâle se rencontre à l'épreuve vigoureux et bien conformé, on lui donne pour Femmes dix, vingt, trente ou quarante Filles de celles qui le cherisoient, pourveu qu'ils s'aiment reciproquement. Le Marié cependant ne peut coucher qu'avec deux à la fois, et il ne luy est permis d'en embrasser aucune, tandis qu'elle est grosse.[54]

> In the land whence I come, at sixteen years of age the boys are put into a novitiate of love; it is a very sumptuous palace, which encloses almost a quarter of the city. As for the girls, they enter at only thirteen. There they one and all pass their year of probation during which the lads occupy themselves only with deserving the affection of the lasses, and the lasses with rendering themselves worthy of the attachment of the lads. The twelve months expiring, the Faculty of Medicine comes in a body to visit this seminary of lovers. They examine them all, one after the other, even in to the most secret parts of their bodies, have them couple before their eyes, and then according to how the male meets the test, vigorous and well-formed, they give him for wives, ten, twenty, or forty girls of those who love him, provided they love each other reciprocally. The husband, however, may only lie with two at any one time, and he is not permitted to embrace any one during her pregnancy.

A rather more plausible kind of fiction was perpetrated in England by Henry Neville (1620-1694), who sat in Commonwealth Parliaments, and with James Harrington and Cyriack Skinner sought solutions for England's future in the Rota Club debates of 1659. Neville fabricated *The Isle of Pines,* published 1668, which pretended to be the true story of George Pine, a castaway shipwrecked with four women on an uncharted island in a distant sea. Pine proceeded to embrace his opportunity, and within a brief span of years his descendants by these four women totalled 1,789 persons, who early achieved an advanced state of civil broils and racial hostilities.[55]

Cyrano and Neville are witnesses to the way the concept of polygamy gave form in those years to trains of thought common to many centuries. But if in Western Europe plural marriage was a rare irregularity, for Jesuit missionaries then actively penetrating the Far East it was an all-pervading problem. One of the most publicized cases was their catastrophe in Vietnam about 1630, as reported by Alexandre de Rhodes. His mission there at first had signal success in converting people in Tonkin to his sect, but then ran into difficulties. When the harem women realized that the success of the missionaries meant that they would be discarded as their polygamous marriages were broken up, they set up a scream from one end of the kingdom to the other. In this they were joined by the corps of royal eunuchs, already cheated of their natural aspirations, who saw in the missionary message the end of their professional careers. The king of Tonkin (who had a harem of a hundred) summoned the missionaries whom he had previously tolerated, accused them of undermining his power by reducing the potential number of faithful and fruitful subjects, and so put an end to their public proselytizing. Alexandre de Rhodes' book circulated in an Italian original, and in a loose French paraphrase; and was brought to the attention of Protestant readers by the Dutch controversialist Gisbertus Voetius.[56]

In England during this period, when clergymen commented on plural marriage they were usually brief, sharply and quickly to the point against polygamy; for instance, William Perkins, *The Combate betweene Christ and the Devill Displayed, or a Commentarie upon the Temptations of Christ,* 1613, page 677. Such were the two divines whose works Milton reviewed on Sundays with his nephews: William Ames, *Medulla Theologiae,* 1628, Book II, page 566, translated 1642 by order of the House of Commons as *The Marrow of Sacred Divinity;* and the Swiss Johan Wolleb, *Compendium Theologium Christianae* (1626), popularized in the version edited by Alexander Ross, *The Abridgement of Christian Divinitie,* 1650, page 313. The Baptist sects, contending with the customary libels against anabaptists, several times published declarations against polygamy, 1647, 1678, 1688 (Edward B. Underhill, editor, *Confessions of Faith and other Public Documents Illustrative of the History of the Baptist Churches of England in the Seventeenth Century,* London, Hanserd Knollys Society, 1854).

Sometimes a comment on polygamy comes in so irrelevantly as to suggest that the idea is somehow haunting the speakers. John Goodwin, the Independent preacher who was lined up with Milton so many times in times of revolution and in times of reaction, ran into some cavil by a Cavalier about good men in the Bible on occasion doing reprehensible deeds, as in the practise of polygamy. Goodwin somehow felt it necessary to argue against polygamy, from the Seventh Commandment (against adultery), from Matthew xix, 5, from Malachi ii, 14,15, while conceding the opposing evidence,

> The ancient Fathers were generally Polygamists; yet the plenty of their practise is but a defective proof of the lawfulnesse of Polygamy. In like manner, the actions mentioned, having no testimony of approbation from the Scriptures, may very possibly be workes of darknesse, though done by children of light; yea, though there be no expresse brand of unlawfulnesse set upon them by God: for Polygamy it selfe hath this negative testimony of its innocency.

(*Anti-Cavalierisme, or the Truth Pleading as well the Lawfulness, as the Necessity of this Present War,* 1642, page 13)

A more extended discussion, perhaps significant in the mere fact of its appearance, was formulated by Henry Hammond, (an Anglican theologian, chaplain to Charles I before his beheading), in *A Letter of Resolution to Six Quaeres,* London, 1652 or 1653. Like many other theologians, Hammond treats of polygamy together with the question of divorce. He makes a clear reference to Milton's writings on divorce, but shows no suspicion of Milton's ideas on polygamy.[57]

Over in the Netherlands, during the same general period, Jacob Cats (1571-1660), as a Calvinist and as a would-be creative writer, composed a book, *Houwelyck* ("Marriage", 1625) on model behavior for married folks, and *Trou-ringh* ("The Wedding Ring", 1636), a string of such stories in verse dialogue and prose dialogue. Subsequently he decided to have his moralities rendered into Latin, and for this purpose he invited the collaboration of Caspar Barlaeus (in Dutch, Gaspard van Baerle, 1584-1648) and Cornelius Boyus (in Dutch, Boey, 1611-1665). They partly paraphrased Cats' work, and also contributed new works in prose and verse. Cats' own verses necessarily involved the story of the polygamous patriarch Jacob and his marriage to the two sisters Leah and Rachel, as well as their two maids, which had to be squared with opposition to polygamy.

Barlaeus, who had earned his meed of fame in that age, contributed several entertaining dialogues of his own: one on that once happily married couple Adam and Eve; a debate on whether a philosopher should acquire a wife; another on whether it is advisable to marry a pretty girl. Perhaps in translating Cats' verses into the Latin of *Patriarcha Bigamos,* Barlaeus felt additional clarification was desirable, perhaps there were other reasons; in any case Barlaeus composed a Latin *Dialogue on Polygamy.* In this item, Barlaeus plays host to Sinapius, his friend who has just come back from Turkey, eager for a drink *de cocta Cerere,* an alcoholic beverage not available in the Ottoman Empire, and eager to talk about the custom of plural marriage which was available there. Actually Sinapius is little more than a straw man who only sets up arguments taken from Ochino and elsewhere for Barlaeus to overwhelm in long speeches.

This Cats-Barlaeus-Boyus opus on matters matrimonial came out in 1643 in two editions, elegantly printed, *Faces Augustae* ("The Royal Nuptial Torches") dedicated to Princess Elizabeth, the never-married daughter of Frederick, Elector Palatine and Winter King of Bohemia, and it came out again in 1656.

This story has an obscure but important sequel. Jacob Cats had been Dutch Ambassador to Charles I, and in 1651-1652 returned to London as Dutch Ambassador to Cromwell. As secretary he brought with him his kinsman Jan Van Vliet, a magistrate of Breda. Jan Van Vliet (c. 1610-1666) has long been known to Milton scholars under his Latin name Vlitius, because of letters surviving in which he wrote of his eager efforts to make Milton's acquaintance. Until now the Vlitius story has stopped there, and for the moment will still stop there, except for a few questions. When they met, Vlitius and Milton, would not the *Faces Augustae* have been an appropriate topic for conversation? Is it significant that Edward Phillips, Milton's nephew, in his *Theatrum Poetarum* mentions all three, Cats, Barlaeus and Boyus, with particular mention for Cats' *Patriarcha Bigamos*? Might it be pertinent that Vlitius was most unhappily married, that his friends' letters constantly refer to the "tempest" of his wedded life, which ended in a ruinous divorce case? When Vlitius came back to Breda, what would have been more likely in his conversation than to drop a remark now and then about his visits with Milton, say, perhaps, when chatting with Gerhard Feltmann, of Groningen, who in 1664-1666 came down to be a law professor at the short-lived college of Breda? We shall pick up this thread again when we shall be meeting up with Gerhard Feltmann a few years hence.[58]

The question suddenly becomes much sharper. In 1663, 1667 and 1669 in Germany there appeared three separate extended works entirely and exclusively devoted to disproving the lawfulness of polygamy.

In 1663 at Giessen in Hesse, William Zesch published *De Polygamia Successiva et Simultanea, Partim contrà Tertullianum et Montanistas, partim Anabaptistas, Turcas, Eorumque Sequaces Dissertationes Duae* ("Two Dissertations on Polygamy Successive and Simultaneous, partly against Tertullian and the Montanists, partly against the Anabaptists, Turks and their Followers.") It has all the marks of a strictly academic exercise, presented at the local Academy with Zesch as *praeses.*[59] The first dissertation is directed against Tertullian and the Montanists, both of the third century, who are remote enough. The second specifies among the Anabaptists John of Leyden, John Bochold (as if he were a different person), "Helzer" and David George; lists Ochino separately; rings in the Jews of Justin Martyr's *Dialogue with Trypho,* the Mohammedans of the Koran, and the Chinese; but does not at all make clear who are meant by "their followers." He makes no overt reference to any contemporary event. His dedication to Ludwig, Landgrave of Hesse, may be a mere matter of form, or it may have meaning. This book seems to be a symptom, but we are not sure of what. If it were one of a kind, we would classify it simply with all the other publications in which polygamy had been discussed; but it is not unique.

In March, 1667, at Greifswald in Pomerania there appeared an inaugural or doctoral disputation at the university, published there in book form as *Funus Polygamiae* ("The Burial of Polygamy"), by Conrad Büttner, with Matthew Tabbert as *praeses.* Internal evidence suggests no contact between Büttner and Zesch, although both adhere to a common theory that monogamy was the law of the first Creation; that polygamy was permitted by divine dispensation from the time of Abraham; and that it was banned by Christ who brought things back to the original status. Büttner's disputation has all the marks of an academic exercise, but it also offers some curiously contradictory references to the times. His opening paragraph observes that the question of polygamy among the Patriarchs and Saints of the Old Testament is a matter common enough and vexed enough in the halls of kings, princes, counts and other magnates. To him it is no mere abstract question, but a practical current question of conscience. Several times Büttner speaks of *multi,* "many," who agree with Ochino, never identifying them, once suggesting that he means Anabaptists. On the other hand, in his Fifth Theorem he writes, that, God be praised, he knows of no case of polygamy properly so-called in their century.

Büttner dedicated his opus to Anton Günther, Count of Oldenburg (then a principality crammed in a corner between Bremen and the North Sea), because the Count had just appointed him superintendent of the church in Jehver, but there is as fulsome homage paid to Carl Gustav Wrangel, renowned Swedish military commander, in whose service Büttner had been both palace preacher and military chaplain. In those years Sweden was very intertwined with Germany, parts of which, as in Pomerania, were under Swedish rule. As we shall shortly see, the family of Carl Gustav Wrangel had personal reasons to be interested in the issue of plural marriage: but that is not obvious in Büttner's book.[60]

On March 28, 1669 back in Giessen in Hesse, theologian Michael Siricius (1628-1685) was sending to the printer a 163 page book embodying an exhaustive review of orthodox answers against polygamy, *Uxor Una, ex Jure Naturae et Divino, Moribus Antiquis et Constitutionibus Imperatorum et Regum. Eruta et contra Insultus Impugnantium Defensa* ("One Wife, Derived from Natural and Divine Law, Ancient Custom, and the Statutes of Emperors and Kings, and Defended against the Attacks of Impugners"). Like Zesch, Siricius dedicated his book to Ludwig,

Landgrave of Hesse, but he gives no indication of either having read or not read Zesch's work. Siricius has his own dark hints to throw out of false teachers, seducers of fleshly desire, who try to persuade that polygamy accords with natural and divine law, and should be again introduced by the civil magistrates. In his preface he gives thanks to God that Kings and Princes in the Christian world reject these false teachers, and rather enforce the death penalty on bigamists (as he can vouch as an eye-witness). His book is not an academic dissertation or disputation at all; rather it is inspired by a specific but unspoken motivation, *occasione quadam motus,* "moved by a certain occasion."[61]

Siricius is by far the most thorough of the three; indeed, up to his time the most thorough of any who had dealt with the matter. He will also be among the most quoted and most influential. What we would most like to know, of course, is what was that *occasion.*

It is conceivable that the occasion involved certain events in the Rhenish Palatinate affecting some distant kin of the ruling family of Hesse, events we shall presently review. Or it may be involved with the family problems of Carl Gustav Wrangel, although Siricius gives no evidence of reading Büttner. Or it is conceivable that it was somehow related to talk going around that year about a different Swedish nobleman, guest of the count of Hanau, who amused himself by tempting the court chaplain at dinner table with challenges to the clergymen's invention of monogamy: we hear of that in a stray letter dated August 8, 1669, with no other details or information.[62] The Muse of History is a tease.

11

Polygamy's Prophet: The Gospel According to Johan Leyser

So for a hundred years the very idea of plural marriage has been officially decried and denounced with no defender openly speaking up, until in the 1670's, in the Germanies, there arose the most passionate enthusiast who ever preached a consistent gospel of social salvation through polygamy, Johan Leyser.

Johan Leyser has been all but forgotten, as men far more important have been, but in his day he stirred up a storm which lasted far into the next century. His chosen mission was eccentric, to say the least, and he did not choose the best way to win friends and influence people; but all he did was to teach and advocate, and suffer for it stones, and sentences of banishment, and the burning of his books. He was sadly misguided in the cause he espoused (and that was all he ever espoused) but the practice of repression, as visited upon him, was far more harmful to humanity than any effect his writings may have had.

His story has never really been told, and is hardly likely ever to be told in full. I have been amazed at the number of scattered sources of information I have been able to find, including original letters and documents: but until now no one has ever tried to compile a reasonably complete bibliography of his publications, or a reasonably correct chronology of his career as apostle of plural marriage.[63]

Johan Leyser was born September 30, 1631 at Leipzig in Saxony, the youngest of nine children. He came from a family of famous men. His grandfather Polycarp Leyser (1552-1610), a prominent Lutheran theologian, married Elizabetha, daughter of the painter Lucas Cranach the Younger, and they had thirteen children. Of these, Polycarp Leyser junior, Johan's father (1586-1633) also achieved eminence as a clergyman. Both of these Polycarps were often quoted as authorities in that time, but to Johan they were only shadowy names.

Johan Leyser's mother was Sabina Volckmar. She wrote no books and had no conventionally acknowledged fame, but she must not be overlooked merely because the world sets arbitrary and unfair standards in evaluating the contributions made by various individuals. Her children were: Polycarp 3rd, 1616-1641; Nicolaus, 1618-1632; Lucas, 1620-1672, lawyer, councillor to the Elector of Brandenburg; Friedrich Wilhelm, 1622-1691, preacher at Magdeburg Cathedral; Christian, 1624-1671, pastor at Sangerhausen; Caspar, born 1626; Michael, 1628-1659, a physician whose pioneer studies in anatomy are still listed in encyclopedias (Milton's medical friend, Dr. Nathan Paget, owned a copy of Michael Leyser's treatise on dissection); Sabina Elizabeth, 1629-1673; and Johan, who lost both mother and father by the time he was three.

Whoever became his guardian, Johan does not seem to have been neglected. Since his father had been Primarius-Professor and Senior of the Theology Faculty at Leipzig University, Johan even as a child of six was immatriculated there in the winter semester of 1637, in anticipation of a clergyman's career. But first, as a teenager, he was sent to study at the renowned Landesschule of Pforta (on the Saal River, southwest of Naumburg), being enrolled there from August 23, 1645, and finishing in September 1649 with a valedictory oration on the burning of Sodom and Gomorrah which won praise for wit and good Latin. He proceeded to his predestined studies at the University of Leipzig; became bachelor of arts July 11, 1651; master of arts, January 27, 1653; bachelor of theology, November 9, 1663. From 1659 to 1664 he served as a member of the Collegium Concionatorii Lunatici, the organization of Monday preachers. In May 1664 he was appointed inspector and pastor at that same school of Pforta. He served in that capacity for three years, leaving by March 1667, before his peculiar mission began, and was ever after referred to as "the former inspector of Pforta school."[64]

From here on Leyser leads a rather unsettled life. He was never married; and when he had become notorious as the advocate of polygamy, his puny body, bent from habit, more than once invited the cruel jest that he might have had a hard time satisfying even one wife. Possibly it was some such factor which motivated his monomania: but from a scattering of early sources we pick up gossip that Leyser was drawn into defending this dogma by a Count Königsmarck of Sweden. Official biographies are silent, although the Königsmarcks with their far-reaching cavortings in that century were constantly in the public eye.[65] (At least one of them was a matter of concern to John Milton, but that, and other tempting by-paths, must go into a footnote).[66]

As near as can be determined at this distance, Leyser had become military chaplain in the service of Count Conrad Christopher von Königsmarck, who, about 1670, had let it be known so emphatically how weary he had grown of his wife, Lady Maria Christina Wrangel, that, in the manorial mansions of her clan earnest discussions were under way about how to thwart his threats of remarriage by divorce or by bigamy. Participating in these conferences were a Wrangel family chaplain, Gerlach Siassius, and a visiting pastor from Giessen in Hesse, Balthasar Mentzer, whose father in 1612 had published one of that century's most often quoted religious manuals on marriage. Just before he left Stockholm, Mentzer submitted a memorandum of his views (November 17, 1670). Without Mentzer's knowledge, this memorandum was published shortly after in a little pamphlet of fourteen pages, with a preface dated November 25, 1670, signed by that family chaplain not using his own name but a pseudonym *Getreuester Serviteur* (= Your Most Obedient Servant), which had the same initials as his real name: *Herrn D. Balthasar Menzers Schreiben, zu Stockholm, an einem fürnehmen guten Freund abgegeben, über einem mit ihme gehaltenen Gespräch, betreffend die Polygami und Ehscheidung. Stockholm. Gedruckt bey Nicolaus Wankijff, Konigl. Buchd. Im Jahr 1670* ("Mentzer's Letter at Stockholm, delivered to a distinguished good friend, about a conversation held with him concerning polygamy and divorce. Stockholm. Printed by Nicholas Wankiiff, Royal

Printer, 1670"). It is a slight piece, a sermon on Matthew xix.

In Königsmarck's entourage a rebuttal was drafted, which developed into a *Kurtzes Gespräch von der Polygami*, "A Short Discourse of Polygamy," printed 1671, without indication of printer or place, signed by *Sincerus Wahrenberg,* a pseudonym which may have been a mask for Johan Leyser, or for Leyser-with-others. It was cast as a dialogue between Theodore, who believes in plurality of wives, and Bernardus, who does not. (Is the choice of names sardonic, Theodore for Beza and Bernardus for Ochino, reversing their real positions?) The argument is all Biblical: if Adam and Eve are to be taken as a compulsory model limiting wedlock to two partners, why not by the same token limit communion to twelve, the number who came to the Last Supper? The patriarchs, Jacob, David, Solomon, Gideon, all had many wives not by dispensation, it urges, but by the basic law of marriage; and so on, through Lamech, and Valentinian and the rest.[67]

The Wahrenberg dialogue circulated somewhat in Sweden, and from there into Germany. What really brought it into some prominence was the appearance of two publications designed to oppose it.

The first was a reply by that same Hesse preacher Balthasar Mentzer, *Kurtzes Bedencken Uber Eines von sich selbst also genanten Sinceri Wahrenbergs Kurtzes Gespräch von der Polygami. Darmbstadt, Gedruckt bey Henning Müllern, Fürstl. Buchdruckern. Im Jahr Christi MDCLXXI.* ("Brief Reflections on a Short Discourse of Polygamy by a self-styled so-called Sincerus Wahrenberg. Darmstadt, printed by Henning Müller, Printer to His Highness, In the Year of Christ 1671"). In this booklet Mentzer reproduced his 1670 *Schreiben* with the preface by *Serviteur,* and then reprinted the text of Wahrenberg's dialogue, interrupted paragraph by paragraph with his own critical comments. His preface, dated October 18, 1671 at Darmstadt, indicates that he is back in Germany and that the Wahrenberg pamphlet had been sent to him three weeks before from Stockholm by his good friend there. Mentzer recognized that *Sincerus Wahrenberg* was a pseudonym ("Sincere Mountain of Truth") and commented that Sincerus' style showed that he spoke *hoch-deutsch* (High German) rather less well than the *niedersächsischen* (Low Saxon) dialect, but he gave no other clue, if he had any idea who the author really was.[68]

Meanwhile in another corner of Germany another clergyman, Friedrich Gesenius, much perturbed by the school of natural law developing at the new University of Lund, in Sweden, also read the Wahrenberg booklet, and jumped to the conclusion that the author was a certain prominent professor there. In July 1672 Gesenius had ready for the press, under the pseudonym Christianus Vigil Germanus ("The Vigilant Christian, a German") a rebuttal, under a half page long title beginning *Ad Sincerum Wahrenbergium Suecum Epistola seu Dissertatio super Polygamia Simultanea, in qua Primaevum Conjugii institutum de non nisi una uxore simul habenda* (leaving out eighty-one more words of the title, "Epistle or Dissertation to Sincerus Wahrenberg, the Swede, on Simultaneous Polygamy, in which the primeval institution of marriage of not having unless one wife at a time," etc.)[69]

Vigilant Gesenius groans that atheism grows daily apace, that Christians go running into forbidden fires and mutations in marriage. He serves up the standard citations and the standard arguments. What is remarkable is his tone. Gesenius addresses the pseudonymous polygamophile as "most excellent Wahrenberg . . . most noble Wahrenberg . . . most sincerely sincere and super-scholarly Wahrenberg" ("excellentissime Wahrenbergi . . . nobilissime Wahrenbergi . . . Sinceri Sincerrime Wahrenbergi Polymathestate") until it develops that Gesenius believes that Wahrenberg is really Samuel Pufendorf, or his brother Esaias Pufendorf, or a spokesman for both of them. (His guess was unfounded, but not wholly unreasonable: that will presently be more clear).

Pufendorf was already up to his neck in unsought controversies arising from his major work *De Jure Naturae et Gentium Libri Octo* ("Eight Books on the Law of Nature and Nations") and its sequel *De Officio Hominis et Civis* ("On the Duty of Man and the Citizen"). In both of these, marriage is a minor matter; in both Pufendorf indicated his preference for monogamy; but his objectivity and impartiality with which he had treated polygamy left him open to unfair accusations and malicious whispers emanating from Gesenius and others. Gesenius' attack came out in 1673, about the same time as a colleague of Pufendorf's at Lund published an *Index* of Pufendorf's unorthodox novelties, which was used by Johan Adam Scherzer, theologian at Leipzig, to obtain a rescript from the Elector of Saxony, June 13, 1673 condemning Pufendorf's work. Pufendorf let out a howl, indeed several howls. He did not answer Gesenius separately, but as part of his book *Samuelis Pufendorfii Apologia Pro Se et Suo Libro, Adversus Autorem Libelli Famosi, Cui Titulus Index Quarundam Novitatum Quas Dn. Samuel Pufendorf Libro Suo De Iure Naturae et Gentium Contra Orthodoxa Fundamenta Londini Edidit, Germanopoli, Anno MDCLXXIV* ("Samuel Pufendorf's Apologia for Himself and His Book against the Author of a Defamatory Booklet Entitled Index of Certain Novelties which Samuel Pufendorf Published against Orthodox Fundamentals in His Book on the Law of Nature and Nations at Lund"). Pufendorf reaffirms his preference for monogamy, denies any contact with Wahrenberg, nails Gesenius as a liar, whose flattering phrases are like lips pursed for a kiss so as to hide teeth ready to bite. Pufendorf again answered Gesenius as part of his *Epistola ad Plur*[*imum*] *Reverendum atque Celeberrimum Virum Dn. D. Ioh. Adamum Scherzerum, Theologum apud Lipsienses Primarium, Super Censura Quapiam in Librum Suum Inique Lata, Hardervici, Apud Cornelium van der Bucht, A. 1674,* "Open Letter to the Most Reverend and Celebrated Johan Adam Scherzer, Primarius-Theologian in Leipzig, on a Certain Censure Unfairly Spread About His Book, Harderwyck, at Cornelius van der Bucht, 1674."[70]

Leyser, it may be presumed, has meanwhile continued in the service of Conrad Christopher von Königsmarck. We really do not know what he was doing, except that he seems during 1672 to have composed a fresh dialogue, "A Discussion on Polygamy between Polygamus and Monogamus," using the pseudonym *Aletophilus Germanus* ("German Truth-Lover"). Whether he ever published it himself is a question. The only copies known are in a Latin version published by his opponent and inadvertent booster Friedrich Gesenius, who in 1673 had it printed as *Discur-*

sus inter Polygamum et Monogamum de Polygamia Autore Aletophilo Germano. Prodit jam latine cum Cautione, praefatione, & notis marginalibus Christiani Vigilis, Hujus Epistolae ad Warenbergium subnexus. Anno M.DC.LXXIII ("The Discussion on Polygamy between Polygamus and Monogamus, Appearing Now in Latin, with the Caution, Preface and Marginal Notes of Christianus Vigil, Bound with His Epistle to Wahrenberg").

In his preface dated January 24, 1673, Gesenius moans that in July 1672, three days after he finished his Epistle to Wahrenberg written to prevent the Swedish virus from spreading infection in Germany, there came to him this dialogue by Aletophilus Germanus without indication of its source. Since he had no reason to think it was by the same hand as had done the Wahrenberg dialogue, Gesenius proffers no courtly compliments, but in bare style reprints the text composed by Aletophilus Germanus, even to including Monogamus' capitulation to Polygamus' arguments; and he appends paragraph by paragraph footnotes which merely give citations to the Bible, and to his own prior epistle, which should between them supply instant and automatic refutation.

The Aletophilus dialogue itself is authentically Leyser, foreshadowing in brief the main tenor of all his later writings, but as yet without the pyramid of "evidence" he will be building up in the years to come. Since Monogamus takes his points mostly from the Bible, which is a document composed in a polygamous society, Leyser's (Polygamus') easy retorts make for lively reading. His own arguments afford in their eccentricity their own kind of amusing reading: God bids man increase and multiply; God and nature make nothing available in vain, so a man's procreative power is a talent not to be wasted unused merely because one's (monogamous) wife is already pregnant; by divine ordinance man is lord over womankind; polygamy is the proper means to overcome the sins of this world, especially abortion, infanticide, onanism, sodomy, adultery, etc., etc. He confidently asserts that there are other theologians who know that polygamy is not against divine law; not at this time naming names.[71]

In December, 1673 Count Conrad Christopher von Königsmarck was killed in battle at Bonn, while serving in the Dutch forces. Leyser may thereby have lost his patron, but not his prophetic fervor. What he does for bread, and where, is not recorded; among the orthodox he already has the reputation of a homeless wanderer, reported in France, in Denmark and in the Germanies.[72] To his critics, Mentzer and Gesenius, he offers no reply, nor to another hostile publication, *De Polygamia, Disputatio Politica* ("Political Disputation on Polygamy"), dated February 26, 1674 at Darmstadt in Hesse, with *praeses* Paulus Linsius and respondent Johannes Valentinus Keller, printed at Wittenberg by Johnnes Haken, 18 pages, including complimentary Latin verses by Johannes Deutschmann, Georg Wagner and Linsius. They are disciples of Siricius and Mentzer; they know Wahrenberg and Gesenius, but (apparently) not Aletophilus Germanus; and they cry out, "Bone Deus, in quae nos tempora reservasti? O tempora! O mores!"—Good God, in what kind of times have You brought us? O these times! O these goings on![73]

The Linsius disputation may, however, have suggested to Leyser the title of a new book which he published in that year 1674, *Discursus Politicus de Polygamia, Auctore Theophilo Alethaeo, Friburgi, Apud Henricum Cunrath. 1674* ("Political Discourse of Polygamy, author Theophilus Alethaeus, Friburg, at Heinrich Cunrath's"). It is a duodecimo of 96 pages, composed in an expository format, not as a dialogue; nominally in eighty theses, but Leyser's numbering, here and in later works, is inconsistent and inaccurate. *Theophilus Alethaeus* is his new pseudonym, meaning "God-Loving Truthful". "Cunrath of Friburg" appears on Leyser's title pages for the next five years, but who actually was the printer, or publisher, or where, is another question.[74] In this book Leyser begins his eight year labour of gathering thistles, facts and quotations, arguing that since polygamy has been practiced so many times by so many people in so many places it was indubitably justified by the law of nature, the law of nations, and the law of God, and should be legislated by all ruling powers for the general good of all segments of the population.

That book was in Latin for the learned. For the public at large, Leyser decides to rewrite his German dialogue, the one which now we know only in Gesenius' text, and so with a dedication grandiloquently addressed "To All Gods on Earth, that is All Earthly Powers High and Low Spiritual and Worldly as the Best to Introduce, the Greatest to Promote and the Most Powerful to Defend Polygamy," boldly signing his own name for the first time, he sends them a New Year's Gift for January 1, 1675, *Politischer Discurs, Zwischen Monogamo und Polygamo von der Polygamia, oder Vielweiberey, aufgesezt und mit 100 argumenten erörtet von Joanne Lysero. Gedruckt zu Freyburch, Im Jare Anno 1675. dem 1. Januarius* ("Political Discourse between Monogamo and Polygamo of Polygamy, or Many-wiving, set forth and urged with 100 arguments by Johan Leyser. Printed at Friburg, in the Year 1675, January 1"). The dialogue, closely printed in two columns on forty quarto pages, bears the sub-title *Gewissenhaftes und Schriftmässiges gespräch, Zwischen Monogamo und Polygamo,* "Conscientious and Scriptural Discussion between Monogamo and Polygamo." M, or Monogamo, and P, Polygamo, seesaw back and forth over Adam and Eve, Jacob and David, arguing in this book almost wholly from the Bible. Then stretching his dialogue format out of shape, Leyser presents his century of supplementary arguments, with a third voice joining in (actually E for Ergo).

As the most dedicated of all who ever wrote in favor of polygamy, Leyser achieves miracles of deduction from Scripture. If the prophet Isaiah said (chapter 4, cited by Leyser as 3) that on some future day of catastrophe seven women will seize on one man and beg him to bestow his name on them, Leyser infers that "what is a token of salvation can be no sin" (XCVI, XCVII). Rather, he again asserts, plural marriage will overcome the common sins of whoring, adultery, onanism, infanticide, wife murder.

Reiterating God's command to be fruitful, increase and multiply, Leyser here as in his Latin *Discursus* of 1674 invokes the curse and doom pronounced by the prophet Jeremiah on any who are negligent in doing the work of the Lord. Without any word of apology for his own nonfeasance, Leyser calls down that curse on those who oppose polygamy, not just casually cursing, but cursing in grand style: "The Lord curse you, Satan, the Lord curse you, Asmodai; the Lord who hath redeemed Israel, the Lord trample Satan under our feet, and so in short, Amen."

In preparing for this peroration Leyser has put on the mantle of the pioneer discoverer suffering for truth's sake. He recalls the New Testament story of Nicodemus, who adhered to Jesus, but in secret only, who came to Jesus, but only stealthily by night (John vii, 50), who would not admit openly to the world that he knew that Jesus was come to be the world's savior. And so Leyser prints a list of names of men well-known in his time, who, he is sure, believe as he does, though secretly, interesting names, fifteen names, which, however, we will withhold from the reader for a little while.

This book offers us a surprise, a respite from the dreary and endless repetition of debater's points and dull dogmas. In some copies (the earliest?), not in all, there are two pages of verses printed, in the fashion of that time, which often included stanzas complimenting the author. Only these stanzas are not quite so complimentary. One could sooner understand why Leyser had them omitted from the later copies than why he let them be included in the first place. Two of them are in French, which may reflect Leyser's spasm of somewhat clandestine preaching in that country. One is signed *S.N.* and addressed *A L'Auteur,*

Que Vous estez divin
Devine est vostre Doctrine
Vos recompenses enfin
En seront coups de lime.
Si vous passez jamais
Les villes populaires
Evitez cet arrest
Par la prudence de vous taire;
Et ne vouz ditez autheur
De Vostre Polygamie
Ou, on vous rossera si meur
Que pour une seule vous n'aurez plus d'envie.

Wit, like poetry, is what gets lost in translation, and this doggerel will come across better in a paraphrase:

You who are a minister
Of a doctrine sinister
Just continue with this tale
You'll be horsewhipped without fail.
If you ever choose to pass
Cities where our women mass
You had better duck this sentence,
Pass in prudence, slink in silence.
Don't you ever dare admit
That this booklet you have writ
Urging men to marry many
Or you'll be so shrewdly hit
You won't need to marry any.[75]

P.A. contributed these lines:

Si jamais un Ouvrage merita des Louanges
C'est Celle qua present vous donne aux humains
Il Faut sans doute qu'un esprit d'ange
Vous aye inspires les sentiments divins

Vostre dessein est beaux juste & fort Salutaire
Je preuois mille bien, qui nous en reviendra
Mais aux beaux sexe estent contraire
Aux lieux de recompense l'auteur en patira.

This may be rendered more or less,

If ever a work did merit high applause
Tis this one you now to the human race define.
No doubt an angel spirit was the cause,
Inspiring your sentiments with grace divine.

Your design is fine, just, highly salutary,
I see a thousand benefits will thence to us accrue
But since to the fair sex tis all contrary
Instead of reward the author will be all black and blue.

B.O. contributed eight lines in German which rhyme badly and reason worse, and so may be passed over, but the fourth, a quatorzain, is interesting because it jabs at Leyser from the rear. No one in that era, no matter how accepting of the idea of one man marrying several women, was willing to consider the acceptability of polyandry, of one woman sharing several husbands. Though it was known that some such marriage forms had existed in the past, and were reputed to survive in some places, polyandry was rejected by all writers in Europe, Leyser included. *D. L. B.*, whoever he was, was therefore being thoroughly ironical in this sonnet:

Herr Leyser ihr thut wohl, der nachwelt anzuzünden
Ein liecht, das mann verlescht hat so viel hundert jahr
Und durch viel argument erweist ihr hel und klar,
Das vor der Welt ein Mann sich Kan und ohne sünden
Mit mehr als einer Frau in Ehestand befinden.
Doch were es, deucht mir Wohl so gut; ihr thetet dar,
Als recht, das einer Frau der Manner hab ein par,
Sonst Wird nie das geschlecht eur meinung gut befinden.
Und ich befürchte sehr, das wo ihr komt ins Haus
Da euch die Frau nur kent, so must ihr gleich heraus,
Weil nuhmer über all die Weiber meist regieren.
Drumb ändert euer lehr, erweiset wo ihr Könnt,
Das mehr als einen Mann zu nehmen sey vergönt,
Es wird viel besser seyn vor euch, ihr werd es spüren.

Herr Leyser, you do well to enkindle the gleam
Of that candle, for centuries a snuffed out beam.
Through long debate you prove both bright and clear
How Jack may openly without sin or fear
In marriage join with more than one Jill.
Though truly, so well, it seems, you reckon there,—
For her to take of men a pair—is quite as fair.
Or else that sex your sense will take quite ill.
I greatly fear, where any lady's house you enter,
—She knows your face? Out promptly you must canter.

Since everywhere the ladies now lay down the law
You must change your lore; prove, as only you know how,
To take more than one man you will allow,
So 'twill go better with you: that's the line to draw.

Again a published answer came out to bring further attention to Leyser. Johannes Musaeus, professor of theology at Jena (1613-1681) published, as *praeses,* a *Theological Dissertation on the Controversial Question, Whether Marriage, without infraction of its primeval institution, might be among more than two, namely, one husband and one wife? In which particularly the text of Matthew xix, 9, is vindicated from the falsehoods of Theophilus Alethaeus by which he tries in his Political Discourse on Polygamy to pervert it from its genuine meaning,* in 54 pages, to be discussed by respondent Tobias Nicolaus Herzog, plus 86 pages of *Theses on Marriage* by Musaeus. Musaeus makes a point of identifying the Johan Leyser who composed the German language dialogue with the Theophilus Alethaeus of the Latin *Discursus Politicus,* to which he devotes most of his attention; and his closely argued orthodoxies are added to the reservoir of repetitious dogma from which later controversialists will draw with or without quotation marks.[76]

Leyser meanwhile is going about from town to town, preaching in the marketplaces, and peddling his books, which find a ready sale, if only among husbands out to tease their wives. In 1675 he gets out a Dutch translation of his hundred-argument dialogue, while he works on revising and expanding both his Latin *Discursus* and his German *Discurs.*[77]

On January 5, 1676 at Wittenberg another theological aspirant takes on himself to lay down the final word on this now sharply debated matter: Lucas Kannenberg, of Riga, delivers a *Theological Disputation on Polygamy,* not naming Leyser, but alluding to Musaeus and to "Candidus" Vigil Germanus' *Epistola* against Wahrenberg, and quoting profusely and effusively from his *praeses* the magnificent, most reverend, most ample excellent Professor Abraham Calovius.[78]

Leyser continues to ignore these opponents. In 1676, after much reading in histories and geographies he publishes a revised and enlarged version of his Latin book of theses, now *Discursus Politicus de Polygamia. Auctore Theophilo Alethaeo . . . Editio altera multò auctior. Friburgi, Apud Henricum Cunrath, 1676* ("Political Discourse on Polygamy . . . Second Edition, Much enlarged"). This volume now has 173 octavo pages. The number of theses is now nominally ninety, with ten new sections added V-XIV, and large addenda tacked on to previous theses passim, with the numeration again, or still, not quite precise or accurate.[79]

As in 1674, but with much greater detail and many more references, Leyser calls on all earthly powers and magistrates highest and lowest to become the patrons of polygamy. He marshals his case methodically and in encyclopedic style. With an earnestness positively pathetic he calculates the benefits that would accrue from plural marriage: benefits to married men, growing old happily surrounded by a large loving well-bred family; benefits to young men who could thereby remedy the ill effects of indiscreet impetuosity, or of a less than satisfactory first choice in matrimony; benefits to wives, freed from the common vices of pride, sloth and jealousy, to wax in virtue and in health both of mind and body; benefits to young maidens, who would have easier access to marriage, less risk to health and reputation from marriage missed; benefits to merchants, sailors, travelers of all kinds, whether to far off India or nearby Leipzig Fair, benefits too obvious to spell out; benefits to poor soldiers, driven to enlist by poverty, who could add a rich wife to the one back home; benefits to many a troubled conscience; benefits to old men who could be rejuvenated by a young bride, as old King David was warmed by Abishag cuddling to his senile bosom; benefits to little children, assured of maternal care even if their natural mothers might die or be away; benefits to parents in bringing up their children; benefits to all householders on the farm or in town, who could use more helpful hands; benefits to emperors, kings, princes, counts, barons and all other ranks of nobility, to whom many wives mean authority, power and opulence; benefits to pastors, bishops, all ranks of clergy, whose livelihood would profit from having so many more weddings and baptisms to perform, apart from benefits to the church by wiping out so many sins, and by solving the dilemmas of missionaries like Alexander of Rhodes in Vietnam. In my father's house are many mansions, says the Saviour, with room for many souls; who but the devil foe to man and envious of his prosperity instills hatred of polygamy?[80]

So Leyser, carried away by his enthusiasm, who might more effectively have kept to the examples which he multiplies: from history, as evidences of the law of nature and of nations; from the Bible and from commentators on the Bible; from authorities on the theory and practice of marriage, notably John Selden; from Luther and Melanchthon; from the precedent of Philip of Hesse, of which he knew the little told by Thuanus; from antiquity, Greek, Roman and German; from the habits of sheep and goats and other such creatures of God's handiwork; from Emperor Valentinian and Count von Gleichen; from Commodus the pagan emperor, misplaced in time after the earliest Christian emperors, which is a symptom betraying Leyser's borrowing of erudition; and from the Catholic spokesmen Cajetan and Bellarmine quoted so imprecisely that we can identify the second hand sources from which he has lifted them.[81]

This edition was addressed broadcast to all ruling powers on earth, but Leyser beamed its message at one reigning monarch, at least, in particular. He ordered a special printing of this volume with a different title page, *Discursus Abrahamiticus de Polygamia, Auctore Joanne Lysero. PP. LL. F. E. N. Friburgi, Apud Hinricum Cunrath, 1676* ("Abrahamitical Discourse on Polygamy, Author Johan Leyser," etc.); and with a different preface, dedicated most fittingly to *Defensori Fidei Dexterrimo Carolo II,* the Most Dextrous Defender of the Faith, Charles II, King of Great Britain. Invoking as reverend models Father Abraham, David the man after the heart of God, and Solomon wisest among kings, Leyser calls upon Charles II to follow the counsel given by Melanchthon to his ancestor Henry VIII, to institute a regime of polygamy, filling the earth with true Christians and Paradise with saved souls. King Charles, as it happened, was already doing his personal best along those lines, as an individual, and as an example to his subjects; but whether he ever received a copy of this book from

Leyser, and whether he had any thoughts about it, is one with what song the Sirens sang and what name Achilles took when he hid among the maidens.[82]

Later in 1676 Leyser issued, with some changes on the title page, and with some additions to the text, his German language dialogue, *Politischer Discurs Zwischen Polygamo and Monogamo von der Polygamia oder Vielweiberey, auffgesetzt und mit mehr als 100. Argumenten erkläret. von J. L. Friburgi, Apud Henricum Cunrath. Anno 1676.* Again in that same year Leyser published that dialogue, adding (above the title as just given) a flamboyant line *Das Königliche Marck aller Lander, Das ist: Politischer Discurs Zwischen Polygamo und Monogamo von der Polygamia oder Vielweiberey, auffgesetzt und mit mehr als 100. Argumenten erkläret. von J. L. Friburgi, Apud Henricum Cunrath. Anno. 1676.*

Those words *Das Königliche Marck aller Länder* were variously interpreted by his contemporaries. Some read it as "To the Royal Forums of All Lands," in keeping with Leyser's habitual tone. Others, more precisian in their German, rendered it as "The Royal Marrow for All Provinces," that is, the essential substance of social policy for the German principalities. Some saw in that line a concealed compliment to the memory of his one time patron, Count Königsmarck. But everywhere this ostentatious title became the crown of Leyser's notoriety. From here on he is continuously the focus of hostile pamphlets, and organized persecution wherever he goes.[83]

This hostility rankles, for Leyser in his delusion always saw himself as a benefactor to humanity, while the lords temporal and spiritual of his time manifestly continued to neglect the real problems which he thought he was solving out of their own Holy Scriptures. On his dedication page he inserts the bare citation "Acts xiii, 46," knowing that his readers will turn in their Testaments to read there

> Then Paul and Barnabas waxed bold, and said, "It was necessary that the word of God should first have been spoken to you: but seeing ye put it from you, and judge yourselves unworthy of everlasting life, lo we turn to the Gentiles."

Once again he prints his list of Nicodemuses, those who agree with him but only in secret, adding eight names to the fifteen he first tabulated in his 1675 text, and so we now give that passage in its revised form,

> Ich weiss viel hochgelehrte in Geistl. und weltl. Rechten Hochverständige Männer, als Wagnerum, Museum, Hülsmannum, Rivetum, Diestium, Hahnium, Struvium, Lisetum, Böclmannum, Frenkenst. Bosium, Jungium, Brecklingium, Svisingrum, Haersurtum, Dirschovium, Müllerum, Abendana, Spinosa, Buvendorf, Miltonum, Hausen, Bona, &c., so zum theil in Privat-Discursen all ihr herz mir hierinn offenbahret und bekant, dass die vielweiberey wider Gottes wort nicht sey . . .

> I know many men deeply learned in canon and civil law, men of profound understanding, such as Wagner, Museus, Huelsemann, Rivet, Diest, Hahn, Struve, Liset, Boeckelmann, Franckenstein, Bosius, Jung, Breckling, Suesinger, Haersurt, Derschau, Müller, Abendana, Spinoza, Pufendorf, Milton, Hausen, Bona, etc., to some degree in private discussions unbosomed and made known all their heart in this matter to me, that polygamy is not in conflict with the word of God . . .

Surprise! Twenty-three names here that Leyser enrolls, most rather unfamiliar to us: some of them we shall try to identify in our footnotes, although to unscramble Wagners, Jungs and Müllers from among the legions with those names is almost hopeless.[84] Struve we can identify at once, because Leyser quotes his *Syntagma Juris Civilis,* in the addenda to this edition, that polygamy is not against natural law or divine law. Boeckelmann belongs in this list: Germany has already heard from him, and so shall we, shortly. Spinoza? That gentle heretic may have been talking about matters he chose not to write about; we wish we knew. Pufendorf, his name peculiarly misspelled, we already know, though we have yet to come to those of his writings which most properly earn him his place in this roster. And Milton: Milton surely belongs in the roll call. *We* know that, having his *Treatise on Christian Doctrine* since 1825. But how did Leyser know?

We find the answer, after laboriously tracing out many mazes to dead ends, in a book by Gerhard Feltmann, lecturer in law at Groningen, in a rebuttal to Leyser: *Tractatus de Polygamia, Das ist: Gewissenhafftes und Schrifftmässiges Gespräch Zwischen Weltmann und Sittmann, Dem Gewissenlosen und Unschrifftmässigen zwischen Monogamus und Polygamus, von der Vielweiberey gehaltenen Gespräch entgegen gesetzt. Leipzig, in Verlegung Matthäus Birckners, Druckts Johann Köhler, 1677,* 217 pages, ("Treatise on Polygamy, that is Conscientious and Scriptural Dialogue between Worldlyman and Moralman, against the Conscienceless and Unscriptural Dialogue between Monogamus and Polygamus on Polygamy; published by Matthew Birckner, printed by Johan Köhler"). Feltmann adapts Leyser's words for his character of Weltmann, "Worldlyman," and answers through Sittmann, "Moralman"; but to review all of his points on what really was God's intention would be as dismal as it was futile, although it is testimony to how seriously men did take Leyser's case. In the course of reviewing Weltmann's arguments for plural marriage, Sittman asks him how he came to adopt those views. This exchange ensues, here rendered into English:

> Weltmann. Don't you know Rivet, Diest, Boeckelmann, Pufendorf, Milton, Hausen, Bona, etc., so definitely to a degree spoke their minds to me that polygamy is not against God's word. However, when it would come to public admission, they would not say anything.
>
> Sittman. Fine compliments, I must admit, you pay them, that they are plain hypocrites—which nevertheless I cannot believe. I do not know all of them but I would not suspect them of that.
>
> As for Hülsemann, Havemann in his Book 3, title I, Section 1, *Gamologia Synoptica*, also makes mention of this, that it should be noticed there how he held the contrary. Hahn and Struve speak much more of the customs of the Jews, than of divine law, and have conceded that polygamy was forbidden

> by Christ. Pufendorf bases himself only in that it is not necessary for a man to expend all his potency on one woman, which to you yourself seems to be quite in bad taste. Herr Boeckelmann tries to do what he can in his Defense Oration to rid himself of this stigma. Milton—it is all what I have myself told you, that he became blind, and lived at the park in Westminster. Once in the presence of the Private Secretary of the Dutch Ambassador, and afterward when the son of the latter was there, he had it rubbed into his nose because he alone then persisted that polygamy was not expressly forbidden by Moses the lawgiver and was customary among the Israelites.

The private secretary to the Dutch Ambassador was (we can be fairly certain) Vlitius, Milton's visitor in 1652, and Feltmann's neighbor and colleague in Breda in 1664-1666. That was most likely when Feltmann learned of Milton's views.[85]

When did Feltmann and Leyser meet? There is a strong hint on Feltmann's page 209: Sittmann says that he and Weltmann had not long before made a trip together down the Rhine, and had been swindled by a rascally innkeeper. Any meeting between Feltmann and Leyser must have been before January 1, 1675, when Leyser first mentions Milton. This contact may perhaps be confirmed by Leyser's 1679 Stockholm testimony (of which more anon) that five years earlier his book had been printed at Groningen, which would be 1674.

Our knowledge of Leyser's movements is always fragmentary, and dates are often conjectural. We know that he visited Kiel, where by 1674 the highly orthodox university faculty, under the influence of Christian Kortholt, alert to the currents then in the wind, sponsored disputations against the ideas of Ochino. Leyser brashly went to Kortholt's house, where he was accorded a most uncordial reception. The Pro-Rector and Academic Senate joined with the Consistory to ask the City Council of Kiel to expel this alien agitator. Leyser moved on.[86]

Perhaps earlier, perhaps later, Leyser is reported at Güstrow, in Mecklenburg, where Siricius had been pastor, 1670-1675. He peddles his tracts, he is summoned before the local magistrates, and he is forced to leave town, escorted by the hissing populace and ducking a shower of stones from a mob from whose hands he barely escaped: so we are told by Fridericus Thomas, in his *Analecta Gustroviensia,* "Gustrovian Gleanings," published at Leipzig and Güstrow in 1706, pages 206-207; unfortunately foggy on the date.

In 1676 Leyser is in Denmark, somehow employed there as a military chaplain. He spends some time in discussion with Johan Lassenius, pastor of St. Peter's Church, then as now a congregation of Germans residing in Copenhagen. Lassenius had travelled much in western Europe and it was his pride that he had been received in France by Cardinal Mazarin, in England by John Milton.[87] Leyser spends more time with Severin Walther Schlüter, court preacher to the Queen Mother of Denmark, and theologian at Rostock. The net result is that Schlüter is presently fulminating against him in print, *Theologische Gedancken von der Polygynia, oder von dem nehmen vieler Weiber, auff Veranlassung eines ohnlängst hievon in Lateinischer Sprache unter dem Nahmen Theophili Alethaei heraussgegeben Politischen Discurses, eröffnet durch Severin Walter Schlütern, Ihr. Königl. Majest. der Königl. Frau Mutter in Dennemarck und Norwegen Hoff-Predigern. Rostock, in Verlegung Sehl. Joachimi Wilden Wittib und Erben. Gedruckt bey Jacobus Richeln, E.E. Rahts-Buchdr. An. 1677.* ("Theological Thoughts on Polygyny, or taking many wives, on the occasion of a Political Discourse recently issued hereabouts in the Latin Tongue under the name of Theophilus Alethaeus, presented by Severin Walter Schlüter, Court Preacher to her Royal Majesty the Queen Mother of Denmark and Norway. Rostock. Published by the Widow and Heirs of the late Joachim Wild, printed by Jacob Richel.")

Schlüter writes in German to accommodate the unlearned public; he draws heavily on Musaeus, and expands on Musaeus, whose dissertation had complained of hindrance from other business; he argues natural law and divine law, balances citations against citations, counters Leyser's fallacious inferences by counter-deductions ultimately no less fallacious; cobwebs against soap bubbles. The book is prefixed by multiple dedications to a parcel of assorted privy councillors and court chamberlains: were they only being flattered, or were they being prodded to take action?[88]

That spring of 1677, Leyser (having found Mecklenburg and Schleswig-Holstein so uncongenial) moves somewhat to the west, to the lower Elbe. During the Lenten season and Easter time he is innocently circulating with his pack of books in and around Hamburg, and inevitably stirring up a cackle and a furor. This we know from the appearance of a 99 page quarto, dated April 3, 1677 in the preface, *Eilfertiges Antwort-Schreiben an Seinen guten Freund zu Hamburg, darin eine Summarische Widerlegung des politischen Discurs von der Viel-Weiberey, So ein Atheistischer Huren-Teuffel J. L. Bosshafftiglich aussgestreuet, enthalten ist. Aus Leipzig gesandt von Simplicio Christiano . . . Gedruckt im Jahr 1677* ("Reply Written in Haste to His Good Friend at Hamburg Containing a Summary Refutation of the Political Discourse on Polygamy Wickedly Disseminated by an Atheistical Devil of a Whoremonger J. L., sent from Leipzig by Simplicius Christianus . . . Printed 1677"). Simplicius Christianus purports to be writing from Leipzig to his friend who reported seeing Leyser in military chaplain's garb hawking his pamphlets at six or eight schillings a copy: why Simplicius Christianus wears his pseudonymous mask is not apparent. As his title page betokens, he is hot, heavy handed and harsh. To him J. L. is an *eseL* (an ass), a Hümpler and Stümpler, a bumbler and a bungler, whose hundred points are a hundred lies. Nonetheless he puts down his answers one for one, arguing almost wholly from Scripture. Unlike other opponents of Leyser, Simplicius Christianus offers almost no learned stuffing from scholars or theologians. For instance, Leyser habitually misquotes Jerome's "non damno polygamos" out of context and imprecisely as if it applied to simultaneous polygamy. Most opponents protest in great pain, digging up Jerome's several texts which really refer to successive marriages of monogamous spouses. Simplicius Christianus seems to know nothing about Jerome's texts, and argues not the fact but the principle, to the effect that what if Jerome may not have condemned the *polygamists,* yet he did not condone *polygamy.*[89]

That same Lenten season at Altona, near Hamburg, an evangelical parson Johan Frische is writing another refutation and fretting over publication delays which hold his book up past his preface date of June 12, 1677: *Unvorgreiffliche Erörterung der Frage: was von der Polygamie oder Viel-Weiberey zu halten sey. Einem jeden Vernünfftigen zu fernern Nachsinnen, und beliebiger Beurtheilung fürgetragen von Johann Frischen, Dienern des Göttlichen Worts bey der Evangelischen Gemeine zu Altona. Hamburg, Gedruckt bey Georg Rebenlein, In Verlegung des Autoris, Im Jahr 1677* ("Disinterested Discussion of the Question: what should be understood of Polygamy, or Many-Wiving: offered to every reasonable person for further consideration and more acceptable judgment, by Johan Frische, minister of God's word in the Evangelical Parish of Altona. Hamburg. Printed by Georg Rebenlein, Published for the Author, 1677"). Frische knows Leyser by name, as an alien (eine frembde person) disturbing the tranquillity of Frische's beloved Vaterland, which to him is the city-state of Hamburg. For a laugh Frische reprints some of the verses from that first 1675 edition. He presents his answers in a series of ten axioms, philosophically developed and fortified by palisades of standard citations barricading his vertical margins. His organization of material is thus original but his case is Siricius and Beza against Ochino, Mentzer and Vigil against Wahrenberg, Musaeus against Alethaeus, credit always given where due. He cites the *Harmony of the Gospels* by Grandfather Polycarp Leyser senior with no hint of the relationship. It never occurs to him, as it never occurs to any of Leyser's opponents, to consider the viewpoint or feelings of the woman or her human entitlement to equality in rights: since Leyser thinks polygamy is so fruitful, Frische cites in refutation a burgomaster in Berne who had thirty children by two successive wives, Count Johan of Nassau with twenty-five children by three successive wives, his personal friend Arnold Schepler who had twenty-four children by one single wife, etc., etc., etc.[90]

Meanwhile in March or April Leyser has crossed from Hamburg to Stade in the nearby Duchy of Bremen (which is not the city of Bremen). Perhaps he hoped for help from some members of the Königsmarck family, who held big estates there and ruled the region on behalf of the Swedish crown whenever the fortunes of war permitted. The women of Stade presently made it too hot for him to linger there, but he remained long enough to conduct a dragged out disputation between Easter and May, 1677, with the doublechinned pot-bellied rector of the local school, Johan Diecmann (1646-1720).

Diecmann was startled by the effect that Leyser's temptation had on the impressionable pupils of his school, so about Easter time he composed a *Breve Examen Discursus politici Germanici de polygamia* ("Brief Examination of the German Political Discourse of Polygamy"). Leyser took the aggressive, challenging and provoking, in face to face confrontations, particularly on April 30, so on May 1 Diecmann sent Leyser a manuscript copy of the *Examen* with a formally polite letter praying God to grant him some good sense. On May 10, with the help of amanuenses supplied by Diecmann, though complaining of the distractions at his inn (at the sign of the All-illuminating Sun, in Stade), Leyser replied with his formally polite letter, restating his credo in an *Examen Examinis,* "Examination of the Examination." Leyser concludes by proposing to inscribe a long monumental epitaph above the tomb to which he consigns monogamy:

> Siste viator gradum, paucis Te volo.
> Quaeris quis hic sepultus sit? Monogamia.
> Quaeris quo Patre nata? Phantaso.
> Qua matre? Agnoea.
> Qua nutrice educata? Moria.
> (Quibus statoribus defensa? fratibus ignorantia & Gynaecocratumenis.)
> Quid egit in mundo? (Nihil, Risit) lusit, cucurbitas pinxit,
> Enixa etiam est, nescio quo foetus infandos,
> Infanticidas, uxoricidas, adulteros, Onanitas,
> (Sodomitas) aliosq: (idgeneris) Cyclopas.
> Tandem debilitata & in nihilum redacta est, atq: hic sepulta jacet.
> Si nihil hic inveneris, Benevole Lector, ne mireris, quia hic sepulta est MONOGAMIA UTIS

Stay, wayfarer, your step, a few words with you I pray.
Do you ask who lies here buried? Monogamy.
Do you ask who her father was? Phantasy.
Her mother? The Lady Know-Nothing.
Bred by what nurse? Folly.
By which attendants guarded? The brothers Ignorance and Pettycoatgoverned.
What has she done in the world? Nothing. She giggled, she coquetted, she painted on gourds,
Yet she did bring forth I know not what an unspeakable brood,
Infanticide, wifemurder, adulterers, onanism, sodomy and other monstrosities of that breed.
At last worn out, and to a nothing reduced, and here lies buried.
If nothing is what you find here, dear reader, be not astounded, for here is buried
MONOGAMY

Diecmann spent the rest of the year revising a book of counter-rebuttals. It was substantially ready by the end of the summer, but first, on September 13, at 8 A.M., as *praeses,* with Joachim Lehment, respondent, he issued a *De Rigore Legis Monogamicae, in politia Judaica ab ipso Deo Relaxato, Dissertatio Biblica* ("On the Rigor of the Law of Monogamy in the Jewish Polity Relaxed by God Himself, A Biblical Dissertation"), printed in twenty-nine pages at the press of Caspar Holwein at Stade. Diecmann sidesteps the pit into which many orthodox fell, including Simplicius Christianus, of trying to evade the fact of polygamy among the patriarchs. Diecmann simply concedes the point, developing the old theory of the three epochs: monogamy the law of God from Adam's time, polygamy permitted by special dispensation from Abraham's time until Jesus restored monogamy to the end of time.[91]

His major work was printed early next year, the preface dated January 28, 1678, at Caspar Holwein's press, *Vindiciae Legis*

Monogamicae ("Defenses of the Law of Monogamy"), including, as his complex title pages advertises, his own May 1 letter, his *Breve Examen,* (1-24); Leyser's May 10 letter and *Examen Examinis* (25-46); and (47-270) the *Iteratae Vindiciae Legis Monogamicae seu Responsio Apologetica, Lyseriano Examini Examinis Opposita* ("Repeated Defenses of the Law of Monogamy, or Response and Defense against Leyser's Examination of the Examination") by Diecmann.

In a Latin style peppered with proverbs, rather easier to read than the leaden prose of most of his contemporaries, Diecmann pounds away at Leyser's evidence, with bows to Siricius, Mentzer, Christianus Vigil and Pufendorf, Musaeus, Feltmann, Frische and Simplicius Christianus, Heroldus and Sharrock among many others. Diecmann is a schoolmaster familiar with libraries, so he supplies not one but three quotations from Jerome to rebut Leyser's misquotation (page 69). He has checked out Leyser's citations and nails him for sloppily garbling the names of Archbishops Theutgaudus and Guntharius into Tengualdus and Contrarius (page 44, in the ninth century divorce case of King Lothar). He maneuvers Leyser into a corner by matching lines from the German *Discurs* with the same phrases in Wahrenberg's dialogue, a flagrant plagiary. Leyser, for whatever reason, never chose to accept responsibility for "Wahrenberg"; in his conversations with Diecmann hemmed and hawed, as if Wahrenberg lifted from him. "It is well for you, Leyser," says Diecmann ironically, "that Wahrenberg as you believe, is no longer among the living, because he would not let this injury pass unavenged, nor would he care to be indebted to you for anything" (page 199). Diecmann, it is clear, knows something about Leyser at Pforta and his church jobs, perhaps from Calovius, to whom this book is dedicated, and he clearly associates Wahrenberg and Aletophilus Germanus as well as Theophilus Alethaeus with Leyser.

Like many Lutheran clergymen of the time he refuses to believe the fact of Luther's consent to Philip of Hesse's bigamy, arguing that Thuanus' account does not name him or any other pastors consulted. But in any case, for the most part Diecmann's erudite and elaborate structure, resting on a stack of over two hundred authors in theology and history, has in the end all the substantiality of a child's mud castle on the beach, carefully constructed complete with turrets and courtyards, which still the first returning tide crumbles again into shapeless wet sand.

One of these two hundred authors was John Milton, mentioned in passing for his peculiar book in favor of divorce on the ground of intolerable behavior and disparity and opposition of minds (page 173).[92]

Diecmann also tells us (page 245) not only that Leyser has been ordered out of diverse and celebrated German cities (we know at least Güstrow and Kiel) but that the King of Denmark has put a ban on Leyser throughout all his domains. What specifically happened at the royal court of Denmark is perhaps recorded somewhere, but until by repeated inquiry I coaxed the Danish Royal Archives to track down the manuscript text of the decree for me, perhaps no one had turned to that page since it was entered by hand on May 15, 1677, with no information as to any trial, hearings or proceedings:

> We, Christian V, by the Grace of God, King of Denmark and Norway, &c., announce to all and sundry: seeing that We have learned that a certain Johan Leyser has written a scandalous book entitled *Das Königliche Marck Aller Länder,* and that book printed in 1676 at Friburg in Germany he has been importing into our realms: We wish by this our edict severely to prohibit that book from being sold in the lands under our sovereignty, or being kept or concealed by any of our dear and faithful subjects. Thus we most seriously admonish all persons that not only they shall abstain from reading it, but, in addition, if they have any copies, they shall deliver them, in our towns to the Mayors and Councils, or in the countryside, to the Prefects, who shall transmit all of them to the Chancellery, whence after they have been gathered they are to be handed over to the hangman for public burning. If any be found to conceal a copy thereof, he shall be fined in the sum of 1000 rixdollars, of which one half shall be assigned to the use of our military hospital and the other half to the poor

who abide in the locality where the crime is committed. If the delinquent lacks the means to pay the fine, he shall suffer corporal punishment, according to his condition. Furthermore We command that the aforesaid Johan Leyser forthwith depart from the territories under our sovereignty and never again to appear therein, unless he wishes to suffer capital punishment. Ordering Our Lord Lieutenants, Prefects, Mayors and Councils, Bailiffs, and all other Functionaries properly to supervise and everybody else most humbly to conform to it and to avoid coming to harm. Given at Our Castle, Copenhagen, May 15, 1677.[93]

Leyser moved on; but from May 22, 1677, when he sends Diecmann a letter from Hamburg, the record is blank all through 1678. From later testimony we know that before June 1679 he has travelled to Abo in Finland and to Riga in Courland (Latvia), and has in due course been expelled from both; but exactly when we cannot say.

For New Year 1679 he appears again in print under a fresh pen-name on a innocuous title page: *Vornehmer Leute Gedancken vom Ehstande, Zusammen getragen von Gottlieb Warmund. Gedruckt zu Friburg durch Henricum Kunrad. 1679* ("Thoughts on Matrimony, to Estimable Gentlefolk, brought together by Gottlieb Warmund. Printed at Friburg by Henrich Kunrad"). *Gottlieb Warmund,* God-loving Truth-mouth, hardly conceals itself as the German equivalent for Theophilus Alethaeus, and the text within is once again the *Gewissenhafftes und Schrifftmässiges Gespräch zwischen Polygamo and Monogamo;* only the dedication and preface are different from the 1675-1676 German *Discurs.* In place of the appeal to all powers on earth, the dedication is now addressed "To All Dispassionate Lovers of the Truth, for Further Consideration in the New Year," but the preface shows a higher degree of passion on his own part. This preface is a six page expansion on the two page addenda printed with the later 1676 issues of the *Discurs.* Reinforcing his catalogue of Nicodemuses, the preface emphasizes as fellows to his opinion the names of Rivet, Diest, Milton, Selden (added to the roster), Hahn and

Struvius. He mentions "cases," the case of that Amsterdam mariner, and a new "case:" "Forty years ago a Bishop in England had 2 wives without contradiction"—not identified as to name or source. Most significant is an expansion of reliance on Luther, and a sudden familiarity with the case of Philip of Hesse. Through an unnamed friend he has learned about a text of the Bucer Memorial, and the signatures of Melanchthon, Bucer, "Menius," Leningus, "Raud" and others, in the library of the Hessian theologian Steuber: obviously, he has learned something, but not very accurately. Unintentionally funny, in his rarely funny writings, "Gottlieb Warmund" tells us that he is transmitting the text of the epitaph sent by the "author of the Political Discourse" to a certain Rector, and then revises the text, blasting the anonymity.

Later in 1679 Leyser put out another printing of this volume, still the same dialogue, but revising and enlarging the preface and changing the title page: *Gewissenhaffte Gedancken vom Ehstande zusammen getragen von Gottlieb Warmund. Friburg. Gedruckt durch Henricum Kunrad, 1679.* ("Conscientious Thoughts on Matrimony, brought together by Gottlieb Warmund"). The Philip of Hesse case is expanded, adding the names of Corvinus and Melander as well as Luther. The "epitaph" is still further revised, now with the addition of a misogynous catalogue of female frights all to be blamed on monogamy: monstrous Lalages, morose Xantippes, arrogant Vashtis, imperious Semiramis, husband-killing Medeas, poisoning Lamias, abominable Drusillas, nameless Furies and many more.[94]

Against Leyser in this year 1679 the ten year old book by Michael Siricius, *Uxor Una,* comes out in a second edition, now received as an anti-Leyser tract. Also early in that year a Norwegian minister, Johan Brunsmann, brought out the last of the major books against Leyser: *Johannis Brunsmanni Nidrosiensis, Monogamia Victrix, sive, Orthodoxa Ecclesiae Christianae Sententia, de Unis duntaxat eodem tempore concessis Christiano Nuptiis: a Criminationibus Vindicata quibusvis, quas Gemino collectas Scripto novus quidam Planus suas fecit . . . Francofurti, Pro Sae. Rae. Mtis Daniae ac Norwegiae Librario, Daniele Paulli. Anno MDCLXXIX.* ("John Brunsmann of Nidrosia, his Monogamy Victorious, or the Orthodox Judgment of the Christian Church on Single Wedlocks only at one time granted to a Christian: Vindicated from Any Charges, which Collected in a Twin Publication some New Charlatan Makes his own, Frankfurt, for Daniel Paul, Bookseller to His Royal Danish & Norwegian Majesty.") Brunsmann seems to have composed his book independently of earlier anti-Leyser books, none of which he cites. With ponderous competence he postulates the churchmen's dogmas for monogamy (chapters 1-7) and devotes chapters 8-29 to ingeniously trying to unravel Leyser's knots, carefully citing each point from both the Latin and the German treatises. He draws on Vesalius and Bartholin for scientific precision on the number of ribs in men and women. He reaches into the Hebrew Midrash, the *Chronicles of Moses,* (a book rarely read even by rabbis) for details on Moses' marriages.

He relies very little on the theory of the patriarchs' dispensation, (naively? wryly?) observing that the absence of Biblical censure on their other peccadilloes, incest, lies, etc., is no warrant for following their practice in polygamy either. He does not believe the reports of Luther's share in the Philip of Hesse bigamy: in the spring of 1679 that was still possible, though not much longer.[95]

This same year 1679 Leyser crossed into Sweden, carrying a cargo of copies of his *Gottlieb Warmund* books. At Stockholm he took lodgings with a German apothecary and industriously set about peddling these books, and so very soon was facing criminal charges: offending against the established religion, against the laws of the realm, and by consequence, of lese majesty. The crabbed minutes of the Stockholm ministers' Consistory have survived in their wretched handwriting at the Municipal Archives there, with several letters by Leyser, so that we can now offer a detailed contemporary account.[96]

On June 4, 1679, the Consistory, being apprised of a pernicious tract being pushed by that little man at the German apothecary's, summoned him to appear before them at 10 A.M., Friday June 6. On that day, the book, or parts of it were read to the Consistory, whose members found it wicked, offensive, and likely to create dissension among married couples. Leyser was then questioned in person. He readily acknowledged that he was the author; that he had printed it at "Sell" (Celle? Zelle?) and that he had brought 250 copies to Stockholm. He had given a copy to two high dignitaries, the rikskansler and to the hovkansler. Unabashed Leyser presented a copy to each member of the Consistory, and so was permitted to leave the hearing; but the Consistory resolved to call upon the Governor General of Stockholm to arrest him and confiscate his books.

Pentecost (Whitsuntide) seems to have interfered. On June 21, after the holy days, Leyser was again interrogated at the Consistory. Perhaps the Governor General had required more particulars: certainly the minutes are now more explicit. Leyser testifies about his father, the one time professor primarius and church superintendent at Leipzig; about his twenty-five years as clergyman; his clandestine preaching in France, and his coming to Sweden to advance the glory of God and to put an end to the grievous sinfulness there prevailing.

Perhaps the spluttering of the Stockholm pastors disturbed their note taking at this point. The next sentence, important to us, remains ambiguous, though it suggests that Leyser had been in contact with "his Excellency Königsmarck"—which one? when? for a church post, for help in getting ship passage to Calmar?

In further questioning Leyser mentioned printing one of his books five years before at Groningen (this ties in with his contact with Feltmann). He insisted that his views were being readily accepted by public men to whom he had sold the book; and that at Helmstedt University not only students but professors of law and theology accepted the doctrine of polygamy.

The consistory wanted to know more about his adventures in Abo and Riga. Leyser asserted that at Abo he had met with Dr. Enevald Suenonius (or Sveno, 1617-1688, professor of theology 1660-1687) and with the Bishop (this would have been Johannes Gezel, or Gezelius, senior, 1615-1690, bishop since 1664) and his son and successor as bishop, Johannes Gezelius, junior, (1647-1718); that he had preached a sermon in the German church at Abo with the bishop's permission; but that the town councillors had him arrested and deported on a ship bound for Lübeck. A recital at least partly dubious, for Gezelius and Suenonius were very strict in their Lutheran orthodoxy, rigid in pursuit of "heresy" and "witchcraft," dominant in both university and town council as well as in church.

Leyser also conceded that he had been ignominiously expelled from Riga by the city authorities, but he balanced that admission by telling that he had been to Copenhagen three years before, holding discussions with the bishop, with Dr. Lassenius and with the Queen's confessor (Schlüter, likely)—omitting all mention of the Danish expulsion decree of 1677, of which there seems to have been no knowledge in Sweden.[97]

The Consistory solemnly bade him cease and desist from distributing his books, which could cost him his head. They delegated two clergymen to report the case to the Royal Council, and two to call on the Governor General of Stockholm to effectuate their previous motion to arrest Leyser and seize his books.

The Governor General acted quickly, perhaps the same day. One of Leyser's letters, in his large scrawl, in German, is an impassioned appeal for release as a man of conscience who has always served God. In place of a date he wrote *Die Pathmi,* "Day of the Passion," suggesting Christ in the garden. A second letter dated June 25 from his prison cell at Stegeborg Castle pleads for a fair reading of his book, for liberation from jail, for return of his books; not yielding on his views. The Consistory members read this petition, and ruled that no answer need be given. Instead that day their report was filed with the Royal Council, alleging that Leyser had sold 238 copies of his book, and had managed to hide 250 others, that Leyser was eager to resume selling the book because increased demand made it possible to raise the price.

The Royal Council referred the indictment to the mayor and aldermen of Stockholm, and a court trial was held, the charges presented for the prosecution by Gustav Holmström, "fiscal" of the city. Leyser protested that a civil court had no proper jurisdiction, that he was entitled to a church court, or to answer to the Consistory or a judicial commission of churchmen and civil officials. This plea helped not at all. The prosecution pointed to Leyser's previous convictions at Abo and Riga and the penalties imposed there as proof that he knew he was guilty of premeditated criminal violation of the law in Stockholm. On July 11, considering the sentence to impose, the court grimly suggested that he deserved the death penalty. However, since Leyser had sworn that he had not intended any lese majesty, the verdict was limited to the familiar: burn the books, ban the man.

The sentence was published July 14. Next day the books were burned by the public hangman in Leyser's presence (in the pillory?) and presently he was put on shipboard for deportation by army troops; mercifully, it is reported, because they barely saved him from the hands of the infuriated ladies of Stockholm who might have readily tossed his carcass on to the pyre of his burning books.

Where he wandered next is uncertain. In his next and last book, dated "after 1682" on the title page, he speaks of roving in England ("in Anglia versanti") seeking information from bishops and from books: but if he really ever was in Britain it could have been earlier.

This last book was a new issue of the 1676 *Discursus Politicus* greatly expanded to 565 pages plus appendices, by adding a huge hodgepodge of footnotes in tiny print, ostensibly contributed by the editor, Athanasius Vincentius, who greatly respects Theophilus Aletheus: a transparent pretext which deceived only a very few.

On the title page Leyser still carried his standard high: *Polygamia Triumphatrix, id est Discursus Politicus de Polygamia, Auctore Theophilo Aletheo, cum Notis Athanasïi Vincentii, Omnibus Anti-Polygamis ubique locorum, terrarum, insularum, pagorum, urbium, modestè & piè opposita. Londini Scanorum. Sumtibus Authoris post. Annum MD.C.LXXXII.* ("Polygamy Triumphant, that is the Political Discourse of Polygamy by Theophilus Aletheus, with Notes by Athanasius Vincentius, Modestly and Piously Opposed to All Anti-Polygamists, of All Places, Lands, Islands, Villages and Cities. Lund in Skane. At the Author's Expense. After 1682"). Leyser used the Lund place-tag for tactical reasons, perhaps to suggest a link to the young university there, but contemporaries identified the printing (better than most of his books though sprinkled with misprints in Latin and in Hebrew) as done in Amsterdam.[98]

The title page is grandiloquent but the book is bitter. The brashness of his earlier writing is now tinctured by resentment. He never deigns to name his opponent-writers, but identifies them by mocking puns and abusive nicknames: primarily Brunsmann, Diecmann and Feltmann; Siricius and Schlüter are identified indirectly without hostility. Gesenius, who called himself "Vigil" (watchful, or wakeful) is always called *Dormitantius,* the sleeper. His other antagonists are given no obvious notice, nor does he take overt notice of two books recently published on his side of the issue, by Daphnaeus Arcuarius (1679) and Vythage (1680).[99]

The footnotes are lucid but bare in style. In contrast, the preface is Leyserian literary at its most lurid: "How rare be, in the nature of things, those things which not only deserve but also attain to be applauded and desired by all; he will say nothing alien to truth who asserts that among them *golden liberty* fills the page on both sides." This hymn to liberty is his overture; liberty prized by all living creatures, hailed by jurists, valued by philosophers; liberty or death, said the prince of orators; an opinion voiced by Agesilaus of Sparta, by Julius Caesar. Why, God himself elects to be called the vindicator of liberty, beginning his Ten Commandments with the reminder that He has led His chosen out of slavery from Egypt; His elect instruments are the liberators Moses, Joshua, Samson, Gideon. Liberty was bought for all men by the blood of Christ; for liberty the tyrant-quellers of Athens and Rome moved every stone.

But into this rodomontade wriggles Leyser's monomania, as he points his accusing finger at wantonly ambitious women who seek to subject men to their servile yoke, who violate Holy Writ which abhors the topsy turvy order where woman wields the symbols of power. "Since therefore there is no heavier servitude than to be subjected to one wife, there will be no greater liberty than to enjoy many at will." Yet such is the wont of this wicked world, wails this "editor," that for the greatest benefits the worst evil is returned; and Theophilus, for his incomparable services to all Christians and to all men, has suffered crosses, persecution, burning at the stake like the earliest Christians.

Leyser's "annotations" inflate this work to many times the length of the 1676 *Discursus,* but they are pertinent commentary only to a small degree, and that highly repetitious. He is so dreadfully serious. He tabulates his model marriage-multipliers, so: among others, Lamech, Valentinian, Gleichen, Philip of Hesse, Oldendorp had two wives; Commodus, Dagobert, three; Jacob, four; Abia, fourteen; David, eighteen; Rehoboam, eighteen plus sixty concubines; Mahomet, seventeen; Kublai Khan, forty, plus concubines; Euenus of Scotland, a hundred; a king of Peru, 250, an Indian king, 500, an East Indian ruler, 600, and Solomon, the record holder, with the divine number of a thousand wives, to be balanced against the statistic that Solomon reigned forty years, or 14,600 available days and nights. Leyser does not specify which calendar he used, but he includes a digression on why 1,000 is a divine number, and on Proculus, who impregnated a hundred virgins in fifteen days. Mostly the additions are mountains of irrelevancies, suggesting a compulsive personality: in alphabetic order, the names of 125 Catholic monastic or "regular" orders; an itemized listing of one hundred and forty different kinds of physical stigmata which in ancient Israel disqualified a man from the priesthood; twenty causes for the seventeenth century currency shortage, with a jolly drinking song in Latin rhyme to illustrate cause number four, excessive fondness for Bacchus.

He quotes many other verses, from Vergil down to neo-Latin nonentities, but most remarkable is the number of stanzas taken from the epigrams of John Owen, more than fifty times, far more than from any other. It is a peculiar coincidence that Thomas Pecke also favored the epigrams of John Owen.[100]

Three times Leyser makes reference to that bigamous bishop he had already cited in his *Warmund* editions: "Forty years ago a certain bishop in England had two wives at once, and they wed by solemn rites, as Baker records in his Chronicle of England, and was told to me also, when roving in England, by several bishops and pastors" (page 533). Leyser does not specify edition or page. Sir Richard Baker's *A Chronicle of the Kings of England* first appeared in 1643; second edition, 1653; five editions appeared during the years when Leyser could have been roving in England, in 1660, 1665, 1670, 1674 and 1679, and these (peculiar coincidence again) were edited by Milton's nephew and pupil, Edward Phillips. If in any of these editions there is record of a bigamous bishop, that has escaped other readers of Baker's *Chronicle*. "Forty years ago" would have been about 1639-1642. It is incredible that in the flood of pamphlets against the bishops in those years such an incident would not have received a great deal of attention. Leyser was often sloppy in citations and not careful in copying; he lifts references and quotations, leaving the impression that he was using the original, only his errors betraying him; he exaggerates; he masquerades under pseudonyms; but it is more in his character to have misunderstood something he heard than to have resorted to fabricating this reference to Baker. We can only wish that we knew for real whether he was actually ever in England, and with whom he spoke there.[101]

Ordained minister as he was, the last of his footnotes is a prayer to the Lord God who sees into men's hearts, to most holiest Jesus, to bear witness that he has sought only the glory of God and the welfare of His church, to strengthen him in His truth, to protect him, always doing God's will, seeking the glory of His name, walking in His ways.[102]

With this book Leyser's fame was at its peak, but it was an ill fame, and brought him only misery. He is reported at Amsterdam, under assumed names, Ludolphus, or Lambertus, ailing, gaunt, unable to pay his room rent. Jean Baptiste Rocolles, a correspondent of Pierre Bayle, wrote that he had met Leyser at the door of the Public Library in Amsterdam, Leyser addressing him in German, but both thereafter conversing in Latin. Rocolles out of pity visited him several times at his inn, bringing him some preserves (Mme Rocolles' charity?) but when Leyser came to their home one Saturday, he scared Mme Rocolles, he looked so like a ghost. Rocolles was (it seems) even more scared that the innkeeper might expect him to pay Leyser's bill.[103]

Leyser is next heard of in France, after a trip somehow made into Italy. For a time he tries his luck in Paris, eking out a bare existence there as a chess expert. At one time or another (late 1682? early 1683?) he applied for aid to Hector Gottfried Masius, chaplain of the Danish embassy in France. Masius, rigidly orthodox clergyman and diplomatic official, declined to admit Leyser to confession or communion without knowing who he was and whence he came. Leyser, still under an alias, indicated that he was an ecclesiastic from Saxony, in enforced exile from there, but kept his true identity secret from Masius. Sometime along in 1684, still suffering from long illness (in *Polygamia Triumphatrix* he mentions a quartan fever for six months), Leyser decided to go to Versailles, to seek out some former supporters there at the court of Louis XIV, who was setting an example of many mistresses, if not of many wives. He managed to reach there on foot, but these former friends only laughed at him. He turned back to Paris, still on foot; collapsed on the way, was carried into some stranger's house, and so died.[104]

12

Prince Charles Louis and His Laurel-Wreathed Bowman

Johan Leyser (rest his poor soul!) has been mentioned in print during the past two hundred years possibly two dozen times. Even more rarely, in footnotes occurring a century apart, one finds mention that there was another defender of polygamy in those years, Daphnaeus Arcuarius; and in the pursuit of this one more pseudonymous polygamophile through dusty tomes in cobwebbed vaults we find ourselves wandering among the ghosts of long-buried lovers and losers, whose tawdry and trivial lives take on the glamour of an operatic libretto because they were born to live in castle walls and palace halls.

Even before Johan Leyser began to run himself ragged promoting his propaganda for polygamy, somewhat similar thoughts occurred independently to a ruling prince, Charles Louis, Kurfürst, or "Prince Elector," of the Rhenish Palatinate: called "Elector," because he was one of the German princes with an hereditary vote in the election of the "Holy Roman Emperor." Charles Louis (= Karl Ludwig) was a son of the ill-starred "Winter King" of Bohemia, Frederick of the Palatinate, and of Elizabeth Stuart, daughter to James I, and sister to Charles I of England. At the very start of the Thirty Years War, in which Frederick lost all "his" domains, Charles Louis was carried out of "their" Rhenish Palatinate as a little child, and he was away through most of those thirty years, until in 1648 the Treaty of Westphalia "restored" him to those domains as their sovereign ruler.

His family crest bore the motto *Dominus Providebit,* "The Lord Will Provide." Most of the family believed in lending a helping hand to the good Lord. During the Civil War years in England,

1642-1648, his younger brothers Rupert and Maurice served their uncle Charles I as commanders in combat against the Parliament. During those same years Charles Louis sat out that war in London under the protection of that Parliament: as a parasite, free-loading on the funds allowed him by the Presbyterian leadership of that Parliament; as a politician, hobnobbing with the Presbyterian pastors in the Westminster Assembly of Divines; while pretender to the Palatinate, intriguing privately to gain for himself the shaky throne of his uncle Charles I; as patron of savants, dabbling in dilettante experiments with the scientists who later became the Royal Society; and as playboy-princeling, dallying with a gentlewoman of Kent, whom he would not marry though she bore his child, a son, Ludwig von Selz, who died a neglected teen-ager in 1660.[105]

In February, 1650, Charles Louis, then barely four months seated on his Palatinate throne, took to himself a dynastic wife: Charlotte, daughter of William V, Landgrave of Hesse-Cassel. Their nuptials were celebrated for ten days with preachings and feastings, with pomps and parades, with hunting the fox, the wild boar and the wolf. In the next three years Charlotte bore him three children: Karl, who ultimately became his successor; Elizabeth, who ultimately married a brother of Louis XIV; and Frederick, who died an infant, not without accusations of negligence being pointed at his young mother. Shortly afterward Charlotte became aware that her husband was not giving her his complete and undivided attention. It was said that she foolishly confided her worries to one of her ladies-in-waiting, Baroness Marie Suzanne Luise von Degenfeld, only too late discovering that her comforting confidante was in fact her rival. There is gossip galore to choose from, fitter for a novel than a history, both Charles Louis and Charlotte contributing to public scenes of humiliation and hostility.

A state of de facto separation followed. They lived apart from about 1657 to his death in 1680. Whether Charles Louis ever "divorced" Charlotte, and whether in any archive there survives some document by which he disassociated himself from her, is a matter of technicality.[106] He never deprived Charlotte of her title as Electoral Princess of the Palatinate; he continued to provide for her maintenance on their estates; but he made it clear that he regarded himself as discharged from any marital duties to her.

In January, 1658 in a religious ceremony conducted by their Lutheran pastor Hiskias Eleazar Heyland, Charles Louis married his Baroness Luise von Degenfeld. She bore him her first son in October, 1658; during their married life she gave birth to eight sons and five daughters, dying in childbed with a fourteenth March 18, 1677.

This marriage of Charles Louis and Luise was morganatic: that is, Luise was recognized by him as his wife, but not as sharing his princely title, and not bearing heirs to that title. This marriage was also generally regarded as bigamous. Charles Louis' letters to Luise before their wedding show that he had little doubt as to the character of their relation. He writes to her about the Bible story of Ahasuerus, King of Persia, who dismissed his first wife Vashti and then married Esther, an example most certainly having divine approval. He invokes an old theologians' distinction then becoming popular among some jurists: some things may be *unlawful* under civil law, or by church regulations, but not *sinful* in the eyes of God. As civil ruler, he could to a considerable degree make or unmake civil law, or dispense with it. Above all, he was delighted to rediscover the then all but forgotten details in the history of Philip of Hesse. On October 31, 1657 he sent Luise a transcript of the documents in that bigamy, notably the *Instruction* which Bucer carried to Luther and Melanchthon, and so wrote to her, "Das buch kompt gleichsam von himmel,"—"this book comes straight from heaven."[107]

Charles Louis suffered from his bigamy even less than Philip of Hesse, whether in conscience or in the exercise of his political powers, but he was rather less successful in getting pastoral endorsements. He had called young Frederick Spanheim to the chair of theology at Heidelberg, accepting him as a worthy scion of the Spanheim family of theologians; but in the matter of this bigamy, Spanheim steadfastly and publicly to his face refused to give him any support.[108]

To a little degree Charles Louis was somewhat better off

among the lawyers. At least one, Johann Friedrich Boeckelmann, could be counted in his corner, somewhat obliquely using the cover of his inaugural dissertation at Heidelberg University to touch on the issues while naming no names. Boeckelmann and his writings on law were later prominent enough to be read and cited well into the next century, but at this time when he was trying to make some indirect statement on behalf of Charles Louis he was still a beginner at the bar, and the reception that his effort aroused from some members of the Heidelberg faculties of law and theology did not encourage further ventures into these maelstroms.[109]

Far more prominent a jurist, then and since, was Samuel Pufendorf, whom we have already encountered several times. At the beginning of his career, with a sharp eye to his future, in 1660, he dedicated his *Elementorum Jurisprudentiae Universalis Libri Duo* ("Two Books on the Elements of Universal Jurisprudence") to Elector Charles Louis, who promptly invited him to fill a professorship newly created at Heidelberg. Charles Louis also has the honor of having tried to convince Benedict Spinoza to accept a professorship in the same university, so that the welcome to Pufendorf may have been purely in recognition of his professional talents.[110] It is also conceivable that Charles Louis took particular interest in such passages as these in Pufendorf's *Elements,* Book II, Observation V, Section 7:

> at vero ut unus pluribus foeminis simul jungatur, etsi lege divina positiva inter Christianos jam credatur interdictum, legi tamen naturae in se haud repugnat. Non enim necessum est, ut quemadmodum uxor nemini viro corporis sui copiam debet facere, praeterquam uni marito; sic et maritus alii foeminae praeterquam unicae uxori . . . At vero ut unius foeminae libidinae mulcendae omnes quis impendat vires quae apud plures soboli excitandae sufficere poterant, haudquidquam à natura praecipi videtur.

But that one man may be united at the same time with several women (although among Christians now believed forbidden by

> divine positive law) is nevertheless in itself by no means repugnant to the law of nature. For it is not necessary, that, just because a wife ought to grant the use of her body to no man but her one husband, that the husband ought to do the same to no other woman besides his one and only wife . . . But in truth that a man should spend upon appeasing the sexual appetite of one woman all the virility which can suffice to raise up offspring among a number of women, does by no means seem to be ordered by nature.

It is conceivable that the episode with Gesenius reinforced his inclination to leave the issue of polygamy a debated open question in his *De Jure Naturae et Gentium.* In any case Pufendorf never supplied Charles Louis with any published apologia for his bigamy.

Neither does it appear whether Pufendorf transmitted his knowledge of Milton's divorce views to Charles Louis: those views, of course, Pufendorf did not accept, although Boeckelmann found them worthy of attention. Charles Louis had previously ample opportunity to hear of Milton the Divorcer in London of 1643-1645; and life being the strange phenomenon that it is, Milton and Charles Louis shared at least one good mutual friend in those London years: Theodore Haak, later the first to translate *Paradise Lost* into German.[111]

One letter to Charles Louis from his mother, Elizabeth Stuart, reads as if his excuses to her might have been borrowed from Milton (Charles Louis had no need, of course, to borrow). Elizabeth Stuart never approved of Charles Louis' behavior in the matter of his two wives, and she wrote him June 2/12, 1658,

> your open keeping of that wench doth you no smale dishonnour to all persons of all coneditions. If euerie bodie could quit their housbands and uiues for their ill humours, there woulde be no smale disorder in the worlde; it is both, against Gods law and mans law, for though you be a souueraine, yett God is aboue you . . .[112]

Milton's name, needless to say, was hateful to Elizabeth Stuart, and presumably to her son, since Milton's books asserted to all

Europe the justice of the execution of her brother Charles I: we can read her bitter hostility to Milton in her letters.[113]

Elizabeth Stuart never stopped reminding Charles Louis how much criticism she continued to hear about his marital vagaries: but all through the years of his marriage to Luise there seems to have been no published effort on his part to influence public opinion in his favor.

Only in 1679, twenty-one years after his bigamous marriage, and some time after Luise was already in her tomb, did a book appear, published privately, almost secretively, distributed anonymously, which was quickly recognized to be a statement of Charles Louis' position, although it nowhere refers to him. Ostensibly it came forth as an impartial contribution to the debate between Leyser and his opponents.

Why Charles Louis finally sponsored such a work at such a belated date is a question that seems to have occurred, without any answer, to two or three persons in the seventeenth and eighteenth centuries. I doubt whether anyone has given it a thought in the past two hundred years since. It may be inferrable that when Luise died, Charlotte moved to re-assume her full status as Electoral Princess, and to ensure the inheritance for her son. While Charles Louis had no reason to disinherit his and her son Karl, he still seems at that late date interested in setting the official record straight according to his own lights.[114]

That book, published in German, was called *Kurtze Doch Unpartheyisch-und Gewissenhaffte Betrachtung des in dem Natur-und Göttlichen Recht Gegründeten Heiligen Ehstandes, in welcher die Seither Strittige Fragen vom Ehbruch, der Ehscheidung, und sonderlich von dem vielen Weiber-nehmen, mit allem beyderseits gegebenen Beweissthumb, Dem Christlichen Leser vorgestellet werden. Durch DAPHNAEUM ARCUARIUM. Anno cIↄIclxxix.* ("Short but Impartial and Conscientious Consideration of Holy Matrimony, Based in Natural and Divine Law, in which the hitherto Disputed Questions of Adultery, Divorce and Particularly of Polygamy, Are Set Forth for the Christian Reader, with All Arguments Given on Both Sides, by Daphnaeus Arcuarius, 1679").

Some first readers saw in "Daphnaeus Arcuarius" still another pen-name for Johan Leyser, but astute classicists at Heidelberg quickly discerned its true meaning: Daphnaeus, quasi-Greek for laurel-wreathed, might be rendered *Laurentius* in Latin, *Lorenz* in German, while *Arcuarius,* the bowman, pointed to the German *Bogner,* or *Böger;* and specifically to Lorenz Beger, a young man hired in 1677 by Charles Louis to be his librarian and curator of antiquities. It was even doubted that Beger had done much more than edit the materials assembled for him by Charles Louis.

The volume appeared in two issues, the second apparently to correct some typographical slips, rather than to meet any great demand.[115] It has been noticed in footnotes on a few occasions in three hundred years, in which its kinship to the Leyser controversy has gone unremarked and its specific defense of Charles Louis has been rather exaggerated.

It opens in all solemn seriousness with an address "To the most serene, high and mighty, highborn, high and well-born, upright, honor- and virtue-loving Christian Females"—using the protocol titles dictated by court etiquette. It makes a bow, with formal respect, to the writings of Mentzer, Siricius, Schlüter, and Diecmann first, and only afterward names Leyser, Ochino, and above all Luther, Melanchthon and Bucer on the opposite side. Elsewhere in the volume Beger referred to others in the Leyser controversy: Feltmann, Musaeus, "Christianus Vigil" and Brunsmann.

The book proper is in four parts, pedantic and pedestrian. The first division treats of natural law, marriage under natural law and divine law, marriage as a divine or civil contract, what is adultery, what is divorce. The second division considers polygamy in natural law, inferences from hens and doves, elephants and goats, the creation of the first woman from Adam's rib, the constitution of marriage in primeval Eden, effects of plural marriage on reproduction, on upbringing and on peaceful society, how a man is to meet his due obligations in sundry situations, the rule of "do not unto others." The third division chews over Scripture texts, in eight chapters. The fourth book reviews Gregory's letter to Boniface, Emperor Valentinian with his Severa and Justina, the evolution of restrictions on divorce and on polygamy, and the advisability of liberalization for both.

Far more influential than this argument was the appendix, which for the first time gave wide circulation to the documents in the old case of Philip of Hesse: the 1539 *Instruction* brought by Bucer from Philip to Luther and Melanchthon; the memorandum signed by Luther, Melanchthon, Bucer and the other ministers, in German and Latin texts; with the marriage lines of Philip and Margaret, also in German and Latin; all attested by Georg Nuspicker, notary public. The bigamy of Philip was up to then not entirely unknown (mainly from Thuanus, as noted by Milton and quoted passim in the Leyser controversy) but the role of Luther and Melanchthon first became common property in historical writings from Beger's book.[116]

Johan Leyser, like many other inspired prophets, did not hail the arrival of a new apostle preaching the same faith. Beger, for his part, had made only one direct reference to Leyser, reserving all his expressions of respect for the opponents he was seeking to refute. Leyser in his *Warmund* books and in *Polygamia Triumphatrix* is at repeated pains to claim prior and independent knowledge of the Philip of Hesse case: there is no other hint that he acknowledged the existence of Beger's work.[117]

Only one of the anti-polygamists discussed by Beger was moved to make a reply: Severin Walther Schlüter, in a "Dialogue of Pyrrhonius and Orthophilus" (*Pyrrhonii und Orthophili Unterredung,* 1680). Schlüter moans: still no end to that scandalous squabble over women! that northland fire which should have consumed Leyser's poisonous screed has left smouldering embers to inflame in many hearts an afterglow of whorelust; and so on again in dreary repetition. In a negative way his dialogue does have one peculiar interest for us: Schlüter, uncertain who "Daphnaeus Arcuarius" really was, but aware that he belonged to the Heidelberg-Palatinate circle, attempts to smear the unknown writer in guilt-by-association with that notorious character the late Benedict Spinoza.[118]

Young Lorenz Beger did not long enjoy the fruits of his sycophantic labor. His patron Charles Louis died August 28, 1680, and was succeeded by Karl, son of the displaced Charlotte. The new era was signalized very soon by the issuance of a *Programma* by the Rector, Deans and Professors of Heidelberg University, November 5, 1680, disclaiming any responsibility for the "Daphnaeus Arcuarius" book.[119]

Karl, the new prince elector, was not a vindictive man. He permitted his half-brothers and half-sisters (Luise's children) undisturbed to retain their properties and their lesser titles of aristocracy. Of Lorenz Beger he exacted a mild, even a funny penance. He required Beger to write another book on polygamy which would refute the case he made out in the first. Beger complied, wrote the second book, and delivered the manuscript to Kurfürst Karl, who, with rare wisdom, chose not to perpetuate a scandal and simply filed the manuscript away into oblivion. Lorenz Beger presently found himself employment with other princes elsewhere in Germany; earned a new reputation, not yet altogether faded today, as a pioneer in numismatics and the study of classical antiquities; married twice, monogamously; and died in 1705 at the rather early age of fifty-two from asthma with complications.[120]

13

Leibnitz Calculates Some Consequences of Dogmatic Monogamy

The disclosure of the Philip of Hesse papers was quickly noticed in Catholic circles, particularly in France. The Abbé René Gastineau cited them almost immediately on their appearance, in his anti-Protestant writings. This "scandal" was particularly useful to Catholic controversialists at a time when the revocation of the Edict of Nantes, 1685, by Louis XIV, was wiping out the rights of Protestants in his domains. So Antoine Varillas, in his six volume *Histoire de Révolutions Arrivées dans L'Europe en Matière de Religion,* "History of Religious Revolutions in Europe", at Claude Barbin, Paris, 1686-1688, volume 3 (1687), pages 116-148, departed in this matter from his usual style of not giving original documents, and spread them at length. (Varillas adds a note that the modesty inherent in the French language would not permit him to translate Thuanus' word *triorches* characterizing Philip's powerful libido). Varillas' work may have reached more readers than Beger's. The review of Varillas in the Leipzig journal, *Acta Eruditorum,* 1687, pages 455-464, focussed at once on the Hesse papers.

These revelations were further broadcast by Jacques Bénigne Bossuet, Bishop of Meaux (1627-1704) in his *Histoire des Variations des Eglises Protestantes,* 1688 ("History of the Variations in the Protestant Churches," printed by the Widow S. Mabre-Cramoisy, Paris), translating the texts into French, Beger becoming Laurent l'Archer. A critical review of Bossuet's *Histoire* was then published by the Huguenot Henri Basnage de Beauval in his periodical *Histoire des Ouvrages des Savans* ("History of the Works of the Learned"), Tome III, 1688, Article IV, 453-456, devoting particular reference to those documents; followed by a book by Basnage, *Histoire de la Religion des Eglises Reformées, etc.,* Rotterdam, 1690. Bossuet countered with a *Défense de l'Histoire des Variations contre le Réponse de M. Basnage, Ministre de Roterdam,* printed by J. Anisson, Paris, 1691. The Catholic anti-Jesuit writer, Antoine Arnauld, in his *Morale Pratique des Jesuites* ("Practical Morality of the Jesuits," 1689), aiming at the missionaries in China, handled the matter secondhand from Bossuet.

From the Lutheran camp, a reply to Varillas, Bossuet and Arnauld was offered by Veit Ludwig von Seckendorf, *Commentarius Historicus et Apologeticus de Lutheranismo, sive de Reformatione Religionis Ductu D. Martini Lutheri,* etc., 1692, published in German as *Ausführliche Historie des Lutherthums und der Heilsamen Reformation welche der theure Martin Luther binnen dreyssig Jahren glücklich ausgeführet* ("Complete History of Lutheranism and of the Salutary Reformation which the Beloved Martin Luther Carried Out Happily for Thirty Years"), 1714, both at Frankfurt by the firm of Johan Friedrich Gleditsch. Seckendorf offered some solace to Lutheran pastors, but he spread the story of Philip of Hesse still further.

It was rather generally known that the Philip of Hesse papers had been revealed to Charles Louis by his cousin Ernst, Landgrave of Hesse-Rheinfels. In those years when the religious affiliation of the reigning ruler could determine the state religion of his realm, Ernst of Hesse-Rheinfels was regarded among many Protestants as one of the most menacing instances of a Protestant prince who had gone over to Catholicism, of which there had been a number in the latter half of the seventeenth century. It was whispered that he had slipped the papers to Charles Louis in the expectation of damaging the Protestant cause. Life in its normal course is full of contradictions and inconsistencies. So in his later years this same Ernst is found engaging in a long correspondence with the mathematician-philosopher Gottfried Wilhelm Leibnitz looking towards a reunification of the Christian church. In this correspondence Antoine Arnauld took part.

Inevitably the issue of polygamy entered into their discussion.

On September 2/12, 1691, Leibnitz wrote to Landgrave Ernst, commenting on the news of Seckendorf's book and his expected answer to Bossuet (Bishop of Meaux):

> Je voy qu'il aura un endroit, où il repondra à Monsieur l'Evêque de Meaux sur l'article de la Polygamie du Landgrave Philippe de glorieuse mémoire, dont les preuves ont esté publiées, comme je crois sur les communications que V. A. S. avoit donné autre fois. Il semble qu'on n'en devoit pas avoir honte, car on a grand tort de s'imaginer que la Polygamie est absolument contre le droit divin ou naturel; et sans cette vision les Chrestiens auroient fait de plus grands progrès dans les Indes, où ils ne reussiront jamais que par la force ou par la permission de la Polygamie, qui y est establie depuis plusieurs milliers d'années; je demeure d'accord que la Monogamie est bien meilleure et plus conforme à l'ordre, mais ce qui est le meilleur n'est pas toujours absolument necessaire. C'est à peu près comme à l'esgard du sentiment des plusieurs Chrestiens de la primitive Eglise, qui trouvoient mauvais qu'un mary eut à faire avec sa femme enceinte, d'autant que c'est "sine spe prolis secuturae". Il est vray qu'il seroit ridicule de vouloir indifferemment introduire la Polygamie dans l'Occident, suivant l'opinion d'un Lyserus, (descendant de Polycarpe) que j'ay connu, et qui a fait plusieurs ouvrages là dessus; mais il ne s'en suit point, qu'elle ne puisse estre accordée et tolerée en certaines rencontres extraordinaires. Si l'Histoire d'un certain Comte de Gleichen, qu'on dit avoir gardé ensemble deux femmes, la premiere aussi bien que celle qu'il avoit amenée de la Turquie, après avoir esté sauvé par son moyen, est veritable, je ne crois pas qu'on y puisse tant trouver à redire.

> I see that there will be a place where he will reply to the Bishop of Meaux on the matter of the polygamy of Landgrave Philip of glorious memory, of which the proofs were published, I believe, from the materials which your serene highness once turned over. It appears that one need not be ashamed of that,

> because it is a great mistake to imagine that polygamy is absolutely against divine law or natural law; and if not for this dream the Christians would have made much greater progress in the Indies, where they will never succeed except by force or by permitting polygamy, which has been established there for several thousand years; I remain in agreement that monogamy is definitely better and more conformable to good order, but what is the best is not always absolutely necessary. It is rather like the case of some of the Christians of the primitive Church, who took it ill when a husband had to do with his pregnant wife, particularly since it was "without hope of progeny to follow." It is true that it would be ridiculous to want indifferently to introduce polygamy into the Occident, following the opinion of a certain Leyser, (descendant of Polycarp), whom I knew, and who composed several works on that proposal; but it does not at all follow, that polygamy may not be permitted and tolerated in certain extraordinary circumstances. If the story of a certain Count Gleichen is authentic, of whom they tell that he kept two wives together, his first as well as the one he had brought from Turkey, after his life was saved by her, I do not believe that very much could be found to say against it.

Leibnitz is giving his opinion, not Seckendorf's. Meanwhile Bossuet was preparing his defense of his *History* in reply to the review published by Henri Basnage de Beauval. On November 13/23, 1691, Leibnitz wrote to Landgrave Ernst with reference to Bossuet's answer to Basnage:

> Il renouvelle aussi le proces de la Polygamie; pour moy je ne voy pourquoy on en fait tant de bruit, et suis très persuadé que le Pape et generalement l'Eglise peut accorder des Polygamies et de veritables divorces *propter duritiem cordis* comme dans le vieux Testament. Ces choses ne sont que contre le droit divin et naturel ordinaire, et ne sont pas absolument mechantes, c'est pourquoy on les peut accorder pour un grand bien; et la Congregation de propaganda fide a grandis-

sime tort, si elle ne tache pas de porter la Pape à accorder la Polygamie aux Chinois et autres peuples semblables; je ne crois pas même que cela soit contraire au Concile de Trent, non plus que les divorces veritables, car les Canons de ce Concile, comme les paroles de la Sainte Escriture, doivent estre entendus selon le droit divin ordinaire.

He is also renewing that business of polygamy; for myself, I do not see why so much of a racket is made over it, and I am convinced that the Pope and the Church generally can grant plural marriges and genuine divorces "because of their hardness of heart" as in the Old Testament. These things are only against customary divine and natural law, and are not absolutely wicked, that is why they may be granted for the sake of a great good; and the Congregation for the Propagation of the Faith is making a great error if it does not try to move the Pope to grant polygamy to the Chinese and other such like peoples; I do not even believe that would be contrary to the Council of Trent, any more than genuine divorces, because the canons of that Council, like the words of Holy Scripture, must be understood according to ordinary divine law.

Leibnitz continued distressed by Bossuet's reply to Basnage. On November 27/December 7, 1691, he wrote to Landgrave Ernst:

Je trouve aussi que ce qu'il dit contre la Polygamie de Philippe le Magnanime Landgrave de Hessen, pouvoit estre exprimé avec bien plus de moderation. Il n'allegue aucune raison solide pour laquelle la Polygamie ne pouvoit estre permise aujourd'huy pour des considerations importantes du bien public, et surtout pour le bien de l'Eglise même; lorsque le Pape accorde le marriage d'un Oncle avec sa Niece, la dispense va bien plus loin. Car la loy de Moyse semble le defendre, comme une chose contraire à la loy de la nature, et ny le vieux Testament, ny l'ancienne Eglise ne donnoient point la dispense là dessus; au lieu que le vieux Testament accordoit la Polygamie, et le divorce estoit permis dans la primitive Eglise pour des raisons assez legeres.

I find also that what he says against the polygamy of Philip the Magnanimous, Landgrave of Hesse, could be expressed with much more moderation. He does not allege any solid reason at all why polygamy could not be permitted today for important considerations affecting the public weal, and especially for the good of the Church itself; when the Pope grants a marriage of an uncle with a niece, the dispensation goes a great deal further. For the law of Moses appears to forbid it, as a thing contrary to the law of nature, and neither the Old Testament, nor the ancient Church gave any dispensation at all for that; whereas the Old Testament permitted polygamy, and divorce was permitted in the primitive church for rather light reasons.

As students of philosophy know, Leibnitz was an inventor of the calculus who turned one philosophical face to the world in public and quite another to his own mirror in his private chamber. His judgment in favor of permitting polygamy remained locked up in his correspondence with Landgrave Ernst, which was not printed until 1847 and since then has hardly been noticed until the present.[121]

14

Returning to Milton's England: The Case of Charles II

There was one other country in that era where a philosophical, or a theological, discussion of polygamy was timely. That was England of the Restoration years, when the question was thoroughly tied up with court intrigue and high politics.

As it happened, King Charles II had no children by his lawful wife and queen, Catherine of Braganza. Therefore the heir apparent to the throne was Charles' brother, the Duke of York, later James II, who was already regarded with disfavor among wide circles long before he began his short reign. Some of these opponents, particularly those who were concerned with ensuring that a Protestant would succeed to the throne, were eager to have Charles II marry again, because any legitimate son of his, born of another marriage, would become heir instead of the covertly Catholic James.

Their maneuvers nearly came to a head in March, 1670, when the Houses of Lords and Commons each debated a bill to let John Manners, Lord Roos, have the kind of divorce which would permit him to marry again: Lord Roos and his wife Anne being scrambled in one of those most racy scandals associated with the times of Charles II, though hardly peculiar to those times. The Roos divorce bill was designed by its proponents to provide a precedent which could be invoked to permit Charles II to divorce and remarry, a somewhat roundabout course, which some high-placed persons felt was the wisest plan. But there were other suggestions and other ideas in the air. In the words of an eminent clergyman who took part in these private discussions, Gilbert Burnet:

> Others talked of polygamy. And officious persons were ready to thrust themselves into anything that could contribute to their advancement. Lord Lauderdale and Sir Robert Murray asked my opinion of these things. I said, I knew speculative people could say a great deal in the way of argument for polygamy and divorce. Yet these things were so decried that they were rejected by all Christian societies.[122]

One of these "speculative people" in 1670 was Gilbert Burnet himself, however much he wanted to hide that fact in later years. In 1670 he was a brash twenty-seven years old, and in his eagerness to contribute to his own advancement, he wrote up a memorandum for Lord Lauderdale, "Resolution of Two Important Cases of Conscience," offering support for either solution, whether divorce of the barren Catherine, or a bigamous marriage. Burnet's first "case of conscience" asked whether a wife's barrenness were a just cause for her husband to divorce or to marry polygamously. He answered that a barren woman is incapable of truly fulfilling a marriage, which should therefore be dissolved by annulment. His second question asked "Is polygamy in any case lawful under the Gospel?" To this Burnet gave an affirmative reply. He used three sets of arguments. First, he cited the Old Testament worthies, Lamech, Abraham, Jacob, David—"David's wives (and store of them he had) are termed by the Prophet, *God's gift to him.*" Burnet's second argument, put very strongly, was based on the practice of levirate marriage (Deuteronomy xxv, 5-10), by which a brother, whether married or not, had the duty to take his deceased brother's widow to wife if that couple had been childless:

> Yea, Polygamy was made in some Cases, a Duty by Moses's Law; when any died without issue, his brother, or nearest kinsman, was to marry his Wife, for raising up Seed to him; and all were obliged to *obey* this, under the *Hazard* of the Infamy if they *refused* it; neither is there any Exception made for such as were married; from whence I may faithfully conclude, that what *God* made *necessary* in some Cases, to any Degree, can in no Case be *sinful* in it self; since God is

> Holy in all his Ways: and thus far it appears, that POLYGAMY is not contrary to the *Law* and *Nature of Marriage.*

Third, Burnet argued from the silence of the New Testament: "a simple and express Discharge of polygamy is no where to be found." He rejected those common interpretations which sought to read into the New Testament some condemnation of plural marriage, and summarized,

> Therefore to conclude this short Answer, wherein many things are hinted, which might have been enlarged to a volume, I see nothing so strong *against* Polygamy, as to balance the great and visible imminent Hazards, that hang over so many thousands, if it be not *Allowed.*

(These "thousands" are to be understood as Protestant Englishmen, and not as unhappily married husbands.)[123]

Another one of those speculative people, of course, was John Milton. On the occasion of the Lord Roos divorce debate in the House of Lords, John Milton the reprobate regicide was sought out in his retirement and "he was consulted by an Eminent Member of that House" . . . "as being the prime person that was knowing in that affair."[124]

As is well known, it was not for nothing that Charles II was called the Merry Monarch. He waited neither for parliamentary debates on divorce nor pastoral permission for polygamy. His mistresses were many, and of his progeny they were prolific. One of these ladies, Louise de Kéroualle, whom he created Duchess of Portsmouth, has particular interest for us.

It was while the pro-Protestant (if it may be so called) Buckingham faction was flubbing the follow-up on the Roos case, the crypto-Catholic (if it may be so called) Arlington faction was maneuvering to tie Charles II tighter into his secret alliance with Louis XIV. Louise had been maid-in-waiting in France to Charles II's sister Henrietta, Duchess of Orleans. She had attracted Charles' roving eye, and so she was shipped over to England as a puppet to be manipulated by the French ambassador Colbert de Croisy. Louise was coy, for a while. Presently she was pressured into yielding to Charles, partly by the seductiveness of the situation, partly by a grim threat of being immured in a French convent. To clinch the cabal, Lady Arlington, who had a reputation for orgies that was outstanding even in that loose era, took advantage of the Newmarket horse race season to assemble a lavish house party at her huge Euston mansion. For entertainment on the evening of October 9, 1671 she staged a wedding ceremony —a mock wedding, or a country wedding, call it what you will —with King Charles as groom and Louise bedecked as bride; performed with all traditional solemnities and all traditional vulgarities, including loosening the bride's garter, and flinging her stocking to the gentle guests: the gentle guests no doubt all quite drunk by that time.

On July 29, 1672 Louise de Kéroualle gave birth to a boy, who was named Charles Lennox, who was accepted by Charles II as his own son, and was brought up as the Duke of Richmond.[125]

To Louise de Kéroualle that pretended wedding ceremony may have served to soothe her superstitious scruples about being a whore (for conscience and morality are surely inappropriate terms in that milieu); for Lady Arlington and her guests, it was a pastime, a play-game, affording vulgar and vicarious participation in the violation of a virginity. But to the eyes of many thousands of Englishmen that ceremony was no mere sport of an autumn evening but a bigamy impure and simple, as testified by pamphlets such as *The Secret History of the Reigns of K. Charles II and K. James II,* 1690, (attributed by Anthony à Wood, though doubtfully, to John Phillips, Milton's nephew), pages 22-23:

> But he was more kind to the D. of Portsmouth, than to any of his Mistresses; and thence it was, that she might not lie under the Scandal of being a Whore, that after he had made her a Dutchess, he made her also his wife; that is to say, he marry'd her by vertue of his Royal Prerogative, at the Lord A's house, by the Common Prayer Book, according to the Ceremonies of the Church of *England.* A thing in some measure justifiable in a Prince, since the Law allows all Men one Wife; and therefore a King, who is above all Law, may surely have two.

Andrew Marvell, Milton's good friend, who also sometimes wrote good poetry, on this occasion spluttered in outraged frustration (so it was said),

> That Carwell, that incestuous punk
> Made our most sacred sovereign drunk
> And drunk she let him give the buss
> Which still the kingdom's bound to curse.

To do Charles II full poetic justice, it took the talent of his own poet laureate John Dryden, celebrating and satirizing him at once:

> In pious times e'r Priest-craft did begin,
> Before *Polygamy* was made a sin;
> When man, on many, multiply'd his kind,
> E'r one to one was, cursedly, confind;
> When nature prompted, and no law deny'd
> Promiscuous use of Concubine and Bride;
> Then Israel's Monarch, after Heaven's own heart,
> His vigorous warmth did, variously, impart
> To Wives and Slaves; and wide as his Command,
> Scatter'd his Maker's image through the Land.
> Michal, of Royal Blood, the Crown did wear;
> A Soyl ungratefull to the Tiller's care:
> Not so the rest; for several Mothers bore
> To Godlike *David* several Sons before.
> But since like slaves his bed they did ascend
> No True Succession could their Seed attend.[126]

So Dryden and the gentlemen at Court laughed at the feats and foibles of their Merry Monarch, and went and did likewise; while sober Milton, being consulted by a member of the House of Lords, privately searched in the Holy Scriptures for precedents permitting lawful polygamy on behalf of a Protestant succession, as he once did on behalf of his own personal needs.[127]

APPENDICES

APPENDIX I

Plural Marriage in Milton's "History of Britain"

The only book which Milton published in which plural marriage crops up was his *History of Britain,* and there always incidentally, in the midst of other topics, at most a symptom of his continuing interest, adding neither new matter nor new clarity.

His one meaningful allusion deals with the customs among the ancient Britons as reported by Julius Caesar. Milton implies his acceptance of polygamy and his disapproval, in contrast, of a social form which his age could not understand, but which (after Lewis Henry Morgan) can be recognized as some variation of group marriage still surviving among the barbarian Britons (Columbia edition, X, 87):

> certain it is that whereas other Nations us'd a liberty not unnatural for one man to have many Wives, the *Britans* altogether as licentious, but more absurd and preposterous in their license, had one or many Wives in common among ten or twelve Husbands; and those for the most part incestuously.

Milton had earlier described these Britons as living

> a lew'd adulterous and incestuous life, ten or twelve men absurdly against nature, possessing one woman as their common Wife, though of neerest Kin, Mother, Daughter or Sister; Progenitors not to be glori'd in. (Columbia edition, X, 51.)

In the course of his chronicle, Milton comes across several bigamous kings, Briton and Saxon. Since none of them were sanctified Scripturally, his comments are either objective or indifferent. They do not bear directly on his case for polygamy. So we hear of a legendary king Ebranc, "a man of mighty strength and stature" who reigned 40 years; "He had 20 Sons and 30 Daughters by 20 Wives" (Columbia edition, X, 16).

Danius, a kinglet in ancient Britain, was succeeded by "Morindus, his son by Tanguestela, a Concubine" (Columbia edition, X, 26). We are told nothing more about Danius, his wife or his concubine, nor is any more to be found if we go back to Geoffrey of Monmouth's account, one of Milton's sources.

Vortigern (X, 117), King of Britain, "though already wiv'd" demands Rowen, daughter of Hengist the Saxon, in marriage. Here "though" might imply a negative attitude, possibly inconsistent with Milton's basic outlook. Actually there are other elements involved in this particular "though." Milton regarded Vortigern as a "proud unfortunate tyrant, and yet of the people much belov'd, because his vices sorted so well with theirs" (X, 113). Years earlier, about 1639-1641, Milton had considered writing a tragedy on "Vortiger marrying Roena," and the doleful consequences that flowed thence, and while he had changed his mind about many matters in the interim, for Milton, Vortigern's bigamy was not at all such as saints and patriarchs used.[128]

King Ida the Saxon, ruling in Bernicia, Northumberland, impressed Milton as a noble king, undaunted in war, mild in peace, who "had twelve Sons, half by Wives and half by Concubines" (X, 131-132); but again we are told nothing more.

The foregoing passages are in Books I through IV, composed 1647-1648. The references in the later books (1668-1670) are in the same spirit.

Kinwulf, a West Saxon king, is killed by Kineard in fighting "at the House of a Woeman he lov'd" (X, 185-186), having "laudably reign'd about 31 years." But in his 1639-1641 manuscript list of topics for dramas, "Kinewulf k. of the West Saxons slaine by Kineard in the house of one of his concubins" (XVIII, 243).

Edward the Elder, son of the great Alfred, "nobly doing, and thus honour'd . . . a builder and restorer, eev'n in War, not a destroyer of his Land. He had by several Wives many children" (X, 230). We are left unenlightened about these several wives, but we are assured that the one of those many children who succeeded to the throne was Athelstan "though born of a Concubine" (X, 231). As ever, in treating of plural marriage, a vital issue was the right of a concubine's child to inherit titles and estates.

King Edwi is treated uncertainly: "he married or kept as Concubine, his neer Kinswoman, some say both her and her Daughter;" found wantoning with her when he should have been busy with his peers, he incurred their wrath with disastrous consequences (X, 241).

King Edgar took Elfreda to wife after killing her husband to get him out of the way. "Another fault is laid to his charge, no way excusable, that he took a Virgin *Wilfrida* by force out of the nunnery where she was plac'd by her friends to avoid his persuit, and kept her as his Concubine"—this after a youth in which "he abstain'd not from Women" . . . "These only are his faults on record, rather to be wonderd how they were so few . . ." (X, 246-247); few on the record, we presume.

Milton's bigamous kings of Britain and England do not ever come up in arguments for polygamy, either his or anyone else's. Not one of them has the status of Valentinian.

APPENDIX II

Milton's Reputation as Polygamophile, 1644-1717

Although Milton himself during his lifetime never printed his private views on polygamy, Milton-the-Divorcer was on a number of occasions associated in print with polygamophiles in publications which somehow (as in the citations above from Leyser and Feltmann) have remained in a forgotten limbo until the present.

It will be remembered that in Milton's century it was a common assumption that divorce doctrine and polygamy doctrine were interrelated. So John Wilkins in his handbook for preaching churchmen, *Ecclesiastes,* (in six impressions, with revisions, between 1646 and 1679) paired polygamy with divorce as judicial or civil aspects of marriage, and in his suggested readings listed Milton's "Treatise, Vindication, Tetrachordon" among other titles under the rubric "Of Divorce and Polygamy." In 1677 Martin Kempe published at Königsberg a bibliography of British theologians, *Charismatum Sacrorum Trias, sive Bibliotheca Anglorum Theologica,* "Triad of Sacred Unctions, or the Theological Library of the English," printed by Reich, published by Martin Hallervord, lifting from Wilkins and others. Misunderstanding Wilkins, Kempe handles *De Divortio* on page 461, *De Polygamia* on page 484, listing Edmund Bunny (who wrote *Of Divorce for Adultery,* Oxford, 1610, 1613) together with Milton under *both* topics. On Milton, who is mentioned elsewhere in this *Trias,* Kempe says under the heading *De Polygamia,* "his writings must be read with care and judgment;" and he quotes Caspar Ziegler's attack on Milton in the preface to *Circa Regicidium Anglorum Exercitationes,* "Observations on the English Regicides" (1653), quite out of context, but made to sound as if Ziegler accused Milton of falsifying Scripture in favor of polygamy.

The Anglican Henry Hammond handled divorce and polygamy together in his *A Letter of Resolution to Six Quaeres,* although his allusion there to Milton's ideas pertains only to divorce. Perhaps it is in this frame of reference that we may better understand the denunciation of Milton in Herbert Palmer's sermon to Parliament on August 13, 1644,

> If any plead Conscience for the Lawfulnesse of *Polygamy;* (or for divorce for other causes then Christ and His Apostles mention: Of which a *wicked book* is abroad and *uncensured,* though *deserving to be burnt,* whose *Author* hath been so *impudent* as to *set his Name* to it, and *dedicate it to your selves*) or for Liberty to *marry incestuously,* will you grant a *Toleration* for all *this?*

(Herbert Palmer, *The Glasse of God's Providence Towards His Faithful Ones,* 1644, page 57). The wicked book is Milton's on divorce. The needle about incest has no reference to Milton, but the dig about polygamy might have. Did Palmer have, as Thomas Young, Milton's former preacher-friend, may have had, some intimation of the proposal to Miss Davis?

We know there was gossip, however malicious and however unfounded, as Anne Sadleir wrote to Roger Williams in 1654,

> For Milton's book that you desire I should read, if I be not mistaken, that is he that has wrote a book of the lawfulness of divorce; and if report say true, he had, at that time, two or three wives living.

(Original in Trinity College, Cambridge; reprinted in John R. Bartlett, *The Letters of Roger Williams,* Publications of the Narragansett Club, 1 series, volume 6, 1874, pages 237-253). Anne Sadleir was hostile to Roger Williams as well as to John Milton; her nephew, Cyriack Skinner, was Milton's good friend.

One person who might have spoken about Milton's ideas on polygamy was Daniel Skinner, who transcribed part of the manuscript of the *Christian Doctrine* in preparation for the aborted publication, but it does not appear in his letters to Samuel Pepys or otherwise. Another was Philip van Limborch, who read the manuscript for the Dutch publishing house of Elzevir, and disapproved of it for its unitarianism; on polygamy, he too left no known public notice.

When Pierre Bayle wrote his note on *Milton* in his *Dictionnaire Historique et Critique,* 1697, he treated the matter as if it were common knowledge, but the context suggests the source of his knowledge, his own *Nouvelles* of 1685,

> Milton n'a donc pas plaidé pour le divorce et pour la polygamie avec le même désintéressement que Lyserus; son intérêt personnel le faisait agir.

> Milton therefore did not plead for divorce and for polygamy with the same disinterestedness as did Leyser; his personal interest made him act.

In 1710 Nicolaus Möller, professor of Church history at Kiel, published an account of notable polygamophiles in his *De Polygamia Omni ab Ipso Juris et Naturalis et Divini Auctore Omnibus et Omni Tempore Prohibita Exercitatio, Dissertationibus aliquot Academicis exhibita* ("A Study of All Polygamy, To All in All Time Prohibited by the Author of Natural and Divine Law Himself, set forth in Several Academic Dissertations"), printed by Barthold Reuther, university printer at Kiel.

Möller reviews Neobulus, Ochino, Leyser (uncertain about Wahrenberg and Vincentius), Beger; and includes Milton twice. Pages 15-16:

> 35. Seculo XVII. currente eandem materiam pertractandam sibi sumsit magnus polygamiae hyperaspistes, *Joh. Miltonus,* Anglus, cujus tamen sententiam, cum ipsummet ejus librum propriis usurpare oculis hactenus non licuerit, ex relatione Perillustris cujusdam Viri, infra Cap. III de dispensatione inter alias plures refero. Cum relatione modò dicta consentit

allegatio, facta à Lamberto *Velthuysio* in Dissert. de Polygamia, p. 218.219. qui & ipse pro more dubitantium ut alibi, ita hîc quoque varius est sibique vix constans.

35. During the seventeenth century that great champion of polygamy, the Englishman John Milton, undertook to treat the same matter; since so far I have not been able to examine his book with my own eyes, I shall discuss his opinion based on the relation of a certain very illustrious man, below in Chapter III, on dispensation, among other matters. With this aforesaid relation agrees the allegation made by Lambertus Velthuysen in his Dissertation of Polygamy, pages 218-219, who in accordance with his habit of hesitation here as elsewhere fluctuates and is hardly constant to himself.

The second passage, on page 92, with reference to recent writers who deny any prohibition of polygamy, says:

> Et huc, ut alios ὁμοδοξος nunc taceam, sec. relationem supra Cap. I. § 35. laudatam, tendere videtur mens Ioh. Miltoni, famosi illius Angli, a Lamb. Velthuysio, suppresso tamen auctoris nomine, ut videtur, allegata in Tr. de Conj. & Polyg. p. 218. sq.

> And, since I pass over now others of the same opinion, according to the account praised in Chap. 1, Sec. 35 in the same direction appears to tend the mind of John Milton, that famous Englishman, as appears to be alleged by Lambertus Velthuysen, in his Treatise on Marriage and Polygamy, pages 218ff., however suppressing that author's name.

Who the certain very illustrious man may have been, Möller leaves unsaid.

We turn to Lambertus Velthuysen (1622-1685), or Velthusius, whose *Opera Omnia* ("Complete Works"), printed by Reiner Leers, in two volumes at Rotterdam, 1680, expanded his 1676 *Tractatus Moralis de Naturali Pudore et Dignitate Hominis, in quo agitur de Incestu, Scortatione, Voto Coelibatus, Conjugio, Adulterio, Polygamia & Divortiis, &c.* ("Moral Tractate on the Natural Modesty and Dignity of Man, in which is treated of Incest, Fornication, Vowed Celibacy, Marriage, Adultery, Polygamy and Divorce, etc."—printed at Utrecht by Rudolph à Zyll, 4°, VI, 146 pages; my photocopy from the British Museum), a commentary on these issues without express reference to current controversy. New York Public Library has John Locke's copy. Columbia University has two issues, differing only in size of margins; in volume I pages 205-221 are on marriage and polygamy, pages 227-240 are on divorce. As Möller says, Velthuysen is a diffuse and rambling writer, verbose and obscure, and if those are really Milton's views which are incorporated in pages 218-219, that would hardly be obvious from reading them or rereading them.

Nevertheless on the assumption that Möller may have known something about Milton that we as yet do not know, we include these pages from Velthuysen's text, and make an effort at rendering them into English, with bracketed interpolations to try to make the thought intelligible:

> Qua adulterii invisa voce uti verentur etiam illi qui tam acriter tuentur Patres, sub lege polygamiâ se peccati reos fecisse, adulterii tamen eos absolvunt; & sub Novo Testamento in eadem polygamia adulterii crimen esse docent: & tamen, quod mirificum est, pugnant pro utraque illa sententia ex prima institutione conjugii, & ex doctrina Christi. Ex illorum itaque sententia unum idemque crimen eadem poena vetitum, à personis in iisdem circumstantiis constitutis perpetratum, in unis erit adulterium, in aliis infirmitatis peccatum.
>
> Nam neque illorum sententiam admittunt, qui docent leges perfectiores legibus Mosaicis à Christo traditas; neque tradunt mulieris dignitati aliquid detractum propter peccatum mulieris ita ut maritus non teneretur eam habere in eadem dignitate, in qua prima creatio illam constituerat, & cui propterea eadem officia praestare non habebat necesse: neque admittunt verba, primae institutionis matrimonii non arguere maritum,

secundam supra primam uxorem ducentem, aut cum libera rem habentem, adulterium committere.

Neque ad ignorantiam Patrum illorum tamquam ad asylum recurri potest: non enim praetendi potest ignorantia non affectata; nam tunc sancti illi Patres omni ea in re peccato caruissent.

Deinde si jure naturae prohibetur polygamia, quo pacto evenit, in re tanti momenti, & in peccato tam enormi, naturam tam cito suae primae institutionis oblitam fuisse, cujus vis apud omnes plurimum valet; et tum maximè cum idoneam complexa est naturam; quae nec consuetudine prohibere solet, quin ius suum teneat, & à qua praecipue specimen naturae capiundum est; praesertim si propius abest ab ortu & divina progenie: quae ergo, ratio suspicandi in sanctis sub V. T. ita illam legem naturae deletam fuisse, ut nulla eius superessent simulachra aut vestigia, sed per ignorantiam inculpatam in mala illa consuetudine versarentur? Erat itaque per ignorantiam affectatam, sed illa non excusat, nec imminuit peccatum; et ita sancti illi Patres, Spiritu Deo acti, tamen ad tantum se proripuerunt nefas, quod morte vindicari solet. Et cum Deus tam sanctas populo Israëlitico tradiderit leges, istius sceleris non tantum nullam prohibitionem prodidit, sed illas leges circa pluralitate uxorum tulit, ut nisi vis primae institutionis viguerit in animis Israëlitarum, vix aut ne vix quidem ullus rem aliter cogitatione complecti potuit, quam eam fuisse concessam.

An non ea sententia superiori forte tolerabilior est, quae docet prima institutione polygamiam non fuisse prohibitam, ita ut ne sub Novi quidem Testamento, ejus prohibitio facta fuerit; & quae Sanctos Patres tanti criminis reos arguit: praesertim cum hic sententiae favere videatur, quod in prima institutione non fiat expressa mentio matrimonii inter duos tantum habendi, neque illatione manifesta id conficiatur; neque enim ex verbis Christi, res in aperto ponatur.

Ostendit equidem Christus, primum conjugium ita institutum, quod individuam vitae consuetudinem continere debeat: quod ideo nullus inire debet nisi animo manendi in eo ad ultimum vitae spiritum; quodque ita repudia sub lege concessa, non mutabant legem illam perpetuam de perpetuo vinculo conjugii, quasi per libellum repudii Judaeis concessum, illata esset conjugiis illa mutatio ut jam non amplius complecterentur perpetuam vitae consuetudinem; & quod possent iniri servata viro libertate se solvendi illo vinculo, quando uxor minus esset facta ad ejus genium et mores: & eo sensu negat Christus repudia convenire cum prima institutione, & ea vitiosa fuisse docet; & Judaeis tantum concessa propter cordis duritiem: concedens pravis eorum moribus, ut cum libertate & potestate repudiandi, quasi matrimonii vinculum esset solubile, conjugia celebrarent.

At Christus ita repudia damnans polygamiae tamen nullam inurit notam, & tacitam praetermittit. Quam si damnasset, essetque adulterium in ea implicitum, ne ad momentum quidem inter Christianos, ubicunque terrarum degissent, tolerata fuisset, et sine dubio *Actor.* 15. institutionibus primae Synodi proscripta fuisset: quod non est factum. Nec est existimandum, ideo illius in Synodo nullam factam mentionem, quia inter eos, qui recens Christianismum amplexi erant, de ea re nulla erat controversia: qua enim veri specie dici potest neophytos illos Christianos de scortatione dubitasse, an esset ponenda in vitio, quae ferme apud gentes omni aevo habita fuit res probrosa; de polygamia tamen persuasos fuisse, illam vitio fuisse vertendam, quae apud omnes gentes Orientales vigebat, & labe carere putabatur?

Nonne verisimilius est polygamiam lege naturae non esse damnatum, neque Christi institutio abolitam; quandoquidem ejus usum in Ecclesia Christiana diu durasse non absurdis argumentis adducti multi credunt? Apostolus, 1 *Tim* 3 imperans ut *Episcopus sit unius mulieris vir,* & ita à polygamia liber sit, seque ab ea contineat, concedet reliquis Christianis potestatem eodem tempore plures habendi uxores: & locus citatus, *Rom.* 7, idem confirmare videtur, quia Apostolus utitur similitudine ducta à muliere, & non à viro; cui alteri viro, priore superstite nubere fas non erat, at virum in exemplum non adducit. Ita ut videatur polygamiam primi Christianismi temporibus non fuisse interdictam; sequentibus tamen aevis illam abiisse in dissuetudinem, & tandem postea fuisse improbatam: quia inter Romanos, quorum imperium longe lateque patebat, & quae eorum imperio parebant, asscisce-bant, polygamia non erat in usu, cum etiam quia progressu temporis nescio quo fato, doctrina & mores Christianorum eo inclinabant, ut etiam concessos congressus, & legitimos concubitus viles, et Christianis parum convenientes duxerint, quasi delicatior & mollior eorum ratio esset, quam Christian-orum gravitas postulat: unde in eorum constitutionibus & decretas natae tot leges, quibus conjugium nota aliqua in-uritur. V. Gr. secundis nuptiis non benedicitur; neque illis, qui ad eas transeunt ad dignitatis ecclesiasticas aspirare licet. Presbyteris in nuptiis bigami prandere non licet: Digami Diaconi, aut Presbyteri nomen tantum retineant, officio tamen non fungantur: Episcopi uxores pro sororibus habeant. Clericus, qui viduam duxerit, degradetur.

Qui itaque tam parum aeque judicabent de justis uxoribus, & conjugiis legitime contractis, quid mirum si ea conjugia dam-narunt, de quibus aliqua dubitatio esse poterat propter qua-rundam gentium consuetudinem, quae ab illis abstinebant. Quid mirum polygamiam ab iis condemnatam, qui secundas nuptias vitiosas ducebant. Denique quomodo poterant con-gruenter suis institutis, polygamiam Christianis permittere, qui in Ecclesiasticis personis congressum cum juxta uxore impurum putabant. Illi itaque, qui polygamiam amplectuntur, non moventur exemplis Christianorum, qui jam à pluralitate uxorum abstinent, sed sibi fas esse aestimant aeque à com-muni illa consuetudine recedere, quam Reformatis licuit an-tiquas conciliorum constitutiones abolere, & Ecclesiasticos in re conjugali eodem iure habere, quo vulgares Christianos.

(Certain commentators opposing polygamy hold self-contra-dicting views; they make assumptions which are objectionable in themselves:)

Even those who regard adultery with greatest hostility, who so sharply indict the Patriarchs as having been answerable for the sin in polygamy under the Law, nevertheless absolve them of adultery, and they teach that under the New Testament the crime of adultery exists in that same polygamy. And yet, remarkably, they fight for each of these opinions from the first institution of marriage and from the doctrine of Christ, deriving from these the opinion that one and the same crime forbidden under the same penalty, perpetrated by persons situated in the identical circumstances, in some would be adultery, in others a mere fault of frailty. Not only do they accept the opinion of those who teach that more perfect laws than Moses' were given by Christ, but they also teach that something was detracted from the dignity of woman because of the woman's sin, so that the husband is not bound to hold her in the same dignity in which the first creation set her, and that therefore he does not need to fulfil the same duty to her; and they assert that the words of the first institution of marriage do not convict the husband of committing adultery in marrying a second wife in addition to the first, or having an affair with a free woman.

(There are further contradictions in ascribing the Patriarchs' polygamy to their ignorance either of the moral law or of the law of nature:)

One cannot seek refuge, as it were, in the ignorance of the Patriarchs, for it is not possible to claim an unaffected ignorance. For the Holy Patriarchs of those times were devoid of ignorance in all matter of sin. Then if polygamy is banned by the law of nature, in what way does it come about in a matter of such moment, and in a sin of such enormity, that nature was forgotten so close to its first institution, when its force was strongest among all, and then especially when nature was suitably embraced, not likely to be overcome by custom but rather maintaining its force as law, by which particularly the ideal of nature is to be grasped; especially when nearer to its origin and its divine creation; what reason is therefore to suspect that among the Saints under the Old Testament the law of nature was so effaced that no images or vestiges remained but that through innocent ignorance they were involved in that custom? So then it was by affected ignorance: but that neither excuses nor lessens the sin; and so those Holy Patriarchs led by the Spirit of God flung themselves into an evil so great that it is customarily punished by death.

(It is an inescapable conclusion that Old Testament polygamy was with divine approbation:)

And when God gave the Israelite people those so holy laws, he provided for that 'wickedness' no such severe prohibition, but enacted those laws about plurality of women, so that if the force of the original institution was not flourishing in the minds of the Israelites, nothing else can hardly or not even hardly be grasped in thought than that it was granted to them.

(Polygamy in fact was never banned by God:)

Is not considerably more tolerable the opinion which teaches that polygamy was not prohibited in the first institution so that not even under the New Testament was its prohibition put into effect, than that which convicts the Holy Patriarchs as parties to so great a sin, especially since it seems to favor this opinion that in the first institution there was no express mention of matrimony as limited between two, nor is it deduced by any manifest inference, nor is the matter clarified in any of the words of Christ.

(Christ dealt with excessive license in divorce, but made no comment on polygamy; and the first Christian Assembly at Jerusalem likewise excluded polygamy from sinful behavior:)

Christ indeed shows the first marriage was so instituted that it should include an inseparable cohabitation; one which no one ought to enter into except with a mind to remain in it to the last breath of life; so that divorces, while granted under the Law, did not change that perpetual law of the perpetual bond of marriage, as if by the writ of divorce permitted to the Jews there was created such a change in marriage so that from that time on no perpetual cohabitation was any longer involved, and which they could enter with the man keeping that liberty of dissolving that bond whenever the woman was less adapted to his spirit and mores; and in that sense Christ denies divorces accord with the first institution and teaches they were wicked and conceded to the Jews because of their hardness of heart, conceded to their depraved standards, so that they, having the liberty and power of divorce, celebrated weddings as if the bond of matrimony was not binding. But while Christ thus condemned divorces, he makes no comment on polygamy and tacitly passes over it. If he had condemned it, and if adultery were involved therein, not for a moment would it have been tolerated among Christians in whatever land they were dwelling. And without doubt it would have been proscribed by the canons of the first synod (Acts xv), which was not done. It is not to be thought, since no mention of it was made in that synod, it was because among them who had recently embraced Christianity, on that matter there was no controversy; for by what true idea can it be said that those neophyte Christians had any doubts whatever as to whoredom, on whether that was to be classed as wicked which among all peoples in every age had been considered a wicked matter; as for polygamy, would they have been, however, persuaded to convert into a wicked sin a practice which flourished among all Oriental peoples, and was thought to be without stain?

(Polygamy continued acceptable during the years of the early church, but became discountenanced during the years when churchmen denigrated all kinds of marriage:)

Is it not more likely that polygamy is not condemned by the law of nature, nor the institution abolished by Christ, when many believe that its practice continued for a long time in the Christian church, convinced by arguments which are not absurd. The Apostle, I Timothy iii, decreeing that a bishop should be the husband of one wife, and so free from polygamy, and refraining therefrom, concedes at the same time to all other Christians the power to have many wives. The text citation Romans vii, 2, 3, also appears to confirm the same, because the Apostle uses a comparison drawn from the instance of a woman and not from a man: she has no right to marry another man while her first husband is still living; but he does not cite a man in this same case.

So as it appears, in the time of earliest Christianity, polygamy was not banned; in the following ages, however, it fell into disuse, and then later became disapproved: because they recognized that among the Romans, whose empire extended far and wide, and under whose power they were subject, polygamy was not in use.

It also became discountenanced because with the passing of time, from whatever cause, the doctrine and practice of Christians so inclined that even licit unions and legitimate copulations were considered vile and little befitting Christians, as if their judgment was more delicate and tender than Christian gravity demands. Whence in their canons and decretals were born many laws which branded marriage with various ignominies. For example: Second weddings were not blessed, and any who entered into them were not permitted to aspire to ecclesiastical dignities. Priests were not permitted to join in celebrating at a bigamist's wedding. Digamous deacons and priests might retain the name, but could not function in office. Bishops treated wives as if they were sisters. A clergyman who married a widow was defrocked.

Among those who held so low an opinion of legal wives, and marriages legitimately contracted, what wonder if they condemned marriages about which there might be some doubt because of whatever custom of the nations who abstained from them. What wonder if polygamy was condemned by those who considered all second marriages to be sinful. In fine, how could they agree to permit polygamy to Christians by their laws, who considered cohabitation with a legally married wife impure to a clergyman.

(As the Reformers restored the right of marriage to the clergy, so polygamophiles may likewise reclaim their original rights:)

> They therefore who embrace polygamy are not moved by the examples of those Christians who now abstain from plurality of women, but judge it is right for themselves to dissociate from the common custom, just as the Reformers permitted themselves to abolish the canons of ancient councils and allowed the clergy to have the same rights in matrimony as ordinary Christians.

The line of argument in these pages of Velthuysen, with the exception of the reference from I Timothy iii, is almost wholly unique. The points from Acts xv and Romans vii are novel. If not for Möller's allusion, there would be no reason to connect any of it with Milton. It is characteristic of Milton that almost any point he makes, or any allusion or text he uses, can be found at least twice somewhere in his works. These points in Velthuysen's text are not found in Milton's writings at all, so we are left wondering what the facts really were.

The uncertainty is heightened by Velthuysen's discussion of divorce. At one point he makes an allusion which might be to Milton (page 237):

> Ex hisce jam liquet quam longe aberrant illi, qui repudia etiam inter Christianos non putant interdicta, sed ea, cum usus postulat, reduci posse in nostras Respublicas. Argumentorum, quae supra attulimus, facilis est depulsio.

> From this it is now clear how far they err who do not think divorces are forbidden among Christians, but that they may be restored as need requires in our commonwealths. Their arguments, which we have given above, are easily crushed.

But when we review those arguments, again they are not the familiar points made by Milton in his books on divorce. In any case, Velthusius has given us another seventeenth century opinion, whether it be Spinoza's, or Vythage's, or Guess-who's.

Möller's 1710 comment, minus the reference to Velthuysen, appears to have been picked up by Gerhard von Mastricht in his notes to the Latin edition of Amyraut, 1712 and 1717, where he says (page 132)

> Nostra aetate Joh. Miltonus Anglus Polygamiae defensor magnus fuisse narratur, scriptum eius quoque non vidi, saltem id quod in favorem introducendi iterum divortii edidit, quod ex Anglico Belgice quoque est versum.

> In our age John Milton, the Englishman, is reported to have been a great defender of polygamy, but that writing of his I have also not seen, nor the one he published in favor of introducing divorce, which has also been translated from English into Dutch.

This reference to a *Belgice* translation (Dutch? Flemish?) of Milton-on-Divorce led me to resume inquiry for the version Aizema proposed, or any other (see Columbia edition, XII, 70-72) but a large number of libraries in the Netherlands, Belgium, Germany, Scandinavia and elsewhere report to me no record of any such translation. It is all the more tantalizing to find not one but two references to such a version in Von Mastricht's notes. On page 108 (1712 and 1717 editions) the footnote reads

> Inventus tamen in Anglia ὑπερασπιστής divortii Joh. Miltonus, qui singulari tractatu Anglico divortium defendit & in Christianum rempublicam inductum voluit; qui & in Belgicum idioma, tanquam dissolutis nostri temporis moribus necessarius, versus est.

> Moreover in England there was found a champion of divorce, John Milton, who defended divorce in a singular

treatise in English and wished to introduce it into the Christian commonwealth; and who has been translated into the language of the Dutch, so much the more inevitable in the dissolute manners of our time.

Needless to say, these references may be mistaken allusions to a ghost, based on misunderstood rumors of the Aizema project. It would not be more bizarre than the obituary article on Milton in the *Allgemeine Schau-bühne der Welt,* "Universal Stage-Show of the World," edited by Christian Juncker, volume 4, 1718, column 1692, (with reference to the year 1674). Among other misstatements of fact it asserts

> Er war ein grosser Vertheidiger der Freyheit der Ehescheidung (wie er sich dann von 6. Weibern hinter einander scheiden lassen) . . .

> He was a great defender of the liberty of divorce (as he himself divorced himself from six wives one after the other) . . .

APPENDIX III

Discussion of Polygamy in England after Milton's Time: M.P.'s and Methodists

1. Michael Mallet, M.P., and his Polygamy Bill in Parliament, 1675

On November 18, 1675 William Denton wrote in a letter to Sir Ralph Verney: "A Bill was brought into the Commons that a man might have as many wives as he pleased, not exceeding 12, by Mr. Mallet." A week later, November 25, 1675, Denton wrote to Verney: "Mallet's bill was certainly offered but would not be received." (Historical Manuscripts Commission, *Seventh Report, Appendix, page 493*).

This incident is not recorded in the official journal of the House of Commons, but it was entered in the journal kept by Anchitell Grey, who was thirty years M.P. for Derby, published as the *Debates of the House of Commons from the Year 1667 to the Year 1694. . . . Printed for T. Becket and P. A. de Hondt in the Strand,* 1769. For November 15, 1675 Grey's text reads:

> Mr. *Mallet* proffered to bring in a Bill to repeal the Act of King *James,* entitled "Felony to marry a second husband, or wife, the former being living."
>
> Mr. *Waller.*] There are some things *that ought not to be named,* even amongst the Gentiles. But is sorry to read that our Saviour was son of a virgin who had but one husband, and that such a thing as this should be reported to be discoursed of within our doors. We cannot do such a thing as this. Let the Gentleman that would bring it in, tell him, whether his dove-house is not better stored, where one cock

has but one hen, than his yard, where one cock has many hens. (Mallet, *in opening the Bill, pretending it was for peopling the nation and preventing the promiscuous use of women.*) 'Tis such an abominable Bill, that it is not fit to be retained.

Sir *Lionel Jenkins.*] Saying, it was against the Canons and Decretals of the Church.

Mr. Mallet.] Said, he knew no Canons nor Decretals it was against, but those of *Rome,* with which *Jenkins* was better acquainted than himself.

Sir Thomas Lee.] The best Question to this purpose is to read the order of the day.

How shall we assess this episode?

Working backwards, Sir Thomas Lee was the parliamentarian who simply sidetracked the question by use of standard procedure. Sir Lionel Jenkins (1623-1685) has his own petty place in history, in particular as being involved indirectly in the suppression of Milton's *Treatise of Christian Doctrine.* His comment here left him wide open to a jab by Mallet directed against Jenkins' political faction. Edmund Waller (1606-1687), who rose so quickly to rebuff Mallet, was the some time poet and long time figure in public affairs, and the confused account of his remarks suggests that he was responding to some things said by Mallet which have not been recorded.

Michael Mallet was a younger son of a prominent Somerset family. His father, Sir Thomas Malet, a jurist of some note, and his elder brother, Sir John Malet, have been somewhat better treated, however slightly, in surviving documents and records. Michael Mallet crosses the stage at odd moments. He was a member of the Rota Club in 1659. As M.P. for Milborne Port, he is heard from time to time in the Opposition, and almost always in a vein of shrewd satire. A 1678 speech of his was baited as "treasonable" to the king, but usually his remarks were safely oblique. For example, on March 6, 1676/1677, he is quoted as saying that he "knows not why we should have so much tenderness for France. He knows not the benefit we have from them, but that they fetch away our horses and our men, and we have nothing from them but wine and women." On May 23, 1677 he was recorded more bluntly in this wise: "King James was said to be 'the *Solomon* of his age.' Our King is heir to his virtues. There is something more recorded of *Solomon*: he fell to strange counsels by strange women. And we cannot repose any confidence in the King, if he puts his Counsel into 'strange women.' If they be left, God will bless his Counsels."

The lawyers in the House of Commons were well aware that bigamy was an offense only in canon law in England before the time of King James, and that it was in his reign that the law was passed making it a penal offense in civil law. Therefore, no matter how much Mallet may have couched his motion in the terms of seventeenth century discussions on population, when he rose to offer his bill every knowing member of the House immediately recognized its barbs aimed directly at Charles II. Unless other evidence is forthcoming, it would be incorrect to read any other significance into this episode.

2. Colonel John Birch, M.P., 1676, Asks for a Bigamous Marriage

Another isolated incident, of a rather different kind, is recorded in a letter of April 28, 1676, sent by Grace, Lady Chaworth, to her brother Lord Roos (the divorce case Roos) about Col. John Birch, M.P. Quoting her letter:

> Colonel Birch came the other day with a woman in his company into a parish Church in the west, and after church service and sermon pray'd the Minister—coming out of his pew—to marry him to that woman, saying that though he had another wiffe yet 'twas a match of his friends and not of his owne making, besides he had had this woman 15 yeares, loved her well tho he had not yet married her, and had good monies with her which was a very good thinge, 20*l*., and a cow, and a horse, and some sheep, and 10*l*., and 10*l*. and 10*l*.; but the morose Minister said he could not marry him

upon those inducements if he had no lysence certificates, &c. of the justnesse of it: and thereupon he said he cared not, he would then marry her himselfe, and so giving her his hand said, 'I John Birch Esqre, take thee Winifrid Maurice for my wedded wife, &c.;' and did repeat the words for her, and all the congregation looked on, laughed, and some writ it for an entertainment of mirth to their friends att London.[129]

3. The Bigamy of Lord Chancellor William Cowper

Rather a good deal more talk was occasioned by the case of William Cowper, Earl of Cowper, 1664-1723, first Lord Chancellor of the united realm of Great Britain. He was reputed to have been a bigamist and to have written a treatise defending plural marriage: both statements must still be qualified as *alleged.* The *Dictionary of National Biography* transmits the version that he seduced Elizabeth Culling of Hertingfordbury Park by a sham marriage, and had two children by her; then legally married Judith Booth in 1688; and later, after Judith died, he legally married Mary Clavering.[130]

In the passing winds of petty politics of that time, Cowper was rated as a "Whig Moderate" whose ability as a lawyer and personal affability helped to make him acceptable to Queen Anne as her Lord Chancellor and Keeper of the Great Seal. Those talents, however, did not render him acceptable to the Tory party; in particular, not to Jonathan Swift, who, not foreseeing that he would in aftertimes be world famous for his *Gulliver's Travels,* about 1710 was pouring his proud and bitter soul into a Tory journal, *The Examiner.* To Swift, Cowper was only a prime figure of the opposing party, and his private past was public property. Swift slips the dirk in by way of a satirical fiction. First he introduces a passing reference in a kind of letter-to-the-editor (*The Examiner,* number 17, November 30, 1710)

If I should add, that my tenants made me very uneasy with their Squabbles and Broils among themselves; he would counsel me to cashier *Will Bigamy,* the *Seneschal* of my Mannor.

In *The Examiner* of January 4, 1710/1711, number 21, Swift pretends to be a different person who is commenting on the prior letter:

> There is another Person whom the same Writer is thought to point at under the name of *Will Bigamy*. This gentleman, knowing that marriage fees were a considerable Perquisite to the Clergy, found out a way of improving them *Cent. per Cent.* for the *Good of the Church*. His invention was to marry a second Wife while the first was still alive; convincing her of the Lawfulness by such Arguments, as he did not doubt would make others follow the same example: These he had drawn up in writing, with Intention to publish for the general Good; and it is hoped he may *now* have Leisure to finish them.[131]

The needle about church fees was an amusing fiction, but the *now* was pointed: Cowper was at this time and for some years out of office. In *The Examiner* for February 1, 1710/1711, number 26, Swift pretends to qualify his praise of the new Lord Keeper with a cavil which really stings Cowper:

> Was any Man more eminent in his Profession than the present Lord Keeper . . . But then it must be granted, that he is wholly ignorant in the Speculative as well as the practical part of Poligamy.

The Cowper case was given wide circulation in a book by Mary de la Rivière Manley (1663-1724), *Secret Memoirs and Manners of Several Persons of Quality, of Both Sexes, from the New Atalantis, an Island in the Mediterranean, Written Originally in the Italian,* first published in May, 1709 and going through seven English editions. These "memoirs" are an agglomeration of gossip and scandal from the times of Charles II through the reign of Anne, using fictitious names but supplying a key to these, even identifying persons still alive.

In Mary Manley's semi-fictional account, Hernando Volpone

(William Cowper) though married, develops a passion for his orphan ward Louisa (Elizabeth Cullen or Culling) but fears he will be sidetracked by a suitor, Mr. Wilmot, (identified in the Key as "Mr. Sambrooke of New Forest that wrote in Defense of Polygamy"). Hernando, his wife, Louisa and Wilmot attend the performance of an opera in which an Enoch Arden second marriage leads the bigamous wife into madness and suicide. Hernando uses the play to introduce "a learned discourse of the lawfulness of double marriages." He suggests that a woman's child-bearing time makes her necessarily monogamous, but a man need not be so restricted. He cites as evidence the law of nature as seen in the customs of many nations and most religions; the precedents in the Bible, and the practice of peoples outside of Europe, whose manners are less corrupting than Europe's refined vices; and the example of Jupiter, whose name, we may suspect, is a stand-in for a more terrestrial monarch. Wilmot falls into a trap in arguing the case for plural marriage, thereby alienating Louisa, who lets herself be deceived by Hernando into accepting *polygamy* by a pretended wedding ceremony, instead of *concubinage*. She continues always convinced that she is lawfully married, though in polygamy, but in the end dies unhappily when Hernando proves entirely unfaithful to her. Hernando's brother Mosco tries analogous maneuvers with another girl, Zara, who drowns herself in despair.

Mrs. Manley's account was also motivated politically, because of her partisan Tory hostility to the Whigs. Her book resulted in a prosecution for slander but she was not convicted. It should be observed that she herself appears to have been involved in the kind of case she wrote of Volpone and Louisa. The *Dictionary of National Biography* states "About this time [1688] she was drawn into a false marriage by her cousin John Manley of Truro, whose wife was then living. This cousin was probably the John Manley who was M.P. for Bossiney borough, Cornwall, from 1701 to 1708, and 1710 to 1714, and for Camelford from 1708 to 1710." Her last will and testament (PCC, 211 Bolton) spoke of "my much honoured friend, the Dean of St. Patrick, Dr. Swift" (*Notes and Queries,* 7 series, VIII, 1889, page 157.)

Since the names in Mrs. Manley's Key are real names, I have sought for Mr. Sambrooke and his defense of polygamy; but the only trace I have found is a handwritten mention of the same name and treatise written in French in an 18th (?) century entry in the New York Public Library copy of Leyser's *Polygamia Triumphatrix,* which may be only an echo of Mrs. Manley.

4. Parson's Palaver and Parlor Prattle, 1725-1742

For some not at all obvious reasons, between the years 1725 and 1742 there was a wide spread of polygamy talk in England, the first such period in which there appear to have been many voices. These dates are not intended to define the beginning and end of an era: they merely happen to be the dates within which the main printed publications fell. In contrast to the discussions which followed upon Neobulus or Ochino or Leyser, these publications did not stimulate a debate, but rather they reflect wide interest in a discussion already going on.

The best summary was supplied by Patrick Delany (1685-1768), a clergyman in Ireland, and sometime friend of Jonathan Swift. Under the pseudonym of Phileleutherus Dubliniensis he published a book against plural marriage in 1737, *Reflections Upon Polygamy, and the Encouragement Given to that Practice in the Scriptures of the Old Testament. . . . London. Printed for J. Roberts at the Oxford Arms in Warwick Lane.* On page one he complains that "Polygamy is a doctrine daily defended in common conversation and often in print, by a great variety of plausible arguments." For specifics Delany lists first of all Leyser's *Polygamia Triumphatrix,* which he thought had been published in London (somehow misreading from its title page *Londini Scanorum,* "Lund in Skane," page 26), and continues with

> another dissertation on the same subject, said to be written by a Lord Chancellor of England, a man of as much sagacity and as fine parts, perhaps, as any that ever presided in a court of equity. To say nothing of the decision of a Christian

bishop of no mean talents upon this point; and the known outcry of Deists and Free-thinkers upon this head, which nobody who hath been any way conversant with them, can be a stranger to.

The Lord Chancellor is, of course, William Cowper, and his (elusive) treatise. The bishop is Burnet, whose 1670 memorandum had been published in 1725, and again in 1727 and 1736 in Bevill Higgons' *Historical and Critical Remarks on Bishop Burnet's History of His Own Time;* in 1733 in *Memoirs of the Secret Services of John Macky, Esq.;* and would be again in Chambers' *Bibliotheca Recondita.*[132] Delany does not mention the 1732 and 1736 publications of Ochino's dialogue in English translation (described elsewhere in this monograph) and regrettably does not specify the "Deists" and "Freethinkers" by individual name.

The "Deists," who were not a unified movement or sect, were not so much concerned with polygamy as with the interpretation of Scripture. They argued: if you insist on literal acceptance of everything in the Bible, you are forced into the ridiculous position of defending polygamy; it is better not to insist on the literal word of the Bible or of Church dogma. For example when Daniel Waterland (1683-1740) asserted dogmatic authority in his *Scripture Vindicated* (1730), he was answered by Conyers Middleton (1683-1750) in *A Letter to Dr. Waterland* (1731):

> your self must be forced to allow a still greater licence; not only a *plurality of wives* but a *number of concubines* into the bargain; unless you will give up some part at least of the Scriptures you are vindicating and condemn the *holy Patriarchs,* Abraham, Isaac and Jacob, and above all, *David, the man after God's own heart;* who had at least *seven wives* and *ten concubines,* without ever being admonished for it by any of the Prophets, or censured by any of the *sacred Writers.*

There were some among the deists, like Henry St. John, Viscount Bolingbroke (1678-1751), who for other reasons asserted that polygamy "is comformable to the law of nature, and provides the most effectual means for the generation and education of children." Bolingbroke saw in polygamy the procedure to offset losses of population in war and epidemics. The apparent failure of polygamy to produce these proper results he blamed on bad statistics, or on the effects of sodomy and abortions. Without divorce, he said, monogamy is an absurd, unnatural and cruel imposition.[133]

Samuel Richardson, writing his novel of contemporary manners, *Pamela,* about 1740, stirs up a silly misunderstanding between Pamela and her husband over this question. Her husband is one of the many gentlemen who are bandying about reasons in favor of polygamy, just at the same time that another woman, a high-born Lady, expresses a willingness to accept him as husband within the framework of that institution. Low-born Pamela is perturbed, but the incident gradually burbles away into nothing (Part II, LXX, LXXI, LXXIV, LXXVII).

About the same time, David Hume, the skeptical philosopher, composed a familiar essay *Of Polygamy and Divorces* (published 1742), a brief exercise in literary wit on a random collection of references rather than any systematic exploration of the topic. It is significant, chiefly, in the offhand manner in which he takes note of the "advocates of polygamy," testimony that the idea had become a matter of drawing room banter. Characteristic of Hume is his acceptance of plural marriage as a fact, coupled with his incisive indictment of its evils: love (which, in its finer manifestations, some people do enjoy) is banished; male sovereignty is a usurpation; children suffer in a polygamous household which stunts their social and psychological growth.

5. *Westley Hall: Misbehavior among the Methodists*

Westley Hall (1711-1776) was a Church of England clergyman, and, it seems, powerfully attractive to the ladies. He began by becoming messily involved in promises of marriage at one and the same time (about 1734-1735) with two sisters of John Wesley and Charles Wesley, the founders of the Methodist sect, with whom for a short time he was doctrinally allied. Hall unscrambled the mess by jilting one sister, Kezziah, and marrying the other, Martha. His career is known primarily through the unsympathetic accounts of the Wesley family and their biographers. *They* allege that in religion Hall became a quietist, an antinomian, a deist, if not an atheist; in personal life, a seducer of seamstresses, an immoral keeper of mistresses, sometimes fleeing from England with his kept woman of the time, sometimes returning to the ever-patient and forgiving Martha (who bore him children ten times); but in all his escapades regarded by the Wesleyans not as a mere rake but as a convinced adherent of the social doctrine of polygamy.[134]

6. The Rev. Martin Madan and His Treatise on Female Ruin

Martin Madan (1726-1790) travelled the other way. He passed from a dissolute youth into the Methodist ministry, publishing hymns and psalms, and denouncing the sin of simony in the rectory of Aldwinkle. Madan was grand-nephew to Lord Chancellor Cowper. Quite possibly he was acquainted with Westley Hall and Hall's ideas. As a Methodist, Madan was distressed to observe the frailties of human behavior among his contemporaries, married and unmarried. Most immediately, as chaplain at Lock Hospital, he was confronted in large numbers with the phenomenon of the "fallen woman," of girls seduced and abandoned, and cast out by their hypocritical parishes into the cesspools of prostitution. In the rigidities of England's marriage and divorce laws, Madan saw one root of these agonies. In the polygamy of the Bible he thought he saw one ready made solution.

In 1780 Madan published *Thelyphthora, or a Treatise on Female Ruin, in its causes, effects, consequences, prevention and remedy; considered on the basis of the Divine Law: under the following heads, viz., Marriage, Whoredom and Fornication, Adultery, Polygamy, Divorce; with many other Incidental Matters; particularly including An Examination of the Principles and Tendency of Stat. 26 Geo. II c. 33, Commonly Called the Mar-*

riage Act. In 1781 he brought out a second, enlarged edition.

Madan does not urge polygamy as an all-embracing panacea. He hardly touches on the probable benefits. He is mainly concerned with establishing that it is proper. His plea is calm, and his style is rational; at least, Madan is as rational as one can be who sincerely believes that the Bible can and should be the pattern for action. Madan of course took off on a fool's errand, honest fool that he was; devout convert that he was, unable to see that church-affiliated folks are supposed to affect to believe in the Bible, but are not supposed to know anything of its historically-dated truths, and above all are supposed to refrain from putting into practice those among its timeless moral principles which are eternally valuable; which taboo incidentally also prevents them from renewing obsolete practices like animal sacrifice, chattel slavery and plural marriage.

His assembly of Bible evidence and commentary is creditable to his preparation for the pastorate, although he owes rather more to Patrick Delany and to Johan Leyser than he admits. He quotes from many sources, including several times from one of his favorite poets, John Milton. Life is ironical. Madan did not know that Milton had preceded him with theological argument for polygamy, but on his title page he inscribed from Milton's prayerful invocation to *Paradise Lost,*

> what in me is dark
> Illumine, what is low raise and support;
> That, to the height of this great argument
> I may assert Eternal Providence,
> And justify the ways of God to men.

All in all the case he presents is rather mild, but nonetheless it did evoke a rash of responses from pious folk bent on grating and pulverizing the Rev. Mr. Madan's book:

—John Smith, D.D. of Nantwich. *Polygamy Indefensible, Two Sermons, occasioned by a late sermon entitled Thelyphthora,* etc., 1780.

—H. W. *The Unlawfulness of Polygamy Evinced, or Observations occasioned by the Erroneous Interpretations of the Passages of the New Testament, Respecting the Law of Marriage lately published in a Treatise on Female Ruin,* 1780 (NYPL).

—*An heroic epistle to the Rev. Martin M-d-n, author of a late treatise on Polygamy.* 1780.

—John Towers. *Polygamy Unscriptural, or Two Dialogues between Philalethes and Monogamus in which some of the principal errors of the Revd. Mr. M-d-n's Thelyphthora are detected,* 1780 (Harvard).

—A Layman. *A letter to the Rev. M. Madan concerning the chapter of polygamy in his late publication entitled Thelyphthora,* 1780 (BM).

—(Edward Burnaby Greene) *Whispers for the Ear of the Author of Thelyphthora in favor of Reason and Religion Aspersed through that Work,* 1781 (NYPL).

—Sir Richard Hill. *The Blessings of Polygamy Displayed, in an Affectionate Address to the Rev. Martin Madan; occasioned by his late work, entitled Thelyphthora, or a Treatise on Female Ruin,* 1781 (Harvard).

—(Sir Richard Hill). *The Cobler's Letter to the Author of Thelyphthora intended as a supplement to Mr. Hill's Address entitled "The Blessings of Polygamy",* 1781 (Harvard).

—T. Haweis. *A Scriptural Refutation of the Arguments for Polygamy Advanced in a Treatise entitled Thelyphthora,* 1781 (Harvard).

—Thomas Wills. *Remarks on Polygamy, &c., in Answer to the Rev. M-d-n's Thelyphthora,* 1781, (Harvard; Union Theological Seminary).

—Anonymous. *Martin's Hobby Houghed and Pounded, or Letters on Thelyphthora,* 1781 (BM).

—John Towers. *Polygamy Unscriptural, or Two Dialogues between Philalethes and Monogamus in which some of the principal errors of the first and second editions of the Revd. Mr. M-d-n's Thelyphthora are detected,* 1781, (BM).

—Henry Moore. *A Word to Mr. Madan, or Free Thoughts on*

his . . . Defense of Polygamy, in a letter to a friend, 1781, two editions (BM).

—John Palmer. *An Examination of Thelyphthora, on the Subject of Marriage,* 1781.

—James Penn, *Remarks on Thelyphthora,* 1781.

—Frederick Pilon, *Thelyphthora, a farce* (1781; ever printed?).

—Anonymous, *A Poetical Epistle to the Reverend Mr. Madan,* 1781.

—Anonymous, *Political Priest, A Satire Dedicated to a Reverend Polygamist,* 1781.

—Anonymous, *Polygamy, or Mahomet the Prophet to Madan the Evangelist, an heroic poem,* 1782.

—James Cookson, *Thoughts on Polygamy,* Winchester, 1782 (NYPL and Columbia University).

Madan was also answered by sundry writers in periodicals of the time, most notably by Samuel Badcock in the *Monthly Review* of London, which also reviewed books by some of his opponents. His Methodist friends were among those who wrote against him, and one of their wealthy patrons, Selina Hastings, Lady Huntingdon (1707-1791), who had helped him to obtain his ordination, now sought to convince him of his error by a petition bearing 3,000 signatures.

Of all the writings occasioned by Madan's idiosyncrasy, only one deserves still to be read today. Madan had a cousin who bore the same name as the eminent Lord Chancellor to whom they were both related, and who was presently to achieve a schoolbook fame as one of England's many good and unread poets, William Cowper. This William Cowper read his cousin Madan's book, and the comments in the *Monthly Review,* and was moved to compose a merry-making satire, 182 lines in mock-heroic couplets, *Anti-Thelyphthora,* 1781. Despite the title, it is not an attack on Madan, but rather a hearty chuckle laughing at the manners of the age as well as at Madan's eccentric proposals for their improvement. In diction somewhat reminiscent of Milton, in tone somewhat reminiscent of Cervantes, Cowper introduces the knight Sir Airy del Castro (= "Castle in the Air"), champion of promiscuity and lover of the fickle lady Hypothesis, whose cavortings were typical of a time which had

> Small need of prayerbook or priest, I ween
> Where parties are agreed, retired the scene
> Occasion prompts, and appetite so keen.

The *mitred few* may be guilty of neglect of their duty to interfere, but Sir Marmadan, Knight of the Silver Moon, rises to the emergency and overthrows Sir Airy.

Madan naturally stuck by his position, in 1782 publishing *Letters on Thelyphthora with an Occasional Prologue and Epilogue*: By the Author; and in 1783, *Five Letters Addressed to Abraham Rees, Editor of Chambers Encyclopedia.* Madan was married once, to Jane Hale, and they had five children. *Their* views have not been publicized, nor those of his brother Spencer Madan (1729-1813) who became bishop of Bristol and later of Peterborough. Madan desisted from further publication on polygamy after 1783, reappearing in the public forum in 1785 in *Thoughts on Executive Justice, with respect to our criminal laws* (two editions), and in 1787 in *Letters to Joseph Priestley,* against the Unitarians. His name, printed as plain Martin Madan with no footnotes, is still to be found with his Hymn 357 in the Hymnal now in use in the Protestant Episcopal Church of the United States of America.[135]

In 1786 his banner was picked up by James Edward Hamilton, in *A Short Treatise on Polygamy, or the Marrying and Cohabiting with more than ONE Woman at the same Time, proved from the Scripture, to be agreeable to the WILL OF GOD. and that Christ was not the GIVER of a NEW LAW. In which are also considered the Just Grounds for Divorce, and what constitutes a lawful Marriage in the SIGHT of GOD* (Dublin imprint, 49 pages; New York Public Library). Hamilton openly lifted his motifs from Madan. He also was of the opinion that Milton had written in support of plural marriage; whether from misapprehension, or from reading Pierre Bayle, cannot be judged, but this is what he offered (page 14)

> Milton having parted from his first wife upon account of contrariety of disposition, determined to marry again during her *lifetime,* and wrote in defense of *such marriages.*

One other tempest in a parish teapot over polygamy took place in a Norfolk, Connecticut, village church in 1780. Here a Dr. John Miner claimed he did not want to propagate a theory of polygamy, but merely to hold the doctrine, claiming that there were others in that church who concurred. He found himself tried and excommunicated by the local yokels. A dozen other village churches in Connecticut were a-dither over this ruckus for a season. Miner left his testimony to posterity in *Dr. Miner's Defense, Being a Concise Relation of the Church's Charge against Him, for Professing the Doctrine of Polygamy, or the Lawfulness of Having a Plurality of Wives,* printed by Hudson and Goodwin, Hartford, Connecticut, 1781, 8°, title page with blank verso, introduction iii-iv, [5]-83 pages.

APPENDIX IV

Discussion of Polygamy in Germany after Leyser: Thomasius, Willenberg

In Germany the "lawfulness" of polygamy rustled intermittently in debate for a century after Leyser and Beger, whose impetus continued operative all through that time, though not enough to more than barely ruffle the somnolence of the universities. Between 1712 and 1717 there was a fresh flutter of controversy, or two separate flutters, in which the chief heretics were Thomasius at Halle and Willenberg at Danzig.

1. Christian Thomasius

Christian Thomasius (1655-1728) was a liberal jurist, somewhat of a follower of Pufendorf, in his footsteps continuing to evolve liberalizing concepts of the law of nature. In a sense Thomasius was a forerunner of the Eighteenth Century Enlightenment.[136] In his day the squabbling Christian sects no longer made battlefield war on each other, but still hated one another most cordially: he pleaded with all of them for mutual forbearance and tolerance. As a lawyer he protested against the continued use of torture to extract confessions. In that age of witch burnings, he critically examined his own prejudice and then denounced that delusion which he had himself once shared. To help break the stranglehold of theological pedantry over serious thought, he changed the language of instruction at his university from Latin to the vernacular German. (In immediate context, a liberation, but at a heavy price. The disappearance of a common and neutral international language of culture and science is no less a loss even if no one feels it, just as the loss of meadow daisies and butterflies and running brooks from our lives is not less a loss because no one even knows enough to miss them.)

Originally Thomasius entered the polygamy debate on the heels of the Leyser controversy, which he saw as one facet in a continuing complex of disputes within the Protestant fold on many aspects of marriage. In his history of the evolution of natural law, *Paulo Plenior Historia Juris Naturalis* ("Rather Fuller History of Natural Law", 1719) he put Leyser into one context with other reverend wrangles over marriage with a sister of a deceased wife (Strauch-Buchholz-Havemann), the wedlock of eunuchs (Hieronymus Delphinus), and other such niceties.[137]

On November 12, 1685, in the year after Leyser's death, Thomasius as *praeses* and Georg Beyer (1665-1714) as respondent submitted a disputation printed in a Latin pamphlet published by Johan Georgius at Leipzig under the bilingual title *De Crimine Bigamiae. Vom Laster der Zwiefachen Ehe* ("On the Crime of Bigamy"). On December 12, 1685 a second disputation of Thomasius and Beyer was recorded in a pamphlet *De Bigamiae Praescriptione. Von Verjährung der Zwiefachen Ehe,* ("On the [Statute of] Limitations for Bigamy," at the same publisher).[138]

As a specialist in the law of nature, Thomasius felt that Leyser had abused that principle by deducing from the wide distribution of polygamy that it must be made mandatory, while Leyser's opponents in their turn had failed to deal properly with the issue because of their lack of understanding of the law of nature and of universal divine positive law.

In these 1685 pamphlets, plural marriage is discussed for the first time from a dispassionate and common sense stand point. Thomasius was dedicated to the separation of denominational religion from politics and from civil law. He here begins with a distinction: polygamy is a theologian's concept, while lawyers deal with bigamy. Bigamy, as every one knows, is commonly treated as a crime, except by extremists, as by Leyser. Bigamy is indeed banned by divine law, and by human (statutory, civil) law, although calm reflection shows that it does not conflict with natural law. Thomasius regards the original divine institution of marriage as monogamous, but under divine "positive universal law." God cannot give a dispensation from "natural law," but He can give dispensations from "positive universal law," and He did so in the case of the Hebrew patriarchs.

To Thomasius bigamy is a practical problem, to be defined with legalistic precision, with penalties to be prescribed, appropriate in degree varying with the offense, rather than an obligatory death penalty for every case, and with a precisely defined statute of limitations for prosecution. Thomasius is extraordinarily uncommon in his insistence on common sense. He may be the first man who ever conceded that bigamy committed by a woman (that "polyandry" so universally abhorred by all polygamophiles) should be regarded on the same legal footing as a man's bigamy, that it is not any more banned by the law of nature, and not any less banned by statutory civil law. Although Thomasius retains the idea of divine law, he remains always the mild voice of realistic experience.

Privately Thomasius sent his two dissertations to Pufendorf, asking for his opinion, with particular reference to his amendment subsuming one-woman-several-husbands under natural law. Pufendorf wrote back from Stockholm, June 9, 1686, politely telling Thomasius what he might very well have known anyway, that he could not expect universal approbation from the learned.[139]

These two pamphlets did not arouse much attention at that time, and across the years Thomasius was generous in supplying his opponents with many more important doctrines on which to attack him. About twenty-five years later there was an upsurge of cackle on this question, centering on later publications by Thomasius. In the interim the polygamy pother bubbled up at irregular intervals, usually in the older traditional vein of dogma, as if Thomasius had never spoken his common sense.

In 1685 (and in 1691) appeared Johannes Andreas Quenstedt's *Theologica Didactico-Polemica* ("Didactic-Polemic Theology") at Wittenberg, a folio of monstrous thickness, in which Part IV, Chapter XIV, pages 458-469, deals with Leyser, whom he considers different from Wahrenberg, repeating chatter from Calovius' *Systema* adding nothing to its authority or authenticity, also deriving from Siricius, Mentzer, Diecmann, Feltmann, Musaeus, Beza-on-Ochino and Selden.[140]

In 1687 and 1688 Johan Meyer's *Uxor Christiana* ("Christian Wife"), against Leyser and Beger, appeared twice. In 1687 Varillas reprinted Beger's papers on the Philip of Hesse bigamy, followed by Bossuet in 1688, and Seckendorf's reply for the Lutherans soon after. Thomasius set down his own viewpoint in his 1688 *Institutes of Divine Jurisprudence.*

In 1690 was published the *Tractatus de Polygamia* written some years before by Melchior Zeidler (1630-1686), preacher at Königsberg Cathedral, in minute detail abstracting from the literature of classical antiquity and of church antiquity on marriage and polygamy.[141]

In 1692 appeared by Hieronymus Bruckner (1639-1693) *Decisiones Iuris Matrimonialis Controversi* ("Decisions in Controversies of Matrimonial Law"), a factual compilation from a lawyer's professional point of view, treating cases and precedents in a balanced fashion, a work therefore of much more significance than the polemics of theologians, and often cited during the next generation.[142]

On January 28, 1692 at Greifswald there was a disputation in traditional style, *Polygamiam Legi Naturae Repugnantem* ("Polygamy Contradicting Natural Law"), Georg Balthasar Mascovius as *praeses,* Georg Bogislaus de Mascou as author and respondent, printed by Daniel Benjamin Starck, 38 unnumbered pages.[143]

In 1694 Thomasius as *praeses* conducted a series of twelve public disputations on forty-eight theses drawn from his *Institutes of Divine Jurisprudence;* not very conspicuous, but nonetheless included, Thesis number 3 in Disputation X, with respondent Christopher Sigismund Richter of Sorau, was stated as: "That male and female polygamy is not banned by the simple law of nature, but by divine universal law, which also binds princes, it is seriously prohibited. Common disagreement with the first clause, and few disagreeing with the latter."

Whether in response to this occasion, or in belated response to the 1685 Thomasius-Beyer disputations, the Elector of Saxony issued a rescript in 1694 forbidding any more disputations on bigamy at the University of Wittenberg, and ordering the confiscation of such tracts from the booksellers of Leipzig.[144]

In 1695 Wilhelm Ernest Tenzel (1659-1707), editor of the *Monatliche Unterredungen Einiger Guten Freunde von Allerhand Büchern und Andern Annehmlichen Geschichten. Allen Liebhabern der Curiositäten zur Ergetzlichkeit und Nachsinnen heraus gegeben* ("Monthly Conversations of Several Good Friends on Sundry Books and Other Pleasant Matters, Published for the Entertainment and Information of All Devotees of Curiosities," printed by J. Thomas Fritsch at Leipzig) applied a large part of his September issue to a critique of Leyser and Beger dated February 22, 1688 by a theologian signing only D. I. W. B., whom we may now identify as Dr. Johan Wilhelm Bajer.[145]

In 1696 Elias Schneegass (a jurist who also wrote under the name Antonius de Mara, deceased 1697) published *Monogamia Triumphans* ("Monogamy Triumphing"), ten theological arguments in seven pages to prove that the New Testament overrode Old Testament precedents for polygamy.[146]

On September 5, 1698 at the University of Leyden, Werner Zur Muhlen veered off the track and delivered an inaugural disputation on "successive polygamy."[147] Also in 1698 a group of Huguenot ministers, exiled from France by the revocation of the Edict of Nantes, collaborated on a series of studies at Amsterdam, at the publishing house of Henri Desbordes, *Vesperae Groninganae sive Amica de Rebus Sacris Colloquia* ("Groningen Vespers, or Friendly Chats on Sacred Subjects"), conversing rather weightily on polygamy in numbers 9 and 10, pages 125-212, and on divorce, in numbers 11 and 25, pages 212-225, 320-330.[148]

On September 10, 1700 at Rinthel University there was ventilated a belated anti-Leyser disputation, *Dissertatio Theologica de Polygamia, praeses* Johannes Kahler, author-respondent Conrad Christopher Neuberg, accompanied by some truly pitiful sets of verses.[149]

In 1701 Jacob Friedrich Ludovici issued his *Delineatio Historiae Juris Divini Naturalis et Positivi Universalis,* published at Halle by Johann Gothofred Renger (8 page preface, 74 pages plus Errata), an unusually lucid "Outline of the History of Divine

Natural Law and Divine Universal Positive Law," setting forth the roots of Thomasius' ideas back to ancient times, spelling out the Pufendorf-Leyser-Gesenius triangle, and offering clarity where many minor writers had left confusion.

In 1701 there appeared in the periodical *Observationum Selectarum ad Rem Litterarium Spectantium,* "Select Observations Regarding the Literary World," published serially at Halle, IV, 406-440 an article *De Vita, Religione et Fatis Bernardini Ochini, Senensis,* "On the Life, Religion and Opinions of Bernardino Ochino of Siena," followed in V, 1-63 (1702), *De Bernardini Ochini Dialogorum Libris,* "On Ochino's Books of Dialogues," and on pages 64-82 *De Bernardini Ochini Scriptis Reliquis,* "Of Ochino's Remaining Writings:" perhaps the first extended treatment of Ochino in print which was not hostile to him; anonymous, but written with Thomasius' knowledge, if not actually by himself.[150]

In 1702 at Greifswald Johan Friedrich Mayer attempted in a dissertation *Utrum B. Lutherus Philippo, Landgravio, bigamiam concesserit?* ("Whether the Blessed Luther Conceded Bigamy to Landgrave Philip?") to raise doubts on the documents because they had come from that notorious convert to Catholicism, Ernst of Hesse-Rheinfels.[151]

In 1703 there was published in six well printed pages under the pseudonym *Henrici Alethaei I.C.T., Eilfertiges Antwort-Schreiben an Einen Hochfürstl. Raht in N. Uber die Frage: Ob die Polygamie mit dem Christenthum Bestehen Könne? Anno 1703* ("Heinrich Alethaeus, Jurisconsult, Hasty Reply Written to a Princely Counsellor in N. on the Question Whether Polygamy Can Stand with Christianity"). "Henricus Alethaeus" simplifies the matter by definition. He limits the matter to Christian dogma, excluding the law of nature and the Old Testament Patriarchs from consideration. Since no Christian sect, no matter how heretical, ever accepted polygamy, and since civil law in all Christian states made it a crime, the customary New Testament texts are fitted into place. Slight as this pamphlet was, it was pirated into a bad reprint; and evoked a counter-reply, an anonymous *Censur* which asked what value could be placed on seventeen hundred years of church unanimity against polygamy when that church had been just as unanimously wrong, until the Reformation, on clergyman's celibacy, and so sought to reduce that case to absurdity. This *Censur* circulated somewhat in manuscript, and apparently was not printed until 1723, which is another story.[152]

In 1705 Thomasius issued the first edition of his *Fundamenta Juris Naturae et Gentium ex Sensu Communi Deducta,* etc., "Foundations of the Law of Nature and Nations Deduced from Common Sense," treating of many matters; to which he appended explanatory notes to his 1688 *Institutes of Divine Jurisprudence,* treating again of concubinage insofar as it had been a lawful form of marriage at certain times and certain places, distinguished from the immoral practices presumably more familiar to his readers.[153]

In 1710 Nicolaus Möller published his *De Polygamia,* reviewing the polygamy literature pro and con, including the notorious polygamophile John Milton, as quoted from Möller elsewhere herein, and the contemporary Thomasius.[154]

On January 9, 1711 at Wittenberg at the Gerdesian Press was published *De Intercessione Conjugum in Delictis Carnis In Primis in Crimine Bigamiae,* "On the Intercession of the Spouse in Crimes of the Flesh, Particularly in the Crime of Bigamy," with *moderamen* (= *praeses?*) Michael Heinrich Gribner, who is always catalogued as the author although the title page explicitly lists as *auctor* Christianus Ludovicus Thilo of Langensalz in Thuringia, pages 3-56, with 14 pages of supplement by dean Johan Heinrich Berger; Ochino, Leyser under his aliases and Arcuarius are recalled; and Thomasius' 1685 writings.[155]

More likely having an effect on Thomasius personally was the publication dated April 14, 1712 of a *Dissertatio Juridica de Polygamia, Incestu et Divortio, Jure Naturali Prohibitis,* "Juridical Dissertation on Polygamy, Incest and Divorce Prohibited by Natural Law," catalogued usually as by the *praeses,* Gottlieb Gerhard Titius, although clearly by the respondent-author Gottfried Pflaume, "Ascaniensis," i.e., of Aschersleben, in Anhalt; printed by Immanuel Titius of Leipzig, [3]-54 pages plus two pages by Gottlieb Gerhard Titius. Titius-Pflaume direct their fire against Athanasius Vincentius and Daphnaeus Arcuarius, following Johan

Meyer's *Uxor Christiana.*[156] They are respectful to Thomasius, while taking a contradicting position. Titius had been a personal pupil of Thomasius, so that dissertation may have helped to motivate Thomasius to restate his ideas.

On April 8, 1713 Thomasius as *praeses* with Erhard Julius Kiechel of Ulm as respondent submitted at Halle a *Dissertatio Inauguralis Juridica de Concubinatu,* "Inaugural Juridical Dissertation on Concubinage," printed by Johan Christian Zahn. Now dean of the law school at Halle (by some opponents called *Hölle,* "Hell"), Thomasius declares that his objective is to cultivate lawyers and jurists who would know the true rationale for law from the spurious and sophistical, so that they would rise above the level of pettifoggers and shysters. Neither defending nor deploring the practice of concubinage, as a particular form of plural marriage, Thomasius seeks to trace the plain facts of its occurrence in history and its place in canon law. Inevitably the conclusion must be clear, since concubinage has existed during long periods of history, and children of concubines throughout these ages have been legitimate.[157]

Thomasius might seek to be the voice of sweet reasonableness, but the clergymen in their *Unschuldige Nachrichten* for 1713, pages 852-853, greeted the appearance of his dissertation with a groan, *Novum ecce scandalum a Jcto notissimi nominis datum,* "see the new scandal contributed by a jurist of noted name;" and announced a counter-blow by Joachim Justus Breithaupt, Abbot of Berga (1658-1732), *praeses,* and Bernhardus Baumgart, Neuhaldersleben, respondent, *Dissertatio Theologica de Concubinatu a Christo et Apostolis Prohibito* ("Theological Dissertation on Concubinage Prohibited by Christ and the Apostles," dated April 29, 1713) another sermon on Matthew xix, insisting that Christ forbade divorce and plural marriage. Thomasius is not named and his arguments are not reviewed.[158]

More directly against Thomasius-Kiechel, and drawing heavily on Breithaupt, in 1713 there appeared an *Examen Philosophico-Theologicum Dissertationis Cujusdam Hallensis de Concubinatu* ("Philosophical-Theological Examination of a Dissertation on Concubinage by Somebody at Halle") by Johan Andreas Grammlich of Stuttgart (1683-1728) with Johan Wolfgang Jäger, (1647-1720) chancellor of the University of Tübingen, *praeses,* printed by Johan Cunrad Reis at Tübingen, 30 pages. Typically, Grammlich ignores Thomasius' historical data. To explain the polygamy of the Patriarchs, he revives an old alibi found in Hülsemann and others: in their case it was permissible because of their pious eagerness to hasten the coming of the Redeemer to be born of their seed. Grammlich also mentions a "recent" pronouncement against concubinage by the faculties of theology and law at Leipzig.[159]

Meanwhile rumor and gossip percolated into the royal court circles in Prussia as if Thomasius were advising men to forthwith acquire concubines to supplement their wives. Many women sounded off to their spouses, but it was the new King Friedrich Wilhelm who was in the tightest spot. His queen came to him in bitter tears, protesting that her happinesss was at an end, wearying him until he consented to send Thomasius some kind of blunt reproof. At the same time, King Friedrich Wilhelm, understanding the facts better, knowing that Thomasius had not broken any law, effectively quashed all punitive proposals moved in his domains, even (August 7, 1713) calling the Halle theological faculty to order for unjustifiably offensive behavior to Thomasius.[160]

On November 4, 1713 a pseudonymous author joined in with *S. Petri Encratitae ad Illustrem Abbatem Bergensem de Concubinatu Epistola* ("S. Peter Encratita's Letter to the Illustrious Abbot of Berga on Concubinage," Utrecht), described by the *Unschuldige Nachrichten* as mediating between Thomasius and Breithaupt (1715, pages 1044-1046). The writer's identity was not known to many; he was Simon Peter Gasser, law professor at Halle, (1676-1745).[161]

Early the next year, a Lutheran preacher in Berlin, Johan Gustav Reinbeck (c. 1683-1741) composed *Die Natur des Ehestandes und Verwerfflichkeit des dawieder Streitenden Concubinats. Aus der Heil. Schrifft, und Anderen Vernünfftigen Gründen Gezeiget, und Wider des Herrn Geheimten Rahts Thomasii Dissertation (De Concubinatu) von Concubinen-halten behauptet* ("The Nature of Matrimony and the Rottenness of That Still Contending Concubinage. Out of Holy Scripture and Other Grounds of Reason Demonstrated and Maintained against the Dissertation on Concubine-Keeping by Privy Councillor Thomasius"), published by J. A. Rüdiger, Berlin, preface dated March 29, 1714. Part One treats of adultery, whoring, incest and other breaches of matrimony, while Part Two is a point by point argument against Thomasius-Kiechel.

Also in 1714, Johan Wilhelm Zierold (1669-1731) put out his *Theologische Gedancken von der Heiligkeit des Ehestandes wider den Unheiligen Concubinatum, aus dem 1 B. Mosis II, 24. auf Veranlassung des Schediasm. Hall. de Concubinatu, entworffen von J. W. Z. D. P. & P. P. 1714* ("Theological Thoughts on the Sanctity of Matrimony against Unholy Concubinage. Based on the First Book of Moses, ii, 24, on the Occasion of the Halle Schediasma on Concubinage, sketched by J. W. Z."). It is short, seven pages, in which Zierold denounces Sadducees and Epicureans who err themselves and mislead others; and plays abracadabra games with the Hebrew spelling of the words for *man* and *woman.*

In support of Thomasius there appeared at Strassbourg in 1714 *Marci Pauli Antonini, Philosophi Tribocci, Confutatio Dubiorum, quae contra Schediasma Halense de Concubinatu Mota Sunt. Argentorati. A. O. R. MDCC.XIV.* ("Marcus Paulus Antoninus, Alsatian Philosopher, His Confutation of the Objections Moved Against the Halle Schediasma on Concubinage. Strassbourg, 1714"). *Antoninus* was Jacob Schmauss (1690-1757) and his forty page pamphlet offers careful and clear summaries of Thomasius, and careful and clear answers to Breithaupt, Grammlich-Jäger and Zierold.

In response to Gasser-Encratita and Schmauss-Antoninus, on November 28, 1714 Reinbeck reprinted his *Die Natur des Ehestandes,* adding a supplement, *Gedoppelter Anhang vom Concubinen-Halten, in welchem I. Petri Encratitae epistola ad Abbatem Bergensem, II. Marci Pauli Antonini confutatio dubiorum quae contra Schediasma Hallense de Concubinatu mota sunt, kürzlich erwogen und die Verwerfflichkeit des Concubinats nochmals wider allerley ausflüchte fest gesetzet wird* ("Double Supplement on Keeping Concubines, in which I. Peter Encratita's Epistle to the Abbot of Berga, II. Marcus Paulus Antoninus' Confutation of Objections Moved Against the Schediasma on Concubinage are Briefly Considered, and the Rottenness of Concubinage Once Again Firmly Demonstrated Against All Kinds of Dodges").

For himself, in connection with the publication in 1714 of a number of his writings, Thomasius brought out a German translation of his 1713 *Schediasma, Juristische Disputation von der Kebs Ehe* ("Juridical Disputation on Concubinage")—"to multiply the scandal," said the *Unschuldige Nachrichten,* 1715, pages 1044-1046. In the same 1714 volume was printed a German translation of Antoninus' pamphlet, *Wiederlegung der Einwürffe welche wieder die Hällische Schrifft von der Kebs Ehe gemacht worden,* to which was added a new *Anhang wieder die letztern Einwürffe des Herrn Reinbecks,* ("Supplement Against the Latest Objections by Mr. Reinbeck").

Reinbeck promptly put out a third section to what had become a three part book, this part a *Nochmaliger Beweiss, dass der vom Herrn Geheimten Rath Thomasio vertheidigte Concubinat ein Sündlicher und Verwerfflicher Stand sey, Wider den Anhang Welcher unter dem Nahmen Antonini ohnlängst wider meine Schrifft von Der Natur des Ehestandes herausgegeben worden, geführet und bestättiget* ("Reiterated Proof that Concubinage Defended by Privy Councillor Thomasius Is a Sinful and Rotten Position, Adduced and Confirmed Against the Supplement Which Was Recently Issued under the Name of Antoninus Against My Book on the Nature of Matrimony").

Grammlich had also come out (preface dated November 14, 1714) with a *Defensio Dissertationis suae de Illicito Concubinatu opposita Marci Pauli Antonini Philosophi Tribocci Confutationi* ("Defense of His Dissertation on Illicit Concubinage Against the Confutation of Marcus Paulus Antoninus, Alsatian Philosopher"), publisher Christoph Andreas Zeitler, Halle, 24 pages, which he added to his 1713 dissertation, printing them together in 1716 as Parts I and II of *Tractatus Philosophico-Theologicus de Moral-*

itate Concubinatus ("Philosophical-Theological Treatise on the Morality of Concubinage") at J. W. Kohles, Frankfurt and Leipzig.[162]

Still other long titled books came out aiming to set Thomasius straight, but through it all Thomasius kept his cool.[163] He continues to reprint his 1685 and his 1713 dissertations; and in his 1718 fourth edition of *Fundamenta Juris Naturae et Gentium ex Sensu Communi Deducta* ("Foundations of the Law of Nature and Nations Deduced from Common Sense") he still asserts that plural marriages are not of themselves necessarily indecent, and may be preferable to vagrant lusts and other common varieties of depravity.[164]

2. *Samuel Friedrich Willenberg*

Somewhat more turbulent, though off in a corner, was the wrangle during the same years occasioned by another jurist, Samuel Friedrich Willenberg of Danzig (1663-1748), who insisted on reading in the Bible what was written there, not what might be read into it in contradiction to its plain words.[165] The Thomasius-controversy literature and the Willenberg-controversy literature flow, in the main, quite apart from each other, although both were reported simultaneously in the pages of the *Unschuldige Nachrichten,* and occasionally both streams did make momentary contact.

In 1709 in his *Sicilimenta Juris Gentium Prudentiae* ("Gleanings from the Law of Nations"), a students' handbook on Grotius in question and answer form, with citations to Pufendorf, Thomasius and others, Willenberg briefly touched on polygamy as not against the law of nature nor against divine positive law.[166] Samuel Schelwig (1643-1715), pastor of Willenberg's parish church of the Holy Trinity, used the occasion of two disputations on the Augsburg Confession, July 18 and July 23, 1709, to retort that polygamy had always been banned, except by divine dispensation in the Old Testament, which Jesus ended by restoring the original law of marriage. Even in Danzig hardly anyone paid them any attention.

Some three years later, Willenberg, who was also professor of history at the Danzig "Athenaeum," or Gymnasium, scheduled an academic disputation on this theme for 10 A.M. on April 12, 1712. As customary, Willenberg had his little folder printed in advance, *De Finibus Polygamiae Licitae, Schediasma ex Lectionibus Publicis Collectum,* "On the Limits of Permissible Polygamy, an Outline Collected from Common Authorities." It is rather shorter than customary, twelve paragraphs on five pages; as customary, announcing himself as *praeses,* with Nicolaus Torner as respondent, and not at all as customary, for once listing the names of the "Opponents," Fridericus Reyger and Carolus Ernestus Pegelau.[167]

Essentially Willenberg repeated that plural marriage was not prohibited by the law of nature nor by divine law, but only by human law. He conceded that there was good and substantial reason for this ban by human law, in general, but he suggested that polygamy might be permitted in cases of urgent necessity, under dispensation from a king or higher magistrate. Inevitably Willenberg evoked hostility from the clergy; not only because he challenged church dogma, but because he urged that the ruling secular prince was empowered to define and dispense in regard to plural marriage as a matter of human law.

As soon as the April 1712 disputation was announced (the theses nailed to church and gymnasium doors), Schelwig, as Willenberg's pastor, hurried to remonstrate with him, without avail. Schelwig sent a note to alert Joachim Weickhmann (1662-1736), pastor at St. Mary's Church in Danzig, and both together got hold of Nicolaus Torner, who was a young theology student. They warned Torner that his participating as respondent would lose him divine grace, render him a candidate for Gehenna, and certainly forfeit him any advancement in his career as clergyman. Torner pleaded that the respondency was merely the usual school exercise, but they sternly scolded him that Bible texts were not given for tongue calisthenics. Torner was intimidated into a tearful withdrawal. Willenberg was annoyed but refused to be terrified, and went on with the disputation, without the respondent. Joachim Weickhmann registered some complaints with the city burgomeisters that Willenberg was exposing the youth of Danzig to danger and that as a doctor of laws he was trespassing on the territory of the doctors of the church in meddling with Holy Writ; without any effect.

Months went by with no further reverberations, when, to Willenberg's surprise, there appeared anonymously a Latin pamphlet *Vindiciae Scripturae Sacrae a Pseudhermenia Quae Passim in Scriptis Patronorum Polygamias, Inprimis Jcti Gedanensis, Viri Excellentissimi Ac Consultissimi Dn. Samuelis Frider. Willenbergs, D. et Professoris, Schediasmate De Finibus Polygamiae Licitae, Committitur. Adjectum est in fine Ipsum Schediasma Willenbergianum. Lipsiae, Sumtibus Haeredum Lanckisianorum. Anno* MDCCXIII, "Vindications of the Holy Scriptures from the Pseudo-Interpretations which are Disseminated Throughout the Writings of the Patrons of Polygamy, in particular of Mr. Samuel Friedrich Willenberg, Danzig Attorney, a Man Most Excellent and Learned in the Law, Doctor and Professor, Expressed in the Schediasma of the Limits of Permissible Polygamy. At the End is Appended that Same Schediasma of Willenberg. Leipzig, published by the Firm of Lanckisius' Heirs, 1713."[168] These Vindications serve up the standard clichés in rebuttal to Willenberg's Bible citations, sauced with the charge that he must be a disciple of Ochino the unitarian heretic and of Leyser who was rendered forever beyond the pale of respectability by the ban of the King of Denmark.

Willenberg took a deep breath and replied with his own Latin pamphlet, *Praesidia Juris Divini, Quibus Tuetur Thesin in Schediasmate Suo de Finibus Poligamiae Licitae Contra Imbelles Conatus Quos Post litem bis depulsam, quam superiore anno contra illam moverant Duo Theologi Gedanenses in Vindiciis Scripturae Sacrae a Pseudhermenia Patronorum Polygamias &c. De Novo ostendit Theologus Anonymus. Francofurti ad Viadrum. Apud Jeremiam Schrey, MDCCXIII,* "Bastions of Divine Law, Supporting the Doctrine Set Forth in His Outline of Permissible Polygamy Against the Feeble Efforts, which after being twice defeated in legal motions which last year two Danzig Theologians moved against him, an Anonymous Theologian Anew Sets Forth in Vindications, etc. Frankfurt on the Oder, at Jeremiah Schrey's,

1713."[169] Willenberg guessed that Schelwig and Weickhmann were responsible for the *Vindiciae,* and about as said so, but chose to seize on the anonymity as a stick to beat them. He denies having previously read either Ochino or Leyser, whose works he is now looking into. He affirms that he had relied only on Holy Writ, on proper theologians, on jurists of stature. He denies any intent to institute universal polygamy, and winds up his counter-citations with "Credunt vetulae, non credunt viri docti, rem tantae abominationis esse polygamiam defendere"—Let old women, not men of education, believe that it is such an abomination to defend polygamy.

Weickhmann, who was the actual author of the *Vindiciae,* now felt that he had to reply under his own name, and so came out with *Justitia Causae, in Controversia De Polygamia Simultanea, Nobilissimo, Excellentissimo & Consultissimo, Dn. Sam. Frider. Willenbergio, J.U.D. ejusdem & Historiarum Professori & Athenaei Gedanensis Inspectori, in defensionem Vindiciarum Scripturae Sacrae &c. quas Hic in Praesidiis, ut vocat, Juris Divini, impugnatum ivit, opposita. Cum appendice Responsorum Theologico-Juridicorum. Lipsiae, Sumtibus Haeredum Lanckisianorum, Anno MDCCXIV.,* "Justice of His Case in the Controversy of Simultaneous Polygamy, in opposition to the Most Noble, Excellent and Most Learned in Law, Mr. Samuel Friedrich Willenberg, Doctor in Civil and Canon Law, Professor in the same and in History, Inspector of the Danzig Athenaeum, in defense of the *Vindiciae,* etc., which he attacks in what he calls the Bastions of Divine Law. With an Appendix of Theological-Juridical Replies, Leipzig. Published by the Firm of Lanckisius' Heirs, 1714."[170]

The *wort-streit,* the verbal duel, is now thumpingly full-blown. Sarcastically he calls Willenberg a poet sans metre rather than a philosopher (page 56). With sanctimonious sophistry he revises Deuteronomy xxi, 15-17 from a clearly polygamous situation into a case of successive monogamous marriages. With wrigglings and squirmings he evades the plain evidence on Luther and Melanchthon. He includes a transcript of testimony by Nicolaus Torner, subjected to the indignity of formal questioning, in which he perforce must pretend to clear Schelwig and Weickhmann of the charge of having intimidated him: no stronger proof of that intimidation needed than this transcript itself. He constructs tables of forced parallels to prove a "harmony" of Ochino, Leyser and Willenberg. In the appendix he prints replies received to questionnaires he had formulated and sent September 27, 1713 to the Law Faculty at Rostock, to the Theological Faculty at Rostock, and the Theological Faculty at Wittenberg; all bound to support his stand in principle and in tactics.

Willenberg read the *Justitia Causae* and was quick with his reply: *Iterata Praesidia Juris Divini Pro Defensione Thesium Suarum de Polygamia Simultanea Viri Summe Reverendi Et Excellentissimi Dni. Joachimi Weickmanni, S. Theol. Doctoris & Pastoris ad Aedes B. Mariae ac Reverendi Ministerii apud Gedanenses Senioris Justitiae Causae ut Vocat, Qua Illas Ulterius Impugnatum Ivit Opposita. Adjectum In Fine Extraneorum Jctorum Judicium de hac Controversia. Francofurti et Lipsiae A. MDCCXIV.*—"Reiterated Bastions of Divine Law for the Defense of His Theses of Simultaneous Polygamy, in Opposition to that Most Reverend and Excellent Man, Mr. Joachim Weickhmann, Doctor of Sacred Theology, Pastor of the Church of the Blessed Mary, Senior among the Reverend Ministers of Danzig, His *Justitia Causae* as he calls it, in which he attacks those Theses Further. To which is Added the Judgment of Foreign Jurists on this Controversy. Frankfurt and Leipzig, 1714." Mostly Willenberg lobs and backhands each of Weickhmann's serves, on Luther and on Lamech. He mocks Weickhmann's Leyser baiting by setting up a harmony of Leyser-Weickhmann, showing how easy it is to find false parallels. He hints that a reply to a questionnaire from the Königsberg Law Faculty was omitted by Weickhmann because it was less favorable: an erroneous supposition, this. Willenberg introduces two new witnesses to whom he had alluded in the previous *Praesidia.* These were two former teachers of his, whose writings he felt reinforced his analysis: Joachim Hoppe (1656-1712) in his comments on marriage in his *Succinct Comments on Justinian's Institutes;* and Johann Schultze, in a March 9, 1690 disputation, *De Eo Quod Non Vetat Lex, Vetat Pudor in Matrimonialibus*—"On that Which the Law Does Not Forbid in

Matrimony, Modesty Forbids." Although Willenberg never lines up with Thomasius' common-sense-on-bigamy, he quotes from several of his works (so too does Weickhmann on occasion). In the appendix he prints a letter from the Law Faculty of Halle, necessarily therefore from Thomasius, restricting Matthew xix to discussion of divorce, and the polygamy ban to human law.[171]

Meanwhile seventy-one year old Samuel Schelwig joined in the published debate with *D. Samuelis Schelguigii De Polygamia Ab Universa Christi Ecclesia Inde a Primis Novi Testamenti Initiis, Usque ad Nostra Tempora, Ex Agnito Monogamiae Praecepto, Per Totum Orbem Constanter Profligata; Adversus Themistium, Virum Nobilissimum, Excellentissimum et Consultissimum, Commentatio. Lipsiae, Impensis Friderici Lanckisii, 1714.*—"Dr. Samuel Schelwig's Dissertation on Polygamy Constantly Cast Down by the Universal Church of Christ, thence from the First Beginnings of the New Testament until Our Times by the Acknowledged Law of Matrimony through the Whole World Argued against Themistius, a Man Most Noble, Most Excellent, Most Learned in the Law. Leipzig, published by Friedrich Lanckisius, 1714."[172] Schelwig has compiled an anthology of paragraphs from the early Christian times of Ignatius and Polycarp through the centuries from men as famous as Aquinas, Wicklif and Huss, and as obscure as Euthymus Zigabenus, over 150 in all; as a display of theological erudition, as spectacular as a burst of sparkling fireworks, as insubstantial and as fleeting. For instance, Schelwig cites a law of Charlemagne's forbidding remarriage to divorced men and women, but he forgets to remember Charlemagne's own foursome of concubines.

In a separate printing Schelwig got out a supplement, *D. Samuelis Schelguigii Reliqua de Polygamia, Adversus Themistium, Virum Nobilissimum, Consultissimum et Excellentissimum. Lipsiae, Impensis Friderici Lanckisii.*—"Dr. Samuel Schelwig, The Rest of the Dissertation on Polygamy Against Themistius, A Most Noble Man, Most Learned in the Law, Most Excellent. Leipzig, published by Friedrick Lanckisius."[173] For reasons of tactics, perhaps of tact, Schelwig uses substitute names, *Themistius* (from Themis, spirit of law) for Willenberg, *Eusebius* for Torner. In this supplement he deplores the discussion as a scandal in which Themistius exposes himself to the contempt of theologians, the censure of jurists, the punishment of magistrates.

Willenberg promptly responded to Schelwig's two pamphlets with *De Polygamia a Christiana Ecclesia ex Supposita, sed Non Probata Lege Divina Monogamica, Prohibita Adversus Meletium Virum Summe Reverendum et Excellentissimum Exceptio. Francofurti et Lipsiae. A. MDCCXIV.*—"Objection Moved against Meletius with Regard to the Prohibition of Polygamy by the Christian Church by a Supposed but Not Proved Divine Law of Monogamy."[174]

Willenberg returns the compliment by calling Schelwig "Meletius," honeyed, from the Latin, *mel,* honey; but with a subtle reference to Psalms xix, where the Lord's judgment is sweeter than honey. He tallies 27 of Schelwig's quotations as wholly irrelevant; if the other quotations confirm that polygamy has always been banned by the church, that is well known, but that does not prove that it is banned by divine law.

By this time the verbal duel of Willenberg and Weickhmann had become a source of amusement to some and of annoyance to others in Danzig. Willenberg mentions an anagram in circulation making fun of him, and there is trace of a lampoon against his opponent, *Weickhmanniana,* which came out in 1714 and was quickly suppressed by the authorities, who were rather under pressure from Weickhmann.[175]

About the same time there also appeared a little 16 page brochure, *Kurtzer Beweis dass unnütze Fragen dem Christenthum schädlich sind. Aus dem Englischen in Deustche übersetzet. Cölln, Anno 1714.*—"Short Demonstration that Vain Questions Are Hurtful to Christianity, Translated from the English into German. Cölln, 1714." It is anonymous, and appears to be, as the title page says, based on an English original. The British author bemoaned debates which tend to destroy a believer's simple faith in Scripture, and which tend to encourage unitarian thought ("Arianism," "Socinianism," "Dr. Whiston's terrible book"). The main example offered, among others, is the disagreement between theologians (who claim the Bible bans polygamy or permits it only by divine dispensation), and lawyers (who demand to see the parchment on which the law or the dispensation is engrossed). The unknown author wishes that the theologians would come to terms with the lawyers.[176] Despite its original focus, the *Kurtzer Beweis* circulated in Danzig as a vernacular voice against Weickhmann, who wanted the authorities to suppress it also. Up to that time the debate had been entirely in Latin, which limited its effect. Now, on Michaelmas day, September 29, 1714 Weickhmann preached a sermon against the Dragon: he might not name Willenberg, he might not even mean Willenberg, but some people so interpreted his sermon. Johan Schelwig, deacon at the Church of St. John, preached there less obliquely, invoking anathema on this Mohammedan disorder, so that Willenberg began to hear that he was becoming a bogeyman who was being cursed in beerstubes and fish markets by folks who could never read the Latin books.

Weickhmann seems to have continued to make demands on the town council, asking a ban on any discussion of polygamy at the faculties of law or philosophy, a 100 ducat fine for the sale of polygamophile books and the like. Finally Willenberg gave them a handle, in some offhand remarks implying that Weickhmann was fond of pomps and luxury, of a carriage with horses and a lackey, of not properly comporting himself in the matter of a call to preach in Dresden. After a series of hearings and talks back and forth the Council issued a statement expressing their confidence in Herr Weickhmann: a six page folder, *E. Hoch-Edlen Hochweisen Raths in Dantzig, Aus Schluss sämtlicher Ordnungen daselbst, Oeffentliche Declaration der Unschuld D. Joachim Weickhmanns, Bey denen Beschuldigungen, mit welchen Er von D. Samuel Friedrich Willenbergen angegriffen worden. Leipzig. In Lanckiscken Buch-Laden,* "Public Declaration of the Honourable Most Judicious Council in Danzig, by Decision of the Joint Orders There, on the Innocence of Dr. Joachim Weickhmann of the Accusations with which He Was Attacked by Dr. Samuel Willenberg."[177] Dated October 19, 1714, signed by the Burgomeisters and Council, the statement clears Weickhmann from the imputations of less than exemplary conduct as pastor, and completely dodges the issue of plural marriage.

Early in 1715 there appeared a blast against Willenberg from an altogether different quarter. A Catholic writer, in Poland, under the pseudonym Lucius Verus, published *Equus Effrenis Fallax ad Salutem, Psal. 32. In Stabulo Epicuri Enutritus, Pluralitati Uxorum adhinniens, Samuel Fridericus Willenberg, Doctor Juris, atq; simul Professor, In Auditorio Athenaei Gedanensis. Polygamiae Simultaneae Propugnator Ex merito castigatus & infrenatus, a Lucio Vero Theologo Romano-Catholico. Anno Domini M.DCC.XV. Cum Superiorum Permissu*—"The Unbridled Horse, Deceiving in Salvation, Psalms 32:9, Bred in the Sty of Epicurus, Neighing for Plurality of Wives, Samuel Friedrich Willenberg, Doctor of Laws and also Professor, in the Auditorium of the Danzig Athenaeum, Champion of Simultaneous Polygamy Deservedly Chastised and Bridled, by Lucius Verus, Roman Catholic Theologian. 1715. With the Permission of His Superiors." The title page tells the tone of the whole, which is an attack in detail on the original *Schediasma* of Willenberg's theses, in immoderate terms, urging that this beast of a sensual slave ("furis veneris bellua," as he half spells Willenberg's name into an anagram) should be punished by public whipping.[178]

That penalty was too mild, in some opinions. Danzig was then, as since, at times, within the sphere of Polish influence; and so in April 1715 the Supreme Court of the Polish realms, then situated at Petricov (or Peterkau, halfway between Minsk and Kiev) ordered that Willenberg's books be burned in the marketplace in sulphur flames to the sound of trumpets blown, and that not only Willenberg should be put to death by the garrote and burning at the stake but that the same death penalty should be imposed on the (nominal) respondent Torner, and equally on the two opponents Reyger and Pegelau, apparently for allegedly taking part in the discussion even though in opposition. The court further directed the city authorities of Danzig to confiscate and burn all copies of those books, and to guarantee no more would be printed, under penalty of a municipal fine of 100,000 Hungarian gulden.

On April 28, 1715 the Catholic Archbishop of Gniessen, Stanislaus Szembek, then metropolitan primate of Poland and Lithuania, laid a church anathema on these books, and called on all to surrender their copies, not to hide any, to preserve any or to sell any. The bishops were directed to publish this proclamation. Accordingly the Bishop of Posen posted the decree on every church door, and these placards remained hanging for months.[179]

The extremism of the Petricov decree led to some protests in print. One pamphlet asked a rather plaintive question: *Frantz Dietrich Freudenhöfers Gründliche Erörterung Der Frage: Ob es einem Scribentem, wenn seines Gegenparts Streit-und Schutz-Schrifft eine auswärtige Obrigkeit durch den Hencker verbrennen lassen, zu einer Ehre und Rechtfertigung seiner Sache, seinem Gegner aber zu einer Unehre und Zernichtung seiner Sache gereichen könne?*—"Frantz Dietrich Freudenhöfer's Fundamental Inquiry into the Question: Whether It May Be Considered an Honor and Justification to a Writer When His Adversary's Debate-and-Defense-Dissertation is Burned by the Hangman of a Foreign Government, but to His Adversary a Dishonor and Disparagement?" Freudenhöfer answers academically and legalistically: a man may derive honor or dishonor from his own conduct under the law of nature; he may also derive civil honor or dishonor, because he lives in a civil society, in which, however, his right of self-defense should protect him in a published debate; but on no account can a foreign state cast dishonor on a man who is not its citizen. Freudenhöfer is not identified in his pamphlet, but tradition says that he really was Christian Thomasius.[180]

The other protest was signed Constantinus Wiernowsky, which catalogues also say was a pseudonym; when it came out, some thought he was really Samuel Willenberg, or at least inspired by him. It bore the title *Consideratio Inculpata Decreti Tribunalis Petricoviensis in Polonia quo Ob Defensam In Gymnasio Gedanensi Thesin: Polygamiam Simultaneam In Lege Divina Non Esse*

Prohibitam, Auctor ejus cum Respondente & Opponentibus ad infamiam, laqueum & rogum condemnati, illiusque scripta hanc in rem edita per Carnificem Petricoviae combusta Edita a Constantino Wiernovvsky. Varsaviae MDCCXV.—"Innocent Consideration of the Decree of the Court of Petricov in Poland, by which, Because of His Defense in the Danzig Gymnasium of the Thesis that Polygamy Is Not Prohibited in Divine Law, the Author together with the Respondent and the Opponents Were Condemned to Infamy, the Noose and the Fire, and His Books Published on this Topic Burned by the Petricov Executioner, Edited by Constantinus Wiernowsky, Warsaw, 1715." Wiernowsky denies that the Petricov court had any jurisdiction over Danzig. He denounces its proceedings, the accused not heard, not even summoned to a hearing, condemned on mere accusation, sentenced with a severity out of line with the alleged offense, condemning the opponents—in effect, Weickhmann—with the advocates. He goes over to the counter-attack, citing Catholic authorities for polygamy, Cajetan, Gregory III, Durandus, Alphonsus—and Bellarmine—showing that he is deriving from the Leyser literature and not from original sources. Writing as a Catholic to Catholics, he suggests that the same papal power which can give dispensations on degrees of kinship otherwise barring a marriage could similarly serve to give dispensations for plural marriage. He ends by quoting another writer, Wilhelm Ignatius Schütz, "non igne et ferro, sed moribus atque doctrina," —not by fire and the sword, but by conduct and doctrine.[181]

All this while Weickhmann has continued to labor mightily in his study. By October 1715 he came out with *Apologiae, qua Justitiam Causae Suae, in Controversia de Polygamia Simultanea, Adversus Scriptum Mordacissimo Sali Involutum, quod Nomine Viri Consultissimi et Excellentissimi, Dn. Sam. Frider. Willenbergii, J. D. Doctoris, Ejusdemque et Historiarum P. P. et Athenaei Gedanensis Inspectoris; et Titulo: Iterata Praesidia Juris Divini, Sese Effert et Luxuriatur, Modeste, Sed Solide Protegit ac Tuetur, Pars Prior Ipsius Doctrinae Veritatem et Pondus Sistens. Appendix Inclutorum Civitatis Gedanensis Ordinum Declarationem Innocentiae Autoris Injuste Laesae, Juxta et Responsum*

Juridicum Regiomontanum Exhibet. Accessit Index Tripartitus. Lipsiae, Sumtibus Haeredum Lanckisianorum, Anno MDCCXV. —"First Part of Joachim Weickhmann's Apologia, by which—Citing the Truth and Weight of the Doctrine Itself—He Modestly but Solidly Maintains and Defends the Justice of His Cause in the Controversy on Simultaneous Polygamy, against a Book Rolling with Biting Wit, which in the name of a Most Worthy Gentleman Most Learned in the Law, Mr. Samuel Friedrich Willenberg, Doctor of Civil and Canon Law, Professor of the Same and of History and Inspector of the Danzig Athenaeum, entitled 'Reiterated Bastions of Divine Law' Puffs Itself Up and Runs Riot. The Appendix Exhibits the Declaration by the Celebrated Authorities of the City of Danzig on the Innocence of the Author, Unjustly Maligned, Together with the Response of the Königsberg Jurists. A Three Part Index Follows. Leipzig, published by the Firm of the Heirs of Lanckisius. 1715."[182] It is a 345 page mass of debater's points, carefully organized and outlined, digested into syllogisms (of which he is fond), but in substance mere repetition. The only new matter is the 1713 letter of support from the Law Faculty of Königsberg.

With the next surrebuttal the debate takes a slightly different turn. Just after Easter 1716 there appeared a short 28 page pamphlet *Unpartheysche Gedancken über den bisherigen Wort-Streit Herrn D. Weickmanns, mit Herrn D. Willenberg, in der Materie von der Polygamie. Wobey zugleich der gantze Streit von Anfang biss gegenwärtige Zeit aufrichtig erzehlet, und zugleich gründlich erwiesen wird, dass Herr D. Willenberg klüglich handele, wann er seinem Gegner nicht mehr antwortet. Entworffen von J. A. E., Franckfurt Anno 1716.*—"Impartial Thoughts on the Recent Debate of Herr Dr. Weickhmann with Herr Dr. Willenberg on the Matter of Polygamy, Wherein the Entire Dispute from the Beginning to the Present Time is Candidly Narrated and By the Same Token It Is Soundly Established that Herr Dr. Willenberg Would Do Wisely Not to Answer His Opponent Any More. Outlined by J. A. E. Frankfurt, 1716."[183]

In a sequel "J. A. E." later explicitly denied that he was Willenberg or acting for Willenberg, but his impartiality extends mainly to using "Themistius" for Willenberg and "Gratian" for Weickhmann. He reviews the sequence of events from the start up to the Polish decrees and Lucius Verus' "stink bomb," briefly castigates Weickhmann's tactics and concludes that further exchanges would be futile.

While "J. A. E." was seeing his pamphlet through the press, in February 1716 another flank attack struck at Willenberg's position, *Summam Sanae Doctrinae de Polygamia, auspiciis Serenissimi Principis atque Domini, Domini Friderici Augusti Ducis Sax. et Elect. Saxon. Heredis, etc. Praeside Gottlieb Wernsdorfio SS. Theol. Doct. et Prof. Publ. Aedis Primar. Praeposito, et Senat. Eccles. Assessore, In Academia Vittembergensi Die Feb. 1716, a recentiorum maxime corruptelis et cavillationibus, Vindicatam dabit Jo. Christophorus Greibziger, Servesta-Anhaltinus. Ex Officina Viduae Gerdesianae*—"Summation of Sound Doctrine on Polygamy. Under the Auspices of the Most Serene Prince and Lord, His Grace Frederick, Duke of Saxony and Heir to the Elector of Saxony, etc. Praeses, Gottlieb Wernsdorff, Doctor of Theology and Supervisory Professor Primarius in the Public School, and Assessor of the Ecclesiastical Senate. At Wittenberg University, February 1716, to Be Vindicated from Recent Extreme Corruptions and Mockeries, by Johan Christopher Greibziger of Zerbst, Anhalt. At the Widow Gerdes', Wittenberg"—the 76 pages adding nothing of moment to the current debate, but of value to us because Wernsdorff printed the text of Archbishop Szembek's condemnation, and of the 1679 Stockholm court order against Leyser.[184]

In 1717 Weickhmann once more rolled out his most ponderous artillery, for the first time in the German language: *Apologie, Anderer Theil, oder Abgenöthigte Rettung der göttlichen Warheit: dass Gott in seinem Wort die vielweibige Ehe verbothen; Als auch: seiner beleidigten Unschuld, wider Den Wol-Edlen und Rechts-hochgelahrten Herrn Samuel Friedrich Willenbergen, J. U. D. und P. P. auch Inspectorem des Gymnasii zu Dantzig, in Deutscher Sprache verfertiget, Auf Veranlassung einer Deutschen von J. A. E. entworffenen Schrifft: Unpartheysche Gedancken über den bisherigen Wort-Streit u. Welche, als auch, was von denen Iteratis Praesidiis zu beantworten noch übrig ist, hier völlig abgefertiget wird; Nebst einem Anhange unterschiedener Schrifften, denen eine deutsche Ubersetzung der Vindiciarum des Autoris beygefüget ist. Leipzig, in Verlegung Friedrich Lanckischens seel. Erben, Im Jahr 1717.*—"Apology, Second part, or the necessary Vindication of the Divine Truth: that God in His Word Forbade Polygamous Marriage; and also his insulted innocence, against the Most Excellent and Most Learned in the Law Mr. Samuel Friedrich Willenberg, Doctor of Canon and Civil Law and Professor, also Inspector of the Danzig Gymnasium, Composed in the German Language, on the Occasion of a German Publication Outlined by J. A. E.: Impartial Thoughts on the Recent Debate, Which, as well as what still remains to answer on the Reiterated Bastions, is here fully dispatched; together with a supplement of various Writings, among which a German translation of the Vindiciae of the Author is Appended. Leipzig, Published by the Heirs of the Late Friedrich Lanckisius. In 1717."[185]

With increasing bitterness and sharpness Weickhmann gives his account of the sequence of events; treads again all over the ground he covered in his *Justitia Causae;* cross-criticizes "J. A. E."; tries to minimize the evidence on Luther. As his title page shows, he reprinted the supporting statements of the university faculties; the Danzig town council Declaration; the Torner testimony; his own *Vindiciae* done into German by a friend; and a German version of the original Schediasma, 594 quarto pages in all.

Consequently Willenberg or his alter ego broke his resolution, again appearing under the initials J. A. E. with a *Continuation der Unpartheyischen Gedancken Uber den fortgesetzten Wort-Streit Hernn D. Weickmanns, Mit Herrn D. Willenberg, in der Materie von der Polygamie. Womit die in dem ersten und letzten Theil der teutschen Apologie Herrn D. Weickmanns vorkommende böse Folgen, vorsetzliche Verstümmelungen, nichtiges Einwenden und ungegründete Auflagen erwogen, und dessen Beantwortung meiner unpartheyischen Gedancken in dritten Theil in zulänglichen Anmerckungen untersuchet werden. Entworffen von J. A. E. Franckfurt Anno 1717.*—"Continuation of the

Impartial Thoughts on the Previously Set Forth Debate of Herr Dr. Weickhmann and Herr Dr. Willenberg in the Matter of Polygamy, whereby the Successive Evil Conclusions, Deliberate Mutilations, Vain Objections and Unfounded Revisions in the First and Last Part of the German Language Apology of Herr Dr. Weickhmann are Considered, and His Answering to My Impartial Thoughts in His Third Part Examined with Sufficient Comment. Outlined by J. A. E. Frankfurt, 1717;" again short, 52 pages.[186]

"J. A. E." is somewhat equivocal on the responsibility for this *Continuation,* or his preceding pamphlet: he says that Gratian's opinion naming Themistius as the author is "ungegründet," without foundation. There is more than one hint that Willenberg may have had reason to fear some action by the "secular arm" instigated against him by Weickhmann or others. But it is in the nature of these controversies to start in a trivial fashion, flare up for a while, and soon splutter out. Weickhmann lived to 1736, Willenberg to 1748, but they rumble no more at each other. Among other writers echoes go on for years.[187]

3. *Once Again: Why?*

Nowhere in the books by, for and against Willenberg or Thomasius is there given any overt or objective reason for their attention to the issue of plural marriage. Neither Thomasius nor Willenberg had a *case* to defend or justify, no Philip of Hesse, no Charles Louis. Neither was concerned with converting the heathen of Asia or Africa.

In his 1712 *Schediasma* Willenberg suggested several type situations as deserving dispensations: conversion of a Moslem from Islam to Christianity; a captive (the Gleichen case); a wife barren, invalid or frigid (always the woman being held to blame!); or a wife inadequate to her husband's libido (the Philip of Hesse case). These instances rather summarize the precedents he could cite, than explain the reasons for his interest in the argument. In later writings he mentions the practical problem of a ruling family in danger of dying out for lack of a male heir, a problem not unusual among the German principalities of that time (Willenberg, *Praesidia,* page 38)

The fact is that these discussions on plural marriage did take place. To understand the evolution of this, or any particular idea, requires the examination of an interaction: the stimuli of complex objective conditions upon the thinking process which operates in an historically conditioned manner. In the Thomasius and Willenberg question, several possibilities may be suggested, all of which may have been operating.

First, for the objective factor may be postulated the persistence, or the reappearance, of biologically inherited tendencies, transmitted like the rest of our biological inheritance, from the primal horde in the days when the species "Homo" separated off from his next of kin. This hypothesis could be helpful, if there were any evidence to support it other than the writings themselves. Without other, external, evidence, this hypothesis remains a guess.

Second, it might appear that, in the ideological climate then existing, beginning to challenge the divine right of state power and church power, with continuing difficulties in regard to divorce, some princely rulers and some private citizens played with the plan of legalizing plural marriage, either generally, or within limits for themselves, while letting the parsons continue the prohibition for the general public. Willenberg himself does not say so, but Schelwig alleges that in private conversation Willenberg asked "Is it not better for kings and princes whose love for their wives has cooled to add a second spouse instead of indulging in vagrant lusts?" (*De Polygamia,* page 11). Thomasius and Willenberg, and indeed all who wrote or privately whispered in favor of plural marriage in the years 1500-1750, were living in the era when reigning princes aspired to rule as absolute despots whenever they could manage it; when all reigning princes were bound to marriages dictated for political and military alliance, ignoring their personal feelings; while mere commoners were achieving for themselves freedom of choice in wedlock as they were achieving a measure of freedom of choice in economic contract. In some countries a ruler might permit himself the licenses of a Louis XIV or a Charles II, but where he had to trim his sails to suit a more straitlaced population, he might well seek the solutions which were discussed by these liberal jurists. We may infer as much from the tolerance extended to both Thomasius and Willenberg, but again, more positive evidence would be desirable.

Third, the occurrence of this discussion may be explained as an episode in the development of the intellectual climate to which we have referred, as an eddy in the wind currents of a changing weather.

In his final Section XXXV of his 1713 dissertation *De Concubinatu,* with Kiechel, Thomasius poses the question: Why is such a discussion needed? Is it not enough for the law student to be taught that concubinage is illegal and prohibited? It matters a great deal, he answers. A law student must learn to investigate the real reasons for laws, to distinguish the true rationale from spurious reasons, or from less valid reasons; otherwise he is no jurist, but a mere quibbler or worse. That, for Thomasius, is fundamental. As for the specific matter in hand, he declares, it is about time that the highly confused doctrine of matrimony be freed from confusions. If concubinage is to be tolerated, or reintroduced, or banned, in the Christian Commonwealth, insufficient reasons must be rejected, genuine and clear reasons given. To be guided by sound thinking, as a Christian, he says, it is important that dissenting opinions, or the *res judicatae* (decided issues) of other peoples, whether applying to concubinage or to other differing customs, should not be judged by pedantry, by feigned piety, by dogmas of covert papistry, or by magistrates usurping powers not rightfully theirs. (There are other uses of this discussion, he finishes, on which he remains silent).

What seems odd, under these circumstances, is that the "enlightened" jurists come forward as partisans of the obsolete practices of concubinage and polygamy, which belong to olden barbarous times, while the Bible-bound priests and pastors were the unshakable defenders of monogamy. Should not the roles have been reversed, with the pastors defending the Bible practice while the "enlightened" jurists should have demanded monogamy based on freedom of choice and full consideration to the feelings of the marrying pair? But life moves in zigzags and contradictions. When the jurists asked that law, morality, rules of conduct should be based on the facts of social practice, without prejudgment or parochial preconceptions, the Bible became just another piece of evidence among all the rest. Their courtroom called for the truth, the whole truth and nothing but the truth. The Bible testimony happened to fall on the side of plural marriage. For the pastors, tradition was all; local custom was all. Formal monogamy was traditional, no matter how or when it came about, no matter how hollow or hypocritical; any other practices were necessarily deviations from their norm. For the pastors their whole existence was bound to tradition, and Bible facts had to be adapted to tradition, not the other way round.

The jurists, on the other hand, saw that what was law or custom in the Lutheran states of Germany was not the norm for all peoples. Instead of brushing the alien heathen aside, these jurists subsumed their practices under the abstractions of the "law of nature" and the "law of nations," to break out of the bonds of Lutheran orthodoxy, out of church dogmatisms in law, out of the rigidity of outlook that refused to see beyond the village churchyard. Since the Bible, read as documentary evidence, supported their case, they read it so, as literally as the provisions of a deed for real estate or the terms of a legacy in a will. Nowhere do they say that by this stand they are philosophically undermining all dogmatisms, that while their focus was on the limited issue of polygamy, their ultimate outlook was far broader, that this discussion for them was a broom to shake the cobwebs out their windows and doorways. Perhaps they did not even see that; but forgotten as they are, they helped clear the way for the world of Voltaire, and of Diderot, for the eighteenth century enlightenment and beyond.

APPENDIX V

Latter Day Polygamophiles

During the nineteenth and twentieth centuries, some eccentrics here and there in Europe and America have written in favor of polygamy, most of them not worth the mention. One of these quacks will be enough: this was Philip L. Anthony, who in 1866 submitted a memorial to the State legislature of Arkansas, *The Marriage Relation, Polygamy and Concubinage, The Law of God,* printed at Little Rock, 80 pages. He proposed, basing himself on his Holy Bible, that there be two degrees of marriage, introducing concubinage by contract for life or for a term of years, to a maximum of seven wives and concubines; any union between persons of "differing race" strictly forbidden; and public morals to be supervised by an appointed censor who would be paid $800 a year. Anthony also drafted a constitution for a Society of the Polygami to propagandize his proposal throughout the country.

Symptomatic of the times, but of no lasting significance were the scattered experiments in "free love" and other marital variations during the nineteenth century, some by individuals, some in utopian communities and some in new sects of religious enthusiasts (see: William Hepworth Dixon, *Spiritual Wives,* two volumes, London, 1868, for some).

Most conspicuous was the spasm of plural marriage on a large scale among the Latter Day Saints (Mormons) in Utah, with its concomitant mass of literature for, against, and making fun of, their peculiar institution.

This sect, like many other religious groups, holds to a book of revelation, which (it believes) is divinely inspired. This revered Book of Mormon, as originally printed by Joseph Smith,

Jr., the founding prophet of the sect, and as it has been often reprinted, explicitly condemns "the wicked practices, such as like David of old desiring many wives and concubines, and also Solomon his son" (Book of Jacob 1:15). The following chapter, Jacob 2:24, 27 absolutely forbade polygamy,

> Behold, David and Solomon truly had many wives, which thing was abominable before me, saith the Lord . . . Wherefore, my brethren, hear me and hearken to the word of the Lord: For there shall not any man among you have save it be one wife, and concubines shall he have none.

This commandment is reiterated verbatim in Jacob 3:5, and its spirit is conveyed further in Mosiah 11:1-4, 14 and Ether 10:5, these being segments within the Book of Mormon. In this respect the adherents of this sect are consistent with the practice of adherents of other religious sects, in that precepts have been honoured rather in the breach than in the observance.

To smooth over the contradiction, when the founders of the sect had adopted their singular attachment to plurality of wives, a supplementary revelation, the *Doctrine and Covenants,* in July 1843 pronounced a revised verdict on David, and lumped monogamous Isaac together with many-wived Abraham and Jacob to justify polygamy. For some fifty or sixty years this peculiar institution was interlaced with all Mormon social, economic and doctrinal activity; although it is said that at most only about 10% of the men were polygamous, most of these "only" bigamous, only a few top leaders having more wives; and that this was not a polygamy of harems and eunuchs, but fostered as much by conditions of famine and the harshness of the exodus into the desert, as by religious delusions. About 1890 this revelation of 1843 "was withdrawn" (so it was expressed to me by a Latter Day Saint spokesman at their religious center in Salt Lake City) and the practice generally abandoned by 1900, mainly because it interfered with the merging of Utah's economy with the national corporate structure of business, and of Utah politics with the national political party machinery.

Splinter offshoots, perhaps numbering in the thousands of persons, have continued to maintain religiously-sanctified polygamous households and families in isolated communities in Utah and Arizona to this day (1973) although officially repudiated by the main body of Latter Day Saints and in spite of sporadic efforts by law enforcement authorities to interfere. These are genuine United States of America polygamists, not visitors from Asia or Africa.[188]

Other instances of genuine Americans practicing polygamy are recorded among Indian groups, although the exact nature of their various family organizations requires a more precise description than that term affords.[189]

A thorough study of present day practices around the world is beyond the scope of this work, but our perspective may be improved by examining some of the data that have come into my hands during the years since I first became interested in "Milton on polygamy." Mostly these are items which have appeared in newspapers, random reports, constituting empirical evidence rather than verified scientific observation, but these items appear to be authentic. They stand as testimony that such matters of human behavior are highly complex, and that among women and men of different cultures, these phenomena generate highly diversified opinions.

It must be noted that the term "polygamy," today as in the past, does not denote one particular form of marriage, but rather includes a variety of different forms in different societies. It must be noted that within those societies where plural marriage is extant, it is not considered "polygamy." It is considered "marriage."[190]

New York Times, May 8, 1946.) At a session on the status of women, in the United Nations Commission on Human Rights, Angela Lurdak of Lebanon proposed a ban on polygamy. Mme Marie Helene Lefaucheux of France spoke in opposition, because of the huge regions then under French colonial rule where polygamy was customary.

New York Times, September 9, 1949.) "Tel Aviv, Israel, Sept. 8. Premier David Ben-Gurion indicated to the Knesset

(Assembly) today that the Government shortly would introduce a bill outlawing polygamy in Israel. When someone said that the move would be against Islam, Mr. Ben-Gurion declared: 'Islam permits Moslems to take four wives but does not require them to do it.' "[191]

New York Times, February 9, 1950.) "Istanbul, Turkey, Feb. 1. Polygamy, forbidden by law since 1926, has not yet been entirely eliminated from the social structure of the Turkish republic. This was indicated in a law enacted today by the National Assembly that authorizes the registration of children born out of wedlock.

"The law against plural marriage superseded the Islamic code under which one man may have four wives. In the more backward parts of the country, where polygamy is not frowned upon socially, a simple way was found for continuing the practice while respecting the letter of the law.

"A married man who wants to add another woman to his household first obtains the consent of his legal wife who can veto the arrangement by bringing action for adultery. A religious ceremony may formalize the second marriage in the eyes of the community, but does not constitute bigamy in the eyes of the law, since only a civil ceremony is legally binding.

"There are also peasants who leave their wives to run the farm during the winter and go to the towns or cities to find work. Some of them establish a second household in the city."

United Press, May 5, 1950, in the *New York Journal American* of that date, reporting an interview with Begum Liaquat Ali Khan, wife of Pakistan's prime minister: "The Begum said polygamy gradually is dying out in Pakistan . . . The Begum explained that plural marriages are arranged because of economic necessity or a desire for heirs. But, she added with a laugh: 'Some, of course, will have more than one just for the fun of it. You get that type everywhere.' "

New York Times, February 10, 1950. "Lake Success, Feb. 9. A special mission reported back to the United Nations today that it had looked into the marital affairs of West Africa's famed Fon of the Bikom tribe and his 110 wives and had come up with the conclusion that maybe polygamy, at least in Africa, wasn't such a bad idea, after all. The four-nation group said that all concerned seemed to be very happy with things as they are, and perhaps the world organization had better forget all about the Cameroon chieftain and his wives. The investigation group, set up last year by the Trusteeship Council to visit West Africa and survey the political and social progress in Togoland and the Cameroons, made a special point of checking up on the now-famous case of the much wedded Fon . . .

"It is common for the chiefs of the Tikar communities to take as wives all the first-born daughters and all female twins of certain families within their tribes, or to give the girls in marriage to their sons or personal attendants, according to the report . . . The Fon of Bikom, it was said, had 110 wives within his compound, forty-four of whom had been inherited from a previous Fon. The visiting mission said that the polygamous custom stemmed from economic necessity and that the wives were among the strongest champions of the idea . . .

"Plural marriage, the mission said, is partly a means of sustenance to the women, and is a 'type of social security' that will have to remain until Western civilization through education convinces the Africans that other ways are better and preferable."[192]

A somewhat contrary orientation was reported in the *New York Times,* August 3, 1969. "Algiers. July 29. Polygamy is among the African traditions whose merit has been fervently reaffirmed at the 30-nation Pan-African Cultural Congress being held here. 'The tendency on the part of some Christians to equate polygamy with a total lack of masculine respect for the female needs to be challenged', the chief Ghanaian delegate, Dr. Seth Cudjoe, said in a speech to the other representatives this week. A burly, once-married widower, Dr. Cudjoe told African intellectuals gathered at the Palais des Nations outside Algiers that 'clearly the hypocrisy of secretive extra-marital relations on which monogamy survives precariously in Europe cannot be maintained in African societies, which from the very beginning have never had any real quarrel with plural relationships.'

"Instead, like most Africans at the 12-day meeting sponsored by the Organization of African Unity, he urged a prideful emphasis on indigenous African ways of life—in this case, the taking of more than one wife . . . Polygamy is not outlawed in Ghana or most other African nations.

"Unlike most of the speakers at the symposium, Dr. Cudjoe did not rest his argument on political grounds. Instead, he contended that the spread of monogamy in colonized African societies had brought a painful increase in illegitimate children sired by men 'whose current marital status legally restricts them to one woman only, irrespective of whether or not she is capable of bearing children.' Polygamy, he contended, offers 'strong protection for both the unmarried and married woman against philanderers.'

"Interviewed at the Palais after his address, he said that missionaries' influences, admiration of European ways, and the pride of modernized woman had contributed to the curtailment of polygamy in his own and other African countries. Even the institution of polygamy, he said, has suffered from a general loosening of traditional family ties and has 'degenerated into promiscuity of a singularly irresponsible kind.'

"Dr. Cudjoe, who was trained at Edinburgh University, heads a Ghanaian Government research unit analyzing family customs in his country. In the interview he said that an advantage of a largely polygamous society was that it did not exclude monogamy for those who preferred it. The best social policy, he concluded, is to foster enduring polygamous marriages by insuring that polygamy remains acceptable in the participants' eyes."[193]

New York Times, April 11, 1966.) "Ivory Coast Acting to Eliminate Polygamy and Bride Purchase. Abidjan, Ivory Coast, April 10 . . . The new civil code, approved by the National Assembly in 1964, is gradually being implemented . . . The most significant result will be the suppression of polygamy and the matriarchal system as the code takes effect. Under polygamy the woman is more of an economic factor—an extra pair of hands—than a person. She also is often a status symbol her husband cannot afford. Under the new code the wife can marry whom she likes and she is encouraged to seek education and to play a constructive role in Ivorian society."

New York Times, October 9, 1969. "Dar Es Salaam, Tanzania, Oct. 4 . . . The most burning issue in Tanzania at the moment is marriage. Several weeks ago, the Government issued a white paper on the subject, setting out a series of steps designed to give more rights to women so that Tanzania does not deviate from the path of progress. In a country that believes in the equality of all human beings, the paper states, it is intolerable that a wife does not have the same rights and remedies in matrimonial matters as the husband.

"The new laws are also aimed at eliminating the conflicts in the civil and religious laws governing marriage. At present, Asian Moslems, African Moslems, Hindus, Christians and nonbelievers are covered by different codes. Among the Government's recommendations were the following:

"More orderly divorce procedures, including an end to the practice among some Moslem men of dissolving their marriage by simply repeating aloud three times the phrase 'I divorce thee'.

"Legal polygamy for Christians as well as Moslems—but with the proviso that the consent of the first wife must be obtained.

"Minimum marriage ages . . . A restriction in the bride price . . . and provision for an installment plan . . .

"When the Attorney General Vark Bomani unsuspectingly appeared at a meeting of the Tanzania Women's Association in Mwanza on Sept. 5, he was beset with demands for modifications —including the insistence by two suffragettes that the law give women the right to more than one husband. The Government immediately decided to postpone parliamentary debate until December. Women are rather emotional, Mr. Bomani said this week.

"Polygamy is the most controversial idea. It is defended by Moslems, whose religious law permits a man up to four wives, and attacked by Christians. The Lutheran Bishop of Moshi in northern Tanzania, Stefano Nkuu, insisted that the new law would inevitably lead to bribes or threats against first wives as husbands sought to gain their consent. One thing is already clear—there are very few men in Tanzania who would be willing to accept what people here are calling reverse polygamy. In a letter to the editor, A. R. Mtui of Dar es Salaam wrote: 'No sane man would enter a contract to share a woman with another man when he could have a whole wife or two to himself.' "

Detroit Free Press, July 21, 1969, from the *London Express.*) "Hong Kong. Britain's colonial government in Hong Kong has moved to outlaw the ancient Chinese custom of taking a second, third and fourth wife.

"Rich Chinese businessmen who can afford a modern-day harem, are, predictably, gloomy. 'Ah, it is a case of you Europeans not understanding our old Chinese customs,' one of them said. He is a man in his 70's, educated in England, who took a second wife more than 20 years ago. 'Often when a wife has no son, the mother-in-law will beg the husband to take a concubine so the family line can be continued. A concubine has the same legal rights as a first wife. That's a lot better than taking a mistress, which is the European way. With mistresses you get bastards. With concubines the children are legitimate,' he said.

"The least vociferous women in the campaign to ban concubines have been the No. 1 wives. Apparently they would rather know about their husband's choice of extra partners than not."

New York Times, December 5, 1969, in an article by C. L. Sulzberger, on sociological changes discussed in Parliament in Denmark: "An even more audacious bill was proposed by the Socialist People's party which called for legal 'marriage' between persons of the same sex, between brother and sister or between one man and an unlimited number of women. This proposal was turned down. Nevertheless, what are called 'megafamilies'—groups of unrelated adults of both sexes and their children—are now an accepted phenomenon on the contemporary scene."

New York Times, June 22, 1970.) Jakarta, Indonesia, reporting the death June 21 of former President Sukarno. "He died early this morning, with five wives and eight children at his bedside."

New York Times, August 24, 1970, despatch by Alden Whitman, discussing customs in southern Mindanao, in the Philippines: "In many tribes, a man of wealth—measured by his landholdings and the crops he can sell or barter—has more than one wife. This, of course, adds to his status,—as well as to the size of his work force. A chief, as in Ma Falen's case, is likely to have as many wives as he can afford, and set each one up in a house of her own. To display impartiality, a husband usually stays a week with each wife in turn.".

New York Times, July 10, 1964.) "Bangkok, Thailand, July 9. Premier Thanom Kittikachorn has disclosed that his predecessor, Field Marshal Sarit Thanarat, left an estate valued, for the moment, at $140 million . . . Preliminary findings of a special investigating committee indicated that most of the former Premier's holdings were acquired since 1952 when, as a rising young army officer, he became chairman of the State Lottery Board . . .

"Field Marshal Sarit, a vigorous, hard-drinking man who made no effort to conceal his private life, ruled Thailand with a decisive hand from 1957 when he seized power in a bloodless coup d'etat until he died last Dec. 8 at the age of 55 . . .

"During his rule Thailand was the firmest ally the United States had in Southeast Asia, and he worked closely with Washington in efforts to contain Communist expansion. The United States gave millions of dollars in economic and military aid to Thailand.

"The existence of Marshal Sarit's estate was first mentioned widely in February when his first wife and two sons initiated court action to prevent Lady Vichitra Thanarat, his second wife, from administering the estate . . .

"Mr. Phra [chairman of the investigating committee] also said that 'it was certain' that part equivalent to $600,000 from Funds for Secret Work was given to women who were called 'minor wives' of Marshal Sarit. Court evidence has disclosed that there were more than 20 of these young women. Many of them said they had a 'wedding' ceremony with the marshal. Almost all of them had been given houses, cars, and money."

New York Times, October 27, 1969). "Vientiane, Laos. Oct. 20. A short, wiry Meo mountaineer who speaks French like a Foreign Legion drill sergeant and English like a foreign born G. I. is the toughest commander on the anti-Communist side in the Laotian civil war. Maj. Gen. Vang Pao, or V.P. as he is referred to by his American admirers here, is the recipient of large-scale direct American assistance to keep his followers, the Meo hill people, in the fight against the Communist-led Pathet Lao forces and their North Vietnamese allies, who have been trying to take over Laos for years. Although American officials are not permitted to discuss the subject, their occasional lapses leave little doubt that the general's backing comes from the United States Central Intelligence Agency. . . .

"He has further solidified his position by choosing his wives, estimated at five or six, from influential Meo clans. Polygamy is widespread among the Meo and other mountain tribes."

NOTES

1. *The Works of John Milton,* Columbia University Press, New York, 1931-1938, is the most complete edition, herein cited as Columbia edition. Milton's major discussion of polygamy is in his *De Doctrina Christiana,* ("Treatise on Christian Doctrine") Book I, Chapter X, in volume XV (1933) of the Columbia edition. Regrettably the Hebrew words there, as elsewhere in that edition, are often misprinted. He also has a passing reference in Book II, Chapter II.

   In I Corinthians vii, 15, in reference to a mate who leaves a believing (Christian) spouse, Paul's words are "But if the unbelieving depart, let him depart. A brother or a sister is not under bondage in such cases: but God hath called us to peace" (King James version). Milton's interpretation (Columbia edition, III, 491) is an inference from this verse. The reference, but not the inference, is repeated in his *Christian Doctrine,* Book I, Chapter X, in Columbia edition, volume XV, 174.

   Alan Rudrum, "Polygamy in *Paradise Lost,*" *Essays in Criticism,* XX, January, 1970, pages 18-23, demonstrated the correct interpretation of *Paradise Lost,* IV, 761-762, by showing that it echoes the same passage from Paul to the Hebrews, xiii, 4, which Milton cites to justify polygamy as lawful in his *Treatise on Christian Doctrine.*

2. The original manuscript of the *Commonplace Book* is in the British Museum, where I had the pleasure of studying it in 1961. Milton titled his notes *Index Ethicus, Index Oeconomicus, Index Politicus.* The present quotations are taken from the 1876 autotype facsimile issued by Alfred J. Horwood, who gave it the title *A Common-Place Book of John Milton.* The text is most easily available in the Columbia edition, volume XVIII, but somewhat edited from the original. Milton kept other notebooks, including an *Index Theologicus,* which are not known to have survived.

   James Holly Hanford, "The Chronology of Milton's Private Studies," *Publications of the Modern Language Association,* XXXVI, (1921), pages 251-314, most ably laid down the basic considerations for dating each entry within a limited span of years, but some of his dates may need reconsideration.

3. Justin Martyr's *Dialogue with Trypho* set forth the views of a second century advocate of Christianity in contrast to the views which he represented as being held by certain tendencies among some of the Jewish people of that time. Milton's references to pages 364 and 371 indicate that he was using a specific edition of Justin's *Works* which appeared in Greek and Latin in 1615 at Paris and was reprinted with the same pagination in 1636 and in other years, *Sancti Iustini Philosophi et Martyris Opera* ("The Works of Saint Justin the Philosopher and Martyr").

   Readers of the Yale University Press edition of the *Complete Prose of John Milton* may wish to delete from its Volume I, page 397, fourth line, its incorrect translation "because of the diverse secret rites" for the Latin "propter varia mysteria" and substitute a correct version such as that given in the present text, or the approximately similar translation in the Columbia edition, XVIII, 149. The reason will appear from the passage on page 364 of the 1615 edition of Justin's *Opera* ("Works"), which reads in the Latin:

   Connubia Jacobi rei per Christum perficiendae figurae

erant. Duas sane sorores eodem tempore ducere Jacobo fas non fuit. . . . Sed enim Lea populus vester est, et synagoga; Rachel, ecclesia nostra.

The marriages of Jacob were a type of what Christ was to carry out. Certainly it was not right for Jacob to marry two sisters at the same time. . . . But then Lea represents your people and the synagogue; Rachel, our church.

Readers of the Yale edition, volume I, page 397, may choose to delete from note 16 the phrase which identifies Justin's straw man Trypho with "the famous Jewish Rabbi Tarphon." Apart from the inconsistency in ideas between Tarphon and Trypho, the identification is chronologically improbable, and is rejected not only by Jewish scholars but by Catholic scholars (see Thomas B. Fall, *Saint Justin Martyr,* New York, 1949) and by Protestant scholars (see L. W. Barnard, *Justin Martyr, His Life and Times,* Cambridge, 1967).

Readers of the Yale edition, Volume I, page 397, may choose to delete from note 17 the second sentence which says, incorrectly, "One of the speakers in the *Dialogue* says (p. 364) that polygamy was forbidden because sons of concubines and sons of the wife were regarded with the same honor." I subjoin the Latin text and a translation:

rursum nunc utrotumque, & liberorum, & qui inter eos sunt servorum filiorum, restituendorum causa advenit Christus: eodem loco habens omnes praecepta sua servantes, quemadmodum & qui Jacobo tum ex liberis, tum ex servis progeniti sunt filii, omnes eodem iure & honore fuere. Iuxta ordine autem, & iuxta praenotionem qualis quisque futurus fuerat, praedictum est.

now again, Christ came for the sake of restoring the sons on both sides, both the freeborn and those among them born of slaves; in the same place propounding his teachings that all are his servants, even as the sons born to Jacob as much from the free (wives) as much as from the slave (concubines) were all of the same right and honor. In like manner, moreover, the order, and in like manner, the foreknowledge what and who was to come to be, was appointed beforehand.

On page 371 of the 1615 edition, Justin says (Latin text) and Milton read:

> Et rursus unum et ipsum Davidis in Uriae coniuge delicti factum, o viri, inquam, ostendit (poentitentia vera opus est, &) non tanquam fornicantes patriarchas plures habuisse uxores: sed oeconomiam quandam et atque dispositionem fuisse, & mysteria ac sacramenta omnia per eos peracta esse, nos existimare debere. Nam si permissum esset, quam quis vellet, atque ut vellet, & quot vellet, habere coniuges: quemadmodum faciunt populares vestri, per terram omnem ubicumque peregre sunt aut quocumque proficiscuntur sub matrimonii nomine mulieres sibi copulantes: longe magis id in Davide hoc permissum fuisset.

To understand this passage it is helpful to refer to the standard dictionary of medieval Latin, the *Glossarium Mediae et Infimae Latinitatis* of Charles Dufresne DuCange (1610-1688), for the key words *oeconomia* and *dispositio,* which may be found under the word *dispensatio*:

> Dispensatio: Dei dispositio et providentia, qua vocare gentes ad verum dei cultum et universum humanum genus per incarnationem, nativitatem, mortem, et resurrectionem Christi salvum praestare decrevit. Hanc dispositionem per excellentiam SS. Patres οἰκονομίαν simpliciter vocant, quidam ex Latinis *Dispensationem.*

> Dispensation: God's disposition and providence by which he decreed to call the nations to the true worship of God and the universal human race to be saved through

the incarnation, nativity, death and resurrection of Christ. This "dispositio" the holy fathers admirably called simply *oeconomia,* or as in the Latin *dispensatio,* management.

Compare *The Works of Samuel Clarke,* London, 1738, volume 4, page 186, section xlvi, "For the Great Oeçonomy, or the Whole Dispensation of God towards Mankind in Christ, consists and terminates in this."

The passage on page 371 of Justin's *Works* therefore reads in English:

> Indeed, gentlemen, this one transgression of David in the instance of Uriah's wife, I say, shows (that there was need of true penitence and) that we ought to understand that the patriarchs took many wives not as if for fornication but to be a certain providence and dispensation, and that certain mysteries and sacraments be acted out. For if it had been permitted that any have as wives whom he wants, as he wants, and as many as he wants: as your countrymen do in every land and wherever they are or wherever they travel abroad, coupling with women under the name of matrimony, much more would this have been permitted in the case of David.

Having considered the foregoing, the careful reader may want to delete the following sentences from note 17, volume I, page 397 of the Yale edition:

> Another speaker says that the offense of David in taking Uriah's wife "shows, not so much that the fornicating patriarchs had several wives, as that the custom had a certain economic aspect and we ought to consider all the mysterious sacraments that were performed among them. For if it were permitted to have many wives, whoever so desired and as he desired and as many as he desired, your people would do the same thing throughout the whole land, wherever they went, taking women under the name

of marriage, for it had long been permitted under David." To this Tryphon then replies.

4. Valentinian's law of bigamy is mentioned by Melanchthon in his paper on the case of Henry VIII, and by Bellarmine in his discussion of polygamy in his *De Controversiis Christianae Fidei Adversus Huius Temporis Haereticos* (On Controversies of the Christian Faith, Against the Heretics of This Age), both discussed below.

   Another who believed Valentinian's law was an historic fact was Milton's friend and boyhood tutor, Thomas Young, through whom Milton became involved in political pamphleteering in 1641-1642, and from whom Milton became alienated in moving leftward in politics. The fact that Thomas Young dragged in an allusion to Valentinian in a 1643 sermon may possibly indicate that he and Milton had been privately arguing over polygamy. Young's allusion follows (taken from: *Hopes Incouragement pointed at in a Sermon Preached In St. Margarets Westminster, before the Honorable House of Commons, Assembled in Parliament: at the last Solemn Fast, February 28, 1643. By Tho. Young. . . . Published by Order of the House of Commons. Printed at London for Ralph Smith, at the Signe of the Bible in Cornhill, neere the Royal Exchange, 1644,* page 32):

   > Eminent governors have stained the glory of their government by enacting Lawes which stand in opposition to God's Law: Valentinian the Great beginning to alienate his affection from his royall Consort (the cause I spare to relate) casting his affection upon Justina, thereupon makes it free by Law for any, that would, to have two wives, and after the promulgation of that Law presently he married her: how inconsistent his Law was with the Law of God, I need not speake.

   Readers of the Yale edition of Milton's prose works may wish to delete from note 26 on page 400 of Volume I the five sentences about the life and character of Valentinian III, which are irrelevant, because the emperor to whom Milton refers was Valentinian I.

It may be convenient at the same time for the careful reader of the Yale edition to mark that in note 1 on page 430 of Volume I the ambiguous reference to Valentinian should be to Valentinian I, so that the misleading reference there to Valentinian III, "(above, p. 375)" may be deleted together with the phrase "who had been denounced as an Arian."

Note 1, page 430, further asserts that Valentinian "was asked for his interpretation of 'identical substance' in the communion." This was not what he was asked. The issue of substance in the communion (more accurately, the real presence) was a nominalist-realist dispute centuries later among the Schoolmen, and still later between Protestant Reformers and the Catholic Church. What Valentinian was asked by certain Athanasian bishops was whether he would deign to take interest in the correction of matters of church dogma. These bishops were identified as Athanasian, in the phrase of the *Historia Miscella, quicumque consubstantialem patrem ac filium praedicabant,* "whoever preached the consubstantiality of the Father and the Son", which was the nub of their controversy with the Arians. Milton used the historically precise Greek slogan-word *homoousia* for the Latin *consubstantia;* rendering it into the English *identical substance* destroys the force of his allusion.

It would have been helpful if Note 1, page 430, of the Yale edition, had made clear that the incidents it cites from pages 351 and 354 of the *Historia Miscella,* by Landulphus Sagax and others, took place at different times and different locations, and that the material taken from page 354, printed in quotation marks in the Yale edition, is only partly quotation, being partly summary.

The reader may also want to turn in the Yale edition to Volume II, page 462, note 1, and there delete the incorrect references and dates of Theodosius I and Valentinian II, and substitute instead the names of Theodosius II and Valentinian

III who were the emperors who did proclaim the Code of Theodosius.

The Columbia edition, XVIII, 150, mistranslates the word *digamia* in Milton's quotation as "a second marriage after the death of the first wife", a meaning which the word *digamia* often has, but not in this context, as the story is told by Socrates Scholasticus.

5. John Owen (1560?-1622) was a facile composer of clever epigrams, forgotten now because he wrote in Latin. He published several volumes between 1606 and 1613, which went through repeated editions later in the century, and were translated into French, into German, into Spanish and at least five times into English. Of one translator, Thomas Pecke, there will be more to tell. Owen had a cavalier Elizabethan or Jacobean attitude to matters like marriage, and did not write seriously on bigamy or polygamy in his verses.

   Milton and some others who defended polygamy drew the inference from the ban on polygamy for bishops that it was permitted to any who were not so largely involved in church management.

   Claude de Saumaise, one of the major European savants of the seventeenth century, had no particular interest in polygamy, but in his *Dissertatio de Foenore Trapezitico* ("Dissertation on Money Usury," preface dated 1640), pages 50-58, he digressed to consider this text in judging inferences from Bible pronouncements. He was inclined to accept the inference that the ban on bishops left the laity free to marry more than once, but only by successive marriages, as in the instance of a widower or a widow, not by cumulative polygamy. This opinion of de Saumaise, or Salmasius, as he was known in Latin, was quoted by other seventeenth century writers, but it rates notice now mainly because Milton, in his most successful Latin prose work, the *Defense of the People of England* (1651) rebutting Salmasius' *Royal Defense* of King Charles I, applied so much of his talent to the effort of destroying Salmasius' reputation for learning, that he saved Salmasius' name from the total oblivion to which by this time it would have been consigned.

6. The twenty-third chapter of Ezekiel is an out-of-the-ordinary citation in favor of polygamy. Almost every other Bible citation for, or against, polygamy, can be found repeatedly in the various authors who wrote in this field, whether they copied from one another, as many did, or whether they simply went to the same Book for their texts. One reason why Milton used it may be that it appears in Beza's *Treatise of Polygamy* (discussed below) in the section against Tertullian; which is also the source for that reference in the notes added by Gerhard von Mastricht to the Latin version of Moyse Amyraut's *Six Considerations on the Law of Nature Which Regulates Marriage* (of which more hereafter) refuting the argument from that text.

7. That Franciscus Junius (1545-1602) doctored his version of Leviticus xviii, 18 to supply a case against polygamy was conceded by Frederick Spanheim, *Dubiorum Evangeliorum Pars Tertia* ("Evangelical Doubts, Part 3") 1639, page 623; and by the Huguenot ministers who edited *Vesperae Groninganae* ("Groningen Vespers"), Amsterdam, 1697, of which more below.

8. *MOSES' CUSHITE WIFE:* Milton's speculation about Numbers xii is entirely his own, as shown by his reservation, *ni fallor,* "unless I am mistaken." As often in the Bible, the story in Numbers xii is obscure. Milton infers that at this late date in his career Moses acquired this additional wife. In the Bible *Cushite* usually means "Ethiopian." Rashi, the foremost Jewish commentator on the Bible, with typically medieval mind, read "Cushite" as an anagram for "beautiful", mystically substituted to avert the Evil Eye, and so identifies her with Zipporah, Moses' temporarily repulsed wife.

   There are several extra-Biblical traditions about other wives of Moses. Milton does not mention the tradition he must have read in Flavius Josephus, *Antiquities of the Jews,* Book II, Chapter X: that Moses in his young manhood as a general in the Egyptian army married as his (first?) wife an Ethiopian princess, Tharbis. Josephus is silent on Numbers xii. Johan Leyser (of whom much more below) took note of Tharbis and Zipporah as Moses' bigamy, but since Tharbis was unscriptural, he held the case inconclusive. There is a different tradition of another wife, Adoniyah, widow of an Ethiopian king, in a marriage antedating and overlapping the Exodus, transmitted in the Rabbinical Midrash *The Chronicles and Demise of Moses Our Teacher May He Rest In Peace,* edited by Gilbertus Gaulmyn and printed at Paris by Toussaint Du Bray, 1628-1629, in Latin as *De Vita et Morte Mosis Libri Tres* with the Hebrew text דברי הימים ופטירתו של מרעה (copy at New York Public Library). This tradition was cited by Johannes Brunsmann, a Norwegian minister writing against polygamy in his *Monogamia Victrix* ("Monogamy Victorious"), 1679, page 138, interpreting "Cushite" as "Edomite" and contending that this marriage was terminated before the marriage with Zipporah.

9. Milton's amanuenses wrote this citation incorrectly in the manuscript of the *Treatise on Christian Doctrine.* Instead of Chapters i and ii of I Samuel, the manuscript has "I Samuel 2.10".

10. Milton's interpretation of King Joash's two wives, II Chronicles xxiv, 2, 3, is literally correct, as may be confirmed from Josephus, *Antiquities of the Jews,* Book IX, Chapter vii. His learned contemporary, John Selden, in his study of Hebrew tradition in marriage *Uxor Ebraica* ("The Hebrew Wife"), 1646, observed that some commentators tried to explain away this bigamy, suggesting that death or divorce had eliminated one wife before the second marriage. Milton takes no notice of this shift. He also does not use some arguments he could have cited in favor of his position from Selden's *Uxor Ebraica,* nor from Selden's *De Jure Naturali et Gentium* ("On the Law

of Nature and Nations"), 1640, although he knew both books. In his *Commonplace Book,* page 110, Milton copied this item from Selden:

> Concubinã unam pmitti in Ecclesiâ antiquâ Christianâ multis patrũ testimoniis testatr Seldenus de jure nat et gent. l. 5 c. 7. p. 573:

> That one concubine was permitted in the early Church, Selden shows by many testimonies from the Fathers. On the Law of Nature and Nations, book 5, chapter 7, page 573.

It should be observed that the various works of John Selden were quoted in Continental Protestant writings on marriage, divorce and polygamy, many more times than Milton was quoted on anything, during the seventeenth century.

LAMECH: Milton does not discuss the instance of Lamech, who was the first polygamist so identified in the Bible (Genesis iv, 19), and who was therefore often cited in theological discussion of plural marriage. Few commentators regarded Lamech as a saint; most called him a sinner. Defenders of Lamech usually had a special reason, like Philip of Hesse; asking approval of his projected bigamy, he listed Lamech among the pious patriarchs (in his 1539 *Instruction,* of which more herein). Luther took a judicial position, suggesting that Lamech took two wives not from lust but for the justifiable motives to increase his family and overcome the effects of the curse of Cain. He added "So to this day barbarous peoples retain polygamy to strengthen and stabilize their economy as much as their polity" (*Vorlesungen über 1 Mose. Kap. 4, 18-21,* "Lectures on Genesis, iv, 18-21", in *D. Martin Luthers Werke. Kritische Gesamtausgabe, Hermann Böhlaus Nachfolger, "Dr. Martin Luther's Works,* Critical Collected Edition published by Hermann Böhlaus' Successors," Weimar, 1911, volume 42, page 233; about 1544). Pierre Allix, *Reflexions upon the Books of the Holy Scripture to Establish the Truth of the Christian Religion,* 1688, judged that Lamech's bigamy was an irregularity, but still proof that he believed in the truth of the promise that the seed of woman would bruise the serpent's head. Theologians were ever spinners of moonbeams.

Milton also makes no use of the levirate marriage commandment in the Old Testament, the law which compelled a brother to espouse the widow of a deceased childless brother. This precept, which necessarily imposed bigamy on the surviving brother if already married, was stressed, we shall see, by Milton's younger contemporary, Gilbert Burnet.

Consistent with his antagonism to church rule by bishops, Milton treats the verses from Timothy and Titus about a bishop-husband-of-one-wife so as to render the terms *bishop* and *presbyter* as interchangeable.

Channing's "Remarks" appeared as a reprint of his unsigned review published in the *Christian Examiner and Theological Review,* Boston and London, III, (1826), 57-77. Most of the first reviews, of which there were many when the *Christian Doctrine* was first published, objected to what they considered Milton's heresies, polygamy included.

WILLIAM BLAKE: Henry Crabb Robinson, who considered Blake an artist, a genius, a mystic and a madman, in his diary for June 13, 1826 wrote that he found Blake "as wild as ever" and "He says that from the Bible he has learned that *eine Gemeinschaft der Frauen statt finden sollte.* When I objected that *Ehestand* seems to be a divine institution, he referred to the Bible—'that from the beginning it was not so' ". Robinson's later *Reminiscences* repeat this entry, translating its German words, "that wives should be in common" and "marriage." If Blake actually referred to the Bible, it could not have been community of wives but polygamy that he meant. Various editors of Blake record the gossip that he talked of adding a concubine, desisting when his wife began to cry. What is perhaps more significant is that Blake (who, as is well known, was intoxicated with Milton) made his remarks to Robinson relatively soon after the publication of Milton's *Christian Doctrine*. For Robinson's notes, and the aforesaid gossip, see Arthur Symons, *William Blake,* London, Archibald Constable & Co., 1907, pages 73-76, 253, 269-270, 303.

11. *DE FACTO POLYGAMY IN WESTERN COMMUNITIES: Monogamy and Polygamy* is the title of a treatise composed by the Norwegian author Björnstjerne Björnson about 1889, concerned not only with formal (Moslem) polygamy, but attacking the many kinds of de facto departures from monogamy prevalent in western Europe and the Americas. Björnson hailed the then recent victory of the anti-slavery North in the American Civil War as a triumph for monogamy over the slaveowners whose abuse of their female slaves was as notorious as it was brutal. Disturbed by "bohemians" who distorted Henrik Ibsen's liberating ideas, and who justified "free love" or "sowing wild oats," or who simply countenanced prostitution, Björnson aimed at uplifting marriage and the status of women by "education," and by a moralizing and civilizing lecture in the spirit of reasonableness. In the space of a single lifetime, Björnson's tractate has achieved the status of a rare book, a fact which speaks for itself, although there still are some people known to me personally who believe in the values of Björnson's ideal monogamy and who practice it.

The Norwegian title of Björnson's booklet was *Engifte og Mangegifte. Et Foredrag* (publisher, Forlag: Bibliothek for de tusen hjem, Fagerstrand pr. Høvik), [3]-45 pages, copy at Harvard. A German version was published by Hermann Lazarus, *Monogamie und Polygamie. Autorisierte Uebersetzung. Mit einem kurzen Vorworte des Verfassers* ("Monogamy and Polygamy, authorized translation, with a short Foreword of the Author's," dated December 10, 1889, 32 pages, copy at University of California, Berkeley). A loose French paraphrase *Monogamie et Polygamie* by Auguste Monnier and

Georges Montignac, preface by Emile Faguet, published by P.-V. Stock, v-xiii, 15-62 pages, appeared at Paris in 1897, copy at Stanford University, California.

Mrs. Attaway and William Jenney were sectarian preachers who left their legally married spouses and eloped, about 1644. Mrs. Attaway had publicly voiced favorable interest in Milton's *Doctrine and Discipline of Divorce,* and so their scandal was laid at Milton's door in Thomas Edwards' *Gangraena, The Second Part,* 1646.

12. *D. Martin Luthers Werke. Kritische Gesamtausgabe. Briefwechsel.* Hermann Böhlaus Nachfolger. Weimar, 1933, volume 4, page 140, letter 1056, ("Luther's Works. Critical Collected Edition. Correspondence," published by Hermann Böhlaus' Successors)

13. The law of Moses that Luther mentions with regard to the kings was probably the law of levirate marriage, which imposed widows on their deceased husband's brothers. Some commentators sought to explain the huge numbers of royal wives among Bible kings on the cumulative effect of this practice. As regards a leprous wife, there were precedents of long standing in the church for permitting a bigamous second wife. At the church synod or council of Compiègne, May 757, which dealt with adultery and other ruptures of marriage, Canon 19 ruled: "Si quis leprosus mulierem habeat sanam, si vult ei donare comiatum ut accipiat virum, ipsa femina, si vult, accipiat. Similiter et vir."—"If a man leper has a wife in good health and is willing to give her permission to take another husband, that woman, if she wishes, may so take. The same for a husband." (Alfredus Boretius, editor, *Capitularia Regum Francorum,* "Capitularies of the Frankish Kings", in *Monumenta Germaniae Historica, Legum,* "Historical Monuments of Germany", Section II, published at Hanover, by Hahn, 1883, page 39). Also see: Herbert Thurston, "Did Pope Gregory II Sanction Bigamy?", *The Month,* London, April, 1931, volume 157, pages 320-331; and Jacques Zoegger, *Du Lien*

du Mariage à l'Epoque Mérovingienne, Thèse pour le doctorat, 10 juin 1915, Faculté de Droit de L'Université de Paris, "On the Marriage Link in the Merovingian Epoch, doctoral thesis June 10, 1915, Law Faculty of the University of Paris."

14. *Luthers Werke. Briefwechsel,* cited above, letter 702, in volume 3, page 230-231. Someone, it seems, had asked Carlstadt about taking a second wife.

15. Martin Luther, "De Captivitate Babylonica Ecclesiae Praeludium", in *Dr. Martin Luthers Werke. Kritische Gesamtausgabe,* volume 6. Hermann Böhlau, Weimar, 1888, page 558.

16. Ibid., page 559.

17. See Ludwig Pastor von Camperfelden, *The History of the Popes from the Close of the Middle Ages,* English edition, London, 1910, volume X, pages 249, 275-277. From the correspondence of Henry VIII with his envoys to the Pope, it is possible to infer that Clement at times offered bigamy as a solution. See the letter of William Bennet to Henry VIII October 27, 1530 in Nicholas Pocock, *Records of the Reformation: The Divorce* (Oxford, Clarendon Press, 1870), volume I, pages 448-460, from British Museum Add. Mss. 25114, fol. 36 to 46; and Public Record Office, *Letters and Papers, Foreign and Domestic of the Reign of Henry VIII,* edited by J. S. Brewer, volume IV, Part II, document 3422, page 1553, and document 4977, pages 2155-2159; volume IV, Part III, document 6627, page 2987, and document 6705, pages 3021-3023; and appendix 261, pages 3188-3189. Catholic writers have been at pains to argue the opposite, suggesting that while Cajetan held polygamy acceptable within natural law, he knew it was banned by church law; e.g., Norman Hardy, "Papal Dispensation for Polygamy", *Dublin Review,* volume 153, 1913, 266-274; and N. Paulus, "Cajetan and Luther über die Polygamie," *Historisch-Politische Blätter für das Katholische Deutschland,* edited by Franz Binder and Georg Jochner, Mun-

ich, 1905, volume 135, pages 81-100 ("Historical-Political Leaflets for Catholic Germany"). The Pope's council did decide against the proposal of bigamy.

18. *Philippi Melanthonis Opera Quae Supersunt Omnia* ("All the Works of Philip Melanchthon which Survive"), edited by Carolus Gottlieb Brettschneider, Halle, volume 2, 1835, column 526.

19. On page 110 of the *Commonplace Book,* with the marginal notation *nothi dicti,* "so-called bastards", Milton copied, at various times, observations that Charles Martel (grandfather of Charlemagne, whose four concubines are recorded higher on that same page) was son of a concubine; that King Ferdinand of Naples (1423-1494) succeeded to his father's crown though the son of a concubine; and that not till the accession of Hugh Capet to the throne of France were bastards there deprived of equal rights, while in Italy no great distinction was made. The item on Italy came from the *Mémoires* of Philippe de Comines, while the preceding data was taken from *L'Histoire de France* by Bernard de Girard, Seigneur du Haillan.

On page 109 of the *Commonplace Book,* Milton entered a note, also taken from Girard, that Childeric, king of France, had two wives. This entry is tacked on to a partly filled line, using up space left after a prior note from Caesar's *Commentaries* that the ancient German Ariovistus had taken two wives. Since there is no reason to date the entry from Caesar before 1643-1644, the date suggested for the Childeric entry, in the Yale edition of Milton's *Complete Prose,* volume I, page 400, note 28, "1639-1641 (?)" is unacceptable. The Yale edition date seems to derive from an unclarity in James Holly Hanford's "The Chronology of Milton's Private Studies," *PMLA,* XXXVI, 1921, which separates the Girard citations among Milton's notes into earlier and later groups.

In this instance the fact that Milton wrote the Childeric entry onto the unfinished line from Caesar rules out any dating of the Childeric item as before the Ariovistus item.

Therefore I did not include the Childeric item above in discussing Milton's notations (presumably) written in before his marriage.

It may be because of the same unclarity that the Yale edition, volume I, page 461, note 10, offers the date "1642-1647 (?)" for the first group of Girard entries on Milton's page 186, instead of "1644-1647 (?)" as it does for almost all other Girard readings. Actually the distinction that should be made is that Milton's entry following the words *L. 1, p. 19, in fol.* was made at a later time than the entry which precedes those words.

Readers of the Yale edition may want to delete from that note 10 on page 461, volume I, the following sentences: "Most of Milton's entries from Girard's *Histoire* are in Latin. In this one and in the two notes from Girard immediately following, he uses English, except where, in two of the three entries, he introduces a French phrase or sentence, showing that he is quoting." The facts are otherwise. Milton quotes or cites from Girard on ten pages in the *Commonplace Book.* Depending on how one may consider his grouping of points, there are twenty-one entries more or less. These entries make reference to thirty cited pages from Girard. Of these, ten entries, with nineteen page citations, total thirty-three and a half lines of Milton's script, are in English; six entries, with six page citations in eight lines of Milton's script are in Latin; two entries with two page citations in four and a half lines of script are in French; and three entries, with three page citations in six lines of script are intermingled English and French.

20. The emendation to "Gregory" was cited by W. W. Rockwell (see note 23 below). Gregory I's counsel to Augustine may be found in its chronological place in any edition of Beda's *Ecclesiastical History of the English Nation.* On Gregory II's letter, see Thurston, cited in note 13 above; A. Vacant and E. Mangenot, *Dictionnaire de Théologie Catholique,* Paris, 1920, volume 6, articles on Gregory II and Gregory III; Jacques Paul Migne, *Patrologiae Cursus Completus,*

LXXXIX, columns 524-525. This document is sometimes called *quod proposuisti,* sometimes *quid posuisti* (both phrases mean "what you are raising as a question"). It was attributed to Gregory III by Gratian, the authority on canon law, and is almost always so attributed in the literature of the sixteenth, seventeenth and eighteenth centuries, when it was frequently cited and discussed. As to whether it was written by Gregory II or Gregory III, I leave to the doctors of the church to decide; some of them debate its meaning, but none of them doubt its authenticity as the letter of a Pope.

21. See article "Gleichen" in Pierre Bayle, *Dictionnaire Historique et Critique,* 1697 and other editions; Louis Moréri, *Le Grand Dictionnaire Historique,* Paris, 1674 and other editions, "Gleichen"; Eberhard Sauer, *Die Sage vom Grafen von Gleichen in der Deutschen Literatur* ("The Tradition of Count von Gleichen in German Literature"), Strassbourg, 1911; Magdalene Pernice, *Drei Gleichendramen aus der Zeit des Deutschen Idealismus* ("Three Gleichen Dramas from the Time of German Idealism"), Greifswald, 1925; Hans Tümmler, *Die Geschichte der Grafen von Gleichen von ihren Ursprung bis zum Verkauf des Eichsfeldes, ca. 1100-1294* ("The History of the Counts of Gleichen from their Origin to the Selling of Eichsfeld"), Neustadt-Orla, 1929, an historical account of the real von Gleichen family. It is characteristic of the Gleichen fiction that almost all sixteenth and seventeenth century accounts give a wrong date for the crusade of Frederick II, "1227."

The medieval church permitted certain kinds of marital dissolution and annulment in lieu of divorce, using the excuse of kinship or other "impediments," allowing remarriage of the parties to other spouses. Since aggrieved families sometimes refused to accept the dissolution, such situations have given rise to confused references in many authors to so-called bigamies among royal and noble families, which would take far more time to elucidate than they are worth. See: Michel du Perray, *Traité de Dispences de Mariage* ("Treatise of Marital

Dispensations"), Paris, 1719, for some examples of bigamies by error, mischance and other kinds. The possibility of papal dispensation for bigamy was seriously discussed by a fifteen century legal expert Jean Montaigne in his treatise on bigamy, printed on folios 121-132 in *Tractatus Illustrium ın Utraque Tum Pontificii Tum Caesarei Iuris Facultate Iurisconsultorum, De Matrimonio & Dote* ("Treatises of Jurists Illustrious in Both Papal and Imperial Law, on Marriage, Dowries," etc.) Tomus IX, Venice, 1584 (copy at Columbia University Law Library). Montaigne's opinion, in a work published with the consent of Catholic church authorities, was that bigamy was not against the law of nature, but a concept invented by magistrates; and that if there might be any authority anywhere in his age to dispense for bigamy, which he doubted, such authority could only be vested in the Pope and not in any mere bishop.

22. Dr. Ernst Ludwig Enders, *Dr. Martin Luthers Sämmtliche Werke. Briefwechsel* ("Luther's Collected Works. Correspondence"), Frankfurt am Main, 1903, IX, page 80, from the Marburg Staatsarchiv manuscript. A somewhat different version with the same essential meaning is given in *D. Martin Luthers Werke. Kritische Gesamtausgabe. Briefwechsel.* Weimar, 1935, volume 6, page 179: "Antequam tale repudium probarem, potius regi permitterem alteram reginam quoque ducere sive facere, et exemplo patrum et regum duas simul uxores seu reginas habere"—"Before I approve such a divorce, I would rather permit the king to marry or make another queen, and have two wives by the example of the patriarchs and kings."

23. The documents in the case of Philip of Hesse are printed in *Dr. Martin Luthers Werke. Kritische Gesamtausgabe. Briefwechsel.* Weimar, 1938, volume 8, pages 628-644, including Philip's memorandum of "Instruction" for Bucer to transmit to Luther and Melanchthon, and the dispensation by the ministers. These two documents and the text of Christina's

consent are also available in *Philippi Melanthonis Opera Quae Supersunt Omnia,* edited by Carolus Gottlieb Brettschneider, Halle, 1836, volume 3, 849-865.

The most complete accounts are in William Walker Rockwell, *Die Doppelehe des Landgrafen Philipp von Hessen* ("The Bigamy of Landgrave Philip of Hesse"), published by N. G. Elwert'sche Verlagsbuchhandlung, Marburg, 1904; and in Hastings Eells, *The Attitude of Martin Bucer toward the Bigamy of Philip of Hesse,* Yale University, 1924. Briefer accounts, more easily available, are in: Preserved Smith, *The Life and Letters of Martin Luther,* Houghton Mifflin, Boston, 1911; and in Arthur Cushman McGiffert, *Martin Luther, The Man and His Work,* Century, New York, 1912.

With the passage of time, the details of this episode were forgotten and the documents filed in the private archives of Hesse. The manner of their reappearance is part of this history. It is open to question whether Milton knew much more than what he read in Book 41, section xxiii of the *History of His Own Times* by Jacques Auguste de Thou (published in Latin, Jacobus Augustus Thuanus, *Historia Sui Temporis*). That text follows, with my English translation after:

> Addam, quod plerisque risu dignum, mihi silentio minime praetermittendum visum est, ipsum tam inexhausti ad venereos usus succi fuisse, ut cum uxore sola uteretur, et illa toties eum admittere non posset, vir alioqui castus, quique vagis libidinibus minime oblectabatur, ex ejus permissu, negotio cum pastoribus communicato, concubinam unam superinduxerit, cujus consuetudine ardore aliquantum perdomito parcius ac moderatius cum uxore versaretur, tandem hoc anno, qui illi climactericus fuit, postridie Paschae mortalitatem exuit, inspecto à medicis corpore triorches repertus.

> I add, what to some may be worthy of laughter, for myself hardly to be passed over in silence, he [Philip] was so inexhaustible of fluid for venereal uses, that when he

> made use of his wife alone, she could not admit him so many times; being a man otherwise chaste, who was hardly pleased by vagrant lusts, with her permission, having taken the matter up with his pastors, he bigamously married a concubine, by whose intercourse his ardor somewhat subdued, he could be occupied more sparingly and moderately with his wife. Finally in this year [1567] which was climacteric to him, the day after Easter he died; when the doctors examined his body, they found him *triorches* [literally, three-testicled; metaphorically, over-developed].

Readers of the Yale edition of Milton's *Complete Prose,* volume I, page 404, note 5, in the clause "the fact which Milton records as something worthy of laughter" may wish to delete the words "which Milton records" to eliminate the ambiguity, which seems to impute Thuanus' phrase to Milton; and may also wish to delete the description uncritically taken from Thuanus of Philip of Hesse "as a chaste person not given to promiscuous relations." Martin Luther complained unhappily soon after the bigamous marriage that if he had been aware of Philip's other concubine in Esschweig, he would have insisted that Philip marry her rather than Margaretha. See: John Alfred Faulkner, "Luther and the Bigamous Marriage of Philip of Hesse," *The American Journal of Theology,* 1913, 17:206-231.

24. Hastings Eells, *The Attitude of Martin Bucer to the Bigamy of Phillip of Hesse,* Yale, 1924, pages 177, 181-186, concludes that the weight of circumstantial evidence, which he adduces, points to Johan Lenning as the main author of the Neobulus *Dialogus,* although Bucer had seen Lenning's manuscript and made some corrections.

    Bucer's own analysis of the issues, written in German, remained in manuscript until it was first printed in 1878 at Cassel, Germany, by a scion of the aristocratic house of von Löwenstein, who signed himself simply "L," so that his full name and identity remain obscure. The title reads *Argumenta Buceri Pro Et Contra. Original-Manuscript Bucers, die Gründe für und gegen die Doppelehe des Landgrafen Philipp des Grossmüthigen de anno 1539, veröffentlicht durch v. L.* Cassel, 1878, Verlag von Theodor Kay, Königl. Hof.-Kunst.- und Buchhandler ("Bucer's Arguments For and Against. Original Manuscript of Bucer's, the Grounds For and Against the Bigamy of Landgrave Philip the Magnanimous, of the Year 1539, published by v. L., Cassel, 1878, House of Theodor Kay, Dealer in Art and Books to the Royal Court"). There are copies at Harvard Andover Theological Library, Princeton Theological Library, and a photostat of the British Museum copy at Yale University (Beinecke Library), iv, 56 pages, printed by Friedrich Scheel, Cassel.

My microfilm of Neobulus' *Dialogus* is from the University of Göttingen library, and I have used the copy at Krauth Memorial Library, Lutheran Theological Seminary, Philadelphia; 189 unnumbered pages, no paragraphing, but subdivisions for Natural, Imperial and Canon Law.

25. This passage was discussed by Siegmund Jacob Baumgarten, in his *Nachrichten von Merkwürdigen Büchern* ("News of of Noteworthy Books"), second series, volume 5, Halle, 1754, pages 503-508. Writers against polygamy in the 1540's were mainly concerned with attacking Anabaptism. Rockwell lists one title directed against Neobulus, a short piece in rhyme, *Wider das Unchristlich Gesprechbüchlein, von vile der Eeweiber, so durch eynen geschwinden auffrührischen Sophisten (der sich erdichter weiss Huldreych Neobulus nennen thut) gemacht ist, Eyn kurz Gedicht, Darinnen gemelten Neobulus mit seiner eygnen Farben, gantz artlich aussgestrichen wirt* ("Against the Unchristian Little Book of Dialogue on Polygamy, composed by a hasty inflammatory sophist, calling himself by the pseudonym Hulderich Neobulus, in which Neobulus being painted by his own colors is effectively effaced"). It is ignored by later writers whether pro or con polygamy.

26. A good English translation less literal than mine is offered by Theodore G. Tappert in *Table Talk,* volume 54 in *Luther's Works,* general editor Helmut T. Lehman, Fortress Press, Philadelphia, 1967, page 153. The original text (in manuscript, full of abbreviations and symbols) reflects the bilinguality of Martin and Katherine Luther as well as of Schlaginhaufen; it is printed in *D. Martin Luthers Werke. Kritische Gesamtausgabe, Tischreden.* Herman Böhlaus Nachfolger, Weimar, 1913, volume 2, page 105, item 1461,

> Es wirt noch dahin komen, das ein man mer den ein weib wirt nehmen.
>
> Respondit ipsa Doctorissa: Das glaub der Teufl!
>
> Dixit Doctor: Ursach, Ketha, ein weib kan ein jar nur ein kindt tragen, sed maritus scit plures generare.
>
> Respondit Ketha: Paulus dicit: Quilibet habeat uxorem propriam.
>
> Tunc Doctor respondit: Propria, aber nicht ein einige, das stet nicht in Paulo.
>
> Sic longo tempore iocabatur, ita quod Doctorissa dicebat: Antequam ego patiar hoc, ego potius rursum ingrediar monasterium et relinquerem vos et pueros omnes.

It must also be noted that, since Luther did not at all favor any general practise of plural marriage, on sundry occasions in his writings he expresses the view that Abraham and Jacob were no justifying precedents for bigamy or polygamy.

JOHAN OLDENDORP is a name which occurs in seventeenth century writings as a bigamist; always without any details. Oldendorp (1480-1567) was a lawyer, and a supporter of Luther. Some of his published writings are still extant. In 1518 he married Sophie Lotz, as it turned out, unhappily. Some years later he took himself a second wife, Anna. Luther was not one to make objections, but among the Marburg clergy some busybodies did (notably, Adam Kraft, or Crato). They excluded Johan and Anna from communion, and made further complaint against them. As it happened, at that time, 1554, decisive jurisdiction was vested in Philip of Hesse, who ruled in favor of Johan and Anna, and they seem to have lived happily ever after. What happened to Sophie is obscure. See: Roderick von Stintzing, *Geschichte der Deutschen Rechtswissenschaft, Erste Abteilung* ("History of German Jurisprudence, Part One") 1880, pages 310-321, based on the original documents in the Marburg achives. Florimond de Raemond (1540-1602) *L'Histoire de la Naissance, Progrez et Decadence de L'Heresie de ce Siècle,* also published in Latin as *Historia de Ortu, Progressu et Ruina Haereseon Hujus Saeculi,* both in several editions ("History of the Rise, Progress and Decline of the Heresy of this Century") is the source for most seventeenth century writers whether they accept or reject his account of Oldendorp.

MELANDER, who officiated at Philip of Hesse's bigamous marriage, was said to have three wives. Rockwell's version is that Melander was wed three times, and that his unorthodox manner of disassociating himself or divorcing himself from the first two wives left him open to the accusation of having three at once.

LUDWIG HÄTZER was a radical Reformer beheaded at Constance, 1529, by the Reformation authorities there. His public statements, as quoted in Arnold Meshovius, *Historiae Anabaptisticae Libri Septem,* ("Seven Books of Anabaptist History," printed by Gerhard Greuenbruch, Cologne, 1617, pages 74-76) show him to have been a clearly thought out unitarian. By his adversaries he was called *Hetzer,* "inciter," labelled an anabaptist, and charged with bigamy, which was the alleged crime for which he was executed. Whether this charge was true or false, I am in no position to decide, but the manner in which the charge was used in propaganda is illustrated by comments in the *Table Talk* of Martin Luther, who probably derived them from hearsay. Luther alleges that Hätzer preached to women who valued their chastity that they were guilty of pride, which was of the devil; that he seduced many matrons and virgins persuading them that to achieve salvation they must first be humbled; and that he was "impurus nebulo . . . qui habuit 24 uxores," a dirty rascal who had twenty-four wives. (*D. Martin Luthers Werke. Kritische Gesamtausgabe. Tischreden. Volume 1.* Weimar. Hermann Böhlaus Nachfolger, 1917, page 38, item 100; volume 5, page 548, item 6222; volume 6, page 276-277, item 6932.) Zedler's *Lexicon,* two centuries later, reduces the number of wives to twelve, while J. J. Herzog's *Realencyclopädie Für Protestantische Theologie und Kirche,* third edition, Graz, 1970, shrinks the case to the alleged bigamy for which he was executed.

27. Readers of the Yale edition of Milton's *Complete Prose* may wish to make some corrections to its discussion of Ochino, Castalio and Milton (volume I, page 412). One may wish to delete this statement there: "According to Thuanus and to Milton's note, Sebastian Castalion . . . based his *Dialogues on Sacred History* on Ochino's *Thirty Dialogues.*" Milton and Thuanus said nothing of the sort, since they were referring to Castalio's Latin translation of Ochino's *Thirty Dialogues* from the original Italian. Castalio's *Dialogorum Sacrorum Libri IIII* was an entirely different work, a series of brief dramatic skits from Bible episodes designed to teach schoolboys Christian principles with Latin composition in one book.

    Readers of the Yale edition may further wish to delete its statement "The Dialogues of Castalion (1563) were written for children and were printed six times in Basle, three in London, four in Edinburgh, and four in Germany." The fact is that Castalio wrote still other series of *Dialogues,* incluring *Dialogi IV, De Praedestinatione, Electione, Libero Arbitrio, Fide* ("Four Dialogues on Predestination, Election,

Free Will, Faith") so that the arithmetic in the Yale edition, as well as the 1563 date, is of no bibliographical value at all.

Readers of the Yale edition may further wish to delete its sentence "I find no evidence that Castalion meant to 'turn into Latin' Ochino's *Dialogues,* though he used them as a source." That Castalio did do Ochino's *Thirty Dialogues* into Latin, and did not use them "as a source," is known to every other writer who ever touched on the subject from 1563 to the present.

Readers of the Yale edition may further wish to delete the sentence "Milton's word 'adstruere' in this entry is translated 'to justify' in the Columbia edition. It means simply 'to cover,' which probably comes nearer to what Milton meant." The Columbia edition is correct. Milton meant "to justify."

Further, the reader of the Yale edition may wish to delete the following passage, after comparing the Yale edition passage with the Latin text of Thuanus and with a correct translation of Thuanus given forthwith:

Yale edition passage which should be deleted:

> The question is, in other words, would a follower of Ochino include the contentious problem of polygamy in a book for children? Thuanus, from whom Milton makes his entry, sheds little light on the matter, for he says that "Sebastianus Castalio Allobrox [a Swiss]" met "Bernardino Ochino, whose dialogues he turned into Latin" in 1563, and that he (Castalio) had been said to agree with Ochino, "whereupon many writings with opposite views (*contraria scripta*) appeared between them." Thuanus' word "adstipulari" means "to agree with," but Milton does not use that word.

Thuanus' Latin text,

> a Gallicis et Helveticis ecclesiis, quarum alioqui doctrinam amplectebatur, in quibusdam dissidens; et Bernardino

Ochino segregi, cuius et dialogos Latinos fecit, praecipue in polygamia adstipulari creditus, unde pleraque contraria inter eos scripta emanarunt.

Translation of Thuanus' text into English:

[Castalio] dissenting in some particulars from the French and Swiss churches, whose doctrine in other respects he embraced; (and apart from Bernardino Ochino, whose dialogues he also made Latin) was believed particularly to assent to polygamy, whence a number of writings for-and-against emanated between them [that is, between Castalio and those churches].

Readers of the Yale edition may wish, in regard to the sentence "In Basle, 1563, he published in Latin his *Thirty Dialogues,* in which he was accused by his adversaries of defending polygamy though pretending to oppose it," to delete "in which" and put a semi-colon in place of the comma at that point.

28. Ochino's borrowings from Neobulus were discussed by Johan Georg Schelhorn, *Ergötzlichkeiten aus der Kirchenhistorie und Literatur,* ("Drolleries from Church History and Literature"), Leipzig, 1762, 3 volumes, volume II, pages 766-801, 979-1017, 1141-2034, 2104-2123, and 2136-2194, "Nachlese von Bernardini Ochino Leben und Schriften" ("Gleanings from the Life and Writings of Bernardino Ochino"), especially page 2140. Schelhorn also prints the statement of the Zurich ministers defending their action in expelling Ochino. Volume I includes a correspondence between Pope Gregory XIII, Archduke Ferdinand and others about concubinage among clergy and among laity in Austria and Bavaria in 1575 and 1576.

29. The title page of Ochino's 1563 book read: *Bernardini Ochini Senensis Dialogi XXX. In duos libros divisi, quorum*

primus est de Messia, continetque dialogos xviij. Secundus est, cum de rebus varijs, tum potissimum de Trinitate. Quorum argumenta in secunda utriusque libri pagina inuenies. Basileae. M.D.LXIII ("Thirty Dialogues of Bernardino Ochino of Siena. Divided into two books, of which the first is of the Messiah, and contains 18 dialogues. The second, in addition to various topics, especially on the Trinity. You will find the table of contents on the second page of each book. Basel, 1563"). Copies at Union Theological Seminary and at Harvard (Houghton).

Peter Martyr Vermigli (1500-1562), friend and associate of Ochino, died before the *Dialogi XXX* came out. In his *Loci Communes,* translated into English in 1574 as *The Common Places,* Part 2, Chapter x, The Seventh Precept, pages 418-430, he detailed arguments for and against polygamy, with his own conclusion in opposition.

Theodore Beza's book against Ochino was printed in 1568, 1571, 1573, 1587, 1591, 1595 (Dutch translation), 1610, 1651, etc., sometimes bound in one format with his treatise on divorce under a common title *Tractatio de Polygamia et Divortiis.* Ochino's name was therefore better known through Beza's book than through his own. Beza devoted the first part of his book to Ochino, and the rest to other matters such as the Montanist heresy in the ancient church which regarded any second marriage (of a widow, for instance), as sinful. Beza dealt separately with the topic of concubinage in *Tractatus de Repudiis et Divortiis* ("Treatise on Divorce"). Beza, like Calvin his mentor, and Calvinists generally, did not accept any exceptions to monogamy, unlike Luther.

Note 38 in the Yale edition of Milton's *Complete Prose,* VI, 364, may well be deleted. Ochino had cited from "2 Reg. xii" (= II Samuel xii) the prophet Nathan saying that God gave into David's bosom the wives of his master (King Saul): this passage Milton discusses at length. Beza, having difficulty denying this statement by Nathan, introduces an irrelevant digression about David's wife Aegla (II Samuel iii, 5) and Saul's concubine Rispa, which Milton simply ignores, attending only to Beza's charge that if Ochino is correct, his argument defended incest. (David was son-in-law to Saul, having married Saul's daughter Michal). The Yale edition errs in taxing Milton with inaccuracy and is in total confusion on what Beza says about Aegla.

It has been suggested that Milton was indebted to Ochino's *Dialogi XXX* for ideas on the trinity, on divorce and polygamy; to Ochino's *A Tragoedie or Dialoge of the Uniuste Usurped Primacie of the Bishop of Rome* (English version by John Ponet, 1549) for the conception of Satan's speeches to his fallen angel followers; and to Ochino's *Labyrinthi* for the metaphor of those fallen angels wandering in philosophical mazes, *Paradise Lost,* II, 561, (Louis Aubrey Wood, *The Form and Origin of Milton's Anti-Trinitarian Conception,* a Heidelberg dissertation printed at London, Ontario, 1911). There is no direct evidence to support any of these suggestions, and Ochino is not needed to explain any of Milton's creations, as was correctly pointed out by James Holly Hanford, *Modern Language Notes,* XXXVI, (1921), 121-122.

30. This passage is quoted from the later, revised editions, which added the parenthetical clause and the word "holy" to the text of the 1655-1656 editions. Spelling and capitalization also differ among these editions.

It should be noticed that Thomas Barlow, who attributed the 1657 English version to Francis Osborne, and was sometime bishop of Lincoln, conceded that it was wrong to say that polygamy was against the law of nature. In *The Case of the Jews* (on their admission to England, but referring to a theological issue) he wrote: "That I conceive to be a manifest mistake, for it will evidently and undeniably follow that God permitted usury and polygamy and marrying a sister to the Jews by a positive law, therefore neither of them is, or can be against the Law of Nature, it being a demonstrative Truth and generally confessed by the best Lawyers, Schoolmen and Casuists, That God never did, nor (manente naturâ humanâ eadem) ["Human nature remaining the same." L.M.]

could dispense with the Law of Nature." Barlow was concerned in a complex divorce question in 1671, involving annulment under Catholic law in Italy: whether it was or was not connected with the Roos case (discussed below) is not apparent. See: Thomas Barlow, *Several Miscellaneous and Weighty Cases of Conscience Learnedly and Judiciously Resolved,* London, 1692, at General Theological Seminary, New York.

31. Otherwise there is not much to say for the possibility of Pecke's authorship of the 1657 translation. Close examination of style does not offer much help. Pecke's authenticated writings are exercises in wit, while the *Dialogue of Polygamy* is almost wholly restricted to rendering Ochino in English. If the translations in *The Judgement of Martin Bucer* were not known to be by Milton, would we associate them with the style of *Areopagitica?*

The 1657 translation is a close, often literal, version of the Latin. On occasion it omits a word, a phrase, even a sentence. Sometimes a classical Latin phrase is rendered almost archaicly: *Immo vero,* "nay verily," *sed age,* "but go to." Sometimes the English version is literary rather than literal: *sanctissimi scilicet homines Papani,* "those most holy men (Sir Reverence) the Papists," *quasi vero,* "That's a good one." Spellings are seventeenth century and there are many misprints. Ochino's error, dating the Gregory-Boniface correspondence to 120 years after the Nativity, goes unremarked and unchanged. Renditions of Bible quotations follow the words of Castalio's Latin and are not amended to correspond to the King James version. Some of Ochino's marginal references to location of Bible texts are omitted. The 1657 editor refers in the preface to Charron's "Book of Wisdom." He inserts one marginal note, on the question whether the Earth could support a much larger population: "Our Authour seems not to have heard or not to have thought, when he wrote thus, of the New-found World, nor of many large Tracts of ground in Hungaria, and other parts of Europe unpeopled." Some phrases might echo a legal training (*Uriae nece,* "the matter of Uriah"; *in bellis, in mari, & magistratibus,* "by war, shipwreck and the sword of justice") and some scattered words may be matched in Pecke's writings, but they all add up inconclusively.

Besides the information and sources mentioned in the text there is almost nothing available on Thomas Pecke. Anthony à Wood, *Athenae Oxonienses,* 1691-1692, has an item on Payne Fisher, but treats of Osborne under his account of Henry Cuff, and of Pecke under John Owen, since neither Osborne nor Pecke were Oxford alumni. John Venn, *Biographical History of Gonville and Caius College,* 1897, affords little. Joseph Needham, now Master of that College, writes me that no further research has been done over the years to add to the information furnished by one of his predecessors to the *Dictionary of National Biography,* which even lacks the date of Pecke's death. The Honourable Society of the Inner Temple records show the admission there of Thomas Pecke of Edmonton, Middlesex, June 11, 1657, and his being called to the bar February 12, 1664, but offers no more information (letter from the treasurer's office, Inner Temple, April 7, 1970). My inquiries through local historical societies in England have turned up nothing. I have considered and discarded the possibility of identifying Thomas Pecke with the unidentified "Mr. Packer" who spoke to John Aubrey about Milton's Latin dictionary project, and was some kind of disciple to Milton. Pecke wrote so many complimentary verses in *Parnassi Puerperium* to his acquaintances that the absence of verses to any in Milton's circle is a strong indication of non-contact.

One peculiar coincidence remains. Pecke makes reference to James Howell, author of *Epistolae Ho-Elianae,* as an adoptive uncle, whom Pecke seems to share with a cousin William Blois. In *Parnassi Puerperium* Pecke calls Blois the author of *Modern Policy,* or *Modern Policies,* a book which is usually (after Anthony à Wood) attributed to Archbishop William Sancroft: that may help explain the mystery why William

Blois' name appears in the 1690 edition after seven anonymous editions between 1652 and 1657. *Modern Policy* uses the Greek word *Colasterion* (= birch rod, punishment) several times as sub-chapter heading, from which Pecke picks it up in his *Parnassi Puerperium* lines to Blois. *Colasterion* is also the title of a 1645 pamphlet by Milton.

Donald Wing's *Short Title Catalogue* and other reference works group together several publications under "T.P." or "Thomas Peck." Some of these should be distinguished from the works of Thomas Pecke:

A Sober Guess, 1662, copy at the Library of the Congregational Union of London, and *The Inseparable Union between Christ and a Believer,* a 1658 sermon printed 1671, copy at Harvard, were both by Thomas Peck, M.A., a minister at Prittlewell, Essex. *Usury Stated, Being a Reply to Mr. Jelinger's Usurer Cast. Wherto are adjoyned some Animadversions on Mr. Bolton's and Mr. Capel's Discourses, concerning the same Subject. Written by T. P. . . . London. Printed for Robert Clavelat at the Peacock in St. Paul's Church-yard, 1679,* copy at the Library Company of Philadelphia, argues for moderation in interest-taking on loans, against immoderate usury and against a total ban on interest. It is a learned work, but my reading did not convince me one way or another whether it was by Thomas Pecke.

The latest publication definitely by Thomas Pecke was *An Heroick Poem,* prefixed by a Latin *Epigramma,* contributed in 1660 to the sycophantic chorus of scribblers dedicating hastily composed effusions, as Pecke did on his title page, *To the Most High and Mighty Monarch, Charles II,* etc., etc., etc.

32. The several items in the text from Pepys and Petty are from: Henry B. Wheatley, *The Diary of Samuel Pepys,* London, 1928, for January 28, 1661; October 19, 1661; December 22, 1662; January 27, 1663/64, and April 5, 1663.

33. *Paganus Piscator, vulgarly Fisher* is included by Edward Phillips in his *Theatrum Poetarum* (1675) as an afterthought

in his supplement, with a less than complimentary allusion to Fisher's having written in honor of the "usurper" Cromwell. (J. M. French, *Life Records of John Milton,* 1958, V, 433, cites a reference made by Thomas Manley, Jr., editor and translator of some of Fisher's verses, to a book which might be Milton's. The item is too uncertain.) A copy of the *Poemata,* published by Thomas Newcomb, 1656, is at the University of Pennsylvania.

34. There was formerly a 48 page manuscript translation of Ochino's dialogue on polygamy at Stanford Court, Worcestershire, noticed by A. J. Horwood, in Historical Manuscripts Commission, *Reports,* 1870, volume I, Appendix, page 53, but I am informed by letter June 12, 1969 from H. M. G. Baillie of that Commission, that the manuscripts there were lost in a fire in 1882. Whether that manuscript related to the 1657 translation is doubtful; the few words printed in the 1870 *Report* differ materially.

    My copies of the 1657 *Dialogue* and of Pecke's *Parnassi Puerperium* are from the University of Chicago; there are copies at Harvard, Yale and other libraries. My copies of Pecke's *Cleeveland, Balam's Ass* and the *Heroick Poem* are from the British Museum, which also has Heydon's *Advice.* I have discussed the University of Cincinnati copy of Osborne's *Advice to a Son,* 1656, in another connection in *Explicator,* XXIX, (February 1971), 52.

35. Nicholas Bernard, sometime chaplain to Oliver Cromwell, though also friend to James Ussher, Archbishop of Armagh and Anglican Primate of Ireland, in 1657 published *The Judgement of the late Archbishop of Armagh and Primate of Ireland of the Extent of Christ's Death and Satisfaction, of the Sabbath, and the Observation of the Lord's Day,* etc. Peter Heylyn, Anglican divine and controversialist, in 1658 issued *Respondet Petrus, or the Answer . . . to Dr. Bernard's Book,* etc., with an appendix criticising William Sanderson's *History of the Life & Raigne of King Charles.* Bernard then submitted

"Articles" against Heylyn's book, asking for a sentence of burning it, on the grounds of its "scandalous" teachings on the Sabbath. On June 22, 1658 the Council of State heard these "Articles" read, and directed a committee (including Sydenham, Fleetwood, Wolseley, Jones, the Lord Chamberlain, Lisle and "Mr. Secretary") to read Heylyn's book and report; "also that they consider the book lately published concerning polygamy, and those lately published by Mr. Saunderson and Mr. Harrington and report."

That book lately published on polygamy was (probably) the Ochino translation printed by Garfeild. William Sanderson's *A Compleat History of the Life & Raigne of King Charles from his Cradle to his Grave,* 1658, with a preface by James Howell, printed for Humphrey Moseley, Richard Tomlins and George Sawbridge, was in itself objectionable to the Council, even if Heylyn had his own disagreements with it. James Harrington was the author of *The Commonwealth of Oceana* (1656) and *The Prerogative of Popular Government* (1658): no threat to the regime, he, but only in so far as men in power fear any honest and independent writer or thinker.

The Council drafted a warrant, which Cromwell authorized, for enforcing the various statutes against unlicensed books, and on June 24 and 25 referred the Heylyn book to the attention of the Lord Mayor and the local justices of the peace (*Calendar of State Papers, Domestic*, 1658, for June 22, 24 and 25, which lists no specific action on the other three books). The Lord Mayor promptly quashed the matter in favor of Heylyn, who had at least one additional ally in the Council of State. George Vernon, *The Life of the Learned and Reverend Dr. Peter Heylyn, Chaplain to Charles I and Charles* II, 1682, page 156, mentions but does not name this ally. He may—or may not—have been Sir Charles Wolseley. We meet Wolseley on other occasions: as a participant in James Harrington's Rota Club (1659), along with Milton's friend Cyriack Skinner, and other interesting men such as Michael Mallet and Henry Neville, of whom more anon; in company and correspondence with Arthur Annesley, Earl of Anglesey, another of Milton's friends; as the author, among other works, in 1673, of *The Case of Divorce and Remarriage thereupon discussed occasioned by the late Act for the Divorce of the Lord Roos*—the case in which Milton was consulted by one or more persons from Parliament; and sixty years later Wolseley's 1673 pamphlet is reprinted in one volume with the 1732-1736 translation of Ochino on polygamy and divorce. (On Bernard, Heylyn and the others in this note, see *Dictionary of National Biography* for details.)

36. The 1732-1736 Ochino translation: In 1732 there appeared anonymously *The Cases of Polygamy, Concubinage, Adultery, Divorce, &c., Seriously and Learnedly Discussed. Being a Compleat Collection of all the Remarkable Tryals and Tracts which have been written on those Important Subjects. By the Most Eminent Hands. London. Printed for T. Payne, in Pater-Noster Row; J. Crichley, at Charing-Cross; and W. Shropshire, in New-Bond-Street, 1732* (copy at Columbia University Law School). This issue was announced without comment in *The London Magazine,* I, 266 (1732). Another issue of this book in 1732 was *Printed for E. Curll, in the Strand; T. Payne, in Paternoster Row; J. Crichley, at Charing-Cross; and J. Jackson, in Pall-Mall* (copy at the University of Chicago). In 1736 the book appeared again with a different title page: *Select and Curious Cases of Polygamy, Concubinage, Adultery, Divorce, &c., Seriously and Learnedly Discussed. Being a Compleat Collection of All the Remarkable Tryals and Tracts which have been written on these Important Subjects; particularly the famous Bernardino Ochino's with some Memoirs and Testimonies of his Life and Writings. London. Printed for the Editor, and Sold by Olive Payne, at Horace's Head, in Round-Court in the Strand, over against York-Building. MDCCXXXVI.* These 1732-1736 editions include:

1. An anonymous compilation, i-lvii, of "memoirs" and testimonies on Ochino's character, following the article in Pierre Bayle's 1697 *Dictionnaire,* defending Ochino against

hostile allegations printed in Louis Moréri's *Grand Dictionnaire Historique* (1674).

2. *Advertisement* explaining the present edition.

3. A new translation of Ochino's dialogue of polygamy, pages 1-65. The nameless 1732-1736 editor claims that this version was supplied by "a friend" who began it independently of the 1657 translation which (the editor claims) they did not see until their own 1732 version was in the press. This claim is not quite candid. Comparison confirms that the 1732 version was indeed begun independently, but very early in the process it began to copy freely from the 1657 version, though making some changes towards a livelier and less literal style.

3. The Ochino-Meschinus dialogue on divorce for adultery, transcribed verbatim from the 1657 edition, here pages 67-106.

4. With a separate title page, the discussion between Sir Charles Wolseley and an unnamed bishop, *The Case of Divorce, and Remarriage thereupon discussed. Occasioned by the late Act of Parliament for the Divorce of the Lord Roos, London, 1673,* pages 109-176.

5. *A Treatise Concerning Adultery and Divorce, MDCC* (reprinted), 177-211.

6. *Conjugium Languens, or the Natural, Civil and Religious Mischiefs Arising from Conjugal Infidelity and Impunity. By Castamore. MDCC.* (also reprinted from the 1700 original).

The 1732 and 1736 printings of Ochino have particular significance in connection with the eighteenth century discussion of polygamy by deists and others, of which more hereafter. In keeping with the change of times, there is a feeling of relaxation about it. These editions omit the marginal citations to Scripture texts included by Ochino and the 1657 version. The editors delight in banter. Speakers A and B replace the names of Telipolygamus and Ochino. Where Speaker A says "But by Observation, you may find one Cock to have many Hens; one Bull, many Cows," the 1732 editor supplies this footnote (page 44),

> A blithesome sort of a lass, who protests, she will sooner have a Husband and a Half, than half a Husband, and is now, while I am revising this *Proof,* leaning confoundedly hard over my left shoulder, says, *She never knew before whence came our saying,* of: Telling a *Story* of a *Cock* and a *Bull.*

37. Milton copied from Sir Walter Raleigh's *History of the World,* 1614, Book 2, chapter 4, section 16, the words beginning "by such" up to "seasonably," except for his parenthetical "saith he." The Congo episode occurred in 1491.

What to do about marriage customs differing from European or Christian practice when pagans were proselytized for Christianity was a problem, as we have seen, at least as old as the mission of Augustine sent by Gregory to the Angles and Saxons about 596 A.D., as related by Beda. The foundation of the Roman Catholic position on polygamy and divorce, the *Gaudemus in Domino* decretal of Innocent III, was originally a letter (1201) to help the Bishop of Tiberias cope with these questions among converts (text in Jacques Paul Migne, *Patrologiae Cursus Completus,* CCXVI, Innocentius III, volume 3, columns 1269-1271).

These questions arose with special force when large populations in Mexico and Peru came under Spanish rule (See: Francis James Burton, *A Commentary on Canon 1125,* in Catholic University of America, Canon Law Studies, 1940, number 121). In the middle of the seventeenth century it was a matter of discussion, as a result of the experiences of Jesuit missionaries in China, and particularly following the report of Alexandre de Rhodes on the Jesuit mission in Vietnam (see note 56 below). Among others, Pufendorf commented on polygamy as a bar to conversion in "the Indies" (*On the Law of Nature and Nations,* several editions, Book V, Chapter I, Section xvi).

Willem Bosman, a Dutch observer, writing on the Guinea

coast of Africa in 1704, reported: "Whilst I was here, there was also an Augustin Monk, which came from *St. Thome,* in order, if possible, to convert the *Blacks* to Christianity, but in vain. Polygamy is an Obstacle which they cannot get over. As for all the other Points, they might have got Footing here; but the Confinement to one Wife is an insuperable Difficulty." (*A New and Accurate Description of the Coast of Guinea,* etc., The Second Edition, London, 1721, page 364; originally Utrecht, 1704, Amsterdam, 1709, in Dutch; in English, 1705, in French, 1705.)

These questions have persisted to our own day.

JOHN WILLIAM COLENSO, Anglican bishop in Natal, South Africa, stimulated a mild controversy by urging toleration for polygamous marriages when the parties were converted to Christianity. He did not endorse polygamy in principle, but protested that compulsory dissolution of polygamous households was ruinous to the abandoned women and children. Besides many traditional arguments, Colenso cited American missionaries in Burma who had decided that previously contracted polygamous marriages should not be a bar to admission to communion.

Colenso first attracted attention to his opinion in *Ten Weeks in Natal: A Journal of a First Tour of Visitation among the Colonists and Zulu Kafirs of Natal,* Cambridge, 1855, pages 139-141, which elicited local discussion in Natal newspapers. Colenso then published *Remarks on the Proper Treatment of Cases of Polygamy, as found already existing in Converts from Heathenism. By John William Colenso, Lord Bishop of Natal,* Pietermaritzburg, May and Davis, 1855, 16 pages. He was quickly contradicted by *A Reply to Bishop Colenso's "Remarks on the Proper Treatment of Cases of Polygamy as already found existing in converts from Heathenism". By an American Missionary,* Pietermaritzburg, May and Davis, 1855, 56 pages: this missionary being Lewis Grout, who was soon seconded by *A Review of Dr. Colenso's Remarks on Polygamy, as found existing in converts from heath-*

enism. By the Rev. H. A. Wilder, American Missionary. Durban, J. Cullingsworth, 1856, 42 pages. Colenso replied to Grout and Wilder in *A Letter to an American Missionary from the Bishop of Natal,* (January 1), 1856, printed by James Archbell at the Natal *Guardian* office, Pietermaritzburg, 70 pages. Lewis Grout countered March 27, 1856 with *An Answer to Dr. Colenso's "Letter" on Polygamy. By an American Missionary.* Pietermaritzburg, May and Davis, 1856, 103 pages. Colenso raised the issue again in *A Letter to His Grace The Archbishop of Canterbury Upon the Question of the Proper Treatment of Cases of Polygamy as found Already Existing in Converts from Heathenism,* printed at London and Cambridge, 1862, 94 pages. Henry Callaway (1817-1890) countered with *Polygamy a Bar to Admission into the Christian Church,* published by John O. Browne, Durban, 1862, 115 pages. Callaway noted that Colenso had some supporters in his opinion, but offered, besides traditional theological arguments, vivid descriptions of the actualities of Kafir society as reasons for his opposition. An odd echo was the anonymous pamphlet *Dr. Ross and Bishop Colenso: or the Truth Restored in Regard to Polygamy and Slavery,* printed by Henry B. Ashmead, Philadelphia, 1857, 82 pages, which reprinted Colenso's "Remarks" and discussed them in context with the views expressed in *Slavery Ordained of God,* by the Rev. Frederick A. Ross, D. D., of Huntsville, Alabama.

Colenso was also the center of a storm over his unorthodox views on the literal acceptance of the book of Genesis in the Bible. The *Dictionary of National Biography* has an exceptionally laudatory article on Colenso (1814-1883). Biographies, with details on the polygamy discussion, were written by George W. Cox, *The Life of John William Colenso,* London, 1888, and by Peter Hinchcliffe, *John William Colenso,* London, 1964.

That polygamy continues a barrier to Christian missionaries in Africa, and a cause of the emergence of secessionist sects, is demonstrated in Jomo Kenyatta, *Facing Mount Kenya, the Tribal Life of the Gikuyu,* London, 1938; and in Geoffrey

Parrinder, *The Bible and Polygamy, A Study of Hebrew and Christian Teaching,* London, 1950, 78 pages.

38. This comment was written before 1641 when Browne married Dorothy Mileham with whom he had twelve children. Browne was "Doctor" from 1633, "Sir Thomas" from 1671.

39. Robertus Bellarmine, *Disputationum Roberti Bellarmini Politiani S.J. S. R. E. Cardinalis De Controversiis Christiani Fidei Adversus Huius Temporis Haereticos, Editio Prima Romana. Romae. Ex Typographia Giunchi et Menicanti, MDCCCXXXVIII, Tomus Tertius, Caput X, De Polygamia Multarum Uxorum Simul* ("Disputations of Cardinal Robert Bellarmine on Controversies of Christian Faith against the Heretics of the Present Time, first Roman edition, Giunchi and Menicanti, 1838, volume 3, chapter 10, On Plural Marriage with Many Wives at Once"). Bellarmine (1542-1621) refers to Luther's writings on bigamy for bishops, on Abraham, etc., not on the Hesse case. He offers a very clear position: God can dispense for polygamy (not for one-woman-many-men, however, which is against natural law); that this dispensation was to all peoples, not only the Hebrews, in patriarchal times, but was stopped for all peoples by Christ.

40. Thomas Sanchez, S.J., *Disputationum de Sancto Matrimonii Sacramento Tomi Tres, Liber VII, Disputatio LXXX* ("Three Volumes of Disputations on the Holy Sacrament of Marriage, Book VII, Disputation 80"), Antwerp, 1607, reprinted 1625, 1626, 1652.

    Since the western European church was in incessant controversy before the Council of Trent, it is in the nature of an ex post facto verdict to classify the men cited by Sanchez as either orthodox or heterodox. It is also difficult to define the precise formulations of these clergymen who wrote at different times addressing themselves to diverse situations. Sanchez himself complains that the great schoolmen John Duns Scotus (died 1308) and Gabriel Biel (1410-1495) wrote rather obscurely when they said that plural marriage was not against natural law, though against the Old (Divine Positive) Law. They were original thinkers often in wide disagreement from the tenets of Thomas Aquinas. John Gerson, of the University of Paris (1363-1429) and the Spanish clerics Miguel de Medina (1489-1578) and Miguel de Palacios (sixteenth century) left writings on marriage among other matters, but apart from Sanchez they seem to have had almost no readers. However, Alonzo Tostado (Alphonsus Tostatus, Bishop of Avila, c. 1400-1450) and Durandus de St. Portian (1275-1335) were cited by Bellarmine (see note 39) as teaching that polygamy was not against the law of nature; Bellarmine's citations were lifted, often without credit to him, by Protestant writers opposing polygamy who wanted to defend Luther by pointing at Catholics (e.g., Michael Siricius, *Uxor Una,* "One Wife", 1669, page 30; Melchior Zeidler, *Tractatus de Polygamia,* "Treatise on Polygamy," 1690, pages 42, 131; Samuel Schelwig, *De Polygamia,* 1714, pages 91-96, also on Gerson and Duns Scotus; of these writers, more anon.

Alphonsus of Vera Cruz (Alonso de la Vera Cruz, 1502-1584) was a major missionary in Mexico from 1536 to his death. His *Speculum Coniugiorum* ("Mirror of Marriages," written 1536, published 1546, revised 1567 and 1572 for publication in accordance with the decisions of the Council of Trent), confronted the problem as a practical question in Mexico. Polygamy there, particularly among the aboriginal chieftains, was valued as much as an economic institution, a labor force, a measure of wealth as much as a service of sensual satisfaction, and was a major obstacle to conversion. See Arthur Ennis, *Fray Alonso de la Vera Cruz, O.S.A., 1507-1584,* Louvain, 1957.

DIEGO GARZIA DE TRASMIERA: In 1638 in Spanish-ruled Sicily, a Catholic clergyman and officer in the Inquisition, published in Latin *De Polygamia et Polyviria Libri Tres. Auctore D.D. Didaco Garcia de Trasmiera (etc., etc.) Panhormi, Apud Decium Cyrillium,* "On Polygamy and Polyandry, Three Books, author Diego Garzia de Trasmiera, etc., etc., Palermo, published by Decius Cyrillius;" i-xvi, dedication, preface, censor's approval, complimentary verses, table of contents; text, 1-332; 34 pages of index. My microfilm is from the Newberry Library, Chicago.

As a theologian, Garzia (died 1661) speaks of polygamy and Old Testament patriarchs, but his focus is on the criminal law of bigamy, as committed by a man or a woman. He is unusual in using *polyviria* or *biviria* for a woman married to more than one man at a time, but he cites precedents for that usage (compare note 52).

As an Inquisitor, who among other books wrote *Stimulus Fidei,* "The Whip of Faith," on the obligation to expose suspected heretics, he writes from the standpoint of the Council of Trent, as applied by the Roman and Spanish branches of the Inquisition. He delves in detail into fine points: varieties of violation of the ban on bigamy, cases arising from ignorance, cases of converted heathen, cases involving false testimony as to the death of a spouse, cases of counselling to commit bigamy; considerations pro and con on the use of torture to establish the facts in prosecution; distinctions in penalty according to degree of the offense, according to social status (nobility, commons, men, women); hairsplitting cases of hermaphroditism and sex change; papal dispensations, and so on. From second hand sources, and with relatively slight attention, he condemns Luther for the Oldendorp case, Bucer, "Hetzerus with 30 wives," John of Leyden. He argues against Bodin on divorce, and derives a good deal from Jean Montaigne (see note 21 above), Bellarmine and Sanchez, and Catherinus on Cajetan (see note 41 below).

41. *Thoma de Vio Caietani Opera Omnia Quotquot in Sacrae Scripturae Expositionum Reperiuntur* ("Thomas de Vio Cajetan, All His Works in Which May Be Found Any of his Interpretations of Scripture") published by Jacob and Peter Prost, Leyden, 1639, volume I, *In Quinque Libros Mosis iuxta Sensum Literalem Commentarii,* "Commentaries on the

Five Books of Moses according to their Literal Meaning," Lamech, page 36; Abraham, page 71; Jacob's two wives who were sisters, page 313.

Cajetan's open-mindedness on polygamy is apparent, but whether he equated the law of nature with other varieties of the law of God in this regard is a matter not of record. Protestant theologians, defending Luther against the charge of accepting polygamy, liked to point at Cajetan and cited "quotations" such as "Iure divino non est prohibita uxorum pluralitas,"—plurality of wives is not prohibited by divine law: for example, André Rivet, *Exercitationes in Genesin CXCI,* "191 Studies in Genesis", printed in his *Operum Theologicorum Quae Latine Edidit Tomus Primus,* "First Volume of His Latin Theological Works," Arnold Leers, Rotterdam, 1651 and 1670, volume I, page 179-185; Michael Siricius, *Uxor Una,* 1669, page 29; Melchior Zeidler, *Tractatus de Polygamia,* 1690, page 131. After reviewing and rechecking Cajetan's *Opera Omnia* (1639) and earlier editions, such as *Epistola Pauli,* etc., "Paul's Epistles", 1546 and *In IIII Evangelia,* etc., "Commentaries on the Four Gospels", 1558, I conclude that these "quotations" are spurious. These "quotations" derive ultimately from an attack on Cajetan's opinions by Lancellotto de' Politi (1484-1553), who became Archbishop of Conza in the kingdom of Naples, and who wrote under his clergyman's name, Ambrosius Catharinus Politus, *Annotationes in Excerpta Quaedam de Commentariis Reverendissimi Cardinalis Caietani Dogmata,* "Annotations on Certain Selected Dogmas from the Commentaries of Cardinal Cajetan," Paris, Simon Colinaeus, 1535, page 196, and Catharinus' *Enarrationes, Assertationes, Disputationes,* "Expositions, Vindications, Disputations," Rome, 1551-1552, 1964 facsimile edition, columns 265-268. It was Catharinus who used the words implying that Cajetan taught "iure divino uxorum pluralitas licita est," that under divine law plurality of wives is permissible, based on Cajetan's comment on I Timothy iii, which did not expressly say so. Rivet, in his *Operum Theologicorum,* volume III, page 69, "Summae Controversianum Tractatus Primus," cited Catharinus' page 196 correctly, but earlier in his volume I, pages 179-185, he had given the citation wrongly as "Cajetani Cardinalis Comment. in N.T. folio 196." Siricius and Zeidler also derived from Catharinus, via Sisto da Siena, *Bibliotheca Sancta a F. Sixto Senensi Ordinis Praedicatorum Ex Praecipuis Catholicae Ecclesiae Authoribus Collectae,* "Brother Sixtus of Siena, of the Preaching Order, His Holy Library, Collected from Outstanding Authors of the Catholic Church," Frankfurt, 1675, Venice, 1676, Cologne, 1676, Annotation LXXXII. End of wild goose chase through vellum-bound folios which can now rejoin their forgotten fellows in their dim and dusty repose.

Augustine of Hippo: Augustine was taunted by Faustus the Manichean on the stories of polygamy in the Bible. Augustine replied, "Quando enim mos erat, crimen non erat; et nunc propterea crimen est, quia mos non est"—when it was the established custom, it was no sin; it has become a sin now, because it is no longer the established custom (Aurelius Augustinus, *Contra Faustum Manicheum Libri 33,* "Against Faustus the Manichean, 33 Books", Book 22, chapter 47, in Jacques Paul Migne's *Patrologia,* volume 42, column 428). This epigram is found frequently quoted by both Catholic and Protestant theologians, none of whom ever mention that there was a personal element in Augustine's quip: in his own pre-Christian innocence, while waiting for his affianced bride to grow up, Augustine himself had enjoyed the company of two concubines without benefit of lawful marriage (*Confessions,* Book VI, Chapters 13-15.)

42. Robertus Bellarmine, work cited in note 39, volume 3, "De Sacramento Matrimonii," "On the Sacrament of Marriage," page 1132. Although Bellarmine cited Durandus de St. Portian and Alphonsus Tostatus of Avila as teaching that polygamy is not against natural law, he also cited Pope Innocent III and others in opposition. Bellarmine himself balanced the case in this fashion: "Nam etiamsi coniugium unius viri cum multis uxoribus, non repugnet, primo fini matrimonii, id est prolis

propagationi et educationi, cum facile possit unus vir ex multos foeminos liberos procreare, et alere, tamen aliis finibus aperte repugnat"—"For even if the marriage of one man with many women may not conflict with the first end of matrimony, that is propagation and bringing up of children, since one man can easily procreate children from many women, and nourish them, nonetheless it plainly conflicts with the other ends."

43. Karl Sudhoff and Wilhelm Matthiessen, editors, *Paracelsus Sämtliche Werke,* "Paracelsus' Collected Works," Berlin and Munich, 1933, Part I, volume 14, page 260.

44. *Treatise on Christian Doctrine,* Book I, Chapter X, in Columbia edition, XV, 148, line 8. Milton combines parts of verses 1 and 4 in I Chronicles vii. Compare Note 31 above on the marginal comment in the 1657 Ochino.

45. *THE NUREMBERG POLYGAMY PERMISSION OF 1650.* A great many nineteenth and twentieth century books in English, French and German, which deal with the history of marriage, mention this law, as if it were an indisputable fact. The key phrases *Sollen hinfüro . . . Jedem Mannspersohnen 2. Weyber zue heyrathen erlaubt sein,* "henceforth it shall . . . be permitted to every male person to marry two women" are quoted in various grammatical adaptations, always with the statement that the law was a consequence of the depopulation during the Thirty Years War, but never with any detail as to who sponsored the law, how long it was in effect, and whether any bigamous marriages were performed under its terms.

Many of these references appear to derive from Joseph Alfred Xavier Michiels (1813-1892), *Secret History of the Austrian Government and of its Systematic Persecutions of Protestants, Compiled from Official Documents,* London, Chapman and Hall, 1859, published in 1863 at Gotha in German as *Geheime Geschichte der Oesterreichen Regierung seit Ferdinand II*. Michiels gave the text of three articles of the law, claiming that it had received the approval of several bishops and archbishops. However, Michiels' book was a wartime propaganda scrawl, and he gives no source for his text, or for the prelates' approval, so that he is of no cogent authority.

The earliest mention of this law appears to have been an item entitled *Auszug aus einem merkwürdigen Kraisschluss vom 14 Februar, 1650* ("Extract from a Remarkable Kreis Decision of February 14, 1650"), pages 155-156 in the *Fränkisches Archiv*, volume I, 1790, edited by Heinrich Christoph Büttner, Johann Heinrich Keerl and Johann Bernhard Fischer. The title of their periodical has been commonly taken to mean, literally, "Franconian Archives," Franconia being Franken, part of north central Bavaria.

Prof. Dr. L. Theobald of Nuremberg, writing "Der Angebliche Bigamiebeschluss des Fränkischen Kreistages" ("The So-called Bigamy Decision of the Franconian Kreistag") in *Beiträge zur Bayerischen Kirchengeschichte* ("Contributions to Bavarian Church History"), xxiii Band, 1916, although bound in the volume dated 1917, pages 199-200, said that no session of the Franconian Kreistag met between 1645 and 1664, and that nowhere in the extant archives of Nürnberg, Ansbach or Bamberg, preserving records of Franconian kreis legislation, was there record of such a law. Theobald suggested that the editors of the *Fränkisches Archiv* had misunderstood some draft document of the 1650 period.

In the *Jahresbericht über das 43 Vereinsjahr 1920* of the Verein für Geschichte der Stadt Nürnberg ("Annual Report for the 43rd Year 1920" of the Historical Society of the City of Nuremberg), 1921, pages 13-15, there is the untitled report of a talk by Dr. Alfred Altmann, kreis archivist, in which he characterizes the *Fränkisches Archiv* as merely a popular journal, not an edition of state documents, and describes the tradition as a literary fantasy. My own examination of the *Fränkisches Archiv* confirms Altmann's description. The most serious reason for impeaching the *Fränkisches Archiv* account is the total silence of all seventeenth century writers on polygamy, which aroused my suspicions and led me to seek further. My thanks to Eva Tiedemann, of the Deutsche Bibliothek, Frankfurt am Main, and to Dr. D. Karasek, Universitätsbibliothek, Erlangen-Nürnberg, for help in obtaining copies of the Theobald and Altmann articles (and other books cited herein), and to A. Abbel of the Universitätsbibliothek, Giessen, for a photocopy of the 1790 *Fränkisches Archiv.*

46. The population argument reappears in the eighteenth century, nonetheless. Patrick Delany (1737, 1739) argued that polygamy was no asset to population; Henry St. John, Viscount Bolingbroke, argued that it was; of both, more anon. Graunt (1624-1674) made the first studies; Petty (1623-1687) made his contributions later.

47. For instances, consult: Somerset County, England, *Quarter Sessions Records for the County of Somerset, volume iv (Charles II, 1666-1667)* London, Harrison and Sons, Ltd., 1919, passim.

48. On Frey, the Hutterites and others in this era, see George Huntston Williams, *The Radical Reformation,* Westminster Press, Philadelphia, 1962, a valuable digest of a vast amount of data, with a very few minor flaws; and his *Spiritual and Anabaptist Writers,* Westminster Press, 1957.

It is hopeless at this date to determine the full truth about these sects. A few writers have emphasized their programs, or slogans, for social reconstruction; most notable is Karl Kautsky, *Der Kommunismus in der Deutschen Reformation,* 1895, translated by J. L. and E. G. Milliken as *Communism in Central Europe in the Time of the Reformation,* London, 1897, New York, 1959. Compare Heine's attitude on John of Leyden (mentioned in our next chapter) as described in his *Geständnisse* ("Confessions", 1854). We have learned too much in the 20th century, from the explorations of Sigmund Freud, and from events in Europe and elsewhere, to derive convincing conclusions from the data available for phenomena like Münster.

The supposed Epistle of Clement is available in Paulus Hinschius, *Decretales Pseudo-Isidorianae et Capitula Angilramni* (Scientia Verlag Aalen 1963 reprint of the 1863 Leipzig edition), page 65. It urges that the faithful brethren follow the example of the apostles, sharing all worldly goods; it is the iniquity of appropriating things which brings on division among mortals. "Denique Grecorum quidem sapientissimus, hec ita sciens esse, ait communis debere esse amicorum omnia. In omnibus autem sunt sine dubio et coniuges"—"Finally, indeed, the wisest of the Greeks, knowing that this is so, says that all things should be in common among friends. Moreover, in all things doubtless are also included wives."

49. *PIERRE BAYLE,* in so many matters a rational and clear-sighted thinker, who rejected polygamy as argued by Johan Leyser, nonetheless wrote that only a most unreasonable passion in men, jealousy, caused the desire for *propriété,* individual possession, in regard to women. See his *Nouvelles Lettres Critiques de l'Auteur de la Critique Générale de l'Histoire du Calvinisme* ("New Critical Letters by the Author of the General Critique of [Louis Maimbourg's] History of Calvinism"), 1685, several editions, Letter IX:

> Il faut se désabuser une fois pour toutes de l'opinion que l'on a, que les hommes se sont conduits par les idées de la raison, dans l'établissement des Societez. S'ils avoient consulté la raison, ils n'auroient pas fait ce qui'ls ont fait a l'égard du sexe. Ils auroient vu, que pour n'avoir pas tant de choses à garder, il falloit faire une grand différence entre la possession d'un champ, ou d'une vigne, & la possession d'une femme, puis qu'un champ est une sorte de bien dont un homme ne sauroit recueillir le fruit, sans l'ôter à tous l'autres, au lieu que les femmes sont comme cet arbre d'or de la Sibylle, dont on pouvoit arracher les branches sans qu'ils en restât moins,

Primo avulso non deficit alter
Aureus, & simili frondescit virga metallo.

Ainsi la Raison eut plutôt conseillé la communauté que la propriété des femmes.

Once for all we must get rid of the opinion that is held that men were moved by the ideas of reason in the establishment of societies. If they had consulted reason, they would not have done what they did as regards sex. They would have seen, that in order not to have so many things to take care of, it was necessary to make a big distinction between the possession of a field, or of a vineyard, and the possession of a woman, since a field is the kind of wealth from which a man cannot gather the fruit without keeping it away from all others, whereas women are like that golden bough of the Sibyl [in Vergil's Aeneid]

—The first broken off, no lack of a second
Golden bough, of that same metal blooms another.

Therefore reason would have counselled community of women rather than individual possession.

In Letter XVII, section v, of the same work, Bayle again attributed modesty and the married state to the effects of jealousy, irrational passion and prejudice,

A ne suivre que cette Raison, il est bien certain que l'on ne chercheroit pas plutôt à satisfaire les désirs de la Nature avec une fille, qu'avec une femme de joye, toutes choses étant égales d'ailleurs & qu'on ne feroit pas plus de difficulté de prêter sa femme, que de prêter un livre.

To follow this Reason only, it is indeed certain that one would not seek to satisfy the desires of nature with a maid rather than with a femme de joie, all things being otherwise equal, and that one would not make more ado about lending his wife than lending a book.

50. The text of Rothman's pamphlet is available in: Bernard Rotman *(sic)* "Restitution rechter and gesunder christliche Lehre," in *Neudrucke Deutscher Litteraturwerke des XVI. und XVIII. Jahrhunderts,* "Reprints of German Literary Works of the 16th and 17th Centuries," Halle, Max Niemeyer, 1888. Rothman argued that I Timothy iii (one wife to a bishop) proved polygamy was acceptable for others in Apostolic times.

    DAVID JORIS or David George, was another sixteenth century apostle, who passed through the Münster episode and settled at Basel among disciples who saw in him a reincarnation of King David or of Jesus. He is honored by some as a pioneer for religious toleration who wrote a fervent appeal on behalf of the doomed Servetus, and he is sneered at by Karl Kautsky as a comfortable bourgeois. For two centuries or more his name was a byword for preaching polygamy: so Thuanus, *Historiarum Sui Temporis Tomus Primus,* Book xxii, Chapter vii; Johannes Hoornbeek, *Summa Controversianum Religionis,* 1658; etc. Another Münster offshoot was the splinter group following John of Batenberg, said to be outwardly Catholic or crypto-Catholic, privately preaching polygamy; whether nobly inspired or insanely adventurist, who now can tell.

51. Jerome used that formula several times: "Non damno digamos, immo nec trigamos et si dici potest octogamos" (*S. Eusebii Hieronymi Stridoniensis Presbyteri Adversus Jovinianum Libri Duo,* "St. Eusebius Jerome, Priest of Stridon, His Two Books against Jovinian," in J. P. Migne, *Patrologiae Cursus Completus,* volume 23, column 234; in the *Prologus* to Jerome's *Commentariorum in Jeremiam Prophetam Libri Sex,* "Six Books of Commentaries on the Prophet Jeremiah," Migne, volume 24, column 681; and in his *Liber Apologeticus ad Pammachium Pro Libris Contra Jovinianum, Epistola XLVIII,* "To Pammachius, a Book Defending his Writings against Jovinian, Letter 48," in Migne, volume 17, column 499).

52. *POLYANDRY AS A TERM:* The term *polygamy* had been naturalized into Latin from its Greek roots at least as far back as Jerome, as in the "Prologue" to his Jeremiah Commentary, cited above. By the seventeenth century it had passed into French and English. In German usage one finds the variant forms *polygamia, polygamie* and *polygami,* as well as the pure German *vielweiberey. Polygynaecia,* Latinized from the Greek, is also found, as in Erasmus (who simply brushed polygamy aside with its patriarchal and royal precedents: see his *Christiani Matrimonii Institutio,* "The Institution of Christian Marriage," 1526)

The term *polyandry* has a different history. The Greek *polyandrion* meant a mass grave to the Latin fathers; so Jerome has "polyandrium, id est tumulus mortuorum" (Migne, *Patrologia,* "Hieronymus", volume 7, page 66, section 63; Oscar Weise, *Die Griechischen Wörter im Latein,* "Greek Words in Latin," in Fuerstlich Jablonowski'schen Gesellschaft zu Leipzig, Gekrönte Preisschrift, XXIII, "His Highness' Jablonowski Society at Leipzig, Laureated Prize Essay," 1882, page 497). In its modern sense of one-woman-with-several-husbands, it was used in Greek letters by Caspar Barlaeus, *Dialogus de Polygamia,* 1643; in Greek letters and Greek case forms by Michael Siricius, *Uxor Una,* "One Wife," 1669; in Greek letters and case forms in the books of Johan Leyser, and in the writings of some of his opponents (Johannes Musaeus, 1675, and as late as Johan Andreas Quenstedt, *Theologia Didactico-Polemica,* 1685 and 1691, all to be discussed anon). Leyser also used *polygynaecia* in both Greek and Latin letters, and for polyandry, *polygamia multiviratus* (i.e., many-men-plural-marriage). The German form *vielmännerey* is also found (Gerhard Feltmann, *Tractatus de Polygamia,* 1677, and others). Johannes Diecmann used the forms *polyandria* and *polygynaecia* as Latin words and in Greek letters as Greek words, in his *Vindiciae Legis Monogamicae* ("Defenses of the Law of Monogamy"), published 1678, so that he may have been preceded in print, if not in coinage, by use of those Latin forms by Severin Walther Schlüter, *Theologische Gedancken von der Polygynia,* "Theological Thoughts on Polygyny", 1677. A century later Martin Madan's *Thelyphthora,* 1781, I, 279, refers to *"polyandry,* as it is called", indicating that the term was still in process of adoption into English.

While "polygamous" unions of one-man-several-women have always been easy to recognize and identify, "polyandrous" arrangements of one-woman-several-men as a stable permanent socially sanctioned form have been difficult to identify or to distinguish from various other forms of family which have existed in historical times. In discussions in the seventeenth century, certain examples recur. Some cite Julius Caesar's all too brief description of the marriage customs of the ancient Britons. Some refer to reports of travelers about Malabar or Calecut in India. Some refer to the remarks of Aeneas Sylvius Piccolomini (Pope Pius II, 1405-1464) on the ancient Lithuanians, remarks which they never quote: "Matrones nobiles publicae concubinos habent, permittenibus uiris, quos matrimonij adjutores vocant"—"Ordinary matrons have notorious male concubines, with their husbands' permission, whom they call matrimonial aids" *(Opera Quae Extant Omnia,* "All Extant Works," Basel, 1551, facsimile reprint Frankfurt am Main, 1967, page 417). Tibet, commonly mentioned in nineteenth century discussions of polyandry, was not so cited in the seventeenth century. Christian Thomasius, of whom more anon, was a lone exception in morally equating a woman's bigamy (in effect, polyandry) with a man's bigamy (= polygyny). A creditable effort has been made by H. R. H. Prince Peter of Greece and Denmark, in *A Study of Polyandry,* Mouton & Co., The Hague, 1963, 601 pages; he defines his observations precisely, and identifies and describes (among other forms) polyandrous marriage institutions as products of certain difficult and rare natural and social environments.

53. Balthasar Meisner summed up a great deal of church discussion in his *Philosophia Sobria, hoc est: Pia Consideratio*

Quaestionum Philosophicarum in Controversiis Theologicis, quas Calviniani moverunt orthodoxis, subinde occurentium, "Prudent Philosophy, that is, Pious Consideration of Philosophical Questions which Calvinists have posed to the Orthodox [Lutherans], continually arising." I use the 1621 Wittenberg edition published by Johan Gormann, in the Solger Collection at Nürnberg Stadtbibliothek (thanks to Elizabeth Hetz), 3 volumes; dedication dated March 5, 1611. Part I, pages 630-650, deals with the patriarchs' polygamy and Jacob's two sister wives.

Henricus Brouwer's book was *De Jure Connubiorum apud Batavos Recepto Libri Duo In Quibus Jura Naturae, Divinum Civile, Canonicum prout de Nuptiis Agunt, Referuntur, Expenduntur, Explicantur,* Amsterdam, Gaspar Commelinus, 1665, 718 pages ("On the Law of Marriages in Effect among the Dutch, Two Books, in which Natural, Divine, Civil and Canon Laws as far as they treat of wedlock, are reviewed, examined and explained"). Its second edition, published by Adrian Beman, Delft, 1714, came at a time of revived interest in these matters.

The Cannemaker case is recounted in full detail in Abraham Kemp, *Leven der Doorluchtige Heeren van Arkel, ende Jaar Beschrijving der Stad Gorinchem* (etc.), Paulus Vink, Gorinchem, publisher, ("Lives of the Illustrious Lords of Arkel and Annals of the City of Gorinchem"), 1656, pages 96-97 (New York Public Library). The Cannemaker case is also mentioned as if it were recent by J. Brunsmann, *Monogamia Victrix,* 1679, pages 139 (of whom, more anon).

Matthaeus' book is a commentary on the Digests, or Pandects, part of the Corpus Juris Civilis, the code of traditional Roman law. Columbia University has 1730, 1761 and 1803 editions.

Death as the penalty for bigamy seems generally to have been assumed to be the law in the writings of seventeenth century western Europe, but the facts are not so definite.

In England, bigamy was a canon law matter, and not punished under statutory civil law until the time of James I. In

France there was no legal death penalty for bigamy but executions did take place for the adultery or for the fraud involved. See *Disputatio Iuridica de Polygamia,* Augustin Leyser, *praeses,* Albinus Ernestus Ulricus, respondent, Wittenberg, 1736.

In Germany of the Holy Roman Empire reference was usually made to Article 121 of the laws of Charles V (1532) as if that authorized death (decapitation by the sword, in practice). Actually Article 121 defined the penalties for bigamy in a roundabout manner, so that it would be punished "not less than adultery." This could be interpreted to mean death, or a lesser penalty. (Jacob Friedrich Ludovici, editor, *Caroli Quinti Romanorum Imperatoris Invictissimi Constitutiones Criminales vulgo Peinliches Halsgerichts-Ordnung,* Halle, Johan Gottfried Renger, second edition, 1716, pages 155-158, "Criminal Code of the Most Unconquerable Charles V Emperor of the Romans, in German, Penal Code of the Capital Court").

Johannes Jannsen, *History of the German People after the Close of the Middle Ages,* translated by A. M. Christie, 1902, 1961, volume XVI, 137-141, cites executions for bigamy in 1558, 1560, 1571, and scourging, 1564, but none of these particular cases appear in seventeenth century discussion. Johan Samuel Adami, alias Misanders, *Tractat von der Polygamia oder Vielweiberey,* Weissenfels, 1713, 1715, page 165, supplies these instances: February 28, 1556, at Freyberg, an eighteen year old youth executed by the sword for bigamy; Wilhelm Schmiedefelder, arrested at his second wedding celebration, also by the sword at Freyberg, November 11, 1599; and jumping to 1697, Lübeck, where a trigamist under death sentence said he was dying a martyr.

54. Cyrano de Bergerac, *Histoire Comique des Etats et Empires du Soleil* ("Comic History of the States and Empires in the Sun"), pages 262-263 of the 1676 edition of *Les Oeuvres de Monsieur de Cyrano de Bergerac, Seconde Partie.* This is the real and original Cyrano, whom Edmond Rostand fictionalized

in his romantic drama. "Cyrano le Bigame," a lecture April 6, 1933 by Adrien Huguet in the Bullétin Trimestriel of the Société d'Emulation d'Abbeville, 1933, 328-343, tells of Hiérome-Dominique de Cyrano, 1665-1741, a distant collateral kin to the famous Cyrano, and a bigamist.

55. Henry Neville's book is discussed in Worthington Chauncey Ford, *The Isle of Pines, 1668, An Essay in Bibliography,* Boston, 1920. The book was much reprinted in English, French, Italian, Dutch, German and Danish within a short time. Neville told his tale so aptly that a Warsaw pamphlet of 1715 cited the Isle of Pines as a type of good evidence justifying polygamy, (C. Wiernowsky, *Consideratio Inculpata,* of which more anon.)

Neville's heavy-handed *The Parliament of Ladies* (1647, 16 pages) speaks of M. Sabrin having a concubine in London and a wife in Geneva, but is only satirizing matrimonial matters in London, as he does in the sequel, *The Ladies A Second Time Assembled in Parliament* (1647, 12 pages). These are occasionally mildly funny, which cannot be said for *Newes from the Exchange, or the Commonwealth of Ladies,* London, 1650, 22 pages, attributed to Neville; this is not a satire but a scandal sheet. Referring to the family of the Earl of Pembroke, page 15: "Zounds, we are now in a Godly Family and they that are the only people in the world that know how to order women: for, the Father keeps two wives and a concubine as prisoners." (I do not have the leisure to verify or disprove the attribution of this last pamphlet to Neville).

DENIS VEIRAS: Another satire of that period which relates somewhat to these matters was *The History of the Sevarites or Sevarambi,* which appeared in England in two parts, 1675 and 1679, was translated by the author into French, and appeared also in German, and in more editions. The author, Denis Veiras (or Vairasse d'Allais) was a French Protestant, who spent time in England about 1665, and in his *History* includes an eloquent digression *against* rhyme which would put him into the midst of the Dryden-Howard-(and Milton) debate on blank verse. Veiras is sometimes included among writers describing polygamous societies, but in fact polygamy plays a very small role in his book, even less than might be expected in a book describing a mythical South Pacific kingdom. More conspicuous is Veiras' handling of a shipwreck of a European vessel in the South Seas. The survivors set up a community in which 74 women (nearly all of whom were whores previously) are assigned on a rotation basis to 307 men. The ratios vary in different editions of the book; senior officers get one woman each, while common ranks must wait their turn, five or seven or ten men to one woman, until contact with the mythical Sevarambi provides women enough for a more even distribution. Veiras offers other fanciful institutions: a corps of slave women to accommodate foreign visitors; a community ceremony in which women can choose their husbands, and any so ill-favored as to be rejected at three ceremonies may compel herself to be accepted, however polygamously, by any husband she chooses; etc.

56. Alexandre de Rhodes (1591-1660) was from Avignon, but rather more a Papal subject than a Frenchman. He told his story first in *Relazione de'felice successi della Santa Fede Predicate da' Padri Della Compagnia di Giesù nel Regno di Tunchino alla santità di N. S. PP. Innocenzio Decimo di Alessandro de Rhodes Avignonese della medesima Compagnia e Missionario Apostolico della Sacra Congregatione de Propaganda Fide. In Roma. Per Guiseppe Luna. L'Anno del Giubileo, 1650* ("Relation of the Happy Successes of the Preaching of the Holy Faith by the Fathers of the Company of Jesus in the Kingdom of Tonkin, to His Holiness Innocent X from Alexandre de Rhodes of Avignon, of the same Company and Apostolic Missionary of the Sacred Congregation for the Propagation of the Faith. Rome, Giuseppe Luna, in the Jubilee Year, 1650"), Chapter XXII, pages 186-188. The French account, which varies somewhat in language, was *Divers Voyages et Missions du P. Alexandre de Rhodes en la Chine & Autres*

Royaumes de L'Orient, avec son Retour en Europe par la Perse et L'Armenie, Paris, Sebastian and Gabriel Cramoisy, 1653 ("Divers Voyages and Missions of Father Alexandre de Rhodes in China and other Oriental Kingdoms, with his Return to Europe via Persia and Armenia"), Part II, Chapter XII, page 105. Solange Hertz, *Rhodes of Vietnam,* Westminster, Maryland, Newman Press, 1966, has done the French account into English.

When Rhodes is cited by Protestant writers it is usually from the Latin version in Gisbertus Voetius, *Politicae Ecclesiasticae Partes Primae Libri Duo Priores/Libri Duo Posteriores/Pars Secunda/Pars Tertia et Ultima ("Ecclesiastical* Polity, Part I, Two First Books/Two Latter Books/Part Two/Third and Last Part"), Amsterdam, 1663, volume I, pages 771-774 on Tonkin; Volume II, 1669, page 272, to the same effect about *regno Conchino,* which probably refers to the same matter but was taken to mean Cochin-China by Johan Leyser. Voetius was also cited by Conrad Büttner, of whom more anon. S. Pufendorf, *De Jure Naturae et Gentium,* cites directly from the *Divers Voyages.*

The efforts of Jesuit missionaries to solve the dilemma of polygamous proselytes led to charges by their opponents within the Catholic Church that they were equivocating on the matter; for example, Antoine Arnauld (1612-1694) of the Sorbonne, in his *Morale Pratique des Jesuites,* Troisième Volume, 1689, ("Practical Morality of the Jesuits"), in his collected works, 1775, and facsimile reprint, 1964, volume 33, page 207. In a letter of June, 1673, to Bishop Le Camus of Grenoble, (*Oeuvres de Messire Antoine Arnauld,* 1775, 1964, volume I, page 712) Arnauld summarizes the dilemmas:

> Il n'y a rien, par exemple, qui empêche plus la conversion de la plûpart des nations infidèles, que de ce qu'on ne peut les admettre au baptême qu'en les obligeant de quitter toutes leurs femmes, à l'exception d'une seule. Cependant il n'est pas aisé de prouver, que la Polygamie soit contre le droit naturel; et S. Augustin semble enseigner manifeste-

ment le contraire. Il n'est point évident, que les Patriarches & tous les autres Juifs n'aient eu plusieurs femmes que par une dispense de Dieu; & à ne s'arrêter qu'aux seules paroles de l'Evangile, sans y joindre la doctrine des Pères, on ne convaincroit pas aisément un homme, qui soutiendroit que J. C. n'a point défendu absolument la polygamie. Et ainsi c'est principalement la tradition & l'autorité de l'Eglise qui fait qu'il n'y a personne qui fut assez hardi, pour admettre au baptême un Roi de la Chine, qui ne voudroit se faire Chrétien qu'à condition qu'on lui laisseroit toutes ses femmes.

There is nothing, for example, which hinders more the conversion of most of the infidel nations than the fact that they cannot be admitted to baptism except by obliging them to discard all their wives except one. However it is not simple to prove that polygamy is against the law of nature; and St. Augustine seems manifestly to teach the contrary. It is not at all evident that the Patriarchs and all the other Hebrews had had several wives only by a divine dispensation; and if one sticks to the words alone of the Gospel, without joining to them the doctrine of the Fathers, one would not easily convince a man who would argue that Jesus Christ did not absolutely forbid polygamy. And so it is principally the tradition and the authority of the church which is the cause that there is no one so bold to admit to baptism a King of China who would not become Christian except on the condition that all his wives be left with him.

57. Apart from the 1657 translation of Ochino, the only conspicuous English writer in the field appears to have been Robert Sharrock, LL. D., 1630-1684, of whom Anthony à Wood wrote that he was learned in divinity, law, and vegetables. In 1662 he published *Judicia (seu Legum Censurae) de Variis Incontinentiae Speciebus, Adulterio, Scil. Polygamia et Concubinatu, Fornicatione, Stupro, Raptu, Peccatis contra Natur-*

am, Incestu & Gradus Prohibitis ("Judgments, or Censures of the Laws, on Various Kinds of Incontinence, Adultery, Polygamy, Concubinage, Fornication, Debauchery, Rape, Offences Against Nature, Incest and Prohibited Degrees of Kinship," Oxford, by the university printer H. Hall, for Thomas Robinson). He is strictly orthodox, as befits an archdeacon of Winchester. Although he uses the same Bible material, there is no hint of Ochino, or Pecke, or Milton. This book came out in 1667 in a Tübingen edition, which was thereafter often cited by Continental writers, among whom Siricius, 1669; Mayer, 1674; Schlüter, 1677; Diecmann, 1678; and Schelwig, 1714, will be discussed anon.

AMYRAUT: At Saumur in France, where a Huguenot academy flourished for some years, Moyse Amyraut (1596-1664), spokesman for a somewhat modified Calvinism, published in 1648 *Considérations sur les Droits par lesquelles La Nature a Reiglé Les Mariages,* "Considerations on the Laws by which Nature Has Regulated Marriages," printed by Isaac Desbordes at Saumur, 428 pages plus Errata. Amyraut's version of the "law of nature" is opposed to divorce and polygamy. This book received little attention until it was issued in a Latin version in 1712, reprinted 1717, as *Moysis Amyraldi, Theol. & Philosophi Clarissimi, De Jure Naturae, Quod Connubia Dirigit, Disquisitiones Sex, Ex Gallica Versae à Bern. Henr. Reinoldo, Antecessore Herbornense, ex Bibliotheca Gerh. von Mastricht, J. C. S. B. Qui notas aliaque ejusdem argumenti addidit. Stadae. Apud Henricum Brummerum, Bibliopolam Stadensem. 1712* ("Six Considerations on the Law of Nature Which Regulates Marriages, translated from the French of Moyse Amyraut, Most Noted Theologian and Philosopher, by Bernhard Heinrich Reinhold, Lawyer of Herborn, from the Library of Gerhard von Mastricht, Attorney, Who Added Notes and Other Matter on the Same Topics. Stade, at Heinrich Brummer's, Bookseller at Stade."), 385 pages. These reprints and addenda are significant in our later story. Amyraut, 1648, at Union Theological Seminary; 1712, at Harvard Law Library; 1717, at Columbia Law Library.

58. *Faces Augustae* appeared in both quarto and octavo editions in 1643, at Dordrecht, publisher Matthaeus Havius, printer Henricus Essaeus, copies in my own library; 1656, by Elzevir, Leyden. Barlaeus' *Dialogue on Polygamy* is not mentioned by any disputant on polygamy until it was reprinted as one of the addenda to the 1712/1717 Latin version of Amyraut's *Considérations.* My thanks to Dr. Sonja F. Witstein and Dr. W. Vermeer of the Rijksuniversiteit Te Utrecht and to Dr. P. Tuynman of the Universiteit van Amsterdam for helpful correspondence on Barlaeus, Vythage and Milton-in-Holland.
    Vlitius speaks of his intent to visit Milton in two letters written in December, 1651 and January, 1652, reprinted in volume 3, pages 741-743 of Petrus Burmannus, *Sylloges Epistolarum a Viris Illustribus Scriptarum Tomi Quinque* ("Collections of Letters Written by Famous Men, Five Volumes," Leyden, 1723). Many letters in Burmann's collection involve Vlitius. Are there not other papers of his still extant and unedited?

59. *PRAESES AND RESPONDENT:* According to Zedler's *Lexicon,* article on *Disputirkunst* ("Art of Disputation"), in the university exercises of that time, the *respondent* affirms a proposition which an *opponent* disputes, while the *praeses* was a supporting sponsor of the respondent. In the scores of "dissertations" and "disputations" printed in Germany between 1650 and 1750 which I have examined, no "opponent" discussion is ever printed; only in one instance (Willenberg, 1712, to be reviewed later) is there any information available about "opponents." It is not always clear who is the author of the text of the disputation, the *praeses* or the *respondent.* Sometimes it is the one, sometimes it is the other. Title pages are often misleading. Catalogues often assume that the *praeses* is the author, sometimes wrongly. Wherever possible I have in-

dicated who was the actual author, or what the area of doubt might be.

Zesch (1629-1682) was also known as Zeschius. His *De Polygamia* was printed by Friedrich Karger at Giessen; title page, blank verso, dedication i-ii, 1-44 pages. Although the inner title says "Disputation," no respondent is indicated. My photocopy is from the British Museum.

60. My photocopy of *Funus Polygamiae* is from the Royal Library, Copenhagen. It was printed by Matthew Doischer, university printer at Greifswald, with a title page cluttered with lists of the offices held by Tabbert and Büttner and with compliments to Carl Gustav Wrangel and the Count of Oldenburg. The inaugural disputation date on the title page is March 18, 1667; dedication on verso; three page preface by Büttner, March 8; text, 64 unnumbered pages; a complimentary letter from Carl Gustav Wrangel dated January 29, 1667, in both Latin and German, 3 pages, and a 13 page supplement dated March 17, in the guise of an invitation to burial ceremonies for polygamy, apparently composed in the name of the faculty by Matthaeus Tabbert.

In spite of its auspices, Büttner's book appears to have been little known. In 1677 Heinrich Storning, at Kiel, in his *Ehelichen Keuschheit* ("Marital Chastity", discussed below) complained that he had not been able to see a copy of *Funus Polygamiae* which he attributed to "Tarnovius." This wrong author's name was repeated from Storning by Nicholas Möller in 1710, and again in the 1712 and 1717 editions of Amyraut (both Möller and Amyraut discussed elsewhere herein), so that it cost me many weary hours of hunting for a Tarnovius work until I discovered the truth in a photocopy of the antique handwritten catalogue on polygamy kindly sent me by the Copenhagen Royal Library. The Tabbert-Büttner book was correctly cited by Mascovius and de Mascou in their 1692 dissertation on polygamy, also at Greifswald; by J. S. Adami, *Tractat von der Polygami,* 1713, 1715; and in an undated barely legible note handwritten in the Harvard Law

Library copy of Mentzer's *Kurtzes Bedencken;* on all of these more anon.

61. Siricius' *Uxor Una* (1669) was printed by Joseph Dietrich Hampelius, university printer at Giessen; my photocopy from the University of Chicago. It bears dedications to Conrad Fabricius and to Hartmann Jacobus. Siricius includes a great deal of information from a wide variety of sources but when he refers to "those who favor polygamy" he neglects to name any names. A careful collation of Zesch, Büttner and Siricius tends strongly to indicate that all three wrote independently of each other. Although Zesch and Siricius were both at Giessen and dedicated their books to the same Ludwig of Hesse, Siricius gives no evidence of having known Zesch's book, except for the coincidence that they are both unusual in citing Ludwig Hätzer as a notorious Anabaptist-polygamist, and both spell his name wrong as *Helzerus.*

62. This letter by Philip Jakob Spener (1635-1705) at Frankfurt am Main to Balthazar Bebelius of Strassbourg (1632-1686) was printed in Samuel Schelwig's *Reliqua de Polygamia,* "Rest of the Discussion on Polygamy," 1715, pages 46-48, and thence by Christian Gottlieb Clugius, *Diatribe Epistolica,* "Epistolary Analysis," 1748, pages 4-5, both of whom felt it was a symptom of its time. Of these, more anon.

63. Spelling of Leyser's name: In his letters in his own handwriting, now in the Stockholm City Archives, he signed LEYSER, as did all his family when writing German. *Lyserus* is the form they all used in Latin. The spelling *Lyser* found in English and American library catalogues will probably continue because of inertia.

Brief notes on Leyser were published by those four most valuable encyclopedists: Pierre Bayle, *Dictionnaire Historique et Critique,* 1967; R. P. Nicéron, *Mémoires pour Servir à L'Histoire des Hommes Illustres dans la République des Lettres avec un Catalogue Raisonné de Leurs Ouvrages* ("Memoirs to Contribute to the History of Men Illustrious in the Commonwealth of Letters, with an Accurate Catalogue of Their Works"), Paris, volume 39, 1739, 386-392, but not with an accurate listing of Leyser's works; Johan Heinrich Zedler, *Grosses Vollständiges Universal Lexicon* ("Great Complete Universal Encyclopedia") Halle and Leipzig, 1739; Christian Gottlieb Jöcher, *Allgemeines Gelehrten Lexicon,* ("General Lexicon of Learned Men"), Leipzig, 1750. All four of these magnificent reference works also supply much information about related persons and places.

A longer sketch, much marred by hostility, was included by Johan Joachim Gottlob Am-Ende, in *Memoriam Inspectorum Portensium Dissoluto Inspectionis Corpore Conservare,* etc., ("To Preserve the Memory of the Pforta Inspectors, Now that the Inspection Corps is Dissolved", etc.), published by Johan Joachim Ahlfeld, Wittenberg, 1748, pages XVIII-L and XCVI-XCVIII. Am-Ende had himself held the post of inspector at Pforta, and was later superintendent of the church at Friburg (was this the Friburg near Naumburg in Saxe-Weissenfels?) About the same time was published the only effort hitherto made at a critical review of Leyser's bibliography, a useful work, though quite incomplete: Christian Gottlieb Clugius (= Kluge), *Diatribe Epistolica de Scriptis Io. Lyseri ad Tuendam Suadendamque Polygamiam Editis ad Virum Maxime Reverendum Io. Ioach. Gottlob Am-Ende Pastorem et Superintendentem Friburgensem Perscripta,* "Epistolary Analysis of the Writings Published by Johan Leyser Defending and Urging Polygamy, Accounted to that Right Reverend Gentleman J. J. G. Am-Ende, Pastor and Superintendent at Friburg," printed by Johan Christopher Tzschiedrichius, Wittenberg, 1748; title page with motto on verso, 1-86, iv. My photocopies of Am-Ende and Clugius are from the University of Göttingen library.

64. Since all sources give conflicting dates for members of the Leyser family I subjoin here, as more likely to be correct, the data furnished me from the records of their parish church, the

Thomaskirche, by the office of the Superintendent, letter of November 2, 1971:

	Born	*Baptized*	*Died*
Polycarp II	Nov. 20, 1596	—	Jan. 15, 1633
Sabina Volckmar	—	—	Sept. 29, 1634
Polycarp III	—	Sept. 27, 1616	Nov. 1, 1641
Nicolaus	—	Nov. 13, 1618	Aug. 24, 1632
Lucas	Oct. 23, 1620	Oct. 24, 1620	June 2, 1672
Friedrich Wilhelm	—	Sept. 5, 1622	Aug. 25, 1691
Christian	Sept. 4, 1624	Sept. 5, 1624	Oct. 5, 1671
Caspar	Oct. 26, 1626	Oct. 27, 1626	—
Michael	—	April 14, 1628	—
Sabina Elizabeth	—	Dec. 12, 1629	June 9, 1673 burial
Johann	Sept. 30, 1631	Sept. 30, 1631	—

Polycarp II and Sabina Volckmar were married October 31, 1615. Without the Thomaskirche data we would not know of Leyser's being an orphan, which is not mentioned in any printed source I have seen.

Dr. Renate Drucker, Leiterin des Archivs at Karl Marx University of Leipzig, most graciously opened their archives for me on my visit in July, 1971; in particular *Vetters Collectaneen, Theologische Fakultät,* an eighteenth century manuscript compilation in several volumes by Wilhelm Ferdinand Vetter from the original records of the theological faculty, since lost in war. Vetter gave Johan's birthdate as May 17, 1631, and the death of Polycarp III as 1664. Under his listing of baccalaureates, Vetter wrote that Leyser attained the degree of Licentiate in Theology (a degree intermediate between *magister* and *doctor*) on September 25, 1668, but this is not elsewhere confirmed. Leyser seems to have claimed that degree, but contemporaries (such as Diecmann in 1677-1678, of whom more anon) seem to have doubted whether he was entitled to it.

Polycarp Leyser, Johan's father, was superintendent of

the Thomaskirche, and his portrait now hangs there, with Johan Huelsemann's and others, above the grave where Johann Sebastian Bach (once organist there) lies reburied.

Michael Leyser's classic *Culter Anatomicus hoc est Methodus Brevis, Facilis, et Perspicua Artificiose et Compendiose Humana Incidendi Cadavera,* Copenhagen, 1653, "The Anatomy Knife, that is a Brief, Easy and Clear Method of Skillfully and Efficiently Dissecting Human Cadavers," was number 600 in the auction catalogue of Dr. Nathan Paget's library (my photocopy from the National Library of Medicine, Bethesda, Maryland). He also wrote on kidney stones, and other medical treatises.

Christian Leyser published some disputations; an obituary oration on Elector Johan George of Saxony; and *Consensus Non Consensus Quin Potius Dissensus Lutheranorum & Jansenistarum,* "The Agreement No Agreement, Rather Disagreement between Lutherans and Jansenists," printed by Christian Michaels, distributed by Johan Simon Ficke, Leipzig, 1668, iii, 68 pages, with complimentary verses by Martin Lipen (my photocopy from Concordia Theological Seminary, St. Louis, Missouri).

C. F. H. Bittcher, *Pförtner Album. Verzeichniss Sammtlicher Lehrer und Schüler der Königl. Preuss. Landesschule Pforta von Jahre 1543 bis 1843,* "Pforta Album, Collected Register of Teachers and Students at the Royal Prussian State School of Pforta, 1543-1843" (copy at Harvard University) supplies names of Leyser's contemporaries and confirmation of dates.

The following paragraphs summarize other information I have found on Leyser's activities before his polygamophile phase.

He himself says (*Polygamia Triumphatrix,* page 520) that he had studied with Johan Conrad Dannhauer, theologian of Strassbourg, which had to be before the latter died in November, 1666. Dannhauer had dealings with John Durie, but did not agree with his efforts to unite Lutherans and Calvinists.

Leyser acted in the role of *praeses* in a disputation (December 3, 1653 at Leipzig University), printed in 14 unnumbered pages *Diatribe Pneumatica de Spiritu, quam Infinito Spiritu aspirante & Inclutâ Facultate Philosophicâ annuente, ventilandam, Publice proponit M. Johannes Lyserus Lips., S. S. Theol. Stud., Respondente, Christophoro Hofmanno Kindelbrüccensi, Phil. Baccal. Ad. d. III Decembr. Anno M.DC.LIII. H.L.Q.S. Lipsiae, Typis Henningi Coleri* ("Pneumatic Analysis of the Spirit, which, with the Infinite Spirit Breathing favorably on it, and the celebrated Philosophy Faculty approving, Johan Leyser of Leipzig, student of Sacred Theology, proposes for public discussion; Respondent, Christopher Hoffman of Kindelbrück, Bachelor of Philosophy, December 3, 1653, Leipzig, printed by Henning Coler"). My photocopy is from the British Museum, whose catalogue lists it as by Hoffman. It may more readily be by Leyser (see note 59). The flamboyancy on the title page accords with Leyser's later style. Dr. Renate Drucker of Leipzig University assigns it to Leyser and identifies Hoffman as Bachelor of Arts, August 18, 1653; Master of Arts, March 21, 1654. It is an exercise in scholasticist speculation, choked with citations and lightly sprinkled with Greek and Hebrew.

Henning Witte, *Diarium Biographicum* (published at Danzig by Martin Hallevord, printer David Frederick Rhetius, 1688, 4°), a biographical dictionary of the century arranged by date of death, has notes on Leyser's grandfather, father and brothers Christian, Lucas, and Michael; and lists as by Johan Leyser *De ἀφθαρσία sive Indeficientia Animi. Aphtharsia* is Greek for incorruptibility, imperishability; *indeficientia* is church Latin for an unfailing supply; but without the book it is hard to make sense of the title, whether it means "On the indestructibility or inexhaustibility of the spirit," or relates to the immortality of the soul. Possibly this item may be related to a 1660 publication *De Constitutione Pneumaticae* by Joannes Lyserus catalogued in Burkhard Gotthelf Struve's bibliography *Bibliothecae Philosophicae Struvianae,* edited by Ludwig Martin Kahlius, Göttingen, 1745, I, 445. I have not been able to locate a copy of either.

Witte also lists a *Dissertatio de Theologia Naturali,* "Dissertation on Natural Theology." This is also listed for Leyser in Hiob Ludolph, *Allgemeine Schau-Buehne der Welt, Fünfter Theil,* "Universal Stage-Show of the World, Part Five," Frankfurt am Main, 1731, in 1675-1688, Book 85, Chapter XV, column 319; and in Zedler's *Lexicon;* but I have seen no trace of it elsewhere.

Georgii Christiani Gebaueri Anthologicarum Dissertationum Liber cum nonnullis adoptivis et Brevi Gelliani et Anthologici Collegiorum Historia, Lipsiae, Sumptibus Casparis Fritsch, 1733, "George Christian Gebauer's Book of Dissertations of the Anthologicans, with some additions, and a Short History of the Gellian and Anthologican Societies, Leipzig, published by Caspar Fritsch, Leipzig, 1733," (my photocopy from the British Museum), includes material on Leyser, xlv and lix-lxxi, but the only detail which Gebauer adds relates to Leyser's admission December 9, 1655 to membership in the Anthologicans. These two closely related societies of the learned of Leipzig at times enrolled Samuel and Esaias Pufendorf, Caspar Ziegler, Johannes Adam Scherzer and other minor luminaries; and Gottfried Wilhelm Leibnitz, who in 1691 wrote that he had once been acquainted with Leyser.

Hostile Am-Ende, basing himself on some written notes he says were left by some unnamed erudite man, speaks of Leyser as having neglected his ministerial duties, failing to keep up the register of births, marriages and deaths, and spending his time on horses and dogs. Am-Ende repeats old gossip that Leyser, after leaving his post at Pforta, was arrested and jailed in Hanau, for failing to remit funds he had collected for the Pforta school. Actually Pforta records, cited by Am-Ende, showed that funds collected by Leyser were received from him by his successor about 1670, and were used to buy a new black pall to cover coffins at funerals. The only element in this report that is of potential interest is that it places Leyser in Hanau at the same time as that unnamed Swedish nobleman of Spener's letter. Considering how many books were written against Leyser while he was alive by men who knew he had been at Pforta, if there had actually been such an arrest and jailing, it could hardly have failed of mention: but it is not mentioned by any, and so may be discounted.

Am-Ende, with better grounds, recites another episode of Leyser's career which was not to his credit. It would seem that after three years Leyser had become bored with Pforta, and accepted the post of pastor at a place called Eybenstock; then finding he disliked its mountainous climate, changed his mind. Benjamin Heiden, pastor at Prettin, near Wittenberg, was assigned, unwillingly, to Eybenstock, and Leyser was assigned to Prettin. Apparently Leyser was there about long enough to preach one sermon (eight days); took off for the therapeutic waters of Bad Schwalbach, then a popular prescription for many ailments, having meanwhile discommoded Pastor Heiden's efforts to return to Prettin, leaving a dog-in-manger-like unpleasantness in the air; came back and took the post of pastor and superintendent at Seiden, another village near Wittenberg, walked out of that in three months, and disappeared, until he turned up some years later in his role of polygamy-prophet. Am-Ende bases this narrative on a 1748 book, its author unknown to him, *Alter und neuer Geschichte der löblichen freyen Berg-Stadt Eybenstock* ("Old and New History of the Praiseworthy Free Mountain City Eybenstock"), which I have not seen; but I also find the essentials about Leyser at Prettin and Seiden in Abraham Calovius, *Systematis Locorum Theologicorum . . . Tomus Undecimus* ("Volume 11 of his System of Theological Topics"), published by Johannes Wilkins at Wittenberg in 1677 but written by 1674, page 213.

65. E. von Maltitz, *Geschichte der Familie von Wrangel, von Jahre 1250 bis auf die Gegenwart, nach Urkunden und Tagebuchern bearbeitet,* ("History of the Wrangel Family from the Year 1250 to the Present Day, Compiled from Archives and Diaries"), published by Wilhelm Baensch, Berlin and Dresden, 1887, page 197, says only of Maria Christina Wrangel, wife

of Conrad Christopher von Königsmarck, "Her life with her husband was unhappy" (*Sie lebte mit ihrem Gemahl unglücklich*). Georg Hesekiel, *Nachrichten zur Geschichte des Geschlechts der Grafen Königsmarck,* published by Alexander Drucker, Berlin, 1854 ("Account of the History of the Lineage of the Counts of Königsmarck") mentions the marriage and nothing more. (My microfilm copies of both are from the British Museum).

66. *THE KÖNIGSMARCKS.* Among the many Königsmarcks whose lives and adventures cut across the scenes of our story may be cited these:

John Milton's Königsmarck: Hans Christopher von Königsmarck, 1600-1663, started out in the service of (Catholic) Emperor Ferdinand II in the Thirty Years War; in 1630 joined the Swedish (Lutheran) forces; was held to blame in the sack of Prague, 1648, among other acts of wartime destruction. In the service of Sweden in war against Poland he raised a regiment of Scots mercenaries (1657), was shipwrecked off Danzig, whereupon the troops mutinied and betrayed him to the opposing forces. He was kept a prisoner in Weichselmünde, and so became the subject of a diplomatic démarche from Oliver Cromwell to Danzig, ally of Poland, dated April 10, 1657, asking for his release or at least milder treatment. This letter was done into Latin by John Milton, then secretary for foreign tongues in Cromwell's service. Königsmarck was nonetheless kept prisoner until the war ended in 1660.

He had three sons: Johan Christopher, who died young; Conrad Christopher von Königsmarck, also called Curt or Cord, 1634-1673, who in 1657 married Maria Christina Wrangel (1638-1691), daughter of Herman Wrangel and half-sister to Carl Gustav Wrangel, and who is the Swedish count who supposedly drew Leyser into the polygamy debate; and Otto Wilhelm von K., 1639-1688, who, it is said, made diplomatic history of a sort (introduced to the French court as Ambassador he forgot his prepared Latin speech and ad-libbed his way through in Swedish, confident that most would not know the difference, and that any who might would not dare to challenge him).

Conrad Christopher von K. had four children: Karl Johan, 1659-1686; Maria Aurora, 1662-1728; Amalia Wilhelmina, 1663-1740, according to Krister Gierow, director of Lund University Library, other sources giving other dates; and Philip Christopher, 1665-1694. Of these Amalia led the quietest life. She married Count Carl Gustaf Lewenhaupt (1662-1703) and preserved the letters and records of the others, now at Lund.

Karl Johan is named in Scandinavian encyclopedias as Leyser's polygamy mentor, but he could not have been. He was too young, born 1659. As a young man he fought with the Knights of Malta against the Turks; was nearly drowned in one engagement at sea; tried his luck as a bullfighter in Spain, was gored and survived; and came to England with his younger brother Philip, bearing introductions from the King of Sweden to Charles II. Here he became interested in a young girl, Elizabeth Percy, heiress to the Earl of Northumberland. At the age of eleven she was married to Henry Cavendish, Earl of Ogle, who died within the year. Nicknamed "Countess Carrot" because of her red hair, child as she was, she was a prize catch for a fortune hunter. While Karl Johan von K was off on one of his adventures (fighting the Moors in Tangier?), young Lady Ogle was abducted, some of her own family conniving, and was married off to Thomas Thynne, a member of Parliament, wealthy on his own account; "Tom of Ten Thousand" was his nickname, but he is Issachar in John Dryden's *Absalom and Achitophel*, line 778. Karl Johan returned and surveyed the scene. In giving thought to the altered circumstances, Count Karl Johan asked the Swedish resident minister whether someone who killed Thynne in a duel might legally be able to marry his widow. The answer was apparently not favorable. So Count Karl Johan arranged to have Tom Thynne waylaid in his coach and murdered. It was clumsily done; the killers, devil-may-care retainers of the

Count, George Borosky, John Stern and Christopher Vratz, were caught, were tried, pleaded *not guilty,* were convicted and were hung. Karl Johan von K was tried on the charge of being accessory before the fact, and was acquitted in what was universally regarded as a deliberate miscarriage of justice, for which Charles II was partly responsible. Karl Johan went off to further adventures, and died at Argos in Greece again in war with the Turks. The twice widowed Lady Ogle, still a teen-aged virgin at all reports, was presently and permanently married to Charles Seymour, Duke of Somerset, and achieved the repute of being one of the most virtuous matrons at the Court of William and Mary; which did not save her from being the target, for reasons of party spite, of verses by Jonathan Swift, in anonymous broadsides accusing her of a share in Tom Thynne's death,

> And dear Englond, if ought I understond,
> Beware of Carrots from Northumberlond.
> Carrots sown Thyn a deep root may get,
> If so be they are in Sommer set:
> Their Conyngs mark thou, for I have been told,
> They assassine when young, and poison when old.
> Root out these Carrots, O Thou, whose name
> Is backwards and forwards always the same;

(That palindromic name is Anna, or Queen Anne, who did not take kindly to these hints. *Conyngs* = cunning, spelled so for the allusion but also because these lines are supposed to be from an old parchment manuscript, *The W-ds-r Prophecy,* for which see: Harold Williams, editor, *The Poems of Jonathan Swift,* 1958, Clarendon Press, Oxford, volume I, pages 145-148; and *Jonathan Swift, A Critical Biography,* by John Middleton Murry, 1955.) Tom Thynne remains immortalized in a marble bas-relief at Westminster Abbey vividly portraying the attack on the coach.

Karl Johan's younger brother Philip Christopher was with him in England, and later travelled on the continent, presently arriving at Hanover. Here the ruling prince was the Elector George, and his wife was Sophia Dorothea. Philip Christopher and Sophia Dorothea were soon convinced that no love on earth had ever been to compare with theirs, and for some time they shared the bliss and the woes of an illicit amour. Unfortunately for them, George became annoyed at the situation, because he had dynastic and political ambitions to think about. Commands were given. Suddenly in 1694 Philip Christopher vanished without explanation and without a trace. Sophia Dorothea was subjected to a trial on the technical ground of malicious desertion, before a consistorial court, which pronounced a state of divorce between her and George, who then shut her up in close captivity for the remaining thirty-two years of her life, while he went on to be crowned George I, King of England.

Philip, it will be remembered, had a sister Maria Aurora. When her brother stopped answering letters and was otherwise unheard from, she came over to look for him. She did not find him, but she did meet Augustus II of Poland and Saxony, became his mistress and the mother of Marshal de Saxe (1696-1750), the famous French general—and *his* mistress was the actress Adrienne Lecouvreur, since famous in drama and opera.

There is a large literature on the Königsmarcks. For the above account, most useful have been the ever-valuable Zedler; the *Dictionary of National Biography* (Thynne); Henry Vizitelly, *Count Königsmarck and "Tom of Ten Thousand,"* London, Vizitelly & Co., 1890; Eveline Godley, editor, *The Trial of Count Königsmarck*, London, 1929; *The Trial and Condemnation of George Borosky, alias Borotzi, Christopher Vratz and John Stern for the Barbarous Murder of Thomas Thynn, Esq. Together with the Tryal of Charles John Count Coningsmarck as Accessory before the fact to the Same Murder. Who was Acquitted of the Said Offence. At the Sessions in the Old Bailey, Tuesday, February 28, 1681. London. Printed for Thomas Basset at the George near St. Dunstan's Church in Fleet-Street, 1681;* William Henry Wilkins. *The Love of an Uncrowned Queen. Sophia Dorothea, Consort of George I and her Correspondence with Philip Christopher Count Königsmarck (Now first Published from the Originals),* H. S. Stone & Co., New York, 1901—the originals at the University of Lund; *The Diary of John Evelyn,* edited by E.S. De Beer, Oxford, 1955, IV, 260-276; James Kingsley, "Historical Allusions in Absalom and Achitophel," *The Review of English Studies,* N.S. vi, 1955, 291-297.

67. So far as I have been able to trace, the prime source for the statement that Leyser was involved by a Swedish nobleman was the letter of H. G. Masius of October 31, 1684, printed by Pierre Bayle (see below). From Bayle it was picked up by early bibliographical specialists, who added the names of Königsmarck and Wrangel from rumor and gossip, with expressions of doubt as to whether it was true: Jakob Friedrich Reimmanus, *Versuch Einer Einleitung in die Historiam Literariam,* Halle, ("Attempt at an Introduction to Literary History"), 1708, IV, 615, and his *Catalogus Bibliothecae Theologicae Systematico-Criticus* ("Systematic-Critical Catalogue of the Theological Library"), 1731, Hildesheim, Ludolph Schroeder, page 696. Reimmann was cited by Johan Vogt, *Catalogus Historico-Criticus Librorum Rariorum,* ("Historico-Critical Catalog of Rare Books") publisher Christianus Heroldus, Hamburg, 1753, and so on; the statement is carried down to current encyclopedias with no additional information and usually the wrong Königsmarck.

I was therefore thrilled to find a copy of the 1672 *Kurtzes Bedencken* of Balthasar Mentzer (stowed away in the dark and cramped basement under the dormitory that serves for dead storage for the Harvard Law Library) which had handwritten notes on the title page, on the obverse of the title page and elsewhere, which, while anonymous and barely legible, may be the oldest testimony available. The anonymous writer states that he has the story from the son of the author of—here the script is illegible: it might refer to Tabbert, *praeses* of Büttner's dissertation. The note states that the occasion for the

Mentzer publication was the request of Count Königsmarck's wife, she the daughter of Count Wrangel; identifies the Getreuester Serviteur as Gerhardus Si---us (last name partly illegible) palace chaplain of Count Wrangel; and indicates that the person who wrote under the name Sincerus Wahrenberg was military chaplain to Count von Königsmarck.

In an effort to identify Gerhardus Si—us, I considered and rejected Ernest Gerhard Siricius, son of Michael Siricius, as too young, and then ransacked scores of bibliographies, and other seventeenth century sources. With the cooperation of Gösta Johnsen, librarian at Uppsala University, a search was made through the *Herdaminne* (biographical memoirs of Swedish clergy) for Stockholm, Göteborg, Uppsala, Hernösand, Strengnas, and others; the Swedish genealogical records at the Church of Jesus Christ of Latter Day Saints, Salt Lake City, were checked through the courtesy of Naoma Harker there; Dr. L. Häusler of the Genealogiska Byrån, Uppsala, checked through the Königsmarck and Wrangel papers, including the manuscripts at the University of Uppsala, the Skokloster archives and the Rydboholm collection: there are disputes between Conrad Christopher von Königsmarck and Carl Gustav Wrangel on military matters, disputes on inheritances due to Maria Christina Wrangel, but nothing obviously related to our question. Both Johnsen and Häusler inferred that Si---us was more likely a German name than Swedish. Two years later, after following up a seemingly endless number of blind leads, in reading up on Lassenius (of whom later) I found in Zedler the name of Gerlach Siassius, pastor of the German congregation of St. Peter's Church, Copenhagen, Lassenius' predecessor there. A letter to Rev. Niels Hasselmann, present pastor of that same congregation, brought confirmation that Gerlach Siassius (1631-1676) had been chaplain to Carl Gustav Wrangel some years before coming to St. Peter's church in 1673.

Our anonymous informant on the flyleaf of the 1672 pamphlet was therefore helpful even if he had the name not quite right. A pity he did not also supply the real name of

Sincerus Wahrenberg in the same note: Leyser's name as author was written onto the title page, but by someone else?

Leyser never in his books admitted to being "Sincerus Wahrenberg", and some seventeenth century writers treated them as separate persons. The case for the identification is basically that no other name was ever suggested; that he is the only likely candidate; and that on that basis he was so identified by Kulpis, Thomasius, Ludovici, Benjamin Christophorus Hermann, Clugius, and others, of whom more anon.

Further clues are offered by two churchmen who wrote about their contacts with Leyser. S. W. Schlüter (of whom more below) wrote that Leyser claimed to him that Wahrenberg stood for a secretary to Königsmarck: this constitutes an admission by Leyser of his association with Königsmarck's circle, and suggests that there may have been a collaboration of Leyser with one or more others, which could also be argued from the style. Johan Diecmann at Stade in 1677 baited Leyser by showing that he had lifted sentences out of "Wahrenberg"; Leyser's answer was evasive.

68. My thanks to Mr. Gösta Johnsen of the University of Uppsala library for making available to me both the originals and microfilms of the 1670 *Schreiben,* the 1671 *Kurtzes Bedencken* and the *Wahrenberg* pamphlet. The 1670 *Schreiben* has the *Serviteur* foreword on the verso of the title page and 14 unnumbered pages. There is a copy also at the Stockholm Royal Library. The 1671 *Kurtzes Bedencken* (copy also at Stockholm Royal Library) has title page, Mentzer's Vorbericht (2 pages), title page of the 1670 Schreiben with its text 2-16, and the *Bedencken* with the inter-sliced *Wahrenberg,* 17-75. There is a second edition of *Kurtzes Bedencken,* with the same pagination as 1671 but different typographical ornaments, and different place of publication, which on the title page is *Franckfurt am Mayn, In Verlegung Johann David Zunners, Buchh. Druckts zu Darmstadt, Henning Müller, Fürstl. Buchdr. Anno 1672,* "Frankfurt am Main, published by Johan David Zunner, Bookseller, printed at Darmstadt by Henning Müller,

printer to His Highness, 1672"; copies at Harvard Law Library and at Harvard Andover Theological Library.

The copy of the Wahrenberg pamphlet in the Palmskiold collection at Uppsala is neatly printed on good paper. The title page has *SINCERI Wahrenbergs Kurtzes Gespräch von der Polygami,* the first and last words in Roman type, the others in German Fraktur type, with no other information. It has title page with Wahrenberg's Vorbericht on the verso, and text 3-23. The Vorbericht speaks of the Serviteur pamphlet as published a few weeks earlier, which puts the Wahrenberg pamphlet after November 25, 1670 and before October 1671.

Mentzer's reprinted texts differ from the Wahrenberg original only slightly, in some spellings, punctuation and misprints. Mentzer (1614-1679) also published in quarto *Eine Predigt im Saal des Königlichen Schlosses zu Stockholm Gehalten,* 1670 ("A Sermon Delivered in the Hall of the Royal Castle at Stockholm") and other works.

69. Gesenius' *Epistola* is dated July 1672 in the text, 1673 on the title page. No publisher is named and the place is given as *Germanopolis,* which might be any one of a number of cities. My photocopies are from the University of Illinois and Harvard Andover Theological Library; thirty-six quarto pages. The copy at the University of Uppsala is from a different printing and has an Errata page added. Gesenius was church superintendent at Garleben; died 1687.

70. *PUFENDORF* continued to suffer for nearly a decade from the false allegation that he was "Wahrenberg". To his opponents, whether they were principled or dishonest, the allegation seemed plausible because of his tolerant and undogmatic views on polygamy printed in his acknowledged works.

The *Index Quarundam Novitatum, Quas Dnus Samuel Puffendorff Libro Suo de Jure Naturae et Gentium Contra Orthodoxa Fundamenta edidit Londini Anno M.DC.LXXIII* ("Index of Certain Novelties which Mr. Samuel Pufendorf

Published in His Book On the Law of Nature and Nations against Orthodox Fundamentals, Lund, 1673," copy at Stockholm Royal Library, quarto, title page with blank verso, ten unnumbered pages) was published anonymously. It subsequently became known that it was composed by Josua Schwarz (or Schwartz), a theologian at Lund, for private circulation in manuscript, and (it seems) without his participation printed by Nicolaus Beckmann, a jurist there. The *Index* tabulates Pufendorf's deviations from strict Lutheran dogma on God, Scripture, Original Sin, the Ten Commandments, etc. Item 24 quotes from Pufendorf's discussion of polygamy.

Pufendorf's *Apologia Pro Se* (copy at Stockholm Royal Library) has title page with blank verso, pages 1-86, 4°. His *Epistola* to Scherzer, dated September 17, 1674 is 4°, title page with blank verso, 17 unnumbered pages (copies at Stockholm Royal Library and University of Uppsala).

Gesenius refused to accept Pufendorf's denial of being Wahrenberg, or to swallow the implication that he himself had made false accusations. He therefore published *Domini Samuelis Pufendorfii Juris Naturalis Doct. & Profess. Contra Jus Naturae Iniquitas Inque Illius Scrutinio Infelicitas in Cautionem Pro Incautis et Vindicationem Nominis Publicè ostensa per V. D. M. Qui se contra Sincerum Warenbergium Christianum Vigilem nominare & adversus ἄθεος illius de Polygamia assertiones pro munere sibi in Ecclesia DEI credito debite voluit Vigilare . . . Germanopoli, Anno 1674* ("Mr. Samuel Pufendorf, Doctor and Professor of Natural Law, Against the Law of Nature His Iniquity and His Infelicity in His Scrutiny Thereof, in a Caution to the Incautious and Vindication of His name by V.D.M., who called himself Christianus Vigil against Sincerus Wahrenberg and against that Atheist's Assertions on Polygamy Wished to keep Vigilant according to the Duty Entrusted to Him in the Church of God;" copies at University of Leipzig, Stockholm Royal Library and University of Uppsala, 4°, title page with quotation from Wilhelm Grotius on verso, 1-66 pages, and Errata. Gesenius here cited from Pufendorf's other writings to reinforce the account he had previously given of Wahrenberg.

When Pufendorf reiterated his denial in the *Epistola* to Scherzer, Gesenius came out again with *Christiani Vigilis V. D. M. Christiana Benedictio ad Impiam & Immanem maledicentiam Dni. Sam. Pufendorfii I. N. D. & P. Quam Ille in Epistola ad Celeberrimum Virum Dn. Joh. Adamum Scherzerum Theologum apud Lipsienses Primarium effutiit (etc.) Germanopoli. Anno MDCLXXV* ("Christianus Vigil, V. D. M., A Christian Benediction to the Impious and Monstrous Malediction of Mr. Samuel Pufendorf, Doctor and Professor of Natural Law, Which He Spouts in the Epistola to the Celebrated Gentleman Mr. Johan Adamus Scherzer, Theologian Primarius in Leipzig," 1675; copies at Stockholm Royal Library and Uppsala University; title page with quotation on obverse from I Peter iii, and 32 unnumbered pages). He continues to harp on the alleged identity of Wahrenberg and Pufendorf.

Pufendorf's position at this time was secure enough, and his side of the case clear enough, for a royal order to be issued condemning Beckmann's printing of the *Index* to be publicly burned. Having lost out on his preferment, Beckmann is said to have intrigued against Pufendorf, even to have sought to use the occasion of Swedish-Danish hostilities to have him killed. He certainly continued his pamphlet feud, publishing *De Magistri Samuelis Pufendorfii Professoris Philosophiae in Carolina Schanorum Academia, execrabili Iuris Doctrina, horrendo atheismo, perversis moribus, & belluina vita brevissimè, sed verissimè scribit. Severini de Monzambano & Tenebrionis Asinij justus censor Veridicus Constans, Qui eo sine id facit, ut omnes literati ore, corde, & calamo pestiferam ficti hujus Severini, sivè Tenebrionis Asinij, h. e. Puffendorffij doctrinam exstirpare conentur. In Academia Catoniana calumnijs & risui Puffendorffij contraria* ("Veridicus Constans, the Just Censor of Severino de Monzambano and the Ass of Darkness, Briefly but Truthfully Writes of the Execrable Doctrine of Law, Shocking Atheism, Perverse Conduct and Bestial Life of Master Samuel Pufendorf, Professor of Philosophy in

Charles University in Skane; who does this to that end that all educated persons should strive by word of mouth, by heart and by pen to extirpate the pestiferous doctrine of this so-called Severino, or Ass of Darkness, that is, Pufendorf. In the University of Cato, against the calumnies and sneers of Pufendorf;" no date or place; copy at Stockholm Royal Library, 4°, title page, 14 pages of text starting on the verso, final verso blank.) Among other charges, Beckmann again repeats the allegation that Pufendorf was Wahrenberg. *Severino de Monzambano* was a pen name actually used by Pufendorf. *Cato* was the ancient censor of morals at Rome. *Veridicus Constans* means "constant speaker of the truth."

To this attack, and others, Pufendorf answered in *Samuelis Pufendorfii Epistola Ad Amicos suos per Germaniam, super Libello famoso, quem Nicolaus Beckmannus quondam Professor in Academia Carolina, nunc vero cum infamia inde relegatus, mentito nomine Veridici Constantis superiori anno disseminavit. ANNO MDCLXXVI.* ("Samuel Pufendorf's Epistle to His Friends Throughout Germany on the notorious libel, which Nicolaus Beckmann, formerly professor in Charles University, now dismissed thence in disgrace, last year published under the lying name of Veridicus Constans. 1676" copy at Stockholm Royal Library, 8°, title page with blank verso, 74 unnumbered pages). In addition to much autobiographical data, Pufendorf makes this statement:

"Not only did Beckmann himself know that the Dialogue of Sincerus Wahrenberg was not written by me; but it is well known to him who really is the author of that book, because in Sweden it is well known (*notorius*) who he is"—why did Pufendorf not name this so notorious character?

Pufendorf repeats the assertion that Beckmann knows the real Wahrenberg, in a letter to Gottfried Klinger, January 10, 1676 (printed from a Göttingen library manuscript by Christoph A. Heumann in *Acta Philosophorum,* published by Renger, Halle, Part XVI, 1725, pages 647-658.) Pufendorf wrote: "Uxor mea mihi carissima, & formae sat felicis, paris mecum est aetatis, & Heidelbergae duabus me filiabus parentem fecit"

—"My wife is to me most dear, her looks are good enough, of an age with me, and at Heidelberg she made me father of two girls."

Actually Pufendorf may not have been so sure of that name. In another context he was said to have thought that Wahrenberg was "medicum quendam Suecum"—"some Swedish doctor" (so noted by Christian Thomasius, *Paulo Plenior Historia Juris Naturalis,* 1719, page 94, from Pufendorf's burlesque *Josuae Schwarzii Dissertatio Epistolica ad Eximium Unum Iuvenem Severinum Wildschyssium Privignum Suum,* Hamburg, 1688, "Josua Schwarz's Epistolary Dissertation to One Exceptional Youth Severin Wildschütz His Foster Son").

The Beckman-Pufendorf feud, with references to Gesenius and Schwarz, continues through more long-titled pamphlets for several years, in which the Wahrenberg allegation is blurred into other issues, so that these sequels belong rather to the biography of Pufendorf. Some of Pufendorf's defensive writings appeared in other formats, as in the *Appendix* to his *Dissertationes Academicae Selectiores,* enlarged edition published by Christian Weidman, Frankfurt and Leipzig, 1678 (New York Public Library); and in collected form at Frankfurt, 1686, as *Eris Scandica, Qua Adversus Libros de Iure Naturali et Gentium Objecta Diluuntur* ("Scandinavian Discord, in which Objections against His Books on the Law of Nature and Nations are Refuted") and so reprinted in the 1759 two volume Knochio-Eslingeriana edition of his *De Iure* at Frankfurt and Leipzig. The feud is outlined in Johannes Moller, *Cimbria Literata,* 1744, II, 819-828, article "Josua Schwartz".

This "Wahrenberg"-Pufendorf episode was discussed by Johannes Deckherr, Procurator of the Imperial Court at Speyer, in *De Scriptis Adespotis, Pseudepigraphis et Suppositibus, Conjecturae,* "Conjectures on Anonymous, Pseudepigraphical and Forged Writings," third edition, Amsterdam, 1686, pages 341-342 (Columbia University); by Jacob Friedrich Ludovici, *Delineatio Historiae Juris Divini Naturalis et Positivi Universalis,* "Outline of the History of Divine Natural

Law and Divine Universal Positive Law," published by Renger at Halle, 1701 (British Museum); by Christian Thomasius, *Paulo Plenior Historia Juris Naturalis,* "Somewhat Fuller History of the Law of Nature," etc., Halle, 1719 (Harvard University); and since then has been ignored by writers on Pufendorf.

Pufendorf's *De Jure Naturae et Gentium* brought Milton's ideas on divorce (not on polygamy) to the notice of Continental readers who might never have otherwise heard of them. One of these was Johannes Eccardus Finck, who discussed Pufendorf-on-Milton-on-Divorce in a dissertation *Usum Divortium ex Divino et Humano hocque Civili aeque ac Canonico Jure* ("The Practice of Divorce according to Divine Law and Human Law, that is both Civil and Canon Law") at the press of Heinrich Meyer, university printer at Altdorf, April 28, 1686 (copy at New York Public Library). Another was Christian Thomasius, of whom more herein, in his *Institutionum Jurisprudentiae Divinae Libri Tres,* "Three Books on the Institutes of Divine Jurisprudence," Halle, 1688 and other editions, Book III, Chapter III, Sections 67-70.

71. My photocopies of *Aletophilus Germanus* are from the University of Illinois and from the British Museum. All libraries with copies have only Gesenius' edition, in every case where I have checked. Clugius suggested that it was written by Leyser in German, translated into Latin by Gesenius, and so never published by Leyser himself; strange, but perhaps it is so. The pamphlet has title page; *Cautio et Praefatio,* 4 pages; *Dialogus inter Monogamum & Polygamum,* 11 pages.

Linsius in 1674 and Calovius-Kannenberg in their 1676 *De Polygamia* refer to the author of the *Epistola* to Wahrenber as "Candidus Vigil Germanus," rather than as "Christianus Vigil Germanus". This suggests another issue bearing the signature in that form, but I find no trace of any such.

72. Calovius in his 1677 published account, written 1674 (see note 64 above) refers to Leyser as *sine lare oberrans,* "wan-

dering without a hearth of his own," and mentions France, Germany and Denmark. Leyser also mentions France in his Stockholm testimony, 1679, but I have found no other data on this phase. He did go back to France (Paris, Versailles) just before he died, seeking help from former patrons.

73. My photocopy of Linsius is from the University of Kiel, (thanks to Dr. H. Seyffert). He is not quoted by later writers.

Also published in 1674 at Leipzig, at the press of Johan Erich Hahn, was a dissertation dated October 19 of that year, by Johan Friedrich Mayer, *Admirabile Jacobi cum Duabus Sororibus Conjugium,* "The Remarkable Marriage of Jacob with Two Sisters," out of Genesis xxix. If bigamy was a perennial problem to theologians, Jacob's marriage with two sisters was a most hardy perennial. Mayer speculates on who Cain's wife might have been; echoes the Havemann-Buchholz argument on marriage with a deceased wife's sister (see note 81 below); takes note of Sincerus Wahrenberg "whose mouth the great Mentzer has stopped up;" and hopes to write, or finish, a book on Ochino, which he does not seem to have accomplished. There is a copy of the 1674 text at Heidelberg University, title page with blank verso, 3-60 pages. It was reprinted at a time of revived interest in these issues as *Tractatus Theologicus de Admirabili Iacobi cum Duabus Sororibus Coniugio ex Genes. xxix,* published by Andreas Heber, Wittenberg, 1717; title page with blank verso, 3-64; copy at Universitätsbibliothek Erlangen-Nürnberg.

74. My photocopy of the 1674 *Discursus* is from the Nürnberg Stadtbibliothek; title page, blank verso, 3-96 pages.

Leyser's printers: "Cunrath" and "Friburg" are rated as fictitious names by Emil Ottokar Weller, *Die Falschen und Fingirten Druckorte. Repertorium der seit Erfindung der Buchdruckerkunst unter falscher firma erscheïnen deustchen, lateinschen und französischen Schrifften, Leipzig,* 1864, "False and Fictitious Printing Centers. Repertory of German, Latin and French Writings Appearing under False Firm Names

Since the Invention of the Art of Book Printing."

There was, however, some reason for Leyser's use of these names. The name "Heinrich Künraht" of Hamburg as publisher is found on the title page of Spinoza's *Tractatus Theologico-Politicus,* 1670, and it appears in Pierre Bayle's *Nouvelles de la République des Lettres.* Dr. Josef Benzing, (author of *Die Buchdrucker des 16. and 17. Jahrhunderts im Deutschen Sprachgebiet, Beiträge zum Buch- und Bibliothekswesen,* volume 12, Wiesbaden, 1963, "The Book Printers of the 16th and 17th Centuries in German Speaking Areas. Contributions to Book and Library Science") writes me, October 17, 1969, that "Heinrich Künrath" was the pseudonym of the Hamburg bookseller who issued Spinoza's writings. The name Henricus Kunraht, 1560-1605, is earlier found as the theosophist author of Christian-Cabbalistic-Mystical writings, *Amphitheatrum Sapientiae Aeternae Solius Verae Christiano-Kabalisticum Divino-Magicum.*

There are several places in Germany named Friburg, one near Leyser's home territory (see note 63). Analogous names like "Freystadt" are found on other author's title pages, also meaning "Free City", instead of Halle or other real cities.

In his Stockholm 1679 testimony, Leyser is recorded as saying that his books were printed at "Sell" (Celle?) and at Groningen. Diecmann (of whom anon) believed that Leyser's books (before 1677) were printed at Amsterdam. From their type and ornaments, it should be possible to identify some or all of his printers, but the resources for that effort are inadequate in the United States, I have found.

75. My photocopy of the 1675 January 1 *Discurs* is from the British Museum, which includes the two pages with the verses; title page; dedication, 2 pages of verses, 40 pages printed in two columns. My photocopy from Heidelberg University is identical in all details except that it lacks those two pages with verses. In Johan Frische's 1677 pamphlet against Leyser (of which more anon) he states that the verses were included in the first issue of that 1675 *Discurs* "printed with Dutch char-

acters in the High German tongue" and omitted in later printings. Frische also offers a German version of the first jingle:

Ihr seit furtwahr ein getstlich Mann
Denn diese Schrifft die zeigt es an:
Wist aber Ihr, was Ihr davon
Erlangen werdet für ein Lohn?
Ein hand voll Koth in das Gesicht.
Drumb last Euch ja beträten nicht
In Stäten wo der leute viel,
Sonst spielt man euch ein seltsahm Spiel.
Auch, seyd Ihr klug, so schweigt dabey
Dass Ihr von der Vielweiberey
Der Autor seyd, sonst ists verkerbt
Das leder wird Euch mürb gegerbt:
Und Euch solch Recompens geschenkt
Dass Ihr an Eine Frau gedenckt,
Und nimmer Ihrer Zwei begehrt
So lang als euer Leben währt.

Johan Brunsmann, in his *Monogamia Victrix* (1679) and his *Nuptiae Prohibitae* (1688) indicates he has heard that Leyser printed the French verses in his first edition under the delusion that they were complimentary. Brunsmann offers a Latin version of those lines:

Divine certe dogmata
Divine das, quod exitus
Facti docebit splendidi
Quum singulis rideberis
Ac pulcra gesta faetidas
Tibi rependent gratias.
Vel maxime per oppida
Majora: quà si manseris
Caveto ne te dictites
Mandasse quicquam literis,
De plurimis uxoribus:
Ne nota res quam pessime
Te plectat atque dedolet,

Ut vapulando mollius
Fiat tibi corpusculum,
Quam per coquum muraenula,
Sic ut deinceps unica
Contentus, haud desideres
Plures maritas amplius.

76. My photocopy is from the Copenhagen Royal Library. Harvard Law Library also has one. The full title reads: *Dissertatio Theologica de Quaestione Controversa, An Conjugium, primaevâ ejus institutione salvâ, inter plures, quàm duos, maritum scilicet unum, & unam uxorem, esse possit? Quâ cumprimis Locus Matthaei XIX.v.9. A Commentis Theophili Alethaei Quibus in Suo Discursu Politico de Polygamia, eius sensum genuinum pervertere laboravit, vindicatur: Thesibus de Coniugio, ex Johannis Musaei, SS. Theol. D. et P.P. praelectionibus, publicis & privatis, desumtis, per modum Appendicis adjecta, & sub ejusdem praesidio ventilationi publica exposita a M. Tobia Nicolao Herzog, Aggeripontano, in auditorio Theologico, ad d. Maji. Jenae, Literis Johannis Jacobi Bauhoferi, Anno M.DC.LXXV.* The second half of the title (first part translated in the text) reads, "Theses on Marriage, Selected from the Public and Private Lectures of Johannes Musaeus, Doctor and Professor of Sacred Theology, added by way of Appendix, and under him as *praeses* offered for public discussion by Tobias Nicholas Herzog, in the theological auditorium, on the — of May, Jena, printed by Johan Jacob Bauhöfer, 1675;" Herzog, title page, blank verso, 1-54 pages; Musaeus, title page, blank verso, 1-86 pages. *Aggeripontano* refers to Herzog's home town, Thomasbrück or Thingsbrück in Thuringia. A separate title page for Musaeus' theses gives Bauhöfer as printer and Johan Bielcke of Jena as the publisher. (The British Museum lists reprints in 1696 and 1703; the Royal Library of Copenhagen lists 1703 and 1737.)

77. Leyser's peddling is mentioned in Johan Frische and in Simplicius Christianus, of whom more anon.

The Dutch version has two title pages in my photocopy from Göttingen. The first reads *Politisch Discours tusschen Monogamo en Polygamo van de Polygamia Ofte Veelwyvery, Opgestelt, ende met 100. Argumenten verklaert. Uyt het Latijn en Hoogduyts vertaalt, en nu in 't Nederduyts Overgeset, door Johannes Lyserus. Tot Freyburgh Gedruckt, In 't Jaer Anno MDCLXXV*. (The assertion of a Latin original has no foundation). The second title page is a sales blurb, repeats Leyser's name in Latin, Johannes Lyserus, and adds "Gedruckt voor den Autheur," printed for the author. The text is the same as the 1675 German dialogue but omits the six line prayer at the end; title page, blank verso, 1-48.

78. My photocopies of this *Disputatio Theologia de Polygamia* are from the University of Göttingen and from Dr. Darapsky of the Mainz Stadtbibliothek; in title page, blank verso, and thirty unnumbered pages, printed at Wittenberg by Matthaeus Henckel, university printer, and includes complimentary Latin verses by Johan Hartung, Johan Dietrich Corbmacher, Heinrich Wohlers and Ericus Levinus Numens.

This disputation is commonly attributed to Calovius on the usual assumption that the *praeses* is the author. However, the repeated effusive references to the works of the "Magnif. D. Praesidis" show that it was composed by the respondent, Lucas Kannenberg.

Abraham Calovius (1612-1686) was one of the major Lutheran theologians of that time. In his huge *Systema Locorum Theologicorum* ("System of Theological Topics"), 1655-1677, he dealt with Leyser and polygamy in volume 8, chapter 5, pages 555-569, "On Polygamy," and in volume 11, chapter 3, pages 208-239, "Whether Concubinage or Polygamy Ever Was Permissible". Calovius approves Mentzer's reply to Wahrenberg as adequate, and devotes his attention to a point by point answer to the 1674 *Discursus* by Theophilus Alethaeus, whom he identifies as Leyser. Although his attack was not published till 1677, internal evidence dates it to 1674.

79. My photocopy of the 1676 *Discursus* is from the University of Chicago; title page, dedication, 3-173 pages. There are copies which I have used at Columbia, Harvard, Heidelberg, and elsewhere. It may be the least rare of Leyser's surviving works. Apart from the many additions which are described above, it has one omission from the 1674 text: the seven-women-one-man passage is dropped; in his *Polygamia Triumphatrix* (after 1682), Leyser blames the omission on a printer's error (page 466).

80. Leyser would have been happy to quote these lines from Milton if he had only known of them—they are Leyser's sentiments exactly:

Our Maker bids increase; who bids abstain
But our destroyer, foe to God and man?
(*Paradise Lost,* IV, 748-749)

Leyser in the same passage also speaks, as Milton does in his *Treatise of Christian Doctrine,* of many places on earth uncultivated and empty of inhabitants. These are coincidences, similar thoughts occuring to people of similar views in the same era.

81. Leyser gives no indication of ever having read the Neobulus dialogue, but his failure to mention Ochino (first mentioned by him in *Polygamia Triumphatrix,* after 1682), was surely deliberate; partly, it may be guessed, to avoid association with the anti-trinitarian and other heresies which Leyser did not share, partly because of his desire to be regarded as the original. It is obvious that some of his quotations and references come from opponents of his viewpoint like Siricius, and much from authorities like Selden. He took much material from sources which also supplied his opponents with data. Many titles could be cited which were quoted on both sides of the polygamy issue. Some of these were:

Michael Havemann (or Havemannus, 1597-1672), *Gamologia Synoptica, Istud est Tractatus de Jure Connubiorum,*

"Weddingology Surveyed, that is a Treatise of the Law of Marriages," 1655, and 1672 (two copies at Harvard). He was orthodox, but a running controversy he had with Christoph Joachim Buchholz (1607-1679) and Aegidius Strauch (1632-1682), over the Mosaic laws on marriage with the sister of a defunct wife, contributed to the formation of the intellectual climate in which Leyser wrote; so Christian Thomasius, in *Paulo Plenior Historia Juris Naturalis,* "Rather Fuller History of Natural Law," 1719, and Joachim Weickhmann, *Apologiae . . . Pars Prior* ("First Part of . . . His Apologia"), 1715, page 5. Jöcher's *Lexicon* lists the titles in their battle of the books.

Caspar Ziegler, (*Jus Canonicum,* "Canon Law," Wittenberg, 1669, 1072 pages and index, copy at Harvard), who gathered much of the data on polygamy, observed that while polygamy had been widespread, monogamy was always praised; he ruled that no matter what had been permitted to the patriarchs, their example was not to be followed. Ziegler would hardly attract notice now, except that he wrote *Observations on the English Regicides*, in Latin, 1653, defending the divine right of kings no matter how despotic, to which he prefixed an introduction maligning John Milton (see Appendix II).

Johan Bartholomaeus Herold, *Dissertatio Politico-Juridica de Polygamia Simultanea et Successiva Ejusque Justitia Interna* ("Political-Juridical Dissertation on Polygamy, Simultaneous and Successive, and its Internal Justice"), published by Johan Georg Walther, Frankfurt, 1675; xii, 63 pages; opposed to polygamy but not a controversial work, citing Musaeus of Jena, but cited by Leyser, 1676 *Discursus,* page 166; dedicated to the faculty of Heidelberg, which may be significant to our later story of Charles Louis. There is a copy at the University of Pennsylvania.

82. My photocopy of the *Discursus Abrahamiticus* is from the University of Uppsala; it has three pages of handwritten bibliographic discussion signed by C. B. Lengnich. There is a copy also at the University of Illinois. Both have title page, dedica-

tion, 3-173 pages. Mr. Robert Mackworth-Young, C.V.O., of the Royal Library at Windsor, informs me that the volume is not known there. Leyser calls Henry VIII (not named, but identified as him to whom Melanchthon wrote that polygamy was not against divine law) *proavus,* "ancestor," to Charles II, but Charles II was descended from Henry VIII's sister Margaret.

On page 157 of the 1676 *Discursus,* Leyser says that the 100-arguments-from-Scripture dialogue is out in German, Dutch, Swedish and English: we have seen no evidence of any in Swedish or English.

83. Not being able to assemble all the possible copies of the 1676 German *Discurs* in one place, I am not certain of the number of issues or their exact sequence, but all are after the 1676 Latin *Discursus,* which they mention. One of the changes in the 1676 German *Discurs* is the inclusion of two pages as a sort of supplementary summary argument, under an ornamental border on the first of these two pages. In my microfilm copy of the 1676 *Politischer Discurs* from the Stadtbibliothek Nürnberg, the two pages are at the end. They are also bound at the end in the copy of the same title at Harvard, in which these two pages are in a larger format than the rest, as if from a different issue. In my photocopy of the *Discurs* with the *Königliche Marck* title, from the British Museum, these two pages are bound in at the beginning of the book after the dedication, and the ornamental border is slightly different from the Nürnberg copy. In my photocopy of the *Königliche Marck* from the Herzog August Bibliothek of Wolfenbüttel those two pages have the same ornament as the British Museum copy but are bound in at the end. Otherwise, all copies have title page, dedication, 48 pages. The copy of the *Politischer Discurs* of 1676 at Leipzig University, once owned by Caspar Heinrich Starck of Lübeck, at one time belonged to someone who filled many pages with now illegible handwriting, bound interleaved with the printed text, adding two scribbled pages before and thirteen pages after of additional comment: my inspection

did not yield any ready identification to any of Leyser's known commentators.

The phrase *Das Königliche Marck aller Länder* was often used by Leyser's contemporaries and the next generations as if it were the title of his book, and was perhaps the title most commonly associated with his name. Copies with that line are rather rare.

84. If all the Nicodemuses named by Leyser had left as much of value as Milton, they might be worth the trouble of extended study. Since their surviving works are likely not to include clues to any covert views on polygamy, I limit myself to seeking them mainly in the writings of Leyser and his opponents, and in the ever valuable works of Nicéron, Jöcher and Zedler.

Johan Huelsemann, 1602-1661, theologian, is mentioned by Leyser as his teacher "never to be praised enough" (*Examen Examinis,* 1677, page 27). Johan Diecmann, *Vindiciae Legis Monogamicae,* "Defenses of the Law of Monogamy," 1678, says that Huelsemann conceded that polygamy was not against the law of nature but banned by divine positive law (page 4). Gottlieb Wernsdorff, *Summam Sanae Doctrinae de Polygamia,* etc. ("Summation of Sound Doctrine on Polygamy", 1716), page 46, says that according to Huelsemann, polygamy was a sin only under divine positive law, not a mortal sin under the Ten Commandments.

Georg Adam Struve (not J. A. Struve, as Leyser has), 1619-1691, has 158 titles of publications to his credit listed in Zedler.

Johan Andreas Bosius, 1626-1674, is mentioned in Leyser's *Polygamia Triumphatrix,* page 520) as his one time best friend, a fine philologist; for his life, besides Zedler, see Johan Christoph Rüdiger (= Adolphus Clarmundus), *Vitae Clarissimorum in Re Literaria Virorum,* ("Lives of the Most Famous Men in Literary Affairs"), 1704, and other editions, volume 2; Alexander Chalmers, editor, *The General Biographical Dictionary,* 1812; his works are catalogued in the *Bibliothecae Philosophicae Struvianae,* Göttingen, 1740, II, 226, of

Burkhard Gotthelf Struve (son of Georg Adam Struve). For Bosius' correspondence with Nicholas Heinsius, Emeric Bigot and others, see Burmann's *Sylloges Epistolarum,* and [Johann Ludwig Uhl], *Sylloge Nova Epistolarum Varii Argumenti,* "New Collection of Letters on Various Topics," Felsecker's Heirs, Nuremberg, 1760-1769.

Friedrich Breckling, 1629-1711, was a Boehmenist mystic, a heretic among Lutherans. He is in the *Allgemeine Deutsche Biographie;* in the British Museum Catalogue; and in Johannes Moller's *Cimbria Literata* (1744),

Abendana may be either Jacob Ben Joseph Abendana, rabbinical scholar at Amsterdam and London, 1630-c.1695, or his brother Isaac Ben Joseph Abendana, also a rabbinical scholar in the Netherlands and at Oxford, England, died 1710. Both are in Moller's *Cimbria Literata.*

Heinrich Hahn, 1605-1668, of Helmstedt, a lawyer, teacher of G. A. Struve, much quoted by Boeckelmann in his 1659 *Diversa Iuris Themata,* of which more later, and by Leyser in the preface to his 1679 *Gewissenhaffte Gedancken.* His life is in Johann Friedrich Jugler, *Beyträge zur Juristischen Biographie,* "Contributions to the Lives of the Lawyers," Leipzig, 1778.

Hendrick Diest, 1595-1673, professor of theology, is again picked out for particular mention by Leyser in his later 1679 prefaces. I have seen Diest's *Analysis Apocalypseos Exegetica,* 1673, ("Exegetical Analysis of Revelation"), in which he reads Huss and Luther into the text of Revelation, as well as the ancient Arian, Nestorian, Eutychian and other heresies; and interprets its 144,000-virgins-not-defiled-with-women text as "non corporalis sed spiritualis" ("Not physically but spiritually," page 51). Leyser may have known him better.

Cardinal Giovanni Bona, 1609-1674, was a maverick among Catholics; his life is in Nicéron. Andrea Suesinger, died 1695, was a Lutheran theologian. Less certain of identification is Jungius: Joachim Jungius, polymath, 1557-1667, or Hermann Jungius (died 1678), who are among the few Jungs who Latinized their names that way rather than Junius. "Frenkenst" may be Christian Friedrich Franckenstein of Leipzig, professor of Latin language and history, 1621-1679; or Johan Leonardus Franckenstein, M.A., Leipzig, 1649, in Vetter; both are mentioned by Gebauer.

There are many possible Wagners and Müllers. Gebauer mentions a Thomas Wagner and a Daniel Müller, who are therefore eligible. More likely is Heinrich Müller, of Rostock, 1631-1675, professor of theology, mentioned favorably by Leyser in *Polygamia Triumphatrix,* page 35. Zedler says he studied with Huelsemann and Calovius.

Dirchovius might be Bernard Derschau, 1601-1639, theologian, or Reinhold Derschau, jurist, both of Königsberg; or it may be a misprint for some Kirchovius of no great fame.

Rivetus could be André, 1573-1671, and Museus could be Johan, 1613-1681, although their published positions are so contrary to Leyser's. Each had a brother who was also in the theology business, William Rivet and Petrus Musaeus, who could conceivably be the men whom Leyser meant, and are as unlikely. Leyser respectfully concedes a point of interpretation to Musaeus, citing the latter's dissertation of 1675 against himself in his *Polygamia Triumphatrix,* page 476. When Musaeus in 1675 wrote that dissertation, he had already seen his name in Leyser's list of Nicodemuses, but he seems to have taken no notice of it, unless that dissertation be considered the answer to his inclusion in the list.

Liset, Haersurt and Hausen have been checked in many variant spellings in many possible sources, and I am still looking for them.

Feltmann is the only writer against Leyser who applies himself to that list. Diecmann, *Vindiciae,* page 60, cited Feltmann. Others merely scoff or deny: Simplicius Christianus, page 5, 92; Schlüter, pages 229-230; and Johan Brunsmann, page 212; in their works to be discussed anon. The names added in 1676 were the eight from Jung through Spinoza. In the first 1675 edition some of the names are peculiarly shortened, *Frenkenst., Boclmn,* as if the name were added and squeezed in after the page was set in type. These peculiarities were carried over, with some variations, in later printings. One important word *mir,* "to me," in that passage, is misprinted *mit* in 1676 and in the 1679 *Gewissenhaffte Gedancken.*

85. My photo copies of the 1677 German edition of Feltmann's *Tractatus de Polygamia* are from the Bayerische Staatsbibliothek and from the British Museum; title page, blank verso, 1-217. There are two copies at Erlangen-Nürnberg and copies elsewhere. My photocopy of the Dutch translation is from the text in volume 7 of *Duorum Fratrum Gerhardi et Theodori Feltman, Jurisconsultorum Doctissimorum Opera Juridica,* etc., "Juridical Works of the Two Brothers Gerhard and Theodore Feltmann, Most Learned Lawyers," edited by Johan Jacob van Hasselt, published by H. Möelemann, Arnheim, 1769, pages 159-298 (at Harvard). I have found no trace of a 1676 Bremen edition in Latin or a 1677 Jena edition as mentioned in Johan Fridericus Cotta's notes to *Ioannis Gerhardi Locorum Theologicorum Tomus XV* ("Johan Gerhard's Theological Texts," Volume 15") Tübingen, 1776, page 199.

The reference to Milton in Feltmann follows, first from the German text (there, page 214) and then from the Dutch text (there, page 297):

Milton habe ich alles, was ich dir gesagt, selbst als er blind worden und in den Felden bey Westmünster wohnete, einmal in Gegenwart des Geheimschreibers der Niederländischen Abgesandten, und hernacher als dieses Sohn dabey ware, in die Nase gerieben, da er dann allein dabey beharrete, dass die Vielweiberey nicht ausdrücklich von dem Gesetzgeber Moses verboten, und bey den Israelitẽ im Gebrauch gewesen.

Milton hebbe ik alles, wat ik uw gezegt hebbe, zelfs als Hy blind was geworden en in de velden by Westmunster woonde, eens in tegenwoordigheid van den Geheim-Schryver van den Nederlandschen Ambassadeur, en daar na als desselfs

Zoon daar by was, in de neus gevreven, daar by dan alleen daar by bleef, dat de veelvyverye niet uitdrukkelijk van den Wetgever Moses verboden, en by de Israëliten in gebruik was geweest.

It is a pity Feltmann was not more precise. The "son of the ambassador" might be a son of Jacob Cats or of Gerard Schaep or of Paulus van der Perre who jointly composed the Embassy. It may also be suspected that reference was really being made to the son of an earlier noted ambassador, Constantine Huygens, senior, whose son Lodewijck Huygens was Vlitius' inseparable companion in England, as he is described in: A. G. H. Bachrach, "Mon fils Ludovicq passant en Angleterre," in *Proceedings of the Huguenot Society of London,* XXII (1971), pages 24-40. Prof. Bachrach, of the Sir Thomas Browne Instituut, University of Leyden, confirms for me (letter, 29 September 1971) that Vlitius' name in Dutch was Jan Van Vliet. Vlitius used *Janus* as his Latinized first name. *James,* given in recent American writings as his first name, is incorrect.

One other person who could have had direct knowledge of Milton's views on polygamy may have been Philip van Limborch (1633-1712), professor at the Theological College for Remonstrants, who was given the manuscript of Milton's *Treatise of Christian Doctrine* about 1675 to read on behalf of the publishing firm of Daniel Elzevir. Van Limborch advised them against publishing it because of its unitarian heresy, which shows that he read as far as Chapter V. Did he read on to Chapter X, on polygamy? Limborch's comment was made in 1711 to Zacharias Conrad von Uffenbach, who recorded it in his *Merkwürdige Reisen durch Niedersachsen, Holland und Engelland* ("Notable Journeys in Lower Saxony, Holland and England"), Ulm, 1754, III (edited by Johan Georg Schelhorn), page 585. Neither in his *Theologia Christiana* (1686) nor his *De Veritate Religionis Christianae Amica Collatio cum Erudito Judaeo* ("Friendly Conversation With an Erudite Jew on the Truth of the Christian Religion"),

1687, is there any reference to Milton or any other polygamophile. Van Limborch knew Velthuysen whom we shall presently encounter.

86. There is a byplay and sequel to these events at Kiel. In 1674 Kortholt had made welcome a refugee Protestant from Hungary, Stephen Fequet (or Fekete) who had fled from religious persecution there. Fequet travelled on, to Sweden and elsewhere, carrying letters of introduction from Kiel University. Later, about 1681, Fequet became converted to Catholicism, and thereafter, in anti-Protestant propaganda at Bratislava, asserted that Kiel University was a hotbed of defenders of polygamy; which evoked a pained outcry of denial by Christian Kortholt in a *Send-Schreiben, Worin die verleumbderische Aufflage, ob solte auff der Hoch Fürstl. Holstein-Kielschen Universität die Polygamie oder Vielweiberey öffentlich gebilliget und behauptet werden, gründlich abgeleinet und hintertrieben wird. Kiel. Gedruckt durch Joachim Reuman, Acad. Buchdr., 1682* ("Circular Letter, wherein the Defamatory Charge whether in the University of Holstein Grand Duchy and Kiel Polygamy or Many-Wiving be Openly Sanctioned or Upheld is Thoroughly Denied and Rebutted. Kiel, Printed by Joachim Reuman, University Printer, 1682"), in 36 pages, with date of January 12, 1682, addressed to Wilhelm Ver Poorten, superintendent of the church of Coburg. My photocopy is from the British Museum. This *Send-Schreiben* is our sole source for Leyser at Kiel. Dr. F. A. Schmidt-Künsemüller of the Kiel University Library confirmed my understanding of this byway, but had no additional data or dates (letter, June 24, 1969). Dr. H. Sievert, Archivdirektorin of the Kiel City Archives, informs me, letter, March 18, 1970, that the municipal records are incomplete, with no mention of Leyser's expulsion. The same negative report is given (June 8, 1970) by the Landesarchiv Schleswig-Holstein at Schloss Gottorf, that there is no notice in their archives of action on Leyser by Kiel city, Kiel University or the Duchy of Gottorf, then suzerain over Kiel.

I estimate 1676 for Leyser at Kiel because Kortholt refers to the German *Discurs* with the initials J. L., and does not use Leyser's full name. I put Güstrow next with no great conviction. Fridericus Thomas put the stop at Güstrow before Stade with Copenhagen third, but the latter sequence is less likely. Schlüter (early 1677) says Leyser recently had to leave the neighborhood, and Diecmann (early 1678) says Leyser had been forced out of several cities. That Leyser was in Copenhagen in 1676 is indicated by his testimony given in 1679 at Stockholm, mentioning Lassenius and the queen mother's confessor (that is, Schlüter). Schlüter's text at least three times dates his book to 1677, but does not mention the decree of Christian V, so we estimate it as early 1677, and Leyser's contact with him (at Rostock or at Copenhagen) to late 1676. Güstrow may have followed the stop at Rostock but preceding Schlüter's book. Professor Bernhard Wandt, head of archives at Rostock University, writes me October 26, 1971 that intensive investigation turned up no records of Leyser at the university or the theological faculty there. Other efforts to obtain archival data from Rostock and Güstrow by correspondence have proved unavailing.

87. *LASSENIUS'* contact with Milton, and his pride in it, is recorded in all his biographies and in reference works in Danish and German, but never hitherto in Milton studies. The earliest references to this contact which I have found are in: *Leben und Todt des Weyland Hoch-Ehrwürdigen, Hoch-Edlen und Hoch-Gelahrten Herrn, Herrn Johannis Lassenii,* etc., ("Life and Death of the Late Reverend, Right Honorable and Highly Learned Gentleman, Johan Lassenius"), printed 1693, with an internal date of September 19, 1692; and an undated volume, apparently of the same period, *Lebens-Lauff des Berühmten Theologi Herrn D. Johannis Lassenii* ("Life of the Famous Theologian Dr. Johan Lassenius"), which is several times reprinted in later editions of Lassenius' *Heiligen Perlen-Schatz* ("Holy Treasure of Pearls"); all at Copenhagen Royal Library (my thanks to Nils-Henning Jeppesen

and Herman C. Adama for cooperation there and by correspondence.) I have summarized the available data in "Milton and Lassenius," *Milton Quarterly,* (Ohio University, Athens, Ohio), VI, (December, 1972), 92-95.

88. My photocopy of Schlüter from Harvard Law Library has 8 pages of dedication, 6 of preface, 231 of text, the same as the copy at Erlangen-Nürnberg.

Also (early?) in 1677 there appeared a pamphlet *In Nahmen dess Drey Einigen Gottes Die Wahre und Veste Grundlehre von der Ehelichen Keuschheit Zwischen einem Manne und einem Weibe, auss dem Heil. Wort des Herren dargethan von einem Diener Jesus Christi Henrico Storning . . . Kiel, In Verlegung Simon Beckensteins und Christian Gerlachs, im Jahr 1677* ("In the name of the Triune God, The True and Fundamental Doctrine of Marital Chastity between One Man and One Woman, set forth from the Holy Word of the Lord by a Servant of Jesus Christ, Heinrich Storning, Kiel, Published by Simon Beckenstein and Christian Gerlach, 1677"), ix, 1, 52 pages. Storning says that he had composed his *Fundamentals* and sent copies to friends long before "J.L." came to his notice, so that it was not designed as a refutation. He had not particularly planned to publish it, but hearing that a copy was fallen into the hands of a printer, he decided to put it out himself. He admits to depending on Gerhard (against Ochino) and Musaeus (against Theophilus Alethaeus) and regrets not having seen *Funus Polygamiae* which he attributed to Tarnovius (see note 60 above). Among other matters, Storning is troubled by the spread through Germany of what he calls the French disease, introduced 180 years before through Italy. Willy-nilly, Storning's pamphlet became part of the anti-Leyser literature. My photocopy is from the Deutsche Staatsbibliothek, East Berlin, through the cooperation of Dr. Willy Unger and Hans Kasper.

89. My photocopy is from the University of Chicago; title page, dedication, [3]—99 pages. There are copies at Princeton Uni-

versity and elsewhere. If the identity of Simplicius Christianus was ever made public, it has escaped me. Diecmann says he does not know who he is. The same pseudonym was used by other writers several times.

90. My photocopy of Frische is from the University of Chicago; title page, dedication, ii, 1-67, i. His printing of the verses is in some details better than the text in the 1675 Leyser edition in the British Museum copy. Frische reprinted the verses I have but omitted the first stanza by P. A., and the eight lines by B. O. which I also omit. Frische and Diecmann deal at length with Herold.

Burkhard Gotthelf Struve (Struvius), *Bibliotheca Iuris Selecta,* "Select Library of Law," various editions, lists (Chapter XV) an anonymous *Die Göttliche Ordnung des Heiligen Ehstandes zwischen einem Männlein und Fräulein, Gegen die Unfläter der Heutigen Viel Weibernehmer, oder Polygamiten, Helmstädt. 1677,* quarto ("The Divine Ordinance of Holy Matrimony between a Young Man and a Young Woman, against those Filthy Beasts the Present Day Takers of Many Wives or Polygamists"). It is also mentioned by Johan Friedrich Cotta in his notes to the 1776 edition of *Ioannis Gerhardi Locorum Theologicorum Tomus Decimus Quintus* ("Johan Gerhard's Theological Texts, volume 15"). I have not been able to locate a copy of that Helmstädt tract.

91. Diecmann's portrait is reproduced in *Die Geschichte der Stadt Stade an der Nieder Elbe,* ("History of the City of Stade on the Lower Elbe"), 1956, by Hans Wohltmann, who died in 1968 before I could consult him. The city archives of Stade and the Niedersächsiches Staatsarchiv at Stade inform me, letter of May 20, 1970, that they find no additional recorded data on Leyser or his contacts with Diecmann or the Königsmarcks, partly attributable to the effects of war and military occupation on Stade 1676-1681. A German version of that "epitaph" on monogamy was printed by J. S. Adami, *Tractat von der Polygamia* (1715, pages 171-173), perhaps

taken from a 1687 disputation by Johan Dünnehaupt at Wittenberg, *Conscientia Accusati.* The parentheses in the epitaph, according to Diecmann, *Vindiciae,* page 267, represent revisions by Leyser. Every time Leyser printed it himself in later works, he revised it further.

My photocopy of the Diecmann *Vindiciae* is from the Harvard Law Library. My copy of *De Rigore Legis Monogamicae* from the Nürnberg Stadtbibliothek appears to be the first edition, the title page designating Diecmann as *praeses* and Joachim Lehment of Stade as respondent, the verso containing dedicatory verses by Lehment to the civil and religious authorities of Stade, text pages 1-29. The copy at Harvard Law Library entirely omits references to Lehment, so that we may attribute it to Diecmann, the only name on the title page, with blank verso, text pages 1-29.

UTIS: This last word in Leyser's Epitaph on Monogamy seems to be intended for the Greek ουτις "no one," which was Odysseus' reply to the Cyclops asking his name (Odyssey, IX, 366).

92. The passage with the reference to Milton is as follows:

> Unde via divortiis non cum Christo obstruetur, sed iisdem quia propter talem πορνείαν admittenda sunt, complanabitur, & adeo Johannis Miltoni, haud ita dudum peculiari libro pro divortiis ob mores intolerabiles, atq; disparitatem & renitentiam animorum concedendis pugnantis, causa triumphabit.
>
> Whence the way to divorces is not blocked with Christ, but made smooth by themselves, because such are allowed by this kind of idea of unchastity, and what is more, the cause of John Milton will triumph, fighting in his peculiar book for divorces to be granted on grounds of intolerable character, and disparity and opposition of minds.

Diecmann also tabulates Milton in his index of authors cited and his index of topics, under *Divortium.* He does not indicate the source of his knowledge of Milton's book on divorce. Pufendorf is most likely. Diecmann also cites (page 246) the *Historia Ecclesiastica et Politica* of Georg Horn (1620-1670), so he must also have read in Horn this sentence:

> *Miltonus* merum viri arbitrium, sine uxoris culpa vel judicis cognitione, facit sufficientem divortii causam.
>
> Milton makes the decision of the husband a sufficient cause of divorce, without any fault of the wife or judicial procedure.

(Georg Horn, *Historia Ecclesiastica et Politica,* Leyden and Rotterdam, 1665, page 279; *Historia Ecclesiastica et Politica, editio nova et emendatior,* "new, corrected edition," Leyden and Rotterdam, 1666, page 281, both published by Haak; Dutch translation with addenda by Balthasar Becker and Melchior Leydecker, *Kerkelyke en Wereldlyke Historie,* Amsterdam, 1739, page 305. Horn also lifts from Thomas Edwards' *Gangraena,* 1646, the list of heresies, including #154, a summary of Milton's divorce theory, and #155, lawful bigamy).

93. I am grateful to Edit Rasmussen, assistant keeper, Historical Division, at the Rigsarkivet, Copenhagen, for locating the text of the ban on Leyser in the Sjaellanske Registre 1677, number 165, and producing the bulky folio for my examination; and to Mogens Møller for assistance with translation from the Danish. I do not know whether the Danish text has ever been printed. It cannot have received much circulation. The one text which did receive some circulation was a slightly shorter Latin version printed by Johan Brunsmann in *Monogamia Victrix,* Frankfurt, 1679, (reprinted in his 1688 *Nuptiae Prohibitae*), which is probably the source from which it was reprinted again in the *Observationum Selectarum* ("Select Observations") of Halle, 1702; by Gottlieb Wernsdorff, 1715; and Am-Ende, 1748, all three discussed elsewhere herein. Brunsmann printed it with the date March 15, 1677, and it is

so copied by later writers. The original is clearly dated May 15 in the Rigsarkivet handwritten copy. The decree makes no mention of Leyser as army chaplain or as dismissed from such a post.

94. The letter of May 22, 1677 is mentioned, but not given, by Diecmann in his *Vindiciae,* page 180.

My photocopy of *Warmund: Vornehmer Leute* is from the Nürnberg Stadtbibliothek. My photocopy of *Warmund: Gewissenhaffte Gedancken* is from the University of Chicago. Both have a title page, with dedication on the verso (not identical in text), six pages of preface differing in text, and 48 pages comprising the body of the work. They are on poor paper closely printed with almost no margins. The pseudonym *Gottlieb Warmund,* like *Theophilus Alethaeus,* has been used by other writers. Leyser spelled *Warmund* without an *h.*

The sentence referring to Milton is identical in both issues:

> Der gleichen Meinung führen auch viel andere Hochgelährte in Geistlichem und Weltlichem Stande. Von Riveto Diestio Miltono Seldeno wil ich nichts sagen,

> The same opinion is offered also by many other highly learned men in spiritual and secular circles. Of Rivet, Diest, Milton, Selden I wish to say nothing,

The dedication of *Vornehmer Leute* suggests a late 1678 printing in anticipation of New Year's day 1679. According to E. O. Weller, *Die Falschen und Fingirten Druckorte* (see Note 74 above) there was a 1678 Dutch publication of *Staat-Kundige 't-Zaamenspraak over de Viel-Wyvery* by Wahrmund (sic) at "Freyburg." The title would seem to make it a Dutch version of the *Discursus Politicus* rather than of the other Warmund texts: but I have been unable to locate a copy, or any other reference to it.

Leyser's suddenly enlarged knowledge of Luther's share in the Philip of Hesse case will become more clear when we come to the story of Charles Louis. Leyser makes no reference to that story, but emphasizes his claim to independent knowledge. Steuber the Hessian theologian is (perhaps) either Johann Steuber (1590-1643), or possibly his brother Valentin. Leyser's notes, as often, are inaccurate. "Menius" was not a signer; "Raud" was perhaps the notary Raid. Leyser also prints a Latin epigram, which Diecmann had previously printed in the *Vindiciae,* which is (happily) Leyser's only attempt at verse:

Pauperis est numerare pecus. Quin praestat habere
  Innumeros nummos, innumerosque libros,
Mancipium sese duntaxat mancipat uni
  Unius servus num Generosus erit?
Mille domus septem praestant & praedia mille
                                        decet
  Uxores cur non ducere mille licet
                                        placet.

It's for a pauper to count his cows. Who would not rather own
  Cash beyond counting, accounts beyond counting?
Conveyancing oneself slave to one alone
  Shall the slave-of-one become a noble brave?
Better than seven houses are one thousand, and properties a thousand
                                        proper
  Why should marrying a thousand wives not be permitted
                                        pleasing?

Among his other vagaries Leyser was attracted to the number 1000, which he considered divine, and so discussed in a footnote on Solomon's thousand wives, in *Polygamia Triumphatrix.*

95. The 1679 *Uxor Una* was published at Giessen as one of *Duo Tractatus Aurei,* "Two Golden Treatises." I have not seen this edition.

There were several issues of Brunsmann's *Monogamia*

Victrix. The copy at Erlangen-Nürnberg University Library has title page with blank verso; dedication to Friedrich von Alefeld, with Christian V's decree on the verso; two pages *Lectori,* "To the Reader," text 1-248, plus index, two pages. The copy at Copenhagen Royal Library, a later issue, (whence my photocopy), has the title page in red and black, the dedication to Alefeld printed twice, the decree of Christian V printed twice in different sizes of type, the two pages To the Reader, text 1-248, two pages of index plus errata. In 1688 the unsold copies of this 1679 volume were re-issued with a new title page, a differently set index (table of contents), omitting the preface to the reader, as *Johannis Brunsmanni Nidrosiensis Nuptiae Prohibitae, ubi simul indicatur, quo modo nuptiae Christiano concessae, praemissis sponsaliis, faciendae, polygamia vitanda, quales ritus nuptiales observandi & matrimonium feliciter contrahendum sit, Francofurti. Apud Johannem Justum Erythropilum. Anno 1688.* ("Johan Brunsmann of Nidrosia, Forbidden Nuptials, wherein at one time is indicated in what manner the marriages permitted to a Christian are to be carried out, betrothals in advance, polygamy to be barred, what nuptial rites to be observed, and how matrimony is to be happily contracted, Frankfurt, at Johan Justus Rothkopf's"—a most misleading title page; there is a copy at Union Theological Seminary. Brunsmann's name is also given as Brunsmand (1637-1707). Nidrosia is an old name for Trondheim, when it was a religious center.

In citing Gaulmyn's edition of the Midrash on Moses (see note 8 above) Brunsmann imprecisely transliterated the Hebrew as *Dibre Hajanim Hamosche,* on page 132, but corrected the second word in his Errata to *Hajamim.* Leyser used this matter in *Polygamia Triumphatrix* and betrays his lifting it without credit by reproducing the spelling *Hajanim.*

Erich Pontoppidan, *Annales Ecclesiae Daniae* ("Annals of the Danish Church"), Copenhagen, 1741-1752, volume 4, page 587, gave the date of Christian V's decree correctly as May 15, indicating that he had some source other than Brunsmann's *Monogamia Victrix* (which he cites as if printed 1678).

96. My deepest gratitude to Olof von Feilitzen of the Kungliga Biblioteket (Royal Library) of Stockholm, who, going out of his way, first made available to me photocopies of the original manuscript minutes of the Stockholm Consistory and Leyser's 1679 letters to them; to Carl Fredrik Corin and the staff of the Stockholm Stadsarkiv (Municipal Archives) for hefting up the original folios, with additional documents, including the 1679 trial court record and other reports, for my review; to Nils F. Holm, of the Riksarkivet (Royal Archives, Stockholm) and his staff for making available the folio (Kungl. Senaten Bref 359R and 360) with the Royal Council's order to the Stockholm city authorities to prosecute Leyser, signed by St. Bielke, G. Baner, N. Brahe, C. Rålamb, G. Sparre, G. Gyllenstierna, J. G. Stenbock, L. Flemming and E. Lovisin; and most particularly to Dr. Renate Drucker of Leipzig University for invaluable help in deciphering Leyser's scrawl.

Leyser wrote his letters in German, and nowhere is there any clear reference to his having been in Sweden previously, so his first visit there may have been in 1679. If he was the author, or the major contributor to the Wahrenberg pamphlet, without at that time being in Sweden, that may help explain the inability of Pufendorf to come up with the author's name.

The Swedish authorities in 1679 seem not to have been aware of the edict of the Danish king of 1677; and Leyser's expulsion from Sweden seems not to have been known to Masius (of Denmark) when he wrote to Allix in 1684 (see below). In addition to the Stockholm manuscript sources, I have found printed references with additional information on the Swedish 1679 phase in the following:

Andreas Carolus, *Memorabilia Ecclesiastica Seculi a Nato Christo Decimi Septimi Juxta Annorum Seriem Notata et Convenienti Ordine Digesta,* Tübingen, 1697-1699 ("Ecclesiatical Memorabilia of the Seventeenth Century Since Christ Was Born, Noted Chronologically by Years and Arranged in Convenient Order"), published by Johan Georg Cotta, printed by Johan Cunrad Reis, pages 229-231 for 1679, (copies at Union Theological Seminary and Harvard-Andover). Carolus appears to derive from *Latom. Rel. lxxxiii, p. 71* which I take to have been an issue of the continuation of Sigismund Latomus' *Relationis Historicae,* of which I have not been able to locate a copy.

Vincentius Placcius, *De Scriptoribus Pseudonymis Detectis Liber,* "Book on Pseudonymous Writers Exposed," in his *Theatrum Anonymorum et Pseudonymorum* (Hamburg, 1708), page 614, cites a letter of Johan Heyssig reporting the burning of Leyser's books in front of his face on July 15, 1679.

Gottlieb Wernsdorff, in *Summam Sanae Doctrinae de Polygamia,* 1716, ("Summary of Sound Doctrine on Polygamy," of which more below) printed the text of the 1679 court verdict, in Latin. Am-Ende reprinted this material in his 1748 book, although he did not know Wernsdorff's sources, but he had studied under Wernsdorff and regarded him as highly trustworthy. This Latin text approximates closely to the Swedish manuscript text in the Stockholms Stadsarkiv, pages 214-218, where it is signed July 12 by O. Thegner and nine others.

The story of Leyser's danger from the women may ultimately derive from contemporary accounts, but my sources are Clugius, *Diatribe Epistolica de Scriptis Io. Lyseri,* page 85, and Johan Christianus Klozius (=Klotz), *Disputatio ex Historia Literaria de Libris Auctoribus Suis Fatalibus,* "Disputation from Literary History on Books Fatal to Their Authors," (respondent Ioannes Ernestus Grabergius, December 29, 1727), Wittenberg, published by the Widow Gerdes, page 11-12 (copy at Harvard); both Clugius and Klotz deriving from Samuel Schelwig, *Exercitatio Theologica de Peccatis Post Mortem Commissis* ("Theological Dissertation on Sins Committed after Death"), Section XI, page 21; I have not located a copy, though of Schelwig more anon. The same point was made by Carolus.

The *Dansk Biografisk Leksikon* and other reference works assert that Leyser was flogged at Stockholm. This allegation is found in Samuel Schelwig, *Reliqua de Polygamia Adversus*

Themistium ("Remainder [of the Essay] on Polygamy against Themistius"), Leipzig, 1714, page 32, and in Nicolaus Hieronymus Gundling, *Historie der Gelahrheit* ("History of the Savants"), 1736, IV, 6070. Am-Ende points out that this is not confirmed by the text of the Stockholm court sentence, and may derive from misunderstanding its references to his punishment at Abo and Riga. The pillory at Stockholm is mentioned by J. S. Adami, *Tractat von der Polygamia,* 1715 edition, page 193.

Dr. Emil Schieche, historian of the ancient German Church of St. Gertrud at Stockholm, writes me (October 26, 1971) that the church archives have no data about Leyser (although he must have visited there in 1679). The pastors at that time were Christoph Bezel (Bezelius) and Aegidius Strauch (Strauch's name appears in the Stockholm consistory minutes of the Leyser proceedings). There were three apothecaries members of the church: Christian Heraeus, royal apothecary; Alexander Steckert, admiralty apothecary; and Julius Friedrich Friedenreich (since the Consistory minutes say only "German apothecary," was he Leyser's host?)

97. My efforts to locate firsthand records of Leyser at Abo and Riga have drawn blanks. Olof Mustelin of the Abo Akademis Bibliotek, Turku, wrote me, February 13, 1970, that no records are preserved there, nor within the facilities of the Professor of Church History at Abo, nor at Helsinki. Heikki Eskellinen, of the Turun Yliopiston Kirjasto, Turku, wrote me (February 17, 1970) that church and city archives of Abo were lost in a fire in 1827. Miss Bagrova, of the Lenin Library, Moscow, informed me (March 30, 1970) that extensive search by their staff had turned up no sources of information about Leyser at Riga.

In *Polygamia Triumphatrix* Leyser at least twice refers to reminiscences of Latvia (Courland) but not to his preaching or suffering there.

Helmstedt: In his testimony of June 21, 1679 before the Consistory, Leyser is recorded as answering that he had not "communicated with the theologians of Helmstedt" but that he believed that his views were shared by "Titio.Calixto.Rixer & Doct. Hillebrand: Celle." I identify these as Gerhardus Titius (1620-1681), Fridericus Ulricus Calixtus (1622-1701), Heinrich Rixner (1634-1692), theologians at Helmstedt; Joachim Hildebrand (1623-1691), superintendent of the church at Zelle. Calixtus and Strauch had feuded on other theological questions, which may be one reason for the question. I find another reason in F. J. Lütke's posthumous (1723) *Tractat von der Polygamie,* page 24, citing a 1679 advisory opinion by the Helmstedt Law Faculty stating that the death penalty for bigamy was enacted by human positive law, and so subject to the discretion of the magistrate, since polygamy is not against natural law or holy writ. I have not been able to locate any other details, but clearly Leyser had some basis for his allegation about Helmstedt.

98. My photocopy of *Polygamia Triumphatrix* is from the New York Public Library. I have also examined copies at Harvard, Harvard-Andover, University of Illinois, Princeton, Erlangen-Nürnberg, Heidelberg, etc. The book has title page, blank leaf, 8 pages of preface, 565 pages of text; 14 page addenda devoted to Martin Luther's *De Digamia Episcoporum* (theses "On Bishops' Second Marriages") with Leyser's marginal comments; 7 pages tabulating his Scripture citations, and 13 pages of topical index. Besides typographical errors in Latin and Hebrew, towards the end of the volume Greek quotations are transliterated into Roman letters, as if the printer had run out of his Greek font. Where 1674 and 1676 have *Alethaeus,* this edition has *Aletheus.*

99. Daphnaeus Arcuarius will be discussed in the next section. Cnaeus Cornelius Vythagius (also found as Cornelis Uythage and as Uyterhage) was a doctor of theology and Hebrew in the Netherlands. His learned treatises on reading Hebrew without vowel points, on Hebrew roots, and on the *Pirke Aboth* ("Sayings of the Fathers") as expounded by Maimo-

nides, may be read at Columbia University, the British Museum and elsewhere; but his 1680 *Eine Disputation von Polygamia,* Rotterdam, 8⁰, has so far eluded my search through many libraries. Zedler (citing Sieber's Bibliography, 385), and B. G. Struve (*Bibliotheca Iuris Selecta,* 1720, page 582; 1743, pages 553-556) say that Vythagius contended that polygamy did not contravene divine or natural law. This disputation is not mentioned in any of the works for or against polygamy published between 1680 and 1750 which I have seen.

Possibly it was printed anonymously, and since most library catalogues are by author, it is not found when inquiry is made. The Harvard (Widener) copy of Leyser's 1676 *Discursus* has a note in an antique hand "Confer Anonymi Diss. de Polygamia Iuri Divino nec Nat. contraria. Roterod. 1680"—"Compare the Anonymous Dissertation on Polygamy Not Contrary to Divine or Natural Law, Rotterdam, 1680."

In Vythagius' *Anti-christus Mahometes* ("Mohammed the Anti-Christ"), published by Johannes Ravestein, Amsterdam, 1676, he listed polygamy and its vices among the evils of Islam, and declared that Christ, in revoking the ceremonial law of the Old Testament also banned polygamy and divorce (pages 62, 270-279, copy at Erlangen-Nürnberg).

100. The quotations from Owen are all bunched, almost all before page 280. It is characteristic of Leyser's quotations to be distributed as if he quoted when he had a book available rather than when it was apposite. Many, perhaps most, of the Owen epigrams quoted by Leyser are from books by Owen not translated by Pecke.

101. In *Polygamia Triumphatrix,* page 533, Leyser wrote "Ante quadraginta annos adhuc habuit quidam Episcopus in Anglia binas simul easque solenniter copulatas, uti *Bakerus* de Rebus Anglicanis refert, & mihi etiam, in Anglia versanti, à nonnullis Episcopis, & presbyteris relatum fuit." Leyser makes the same point on pages 461 and 556 and in the index. I

have examined the 1643, 1653, 1674 and 1679 editions of Baker's *Chronicle* without finding this bigamous bishop, or anything which might have led to such an interpretation. I have not seen the 1649 Dutch version. Leyser makes no other reference to Baker, though he might have cited, for example, Edward IV and his three concubines. Perhaps Leyser *heard* something which he misunderstood in his eagerness for any scrap of "evidence."

102. It does not suit our purpose here to dwell further on *Polygamia Triumphatrix* but in that farrago there is so much packed that almost any work dealing with the seventeenth century might find something of use. I will here add only some items of most pertinent interest.

Biographical: Besides references to his friend Bosius and sometime teacher Dannhauer, Leyser indicates acquaintance with Johan Sperling (1603-1658), physician, pedant, scientist of a sort, page 26; page 320, his work in libraries; page 357, a time reference indicating he was working on this book in 1680; page 15, a reference to his being in a maritime city with 50 booksellers but no copy of Pufendorf, which was Amsterdam; pages 119, 121, he quotes Italian proverbs, and on page 138 in Italian what passes for a joke on monks, nuns and miraculous pregnancies: this recalls that Feltmann in his anti-Leyser dialogue assigned to Sittmann an anecdote which suggests that Leyser may have visited Italy before 1675.

On page 468, Leyser makes the only reference in all his writings to Ochino, actually to Beza-on-Ochino. He makes references to Anglican divines Joseph Hall and Henry Hammond because of their role in the seventeenth century controversy over the authenticity of the writings attributed to church father Ignatius: Hall and Hammond owe most of what fame they retain today mainly to their having been the butt of opposing writings by John Milton; ditto Claude de Saumaise (Salmasius), quoted both in the earlier *Discursus Politicus* and in the *Triumphatrix* annotations; but Milton is not mentioned in this volume, although Leyser clearly has read those passages in Pufendorf's *De Jure* which discuss Milton-on-divorce.

Leyser, page 554, corrects his errors on Lothar, which had been pointed out by Diecmann, (and later by Brunsmann, in regard to the Latin *Discursus*) but he makes new errors as gross, as we have seen in the matter of the *Chronicles of Moses,* and, as we shall see, in regard to Sarcerius.

He tinkers again with his epitaph on monogamy (page 116). In his preface he creates a new epitaph available for any of his opponents, which reads as if it were composed in the delirium of his quartan fever. Since it seems to have made an impression on his contemporaries, and was quoted in reference works almost as if it better applied to Leyser himself, we give it here:

Sub hoc lapide jacet sepultus
Homo non homo, vir non vir, mulier non mulier, liber non liber,
ἀνδρόγυνος an γύνανδρος certatur, sanè γυναικοκρατόμενος
Semideus an Semihomo, aut Semidiabolus disceptatur,
certe Diabolus incarnatus, hominum multiplicationi invidens,
hominis naturam evertere, ejusque generationem impediens,
hominis nomine indignus, virorum vires destruens,
mulierum naturam contra naturam evehens,
hostis Dei & hominum adeo ut nec virilis nec mulebris sexus,
nec diabolus sub censu habere desideret,
metuens ne inferno ipsi leges imponat sicuti Christo,
Salvatori nostro, novas affinxit leges,
Spiritus S. verba reformavit,
Apostolorum mentem malitiosè dementavit.
Mancipium Diaboli. Adjutorium Satanae
cui Pater Abaddon, mater Alecto, nomen Legio, nutrix Megaera.
Scilicet horrendum monstrum ac ingens, cui lumen ademptum,

asini sepultura dignissimum, & si viveret,
in Asinariam aut Utopiam relegandum.

Under this stone lies buried someone
Man or not man, male or not male,
woman or not woman, child or not child,
Androgyne or Gynandrone, is in dispute, certainly petty-coatruled,
Half-god, half-man, or half-devil, is in debate,
Surely a devil incarnate, envying man's multiplication,
overturning man's nature, and impeding his generation,
unworthy the name of man, destroying man's virility,
exalting woman's nature against nature,
enemy of God and man so that neither the male nor female sex,
nor the devil himself would want him included in the rolls,
fearing that he would impose new laws on hell itself, as if Christ,
our Saviour, had added new laws,
had reformed the words of the Holy Spirit,
had maliciously demented the minds of the Apostles.
The Devil's Servant, Satan's Helper,
his father Abbadon, mother Alecto, his name Legion, nurse Megaera.
Surely a monster horrid and huge, deprived of sight,
worthy an ass's funeral, and if still living,
to be banished to Assinaria or to Utopia.

(Androgyne, gynandrone: hermaphrodite. As if Christ: Jesus said he came not to make new laws, but to fulfill the Law, which suits Leyser's case that Old Testament polygamy remained lawful under the New Testament. Abaddon: in Revelation ix, 11, the angel of the bottomless pit, in Hebrew *Abaddon* (= Destruction), in Greek called *Apollyon.* Alecto: one of the Furies in Greek mythology, (= Unrelenting). Legion: see Mark v, 9, where the unclean spirit says "My name is Legion, for we are many." Megaera: another of the

Furies (= Envious). A monster: Vergil's line on the Cyclops, from his *Aeneid;* Leyser often uses this image for opponents. Assinaria: kingdom of the asses. Utopia: not More's ideal realm, but simply Nowhere.)

"Athanasius Vincentius" (Leyser's "editor's pen-name") translates into "Immortally Conquering."

103. Letter of J. B. Rocolles to Pierre Bayle, May 17, 1685, in: Emile Gigas, *Choix de la Correspondance Inédite de Pierre Bayle, 1670-1706. Publié D' Après les Originaux Conservés à la Bibliothèque Royale de Copenhague,* 1890, tome 1, page 640 ("Selection of the unedited Correspondence of Pierre Bayle, 1670-1706, from the Originals Preserved in the Royal Library at Copenhagen"). Rocolles (died 1696) was the author of a history of Calvinism, written in opposition to Louis Maimbourg (1610-1686) against whom Bayle also wrote extensively.

During 1682 Johan Brunsmann applied to Pufendorf for a statement on Leyser. Pufendorf's letter in reply tried again to set his record straight "on that question of polygamy, about which that crazy Leyser raises so much commotion." He affirms his preference for monogamy on principle. He thinks that polygamy multiplies poverty; that Moses rather tolerated than approved polygamy; that while polygamy might not be banned by natural law, it might be banned to Christians by other law. Pufendorf's Latin letter was printed, from the original manuscript in the Hamburg Stadtbibliothek, in: Paul Meyer, *Samuel Pufendorf, Ein Beitrag zur Geschichte seines Lebens, von Paul Meyer. Abhandlung zum Jahresbericht der Fürsten-und Landesschule zu Grimma über das Schuljahr 1894-1895* ("Samuel Pufendorf, a Contribution to the story of His Life. Supplement to the Annual Report of the Princely and Provincial School of Grimma for the School Year 1894-1895"), printed by Julius Schiertz, Grimma, pages 29-31.

In 1682 at the University of Abo, Finland, Erik Falander, a local luminary, collaborated with doctoral candidate Isaacus Pijlman on a *Dissertatio Philosophica Disquirens Utrum et*

Quomodo Polygamia Possit Dici Juri Naturali Adversa ("Philosophical Dissertation Investigating Whether and in What Manner Polygamy May Be Said to Be Against Natural Law"), printed by Johannes L. Wallius, printer to the university there. The dissertation was defended March 24, 1682, with Falander as *praeses,* and so (as well as on stylistic grounds) it is attributed to Falander by Otto Brusiin, "Professor Falander och Månggiftet" ("Professor Falander and Polygamy") in *Nordisk Gjenklang* ("Northern Echo"), *Festskrift til Carl Jacob Arnholm, 18 Desember 1969,* Oslo, Johan Grundt Tanum Forlag. However, there are indications that this is one of those dissertations whose real author was the respondent: the dedication to Count Benedict Oxenstierne, on the first seven pages after the title page, is signed by Pijlman; while Falander signs a page of compliments to Pijlman in Greek introducing the section of customary compliments (verses by Jacob Flachsenius, prose by D. Achrelius, three pages). The preface, four pages, and the text, ninety pages, do not settle the authorship; but the page of verses at the end, in Greek by David Lund, and the page verses in Latin, by Isaac Lund and by Gabriel Thauvonius, are to Pijlman. The discussion leans heavily on Grotius and Siricius, evading Pufendorf, who is not mentioned. There is slight attention to Leyser, who is not named, nor is anything mentioned about Leyser's stay at Abo. The preface refers to an unnamed book printed at "Friburg" by Theophilus Alethaeus in 1679, and there is a later note to the dialogue of Monogamus and Polygamus, which leaves it unclear which books of Leyser were being considered. Musaeus and Diecmann are also mentioned. (I am grateful to Olof Mustelin, Abo Akademis Bibliotek, for helping me locate a copy of that 1682 dissertation at the University of Helsinki library.)

104. Pierre Bayle's literary journal, *Nouvelles de la République des Lettres* ("News from the Commonwealth of Letters", published monthly at Amsterdam) devoted much of the April, 1685 number to Leyser: a review of *Polygamia Triumphatrix,*

pages 339-355; a further note (discussed below), pages 355-358; pages 358-362, a French translation of a Latin letter sent by H. G. Masius to Pierre Allix dated October 31, 1684, partly based on his own knowledge, partly on information from a Herr Schuster of Leipzig, telling of Leyser's last years and his end. Masius says that he did not know Leyser's true identity until after his death, when he was able to examine his papers, which seemed to include the draft of still another book. Are Masius' papers extant anywhere, and would there be any Leyser papers among them? These *Nouvelles* (December, 1685, page 1350) refer to one Carrera stating that Leyser's papers included a manuscript listing all the polygamophiles of those times and a narration of all his sufferings: this might be merely a confused account of Leyser's 1676 *Discurs* and the preface to his *Polygamia Triumphatrix,* or it might be a later composition than either.

The *Nouvelles* for December, 1685, pages 1351-1352, reported that Johan Brunsmann had ready for publication twenty-eight theses in a *Polygamia Triumphata* ("Polygamy Overcome") against Leyser's *Polygamia Triumphatrix.* Johan Diecmann also mentions this *Triumphata* by his learned friend Brunsmann, in a passing reference to Leyser, in his *De Naturalismo,* published 1683 by Reumann at Kiel (copy at British Museum, which also has Diecmann's 1684 edition published by Gleditsch, printed by Krüger). The *Unschuldige Nachrichten,* (literally "Innocent Bulletins" or "Righteous Reports," a clergymen's periodical), 1715, pages 79-80, printed a letter from Brunsmann at Copenhagen to Johan Wilhelm Bajer at Jena, December, 1684, complaining that he could not find a publisher for his "Triumphata." Apparently it was never printed.

Pierre Allix's letter to Bayle which transmitted Masius' letter is printed in Emile Gigas, *Choix de la Correspondance Inédite de Pierre Bayle* ("Selections from the Unedited Correspondence of Pierre Bayle"), 1890, 1:127. Pierre Allix (1641-1717) was a Protestant minister at Charenton, France, exiled to England after the revocation of the Edict of Nantes.

Masius (1653-1709) also figures in history as a defender of the divine right of royal absolutism and in controversy with Christian Thomasius, of whom more anon. Masius' life is in Johan Heinrich von Seelen, *Athenae Lubecenses* ("The Learned of Lübeck"), 1719, 1:366-368; in *Dansk Biografisk Leksikon,* etc.

The further note in Bayle's *Nouvelles,* April, 1685, refers to Pufendorf's *De Jure* on Milton-on-divorce. One should not assume, it says, that Leyser's views on polygamy were caused by a desire for changing mistresses, "comme M. de Puffendorf soupçonne que Milton n'a écrit pour le divorce que parce qu'il avoit une femme qui le faisoit détester" ("as Pufendorf suspects that Milton wrote on divorce only because he had a wife who made him detest her"). Bayle wrote up Milton in his *Dictionnaire,* 1697; makes other references to him; and Gigas, 1:579, prints a letter to Bayle from Vincent Minutoli, 1690, saying that cultured Englishmen regard Milton's poem on Adam as the *non plus ultra* of the human creative spirit.

That Milton had been unhappy in marriage (at least for a time) was well known to his contemporaries. Christopher Arnold (a sometime visitor to Milton) writing of various matters to theologian Theophilus Spizelius, in a letter dated Nürnberg, May 5, 1676, makes passing reference to "de infelici item coniugio (quod eruditis ut plurimum peculiare est) Usherii, Miltoni, Heerbordi"—"also of the unhappy wedlock (which is often peculiar to the learned) of Ussher, Milton, Heerbord." This Ussher was Henry Ussher, uncle of the famous James Ussher; Andreas Heerbord is in Jöcher. The full letter is printed by Johan G. Schelhorn, *Amoenitates Literariae,* "Literary Beauties," XIV, 1731, 570-580, with footnotes based on Bayle's account of Milton's writings on divorce and his proposed bigamy.

Hiob Ludolf, *Allgemeine Schau-Buehne der Welt* ("Universal Stage-Show of the World"), Part Five, 1675-1688, Frankfurt am Main, 1731, Book 85, Chapter XV, column 319, in Leyser's obituary says he died in a "Bauern-Schencke", a peasant hut; that is likely, though not authoritative.

105. There is no adequate biographical study yet of Charles Louis, although the bibliography is extensive. The account here constructed is derived from the specific sources mentioned in the text and in footnotes below, and from the following additional sources:

Relatie Van't Ghepasseerde aen't Hof van Cassel, Geduyrende de Celebratie van het Houwelijck van der Doorluchtigen end Hoogh-Gebooren Vorst ende Heere Karel Lodewyck, Pfalz-Grave by den Rhijn, des H. Roomsche Rijcx, Prince Electeur ende Hertogh van Beyeren &c. Gedruckt in's Gravenhage, by Michiel Stael, ende Johannes Breeckevelt, Bouckverkoopers op't Buyterhof, "Relation of the Events at the Palace of Cassel, during the Celebration of the Nuptials of the Enlightened and High-born Prince and Lord, Charles Louis, Count Palatine of the Rhine, Prince Elector of the Holy Roman Empire and Duke of Bavaria, etc., printed at the Hague by Michiel Stael and Johannes Breeckevelt, booksellers at the Buyterhof," 1650, 8 pages, New York Public Library.

Sir Richard Baker, *A Chronicle of the Kings of England,* of which the 1674 and 1679 editions (continued by Edward Phillips and others) have passim items on Charles Louis from his arrival in England in the 1630's, through his allotted place at the coronation of his cousin Charles II as King.

L. V. A., *Die durch Unlust Vergallete Lust des Ehelichen Lebens; im kurtzer Erzehlung fürgestellet an dem Exempel Zweyer unglücklichen Gemahlinnen von Chur-Fürstl. Hause Pfalz; worinnen die Liebes-Intrigues der Baronesse von Degenfeld, und des ungewissenhafften Gewissens-Raths Langhansens Gottlose Händel zu befinden. Von neuem ans Licht gestellet durch L. V. A., Giessen, bey Johann Müllern.* 1720 ("The Joy of Married Life Marred through Misliking set forth in a short narrative from the example of two unhappy wives of the House of the Electoral Palatinate; wherein are to be found the Love-Intrigues of the Baroness von Degenfeld, and the

Godless Conduct of the Conscience-Less Conscience-Counselor Langhans. Anew Brought to Light by L. V. A., Giessen, at Johan Müller's"). On pages 1-25 this reprints from a 1689 original what purports to be the text of Charlotte's appeal to Emperor Ferdinand III against her husband's treatment, four supposititious Latin love letters of Charles Louis and Luise, and letters between Charles Louis and Charlotte, with painful and tawdry details; on pages 26-45, fictional letters represented as between Charles Louis and Luise, and between him and Charlotte, in rhymed verse, attributed to Herr Hoffmanswaldau (presumably Christian Hofmann von Hoffmanswaldau, 1617-1679, whose collected works include fictional verse letters between Graf 'Ludwig' von Gleichen and his wife, between Abelard and Heloise and other romanticized couples); pages 46-47, on the death and burial of Luise and of Charles Louis. The remainder of the booklet is discussed below, note 119. My photocopy is from the British Museum.

Anonymous. *La Vie et Les Amours de Charles Louis, Elector Palatine, à Cologne, chez Jeremie Plantie, 1692* ("Life and Loves of Charles Louis, Elector Palatine", publisher Jeremie Plantie, Cologne, 1692), deriving from the same sources as the preceding (Columbia University Library).

Allgemeine Schau-Bühne der Welt ("Universal Stage-Show of the World"), edited by Hiob Ludolf and others, Frankfurt, 1699-1718, has notices passim year by year on Charles Louis.

Johan Christian Lünig, *Literae Procerum Europae* ("Letters of the Princes of Europe") Leipzig, 1712, I, 700-704, reprinted the four supposed Latin love letters of Charles Louis and Luise, which were exposed as forgeries by Johan G. Schelhorn, *Amoenitates Literariae* ("Literary Beauties," published by Daniel Bartholomaeus, Frankfurt and Leipzig, 1725, I, 262-268), stolen, abridged and edited from the love letters of Eurialus and Lucretia, in a fiction by Aeneas Silvius Piccolomini, available in his *Opera Quae Extant Omnia,* Basel, 1651, 1967 facsimile by Minerva CMBH, Frankfurt, pages 627-631.

Daniel L. Wundt, *Versuch Einer Geschichte des Lebens und der Regierung Karl Ludwigs Kurfürst von der Pfalz,* Genf, bei H. L. Legrand, 1786, ("Attempt at an History of the Life and Reign of Charles Louis, Elector of the Palatinate," Geneva, H. L. Legrand).

Friedrich Peter Wundt, *Entwurf der Allgemeinen Rheinpfalzischen Landesgeschichte von den Ältesten Zeiten an bis zu dem Jubelfeste der Fünfzigjährigen Regierung Karl Theodors, 1792,* Mannheim, 1798 ("Outline of a General History of the Rhenish Palatinate from Oldest Times to the Fiftieth Anniversary Jubilee of the Reign of Karl Theodor, 1792").

Sir George Bromley. *A Collection of Original Royal Letters Written by King Charles the First and Second, King James the Second and the King and Queen of Bohemia, together with Original Letters Written by Prince Rupert, Charles Louis, Count Palatine,* etc., London, 1797.

Johan Friedrich August Kazner, *Louise Raugräfin zu Pfalz,* Leipzig, 1798, in three parts, paginated separately, 154, 165, 168 pages.

Felix Joseph Lipowsky, *Karl Ludwig, Churfürst von der Pfalz, und Maria Susanna Louise, Raugräfin von Degenfeld, nebst der Biographie des Churfürsten Karl von der Pfalz, des letzsten Spröslings aus der Linie Pfalz-Simmern,* Sulzbach, 1824 ("Karl Ludwig, Elector of the Palatinate and Raugräfin Maria Susanna Louise von Degenfeld, together with the Biography of Elector Karl of the Palatinate, last scion of the Pfalz-Simmern Line"). (The title *Raugräfin,* revived for Luise, and inherited by her children, is discussed in Zedler's *Lexicon,* with information on some of her children).

Edward Vehse, *Geschichte der Deutschen Höfe seit der Reformation,* Hamburg, Hofmann und Campe, 1853 ("History of the German Courts since the Reformation"), volume 24, pages 101-113; also data on Luise's children.

Ludwig Häusser, *Geschichte der Rheinischen Pfalz,* Heidelberg, 1856 ("History of the Rhenish Palatinate").

Karl Hauck, *Karl Ludwig, Kurfürst von der Pfalz, 1617-1680,* published by the *Mannheimer Altertumsverein* (Mannheim Antiquarian Society), Leipzig, 1903.

François Ausaresses and H. Gauthier-Villars, *La Vie Privée d'un Prince Allemand au XVIIe Siècle. L'Electeur Palatin Charles-Louis, 1617-1680, Paris,* 1926 ("The Private Life of a German Prince in the Seventeenth Century, Charles Louis, Elector Palatine").

106. Daniel L. Wundt (1786) and F. J. Lipowsky (1824) indicated that some such documents were extant in the family archives. J. F. A. Kazner (1798) printed documents in which Charles Louis charged Charlotte with "malicious desertion" as grounds for their separation. Ausaresses and Gauthier-Villars (1926) speak of a conference October 25, 1658, after Luise's first child was born, at which Charles Louis "explained" to a select group of notables that he could not simply divorce the Electoral Princess.

107. Letter of Charles Louis to Luise, October 31, 1657, and others, in: Wilhelm Ludwig Holland, *Schreiben des Kurfürsten Karl Ludwig von der Pfalz und der Seinem,* in Bibliothek des Litterarischer Vereins in Stuttgart, volume CLXVII, Tübingen, 1884 ("Letters of Elector Charles Louis of the Palatinate and His Family").

A clear contemporary statement of the actual status was made by Ernst, Landgrave of Hesse-Rheinfels, in his obituary on Johannes Ludovicus Fabricius, counsellor to Charles Louis: "son en effet non autre que concubinage avec la Baronne de Degenfeld, avec laquelle cet Electeur pretendoit justement, comme mon bisaïeul, le landgrave Philippe, estre en une legitime Polygamie avec la seconde femme"—"in effect nothing but concubinage with the Baroness of Degenfeld, with whom this Elector pretended, precisely like my ancestor Landgrave Philip, to be in a legitimate polygamy with the second wife" (Johannes Ludovicus Fabricius. *Opera Omnia. Quibus Praemittitur Historia Vitae et Obitus Eiusdem. Authore Joh. Henrico Heidegerro. Tiguri. Typis et Impensis Davidis Gesneri. A. MDCXCVIII,* "Complete Works, to which is prefixed the History of His Life and Death, by Johan Heinrich Heidegger, Zurich, printed and published by David Gesner, 1698," pages 149-154. Newberry Library, Chicago.)

108. A lifetime later, Spanheim's stand is recalled and emphatically praised in the funeral panegyric (*Laudatio Funebris*) delivered in his memory June 6, 1701 by Jacobus Triglandius (1652-1705), printed in volume II of Spanheim's *Works* (Fridericus Spanheim, *Opera,* Leyden, 1701-1703); and in Jacobus Triglandius, *Dissertationum Theologicarum et Philologicarum Sylloge* ("Collection of Theological and Philological Dissertations"), of which I have seen the second edition, Delft, Adrian Beman, 1728, pages 166-167 (Columbia University). Nicéron emphasizes the same point in his sketch of Spanheim (1632-1701).

109. In the *Bibliotheca Realis Juridica,* edited by the successors to Martin Lipen, Leipzig, 1767, volume 2, page 122, there is listed a *Iuris Themata Pro Electoris Palatini Coniugio,* 1659, ("Concepts of the Law for the Palatine Elector's Marriage"). This title is not known to any of the many libraries I have checked, nor is it listed in the biographical essay on Boeckelmann (1633-1681) in Johann Friedrich Jugler, *Beyträge zur Juristischen Biographie* ("Contributions to the Lives of the Lawyers"), Leipzig, 1777, volume 4, pages 274-301, or elsewhere. Perhaps that title was intended to represent Boeckelmann's doctoral disputation of which the title page reads:

Disputatio Inauguralis Exhibens Diversa Iuris Themata Quae Opitulante Christo Opt. Max. Sine Praeside: (Electorali super contraria hujus loci observantiâ impetratâ dispensatione) Pro Summis in Utroque Jure Privilegiis et Honoribus Doctoralibus Rite et Decenter Consequendis Solenni Eruditorum omnium Examini submittit Die Martii horis locoque consuetis Johannes Fridericus Böckelmann Steinfurto-Westphalus Heidelbergae/ Typis Aegidii Walteri Acad. Typogr. Anno MDCLIX ("Inaugural Disputation Setting Forth Diverse Concepts of Law, which, with the help of Christ the Best and the Greatest, without a *Praeses,* (having obtained from the Elector a dispensation from the contrary procedure in this place) for Highest Privileges and Doctoral Honors in Both Branches of Law Duly and Fittingly Following/ Johann Friedrich Boeckelmann of Steinfurt in Westphalia, submits to the Formal Examination of all the Learned on the day of March at the customary hour and place. Heidelberg, printed by Aegidius Walter, University Printer, 1659").

The copy at Columbia University has title page, dedication to Charles Louis on the verso and two following pages, text 1-60; has the date (March 11) written in by hand as "XI"; and appears to be an early state of the printing, the word *tertia* being crossed out in ink with "IV" correctly written in on the caption, (page 37). The title page notes that the exceptional procedure, without a *praeses,* is by special permission (or command?) of the Elector; which we may associate with the unusual printed note dated February 14, 1659 on page 60 in the name of the Dean of the Law Faculty throwing all responsibility on the author. There are six main topics: of civil power in ecclesiastical matters; on law written and unwritten; on *usucapium,* ownership based on continued possession; on the esssential content of marriage, which (he says) is consent, not the bed, and not the priestly blessing, with a few side observations on the status of concubines and the children of concubines; on grounds for divorce, under the Justinian Code, and among Reformation theologians; and on male and female inheritance under feudal tenures.

Subsequently this *Disputatio* was reissued, the caption on page 37 corrected to "Quarta," and in the same format, pages 61 to 124 were added as an *Epistola ad Lectorem* ("Letter to the Reader"); copy at Heidelberg, of which I have used both original and microfilm, thanks to Dr. Wilfried Willer and Hellmut Vogeler there. In this sequel, Boeckelmann takes note of the rumors that he was a defender of polygamy. He attributes the rumor, apart from the ill will of the authors of a satire against him, to his argument that the pastoral benediction was no requisite to a true marriage. He denies that he approves polygamy, and defends his theses in detail against that satire, point by point, with citations for every point. So when he is answering the question whether there may not be grounds for divorce as weighty as adultery or malicious desertion, he quotes twenty-one distinct authors, (some of whom quote others), among whom the last two names are of Englishmen, of whom the twentieth is no surprise, John Selden with his *Uxor Ebraica,* followed by (page 123)

> Iohannes Miltonius Anglus duobus integris libris rationibus & authoritatibus pluribus refertis idem adstruit.

> John Milton, the Englishman, supports the same in two books filled with solid reasons and many authorities.

The satire was by Bartholomew Anhorn and Jacob Meyer under the pen-name Parrhesius Philalethes, with the title *Krigericus Hircander Omnibus Bonis Foetens et Exosus* ("The Fighting Goatman Stinking and Hateful to All Good Men"—Hircander, "Goatman," a pun on Boeckelmann's name; no copy found among all the libraries I have checked). See: Karl Büttinghausen, *Beyträge zur Pfälzischen Geschichte* ("Contributions to Palatinate History"), Mannheim, 1776-1782, volume 2, pages 56-58 (copy at Harvard). The commemorative *Memoria Bockelmanniana* by Alexander Arnoldus Pagenstecher, 1694, printed at Cologne with his *De Praescriptione Feudi Ecclesiastici,* 1700, is laudatory rather than informative (Columbia Law Library).

In Boeckelmann's *Compendium Institutionum Imp. Iusiniani* ("Abridgement of Emperor Justinian's Institutes"), Leyden, Felix Lopez, 1679 (copy at Columbia Law Library; 1685 edition at Harvard), page 34, he notes that the penalty for simultaneous polygamy is death, with no comment. In his *Commentariorum in Digesta Justiniani Imp. Libri XXVII* ("Twenty-seven Books of Commentaries on Emperor Justinian's Digests"), Utrecht, Antonius Schouten, 1694, 2 volumes, copy at Columbia Law Library, in Book xxv, Part iv, Title vii, pages 185-193, "On Concubines," he offers a technical discussion recognizing the legality of concubinage in past times.

110. The invitation, sent by Johannes Ludovicus Fabricius, by order of his master Charles Louis, February 16, 1673, and Spinoza's eloquent refusal, are available in various editions of Spinoza's correspondence. Fabricius sent the invitation unwillingly, because he was hostile to Spinoza's *Tractatus Theologicus-Politicus* (J. L. Fabricius, *Opera Omnia,* 1698, pages 70, 74). We wish Fabricius had commented on Leyser's note on Spinoza.

111. See: Pamela R. Barnett. *Theodore Haak, 1605-1690. The First Translator of Paradise Lost,* 1962, Mouton & Co., 's Gravenhage (The Hague).

112. Bibliothek des Literarischen Vereins in Stuttgart. CCXXVIII. *Briefe der Elizabeth Stuart, Königin von Böhmen, an ihren Sohn, den Kurfürsten Carl Ludwig von der Pfalz, 1650-1662, Nach den in Königlichen Staatsarchiv zu Hannover Befindlichen Originalen. Herausgegeben von Anna Wendland.* Tubingen, 1902, page 92 ("Library of the Literary Society, Stuttgart. Letters of Elizabeth Stuart, Queen of Bohemia, to her son Elector Charles Louis of the Palatinate, 1650--1662. From the Originals in the Royal State Archives of Hannover, edited by Anna Wendland.")

113. In the same collection of letters, page 51, may be read Elizabeth Stuart's letter to Charles Louis, October 16/26, 1654 from The Hague about John Durie's translation of Milton's *Eikonoklastes,* written to expose the fraudulent royalist "King's Book," *Eikon Basilike.* From Elizabeth Stuart's spelling of Milton's name, it would seem that she had heard of him from people speaking French:

> Sonne, I vnderstand that Dury meanes to pass by Heidleberg in his way from Suiss; I hope you uill neither

see him nor suffer him to haue anie kinde of fauour or stay in your countrie, for though he be a minister, he is the basest rascall that euer was of that coat. He uritt and printed a booke, where he aproues the king my dear Brothers murther, which I haue read, and he has translated into french Milletons booke against the kings booke, so as I entreat you, not to see that rascall nor suffer his stay and if it be possible his passage thourough your countrie; I assure you, that if I were now at Heidleberg, and that he passed there, I would haue him soundlie basted, his coat shoulde not saue him, hauing dishonnoured it by his villanie, which is all I haue to say to you at this time onelie I pray, remember the ill condition I ame in who ame

Your most affectionate Mother
E.

Hagh this 26/16 of Oct.

Nachschrift: Cromwell coach horses runne away with him the other day, but his master the Divell saued him from harme onelie a little bruised and a black eye, the oulde rascal did driue himself and fell off the coache box, I hope it is a good omen.

114. To complicate the question, there is extant the text of a long letter addressed to Charlotte by Carl, Landgrave of Hesse-Cassel, after the death of Luise von Degenfeld, urging that Charlotte agree at that late date to a formal divorce from Charles Louis, on the grounds that it would clarify an improper situation; that the death of Luise eliminated questions of pride and pique; and that it was necessary to forestall a challenge to the succession by pro-Catholic claimants such as the Duke of Neuburg, or Prince Rupert, thereby endangering the Protestant church in the Palatinate, with Heidelberg University, and the entire balance of power between Protestants and Catholics in the Holy Roman Empire. A shorter letter to the same effect was addressed by this Carl to the faculties of theology and law at Marburg University, August 27, 1677.

These letters wre published under the title *Gründliche Ausführung einiger Ursachen, warum sich die Churfürstin Charlotta zu Pfalz, Churfürst Carl Ludwigs zu Pfalz Gemahlin, nach absterben der Frau Rau Gräfin, resolviren solle in eine Ehe-Scheidung mit hochgedachtem Churfürsten zu consentiren, nebst beygefügtem Schreiben des Herrn Landgrafens zu Hessen-Cassel, gegenwärtige Schrifft betreffend, de Anno 1677* ("Fundamental Exposition of Several Reasons Why Electoral Princess Charlotte of the Palatinate, wife of Elector Charles Louis, after the Death of the Lady Raugräfin Should Decide to Consent to a Divorce with the Highly Esteemed Elector, together with an Appended Letter of the Lord Landgrave of Hesse-Cassel Concerning the Instant Document"). These letters were printed by Johan Christian Lünig, *Selecta Scripta Illustria* ("Selected Notable Letters"), folio, Friedrich Lanckisch's Heirs, 1723, pages 426-436; my photocopy from Freiberger Library, Case Western Reserve University, Cleveland, Ohio.

115. Siegmund Jacob Baumgarten, *Nachrichten von Merkwürdigen Büchern* ("News of Noteworthy Books"), second series, fifth volume, Halle, 1754, pages 499-503, distinguished the two issues by these features: page 3, preface, *quis iustitius,* second issue, *quis iustius;* page 248 is misnumbered 148 in the first issue. My photocopy is the first issue, from the British Museum, which I have compared with the copy of the second issue at the University of Heidelberg Library. Both issues are quarto; title page with blank verso, four pages dedication, six pages Vorrede, text and appendices, 1-249. The *Errata* tabulated on page 249 of the first issue remain the same in the second; neither includes Baumgarten's two points. Baumgarten noted that some first readers erroneously attributed the book to Boeckelmann.

116. Siricius, Diecmann and other Lutheran writers against polygamy refused to credit the statement that Luther had approved of Philip of Hesse's bigamy, since Thuanus (the

only source before 1679) had not named the "pastors" whom Philip consulted. The texts given by Beger differ somewhat from those printed by Carolus Gottlieb Brettschneider, *Philippi Melanthonis Opera Quae Supersunt Omnia* ("All the Works of Philip Melanchthon which Survive"), 1834-1835, volume 3. Brettschneider's notes indicate the variants. W. W. Rockwell thought that Brettschneider's text derived from a later version, and that Beger's text corresponds more exactly to the original manuscripts in the archives at Weimar and Marburg. I have not the leisure to seek out these manuscripts, nor would it be to our present purpose; but I find that Beger-Arcuarius' version has "einen grafen" while Brettschneider's text specifies "Grafen von Gleichen." Leyser lists the pastors who signed the dispensation for Philip, in his *Warmund* books and *Polygamia Triumphatrix,* with several differences from Beger and from Brettschneider; attributable to his sloppy note taking, or perhaps, as he claims, to his having used still another source, at the Steuber library.

117. Leyser also cited as his source for Luther's share in Philip's bigamy "*Sarcerium* in *Corpore Juris Matr.* p. 27. 36. 274" which sent me off on another wild goose chase to Princeton Theological Seminary, the University of Chicago, Harvard-Andover and elsewhere. Erasmus Sarcerius, Lutheran clergyman, 1501-1559, wrote *Ein Buch vom Heiligen Ehestande,* "A Book on Holy Matrimony," 1553, which appeared, still in German, in 1569, but with a Latin title *Corpus Iuris Matrimonialis,* "Body of Matrimonial Law." Leyser's page numbers troubled me, because they did not correspond to the matter of the numbering of either the 1553 or 1569 editions, which are numbered by folios, not by pages; until I found that Leyser had sloppily lifted those numbers from Siricius' *Uxor Una,* 1669, page 44, substituting "p." for "fol.," and ignoring Sarcerius' actual position on these issues. If Leyser had really known the details of Philip of Hesse's bigamy earlier, it is hard to believe that he would not have made effective use of that information.

118. The full title is *Pyrrhonii und Orthophili Unterredung von der im nechsten Jahr unter dem nahmen Daphnaei Arcuarii Ans Liecht gekommenen Betrachtung des In dem Natur- und Göttlichen Recht gegründeten heiligen Ehestandes, insonderheit so fern Selbige Severin Walther Schlüters, Königl. Hoff-Predigers in Dennemarck, wieder den so genanten Theophilum Alethaeum im 1677ten Jahr eröffnete Theologische Gedancken von der Polygynia angehet. Hamburg, Gedruckt bey Georg Rebenlein, 1680.* (Harvard) ("Dialogue of Pyrrhonius and Orthophilus about the Consideration of Holy Matrimony Based in Natural and Divine Law, published last year under the name of Daphnaeus Arcuarius, particularly in so far as it relates to the Theological Thoughts on Polygyny published in 1677 by the same Severin Walther Schlüter, Royal Palace Preacher in Denmark, against that so-called Theophilus Alethaeus. Hamburg, printed by Georg Rebenlein, 1680"). It includes title page, five page preface, three page summary, 96 pages of text, and five pages of Errata of which one appertains to his 1677 booklet, which seems to have been issued (reissued?) in common format with the 1680 dialogue. Schlüter also suspected that Arcuarius was, or was associated with, Johan Ludwig Fabricius.

S. W. Schlüter's *Propylaeum Historiae Christianae* ("Gateway to Christian History"), published by Johan Georg Lipper at Leipzig and Lüneburg, 1696, lists the major books against Leyser and Beger, but adds no information. (Copy at Swift Library, University of Chicago).

Rather more often cited in later discussion was Johann Meyer's ponderous *Uxor Christiana, sive de Conjugio inter duos deque incestu et divortiis Dissertationes Tres* ("The Christian Wife, or Three Dissertations on Bigamous Marriage and on Incest and on Divorce"), Amsterdam, 1687 issue at Library Company of Philadelphia, 1688 issue at General Theological Seminary, New York. The first dissertation, pages 1-298, is devoted to refutation in minute detail not only of

Daphnaeus Arcuarius but also of Theophilus Alethaeus and of Athanasius Vincentius, whom Meyer treats as if he believed them to be different persons. Meyer was Reformed (Calvinist rather than Lutheran, which at that time often meant no contact) and he appears unfamiliar with Leyser's earlier works. He does not mention Vythagius. Meyer was a professor at Harderwyck, and he lists the names of seventeen respondents who shared disputations with him on these and other topics. He offers a great deal of detail out of the Talmud and from the teachings of the Karaite (non-Talmudic) Jewish sect. His essay on divorce is heavy with Selden, nothing on Milton or Pufendorf. Meyer mentions a 1681 juridical disputation by J. F. Boeckelmann, *De Sponsalibus et Ritu Nuptiarum* ("Of Betrothals and the Marriage Rite") discussing polygamy and natural law, and taking notice of Daphnaeus Arcuarius on Luther's and Melanchthon's roles in the Hesse bigamy.

Meyer's book was reviewed at length in Jean LeClerc, *Bibliothèque Universelle et Historique de l'Année MDCLXXXVII* ("Universal and Historical Library for 1687"), Amsterdam, volume 7 (1688), pages 475-486; and in Henri Basnage, *Histoire des Ouvrages des Savans* ("History of the Works of the Learned"), 1688, volume II, article IX, pages 83-96.

In the clergymen's journal, *Unschuldige Nachrichten von Alten and Neuen Theologischen Sachen* ("Righteous Reports on Old and New Theological Affairs"), printed at Leipzig by Johan Friedrich Braun, 1713, pages 39-42, there was reprinted a brief worldly-wise defense of Luise von Degenfeld's role in the bigamy of Charles Louis, fourteen points defending the bigamy, with a point by point counter-argument: *Kurtze Untersuchung einer Schrifft so vor die Chur-Pf. Degenfeldische Bigamie Gestellet Worden* ("Short Inquiry into a Document Setting Forth the Palatinate-Degenfeld Bigamy"); both points of view anonymous and undated, but the publication of the item testifying to continued interest in the matter and the issue.

119. This *Programma* was printed in Johannes Ludovicus Fabricius, *Opera Omnia* (see note 107 above), pages 461-462. While the Heidelbergers disclaim any connection with the Daphnaeus Arcuarius book, they make no mention of Beger's name and no reference to Charles Louis. The disclaimer was at least partly a maneuver to defend Fabricius from the intrigues of his rivals.

THE CASE OF JOHAN LUDWIG LANGHANS: A peculiar sequel involved Charles Louis' son and heir Karl. Samuel Schelwig, in *Reliqua de Polygamia Adversus Themistium,* Leipzig, 1714, (of which more below) tells of Johan Ludwig Langhans, clergyman and sometime privy councillor to Karl, in 1686 sentenced to the pillory and to twenty years jail for invoking Scripture in defense of an illicit liaison or bigamy. Schelwig cites the account in *Der Ungewissenhaffte Gewissens-Rath* ("The Conscienceless Conscience Counsellor", 1689, 4°). I have not seen this 1689 text but I do have from the British Museum a photocopy of the 1720 reprint by L. V. A., *Der Ungewissenhaffte Gewissens-Rath, Vorgestellet in einer Theologischen Facultät zu Heidelberg Bedencken über etzliche Brieffe Johann Ludwig Langhansens, vormahls bey des verstorbenen Churfürsten von Pfalz Durchl. gewesen Beicht-Vaters, Geheimden- und Gewissens-Rath Darinnen er Ihre Chur-Fürstl. Durchl. zur Desertion Dero Gemahlin, und ungebührlichen Buhlen-Liebe mit einer gewissen Hof-Dame verleiten wollen, Samt einer Vorrede, worinn dessen Conduite, Verbrechen und Bestraffung enthalten* ("The Conscience-less Conscience Counsellor Portrayed in the Considerations of the Theological Faculty of Heidelberg over Several Letters of Johan Ludwig Langhans, formerly Father Confessor, Privy and Conscience Counsellor to the Late Serene Elector Palatine, Wherein He Wished to Mislead His Highness to Desertion of His Wife and into an Indecent Illicit Love with a Particular Court Lady, Together with a Preface on his Conduct, Crime and Punishment with More Details.") The intrigue began when Elector Karl's wife Wilhelmina Ernestine failed to supply an heir. Langhans did not urge any of the usual arguments for bigamy but in veiled language justified a rather hedonistic attitude, here evidenced in the texts of eight letters to Karl, between July 1682 and June 1684, and Latin verses dated March 31, 1683. Naturally he incurred the hostility of Charles Louis' widow Charlotte, and the Heidelberg faculty, whose commentary dated December 7/17, 1684 is by Johannes Ludovicus Fabricius, Johannes Wilhelmus Matthaeus and Johannes Georg Ohm. Karl apparently tolerated Langhans, but soon after his death (May 17/27, 1685) Langhans was prosecuted, pilloried March 2, 1686 and jailed. He was set free in the French invasion two years later. The 1689 booklet was published by those who had pushed his 1686 prosecution. The Langhans case occupies pages 73-148 of the 1720 book (see note 105 above). Langhans has also left several volumes of devotional writings, with no reference to plural marriage in them.

120. Brief biographies of Lorenz Beger (1653-1705) may be found in Nicéron, volume 4, 168-181; Adolphus Clarmundus (= Johan Christoph Rüdiger), *Vitae Clarissimorum Virorum* ("Lives of Most Famous Men"), XI, 1714, pages 143-149; Iohannes Klefeker, *Bibliotheca Eruditorum Praecocium* ("Library of Erudite Prodigies"), at Christian Liebezeit, Hamburg, 1717, 24-26; and others, because of his contributions to numismatics and antiquities, which are readily available in their elegant original editions in major American and European libraries. Beger's first wife was Sophie Clodie, Danish maid of honor to Wilhelmina Ernestine, wife of Elector Karl; she died in 1693. He later married Anne Neuhausen, daughter of Matthias Neuhausen, burgomaster of Berlin. He had no children. Also see Charles Ancillon (1654-1715), *Mémoires Concernant Les Vies et Les Ouvrages de Plusieurs Modernes Celebres dans la République des Lettres,* "Memoirs of the Lives and Works of Several Celebrated Moderns in the Commonwealth of Letters," Amsterdam, 1709, 432-468. Ancillon said that

when Elector Karl died, Beger recovered his anti-polygamy manuscript; but I have not seen any indication whether it has survived anywhere.

121. These letters of Leibnitz are in: Dietrich Christoph von Rommel, editor, *Leibniz und Landgraf Ernst von Hessen Rheinfels. Ein Ungedruckter Briefwechsel über religiöse und politische Gegenstände. Mit einer ausfuhrlichen Einleitung und mit Anmerkungen herausgegeben von Chr. von Rommel,* "Leibnitz and Landgrave Ernst of Hesse-Rheinfels. An Unpublished Correspondence on Religious and Political Affairs. With a Complete Introduction and Annotations edited by C. von Rommel," Frankfurt, Literarische Anstalt, J. Rütten, 1847, volume 2, pages 297-298, 341-342, 346. These letters were incompletely quoted by Julien Schmidt, *Geschichte des Geistlichen Lebens in Deutschland von Leibnitz bis auf Lessings Tod,* "History of Intellectual Life in Germany from Leibnitz to the Death of Lessing, 1681-1781," Leipzig, published by Fr. Wilhelm Grunow, 1862, Volume I, 166. I have carried over the irregularities in the French accent marks from the originals.

Gastineau: His references to Philip of Hesse's bigamy are not in his *La Grande Controverse de la Présence Réelle de Jésus-Christ en l'Eucharistie ou la Suite des Lettres à un Gentilhomme de la Réligion Prétendue Reformée,* Tome II, III, 1679, "The Great Controversy of the Real Presence of Jesus Christ in the Eucharist, or the Sequel to the Letters to a Gentleman of the So-Called Reformed Religion" (Bibliothèque Nationale, Paris). Despite the efforts of my good friend, Pierre LeBailly, and my own search there, no pertinent writings by any Gastineau have been located. (Rockwell, p. 135, cited "Nic. Gastineau.")

122. *Bishop Burnet's History of His Own Time,* 1724, volume I, pages 260-261. Gilbert Burnet (1643-1715) was only 27 in 1670, but already had a considerable reputation. He was elevated to bishop in 1689 in connection with the accession of William and Mary to the throne. Lauderdale and Murray (also spelled *Moray*) were in 1670 in the inner circle of advisers to Charles II.

The Lord Roos scandal is told in detail by Edward Hyde, Earl of Clarendon, *The Life of Edward, Earl of Clarendon, Part II, The Continuation,* in several editions; and in the Journals of the House of Lords and the House of Commons. There is a summary in J. M. French, *The Life Records of John Milton,* Rutgers University Press, 1958, V, 11-15. J. M. French made important contributions to Milton studies; he does not indicate whether he ever considered linking the consultation with Milton on divorce with the concurrent consideration then being given to the alternative of polygamy.

123. The memorandum by Gilbert Burnet is available, with minor differences in spelling and punctuation, in Bevill Higgons, *Historical and Critical Remarks on B[isho]p Burnet's History of His Own Time.* London, Printed for P. Meighan, at Gray's Inn Gate in Holborn. MDCCXXV, pages 232-243; and in John Macky, *Memoirs of the Secret Services of John Macky, Esq.,* second edition, 1733, Appendix, Number II. In line with the then high interest in the question of polygamy, it was reprinted in a number of other books about that time. T. E. S. Clarke and H. S. Foxcroft, *A Life of Gilbert Burnet, Bishop of Salisbury,* Cambridge, 1907, pages 103, and 503, regarded this paper on polygamy as genuine, as the fruit of youthful indiscretion later regretted by Burnet. Osmund Airy, contributor of the article on Burnet in the *Dictionary of National Biography,* rejected its authenticity.

In later years Burnet tried to overcome the effects of this indiscretion. He used the occasion of the death of John Wilmot, Earl of Rochester (1648-1680) to publish an account of his pastoral ministrations to the dying roué and agnostic when the deceased was no longer able to contradict him. Rochester had urged that one should seek every kind of pleasure, so long as one did not hurt another or damage one's own health thereby. "The restraining a Man from the use of Women, Except one in the way of Marriage, and denying the remedy of Divorce, he thought unreasonable impositions on the Freedom of Mankind." (Add Rochester to the roster of polygamophiles). Burnet tells us that he answered Rochester, arguing not from the

Bible but using Rochester's own premises, from the manifest injury to the welfare of women in extant polygamous societies. See: Gilbert Burnet, *Some Passages of the Life and Death of the Right Honourable John, Earl of Rochester, who died the 26th of July, 1680. Written by his own Direction on his Death-Bed, by Gilbert Burnet, D.D. London. Printed for Richard Chiswel at the Rose and Crown in St. Paul's Church-yard, 1680.*

124. The first phrase quoted is from the "earliest" or "anonymous" life of Milton, recently identified by the late William Riley Parker as by Milton's pupil-friend Cyriack Skinner. The phrase is used by Anthony à Wood in his sketch of Milton in the *Fasti Oxonienses,* 1691, together with the second quoted phrase about Milton's competence on this matter. I omit Wood's other phrase "as he was about that time by a chief Officer of State," which is Wood's slurring together Cyriack Skinner's recollection of a different incident. Wood's phrasing has led some to infer that Milton was consulted by a committee of two at the time of the Roos case. Such may have been the case, as it was with Burnet, but we have only Skinner's testimony, which is for one member of the House of Lords. Under the influence of Wood's account, David Masson in his monumental *Life of Milton,* vi, 640, suggested the Earl of Anglesey and Sir Orlando Bridgman, Lord Keeper of the Seal. J. M. French suggested the Earl of Bridgewater (*Life Records of John Milton,* V, 14). Others who should be considered are Lord Lauderdale, with or without Sir Robert Murray; the then Duke of Buckingham, who was son-in-law to Sir Thomas Fairfax, the one-time Parliamentary army commander, and a prime mover in the divorce; John Wilkins, one of the two bishops who voted for the divorce, who included Milton's writings on divorce in his lists of reading recommended for clergymen (See Appendix II, herein, and J. M. French, *Life Records of John Milton,* II, 160, 169, 337), and who was for a time in the 1640's chaplain to Charles Louis; or possibly, Lord Arlington, even though he was of the faction opposed to

the divorce, because he is listed in the House of Lords Journals on each day of the debate in March 1670 as "one of the Principal Secretaries of State" and is the only person so listed there.

125. The story of Charles II and his going through the forms of a wedding with Louise de Kéroualle is told in Osmund Airy, *Charles II,* London, 1901; John Lindsey, *Charles II and Madame Carwell,* London, 1937; Jeanne Delpech, *Louise de Kéroualle,* Paris, 1950; and others.

John Evelyn, the "other" great diarist of that age, was present at Euston that night of October 9, 1671 but staying somewhere else in that huge expanse of isolated wings and apartments, so that he missed the "marriage." In his account (*The Diary of John Evelyn,* edited by E. S. De Beer, Oxford, 1955, volume 3, pages 589-590):

> It was universally reported that the faire Ladye —— was bedded one of these nights, and the stocking flung, after the manner of a married Bride: I acknowledge she was for the most part in her undresse all day, and that there was fondnesse, & toying with that young wanton: nay, 'twas said, I was at the former ceremonie, but 'tis utterly false, I neither saw nor heard of any such thing whilst I was there, though I had ben in her Chamber & all over that Apartment late enough; & was my selfe observing all passages with curiosity enough: however twas with confidence believed that she was first made a *Misse* as they cald these unhappy creatures, with solemnity, at this time &:

(A *misse,* in the slang of that time, was a concubine: Oxford English Dictionary).

The *Histoire Secrette de la Duchesse de Portsmouth* (etc.) *Traduit de la Copie Angloise imprimée à Londrès. Chez Richard Baldwin, en 1690,* "Secret History of the Duchess of Portsmouth . . . Translated from the English Copy Printed at London. At Richard Baldwin, 1690," vii, 192 pages, in at least two printings (copies at Harvard-Houghton) is a fictionalized account using substitute names, "le Prince," "Francelie"; it is no evidence for the fact of the pretended marriage, but good evidence of the popular gossip that it had been sought in good faith by Louise and granted in mock play by Charles.

126. John Dryden, *Absalom and Achitophel,* lines 1-16. Dryden made good use of the Bible story. David stands for Charles, Michal for Catherine of Braganza.

The lines attributed to Marvell were printed in *The Secret History of the Reigns of King Charles II and King James II,* [London], 1690, page 85. The New York Public Library copy has ii, 214, i pages.

127. There is no recorded testimony that the question of polygamy came up when Milton was consulted in the Roos divorce case, or that in any such discussion he would have been motivated by the issue of a Protestant succession; but both are plausible and reasonable inferences from the context of events, as shown by Burnet's recollections, and from the views which Milton expressed in his 1672 pamphlet *Of True Religion.*

128. In his Cambridge Ms., 1639-1641, Milton had listed among his possible subjects for dramatic treatment "Vortiger marrying Roena. see Speed. reproov'd by Vodin archbishop of London. Speed." (Columbia edition, XVIII, 241). John Speed's *History of Great Britain,* which Milton was reading, has only censure for Vortigern, who laid Britain open to conquest by the Saxons, and for his bigamy, Vortigern being "in profession a Christian, whose Religion alloweth neither polygamy nor adultery." Archbishop Vodin spoke for the Briton nobility when he warned Vortigern that he was thereby endangering both his soul and his crown. Subsequent events were gruesome enough to amply fulfill the needs of any Elizabethan or Jacobean historical tragedy.

In the 1698 collected edition of Milton's works, in the text of the *History of Britain,* among other revisions there attributed to Milton himself, Helena, mother of Constantine, is described as the concubine of Constantius, with no further elaboration.

MILTON'S NOTE ON GILDAS: In his *Commonplace Book*, page 114, Milton wrote a note which he understood, but because of his brevity it has hitherto been misunderstood. Probably about 1647-1648 Milton was reading a book by Gildas, a sixth century British monk, *De Excidio et Conquestu Britianniae Epistola,* "Epistle on the Fall and Conquest of Britain," from which he drew extensively for his *History of Britain* (and for his *Tenure of Kings* and his *Defense of the People of England*). Inclined as he was to grasp at any polygamophile straw, Milton took notice of two passages (so his entry shows), here given in Gildas' Latin and in my translation:

> Reges habet Britannia, sed tyrannos; judices habet, sed impios; saepe praedantes et incutientes, sed innocentes; vindicantes et patrocinantes sed reos et latrones; quamplurimas conjuges habentes, sed scortantes et adulterantes; crebro jurantes, sed perjurantes; vouentes . . .

> Britain has kings, but tyrant kings; she has judges, but unjust judges, often penalizing and striking down, but the innocent; defending and protecting, but the culprits and the felons; having many wives, but committing fornication and adultery; often taking oath but swearing falsely; making vows . . .

From the balanced construction, it is clear that the phrase "quamplurimas conjuges habentes," "having (as) many wives (as possible)," corresponds to the first part in each contrasted activity, so that it suggests that Gildas in this construction was not criticizing plurality of wives, but whoring and marital infidelity. (Whether he was condemning adultery by the men or by the women could be disputed.)

The second passage, near the end of Gildas' epistle, referring to the corruption of the clergy, reads:

> I Tim. 3.2 *Oportet ergo huiusmodi irreprehensibilem esse.* In hoc namque sermone lacrimis magis quam verbis opus est, ac si dixisset Apostolus eum esse omnibus irreprehensibiliorem debere Unius uxoris virum. Quid ita apud nos quoque contemnitur quasi non audiretur vel idem dicere & virum uxorum?

> I Timothy iii,2. *It behooves therefore one of these to be free of any cause for reproof.* At this remark we have need for tears more than for words, and as if the Apostle had said he should be more free than all others from occasion for rebuke, the husband of one wife. What is so much contemned among us, as if it had not been heard, or as if he had said the "husband of wives?"

Milton's note combined extracts from both passages, as follows:

> Britanni etiam post fidem receptam conjuges habuere complures, quo nomine a Gilda reprehunduntur quam plurimas conjuges habentes, sed scortas, &c. vid. epist. Gild. et ad finem; unius uxoris virum, quod ita apud nos contemnitur &c ac si apostolus dixisset virum uxorum.

In my translation, I leave Milton's quotations from Gildas in the original Latin, in italics, which will make Milton's intent more clear:

> The Britons even after they had received the faith had many wives, in which regard they are criticized by Gildas *quam plurimas conjuges habentes,* but whores, etc. See the Gildas epistle, and towards the end, *unius uxoris virum, quod ita apud nos contemnitur,* etc., *ac si apostolus dixisset virum uxorum.*

From the fact that Milton uses the feminine *scortas,* "whores," and that he knew the context of the first passage, it is clear that he understood that the focus of Gildas' criticism was not on the men marrying many wives, but on the ensuing adulteries (of the wives, in Milton's interpretation). For Milton, the second passage was further evidence of plurality of wives among the ancient Britons.

The Columbia edition translates the words of the *Commonplace Book* out of their context and so erroneously turns the entry into a criticism of polygamy. The Yale edition knows nothing of the first quotation, garbles the second, and offers confusion, in its note 3, Volume I, page 413.

The passages from Gildas I take from the 1587 edition, pages 121 and 145, in the collection of annals of the Britons, *Rerum Britannicarum,* published by Renatus Potelerius (René Postellier) at Lyons, France; copy at New York Public Library.

129. Lady Chaworth's letter was among the manuscripts of the Duke of Rutland, at Belvoir Castle, published in: Historical Manuscripts Commission, *Report, 12 Appendix,* Part V, 1889, volume II, page 28. John Birch appears passim in Grey's *Debates,* in Pepys' Diary, and other records of the time. The *Dictionary of National Biography* does not report this incident at the church.

My thanks to J. P. Ferris, of the History of Parliament Trust, Institute of Historical Research, University of London, for helpful suggestions on Mallet and Birch.

It has been suggested that Mallet's bill ushered in a century of discussion on polygamy, but this is an unrealistic evaluation: Alfred Owen Aldridge, "Population and Polygamy in Eighteenth Century Thought," *Journal of the History of Medicine and Allied Sciences,* iv, 1949, 129-148; "Polygamy and Deism," *Journal of English and Germanic Philology,* 48, (1949) 343-360; "Polygamy in Early Fiction: Henry Neville and Denis Veiras," *PMLA,* 65, (1950) 464-472; but Aldridge included Beza as an advocate of polygamy, misdated the June

1658 Council of State order, mis-attributing it to Cromwell, and makes other statements which must be discounted.

Part of Aldridge's material reappears in: Geoffrey Bullough, "Polygamy Among the Reformers," in *Renaissance and Modern Essays Presented to Vivian de Sola Pinto,* edited by G. R. Hibbard, London, 1966, 5-23, with fresh errors, Philip of Hesse repentant, Ochino misdated, Neville's book mis-titled "Parliament of Women," and Leyser's 1674 *Discursus* allegedly "issued in English as Polygamia Triumphatrix."

130. John Lord Campbell, *The Lives of the Lord Chancellors and Keepers of the Great Seal of England from the Earliest Times till the Reign of King George IV* (1845-1847 and in other editions) is willing to concede that Cowper had Elizabeth as mistress, and had two children by her, but denies that there was a bigamy on the grounds that he had dropped all correspondence with her before he married Judith Booth.

131. Patrick Delany (of whom more anon) also mentions a book on polygamy written by the Lord Chancellor, but no one ever mentions it as printed.

Voltaire heard about the Cowper case when he was in England and he retailed it with unverified variations. Under the heading "Femme. Polygamie" in his *Dictionnaire Philosophique,* Voltaire asserts that Cowper kept his two wives in an amicable ménage à trois; and he was quite sure that Cowper had composed a little book favoring polygamy. Voltaire also claimed "J'ai connu un des souverains dans l'empire d'Allemagne dont le père, ayant épousé une luthérienne, eut permission du pape de se marier à une catholique, et qui garda ses deux femmes"—"I knew one of the rulers in the Empire in Germany whose father, having married a Lutheran woman, received permission from the Pope to marry a Catholic, and who kept both his wives."

132. So tabulated by T. E. S. Clarke and H. S. Foxcroft, *A Life of Gilbert Burnet, Bishop of Salisbury,* Cambridge, 1907.

In 1739 Delany published a second edition, under the same pseudonym, enlarged with a preface, and dedicated to Hugh Boulter, Archbishop of Armagh. A German translation appeared in 1742, D. Patrick Delany, *Gedancken von der Vielweiberey, aus dem Englischen übersetzt von M. C. E. K.*, Danzig, at Johann Heinrich Rüdiger. It has title page with blank verso; preface by translator, November 1, 1741, 4 pages; Delany's preface, 10 pages; translation based on the second English edition, 1-120. The translator added useful notes of his own but was properly puzzled by Delany's placing *Polygamia Triumphatrix* in London instead of Lund (copy at Columbia University). A French couple, M. and Mme. de Prémontval, dissatisfied with Delany and his German editor, in 1751-1752 published in three volumes *La Monogamie, ou l'Unité dans le Mariage: ouvrage dans le quel on entreprend d'établir contre le préjugé commun, l'exacte & parfaite conformité des trois lois, de la Nature, de Moïse, & de Jésus-Christ, sur ce sujet, par M. de Prémontval. Dedié aux Dames par son Epouse. La Haye, aux frais de l'Auteur, et se trouve chez Pierre van Cleef, MDCCLI* ("Monogamy, or Unity in Marriage: a work in which we undertake to establish, against the common prejudice, the exact and perfect conformity of the three laws, the Law of Nature, of Moses and of Jesus Christ, on this subject. By M. de Prémontval. Dedicated to the Women, by his Wife. The Hague, at the author's expense, and for sale by Pierre van Cleef"). In format the work is a series of letters between Ariste and Eudoxe, ranging all over the field. My microfilm copy is from the Royal Library, Copenhagen. A German version appeared in three volumes at Nuremberg, 1753-1754, *Des von Premontval Monogamie worin wider die gemeine Meinung erwiesen wird, dass das Gesetz der Natur, Moses, und Jesu Christi einstimmung die Vielweiberei verwerfen. In das Deutsche übersetzet von Dorotheen Augusten von Windheim, gebohren von Mosheim.*

133. Henry St. John Bolingbroke, *Works,* printed for J. Johnson and others, (1809 edition), volume 7, pages 475-491. These

remarks are not dated; they appear to be from 1727-1733. An anonymous letter to the *London Magazine and Gentleman's Monthly Intelligencer,* June 1954, volume 23, pages 267-269 of the London edition, pages 294-296 of the Dublin edition, offers a "refutation" of Bolingbroke-on-polygamy; and asserts that George Berkeley, Bishop of Cloyne, the philosopher, had agreed with Bolingbroke, an assertion not supported by Berkeley's published writings.

Another instance of polygamy in common conversation is seen in *The London Magazine,* 1732, I, 461, commenting on a current book *Philosophical Dissertation on Death,* "All national institutions must be try'd by the great Law of Nature. For instance, whether Polygamy be right, or Single Marriage. For, if the Proportions of Males to Females be as 14 to 13 (as the exactest calculations affirm) then it seems to be the Design of the Author of Nature, that one Man should have but one Wife at a Time."

Thomas Rutherforth, D.D., Archdeacon of Essex, discussed polygamy at length from the standpoint of an orthodox opponent in Chapter XV, pages 322-372, of volume I of his *Institutes of Natural Law, being the substance of a Course of Lectures on Grotius de Jure Belli ac Pacis read in St. Johns College, Cambridge,* two volumes, 1754-1756.

Conyers Middleton's *A Letter to Dr. Waterland Containing Some Remarks on his Vindication of Scripture: in Answer to a Book, intituled, Christianity, as old as the Creation, Together with the Sketch or Plan of Another Answer to the Said Book* (1731) is in: *Miscellaneous Tracts by the Reverend and Learned Conyers Middleton, D.D., never before published, to which are added some scarce pieces of the same author, that were printed in his lifetime. London, 1752,* (page 141).

134. Luke Tyerman, *The Oxford Methodists,* New York, 1873, pages 386-411, "Rev. Westley Hall," stated: "He publicly and privately recommended polygamy, as comformable to nature, preached in its defence and practiced as he preached" (page 404). So also Adam Clarke, *Memoirs of the Wesley*

Family (1823 and other editions) and the *Dictionary of National Biography.*

The Gentleman's Magazine and Historical Chronicle of London, for the year 1747, volume XVII, page 531 (copy at the Library Company of Philadelphia) printed an anonymous letter dated October 30, 1747, not naming Hall, but describing him as of "uncommon appearance of sanctity, joined with indefatigable labour in field and house preaching" whose flock followed him as if he were Christ himself, until, after some period of suspicion, a servant maid of eighteen summers, E———h R-g-s, declared herself with child by him. He is quoted as saying, in self defense, "He thought it no harm, but if man's constitution required it, he might lawfully have to do with more than one woman, if not the wife of another;" and he is reported to have preached a farewell sermon to the same effect based on the instance of Elkanah in the book of Samuel. The anonymous letter writer concludes that after Hall on this occasion abandoned his wife and his congregation, in that flock "The fire of jealousy has broke out in many families, where wives or daughters were his followers."

135\. The first edition of *Thelyphthora,* (London, Printed for J. Dodsley, MDCCLXXX), was in two volumes. Volume I has the title page with blank page overleaf, two page "Advertisement," one page "Contents" with Errata overleaf; xi-xxiv, Preface; and text, 1-412. Volume II repeats the title page and blank overleaf; "Contents," one page, with "Memorandum" and Errata overleaf; text, 1-432; index to Volume I, 10 pages; index to volume II, 10 pages.

The 1781 edition adds to the title page "The Second Edition, Enlarged." The title page of Volume I still describes the work as being "In Two Volumes" but the obverse page carries the announcement of a forthcoming Volume III; followed by "Contents" on one page with Errata overleaf; i-iv, address to the officers of the charity organizations; v-xvii, Preface to the First Edition; xviii-xxxii, Preface to the Second Edition; 1-404, text. Volume II has the title page with blank overleaf

"Contents," one page with "Memorandum" and "Erratum" overleaf; 1-382, text; index to Volume I, 9 pages; index to Volume II, 9 pages.

The third volume, 1781, repeats the title page from Volumes I and II, but identifies itself as Volume III; replaces the Milton quotation on the title page by a Greek text from II Corinthians vi, 8, and a quotation from the translators' preface to the King James Bible, with a "Memorandum" overleaf; "Contents," with Errata overleaf; Preface, v-xii; text, 1-402; index, 10 pages. Volume III deals with subsidiary and related issues. Chapter XIII deals with polygamy and concubinage as dispensations of God.

According to the *Dictionary of National Biography*, a Dutch translation appeared in Amsterdam in 1782. The books against Madan marked NYPL (New York Public Library) or Harvard, in the list, I have seen; the other titles are taken from the *Monthly Review*, London, 1780-1782, passim; BM, the British Museum catalogue; and *DNB*.

British Museum supplied my photocopy of *Letters on Thelyphthora: with an Occasional Prologue and Epilogue. By the Author* [three mottoes]. *London. Printed for J. Dodsley, in Pall Mall. M.DCC.LXXXII.* It has title page; Advertisement; two page prologue; 1-167 pages. It includes twenty-eight letters written at various times between April 4, 1781 and May 18, 1782, to some ten or twelve Reverend Gentlemen, one Esquire layman and two married ladies, identified or concealed by using initials only. Since some of these letters refer back to others preceding, they may have been actually composed as real letters, not merely as a literary form. Mainly they deal with side issues; bigotry, prejudice and ignorance of his opponents; the importance of knowing the Hebrew original of the Old Testament; Josephus as evidence for polygamy in practice in Jesus' time; Mazdak, a sixth century Persian advocate of community of goods put to death with many followers, being also accused of advocating community of women. Some of these letters read well, as does the Prologue (rhyming in heroic couplets, after the then fashion on the stage).

The Epilogue, a tetrameter versification of a fable out of Aesop and Phaedrus, a satire, on jungle law justified by wild beasts because they study the ways of man, full of violence and oppression, in style and message would be eloquent in any age.

There are passim comments on Madan and the controversy in William Cowper's letters to William Unwin and John Newman, 1780-1781, in Robert Southey's edition of *The Works of William Cowper, Esq.,* London, 1836, volumes 3 and 4.

136. On Thomasius in general, since the plural marriage issue was a very small aspect of his career, see Zedler's *Lexicon;* Ernst Landsberg, *Geschichte der Deutschen Rechtswissenschaft, Dritte Abteilung* ("History of German Jurisprudence, Part Three"), published by R. Oldenbourg, München, 1898; Nicolaus H. Gundling, *Historia der Gelahrheit* ("History of the Savants"), 1736, IV, 3314-3343; Andrew D. White, *Seven Great Statesmen in the Warfare of Humanity with Unreason,* Century, New York, 1912, pages 111-161.

In recent years there has been a revival of interest in Thomasius, with publication of a series of *Thomasiana* volumes, *Arbeiten aus dem Institut für Staat- und Rechtsgeschichte bei der Martin-Luther-Universität Halle/Wittenberg* ("Works from the Institute for the History of the State and Law at the Martin Luther University of Halle/Wittenberg"). Heft 2 in the *Thomasiana* is an exhaustive bibliography of works by and about Thomasius, by Rolf Lieberwirth, *Christian Thomasius, Sein Wissenschaftliches Lebenswerk, Eine Bibliographie* ("Christian Thomasius, His Scholarly Life's Work, A Bibliography") published by Herman Böhlaus' Successors, Weimar, 1955, 213 pages, an invaluable work, to which in this present study I make a few additions.

The auction catalogue of his library *Bibliotheca Thomasiana,* Halle, July 6, 1739 (copy at Harvard and at Halle) shows that he had owned the writings on polygamy by Ochino, Beza, Leyser, Siricius, Feltmann, Mentzer, Gesenius, Dieckmann, and Beger, and works on marriage by Sarcerius, Selden and others. Of Milton's works he owned the *Epistolarum Familiarum Liber Unus* ("Personal Letters") and a 1676 edition of Milton's State Letters. He also had Salmasius' *Defensio Regia* ("Royal Defense for Charles I") and the posthumous Salmasius' *Responsio* against Milton's rebuttal of the *Defensio Regia.* A particular treasure was his manuscript copy of Bodin's *Heptaplomeres.*

Thomasius was married once and with his wife had six children.

137. Thomasius made this same point in *Paulo Plenior Historia Juris Naturalis,* published by Christopher Salfeld's widow at Halle (copy at Harvard) and in *Institutionum Jurisprudentiae Divinae Libri Tres,* etc., "Three Books on the Institutes of Divine Jurisprudence," Section 20, (page references differ in the several editions; 1730 copy at Columbia University Law Library). See Note 81 above.

Johan Georgius Kulpis, in his *Collegium Grotianum, Super Iure Belli ac Pacis, in Academia Giessensi, XV. Exercitationibus Institutum* ("Course of Grotian Lectures, on the Law of War and Peace, Arranged in Fifteen Studies at Giessen University"), Halle, 1682 and other editions, in Exercitatio IV, Section vi, touched briefly on the Leyser and Beger literature in a footnote. In his text he said that polygamy was not banned by natural law but that monogamy, the better form, was ordained by a universal divine law, waived by divine dispensation in the Old Testament, this license taken away in the New, and he wanted to doubt that it was available to the highest terrestrial powers. This passage is often cited, never quoted, by writers on this subject in the next sixty years.

Also often cited by later writers, though of small import, were the notes on polygamy added by jurist Samuel Stryk (1640-1710) to the third edition (1681?) of *De Jure Ecclesiastico,* "On Church Law" by another jurist Johann Brunnemann (1608-1672), reprinted 1699, 1709, making references to Christianus Vigil, Theophilus Alethaeus and Musaeus-Herzog; these three editions in Harvard Law Library.

138. My microfilm copies of the 1685 edition of these disputaitons are from the Royal Library, Copenhagen, and there are copies at Harvard Law Library. *De Crimine* has title page with blank verso, 47 unnumbered pages. *De Praescriptione* has title page with blank verso, 34 unnumbered pages.

The biography of Beyer (1665-1714) is found in Jugler and in Landsberg, both of whom offer sketches on Ludovici, Gundling, Schmauss, Gribner, Titius and others who figure in the Thomasius story.

139. Konrad Varrentrap, "Briefe von Pufendorf," in *Historische Zeitschrift. Herausgegeben von Heinrich v. Sybel und Max Lehman, 1893, Neue Folge,* "Letters of Pufendorf, in Historical Journal, edited by H. v. Sybel and M. Lehman, 1893, new series," volume 70, 1-51, 193-232, especially page 18.

Luther approached a similar position on a woman's bigamy under certain circumstances; see above, quotation from *Prelude on the Babylonian Captivity of the Church.*

A peculiar reference to Leyser and Milton apeared in Thomasius' periodical *Monats-Gespräche,* in the June 1688 issue (that issue titled *Scherz-und Ernsthaffter Vernünfftige und Einfältiger Gedancken,* "Jesting and Serious Reasonable and Simple Thoughts," published by Christoph Salfeld at Halle, page 737), discussing Gerhard Feltmann on dowries,

> So hat auch unter denen so wieder den nunmehr bekannten Theophilum Alethaeum pro defendenda monogamia geschrieben, keiner eine gute Sache so übel vertheidiget, als der Herr Feldmann, und weis sich solches der Athanasius Vincentius in seiner polygamia triumphatrice trefflich zu nütze zu machen, das so offt ich dieser beyder adversarios gegen einander halte; so offte gedencke ich an das judicium des Herrn Boeclers, welches er in seinem Museo von des Miltoni und des Salmasii Streit Schrifften gefället; quod Miltonus malum causam bene, Salmasius bonam causam male defenderit.

> So likewise among those who wrote in defense of monogamy against the recently notorious Theophilus Alethaeus, no one so ill defended a good cause as Herr Feltmann, as Athanasius Vincentius in *Polygamia Triumphatrix* points out cleverly, turning it to advantage; that as often as I compare these two opponents one against the other, so often I recall the judgment of [Johann Heinrich] Boecler submitted in his *Museum* [*ad Amicum,* 1663] on the books written in the Milton-Salmasius controversy, that Milton defended a bad cause well, Salmasius a good cause badly.

Thomasius repeated Boecler's epigram on Milton, without reference to Leyser, on other occasions; in *Monats-Gespräche,* 1688, page 760, and 1689, page 945. My microfilms are from the Faber du Faur collection of German baroque literature at Yale University.

140. The 1685 Quenstedt edition is at Universitätsbibliothek Erlangen-Nürnberg; 1691 edition at Union Theological Seminary. Contemporary reviews of Quenstedt, Meyer, Varillas, *Vesperae Groninganae* and others in our story appeared from time to time in the *Acta Eruditorum* ("Works of the Erudite") of Leipzig.

141. Melchior Zeidler's book was *Tractatus de Polygamia in quo disquiritur, an sit contra jus naturae, aut contra jus divinum sub N. T. ut circa eam dispensari nequeat?* ("Treatise on Polygamy, in which is examined, whether it be against the Law of Nature or against Divine Law under the New Testament so that there cannot be a Dispensation Thereon?"), 180 pages. It was printed together with *Matrimonio cum Sorore Uxoris Defunctae Disquisitio* ("Disquisition on Marriage with the Sister of a Deceased Wife") by Philippus Jacobus Hartmann (Zeidler's son-in-law), published by Georg Wolfgang Hamm, printer to the University of Helmstedt. My copies are from the Bayerischen Bibliothek, München, and the Royal Library, Copenhagen. Zeidler's book is heavy on Gleichen, Valentinian,

Lothar; attacks Ochino and Cajetan; was it written in the 1670's? Gerhard von Mastricht's notes in the 1712/1717 edition of Amyraut, pages 136-137, give a 1678 date, but his notes are not perfect. Universitätsbibliothek Erlangen-Nürnberg has a 1698 edition.

142. Hieronymus Bruckner's *Decisiones Iuris Matrimonialis Controversi,* 1692, was published at Frankfurt and Leipzig by Augustus Boetius, ix, 1-528, i, 1-312, plus indexes, copy at Harvard Law Library. A revised second edition was published at Gotha by Jacob Mevius, 1705.

143. Mascovius-de Mascou derive from Siricius, Büttner-Tabbert, Quenstedt and Zeidler; focus on *Polygamia Triumphatrix;* and are exceptional in citing Catholic sources, some of which were not included by Sanchez (see note 40.) My copy is from Copenhagen Royal Library. The accusative case in the title is from its grammatical construction there.

144. The list of topics in the 1694 *Disputationes Publicae XII super 48 Thesibus maxime controversis excerptis ex Institutionibus Juris Prudentiae Divinae* ("Twelve Public Disputations on 48 Theses Highly Controverted Taken from the Institutes of Divine Jurisprudence") is included in later editions of the *Institutes* (1717 and 1730 editions at Columbia University, 1730 at Halle).

The text of the 1694 Rescript is printed in M. H. Gribner, *De Intercessione Conjugum,* 1711, page 45; in Joachim Weickhmann, *Justitia Causae,* 1714, page 9; and in Gottlieb Wernsdorff, *Summam Sanae Doctrinae de Polygamia,* 1716, pages 3-4; all of whom to be discussed anon.

145. My photocopy of the *Monatliche Unterredungen* is from the British Museum. The identification of D. I. W. B. is based on Nicolaus Möller, *De Polygamia,* 1716, pages 110-113. Bajer's life (1647-1695) is in Zedler.

146. My photocopy of Schneegass is from the British Museum.

147. Werner Zur Mühlen, *Disputatio Juridica Inaugurali de Polygamia Successiva,* "Inaugural Juridical Disputation on Successive Polygamy," printed by Abraham Elzevir, Leyden, ii, 20 pages; my photocopy from The Hague Royal Library. A dissertation by N. Hougenbouck, *Dissertatio de Polygamia,* 40, Leyden, 1694, no copy located, is listed in Martin Lipenius' bibliography as revised in *Bibliothecae Realis Juridicae Supplementa et Emendationes,* edited by A. F. Schott, Leipzig, 1775.

148. My thanks to Alan and Patricia Day of London who have been helpful in expediting my photocopies of the *Vesperae,* Ludovici's *Delineatio* and other books to me from the British Museum.

149. My photocopy of Kahler-Neuburg comes from Dr. Ursula von Dietze of the Mainz Stadtbibliothek, printed at Rinthel by Herman August Enax, title page, blank verso, 1-22 pages.

150. These articles on Ochino (Volume IV, Observation XX; Volume V, Observations I and II) were attributed to Thomasius by Nicolaus Möller, *De Polygamia,* 1710 (see note 154 below). They are not included among the articles attributed to Thomasius in the list given in Lieberwirth's *Bibliographie.* In Cotta's notes on Gerhard (see note 85 above), pages 191-198, "Observation I" in volume V is attributed to "Struvius" (that is, Burghardt Gotthelf Struve). In the *Unschuldige Nachrichten* for 1716, 705-706, many articles in the *Observations* are identified by author, but not these on Ochino. These articles on Ochino also include material on Leyser. In the 1702 *Observations,* volume VI, Observation II, pages 9-13, there is a note on Jean Bodin's thought on the link between population and polygamy; this is attributed to Thomasius by Lieberwirth.

151. See note 73 above on Mayer's 1674 dissertation on Jacob's marrying two sisters. Mayer's 1702 dissertation is discussed in J. Weickhmann, *Apologie, Anderer Theil,* (of which more below), page 398.

152. My photocopies from the British Museum include a good six page printing, and what appears to be a pirated edition in seven pages with names badly misprinted (e.g. Alathaei) In the antique handwritten catalogue of the Copenhagen Royal Library, it is attributed to H. G. Masius; on what basis it is hard to see. The "Hochfürst Raht" to whom it was addressed is unidentified; Thomasius was privy councillor to the Elector-of-Brandenburg-and-King-in-Prussia, but there is no obvious reference to him in this pamphlet.

The *Censur,* written before 1712, was rebutted by Franz Julius Lütke (1651-1712) whose work was first printed in 1723 as D. Frantz Lütkens . . . *Gelehrter und Ausführlicher Tractat von der Polygamie und Concubinat* (69 more words to the title), "F. J. Lütke's Learned and Thoroughgoing Treatise on Polygamy and Concubinage," printed by Ernst Heinrich Campe, Leipzig and Gardelegen: with six page preface by the publisher; a reprint of the Henricus Alethaeus text, pages 1-8; the anonymous *Censur,* pages 9-30; Lütke's *Widerlegung der vorhergehenden Censur,* "Rebuttal of the Preceding Criticism," pages 31-153, and five pages of indexes. My microfilm copy is from the Bayerische Bibliothek, München. Lütke had been pastor at Cölln an der Spree; a member of the Royal Prussian and Royal Danish Consistorial Councils; palace preacher and professor at the Ritter-Akademie in Copenhagen.

In the Palmskiold Collection at the University of Uppsala Library, I found a handwritten copy of the Alethaeus pamphlet, in 22 pages, signed "Henricus Alethaeus I.C.T." at the end, followed by the text of the anonymous *Censur* in 89 pages, corresponding to the text on pages 9-30 of the

Lütke 1723 publication; its place in the history of these pamphlets unexplained.

153. There are copies of the *Fundamenta* (1718 edition, printed by Christopher Salfeld's widow) at Columbia and Harvard Law Libraries.

154. My microfilm copy is from the British Museum; title page, blank verso, V, 144 pages. Möller seems to be the primary source for Gerhard von Mastricht's notes in the 1712/1717 edition of Amyraut (see note 57). Gerhard von Mastricht's *Historia Juris Ecclesiastici et Pontificii* ("History of Church and Papal Law"), Halle, 1705, had a preface by Thomasius. Their association may have bearing on the revival of Amyraut, with Barlaeus-on-Polygamy and the notes added.

155. My microfilm of Gribner-Thilo is from the University of Göttingen; thanks to Oberinspektorin Eulert for this and other assistance.

156. My photocopies of Titius-Pflaume are from the Royal Library, Copenhagen and the University of Michigan. The book was reprinted in 1720.

Johan Samuel Adami, alias Misanders (1638-1713) wrote much earlier, but although his *Tractat von der Polygamia oder Vielweiberey* was announced in the columns of the *Unschuldige Nachrichten* on the appearance of both first (1713) and second (1715) editions, it was quoted (so far as I have noticed) only once, by Willenberg in his *Iterata Praesidia,* 1714, page 48. The full title runs to over a hundred words; printed by Johann Christoph Brühl for Johann Friedrich Wehrmann at Weissenfels; the second title page adding "Vermehrt und zum andermal aufgelegt"—"Enlarged and Printed the Second Time," but actually both have title page with blank verso, [3]—200 pages. I use the 1713 edition at Erlangen-Nürnberg; the second edition there, at Copenhagen Royal Library and at the University of Pennsylvania; there are copies of both elsewhere. The bulk of the book, chapters 1-7, dates to no later than 1673 or 1674, making reference only to Mentzer and Vigil on Wahrenberg and Aletophilus. The addenda, of various dates, include instances of "interim wives" among Dutch merchants in the East Indies, and other data already cited herein.

157. There were several printings of the 1713 Thomasius-Kiechel dissertation. I have seen three variants. The Harvard Law School copy has a title page with blank verso, 1-52 pages. My microfilm copy from Jena University has the same text as the Harvard copy on the title page, but after the blank verso is set in 1-68 pages. The copy at Columbia Law School is also in 68 pages, but the title page reads *Schediasma Inaugurale Juridicum de Concubinatu, Anno 1713*. This latter title is used by some of Thomasius' opponents.

Both defenders and opponents treat this dissertation as done by Thomasius himself. This dissertation, like many dissertations of that date, but not all, is printed in larger type text and smaller type commentary. The commentary in several places is unmistakably not by Thomasius, so it may be inferred that the text is Thomasius and the commentary by Kiechel, probably in consultation with each other; but see Note 162.

158. My microfilm copies from Harvard and from Jena show two distinct editions of the Breithaupt-Baumgart dissertation, both printed by Orphanotrophaeus of Halle. The title pages differ only in the placing of the year, MDCCXIII; the Harvard copy has a dedication by Baumgart to Carolus de Dieskau on the verso to the title page, text on pages 1-18, and lacks on page 16 one sentence found on Harvard page 22.

159. My copy of Grammlich's *Examen* is from Jena; title page with blank verso, 1-30. Harvard has the same edition. Jäger is usually catalogued as author, and he was so regarded by the earliest participants in the controversy, but Grammlich in later writings took full responsibility and credit.

160. See Walter Bienert, *Der Anbruch der Christliche Deutschen Neuzeit Dargestellt an Wissenschaft und Glaubens des Christian Thomasius,* ("The Beginning of Christian German Modern Times Represented in the Science and Faith of Christian Thomasius"), Halle, 1934, page 177, citing a letter from G. H. Neubauer to Anton Wilhelm Böhme; Gustav Kramer, *August Hermann Francke, Ein Lebensbild* ("A. H. Francke, A Life Portrait"), Halle, 1880-1882, volume 2, pages 151-155.

161. Petrus Encratita was pseudonymous to most of the participants in the controversy, and has remained so in references and bibliographies to this date. I find him identified as Gasser by Johann Georg Walch, *Historische und Theologische Einleitung in die Religions-Streitigkeiten der Evangelisch-Lutherischen Kirchen von der Reformation an bis Jetztige Zeiten* ("Historical and Theological Introduction to the Controversies on Religion in the Evangelical Lutheran Churches from the Reformation to the Present Time"), Jena, 1733, volume 3, 71-78 on Thomasius, page 76 on Gasser. My microfilms of Encratita are from Halle and Jena, title page with blank verso, 1-30.

162. Reinbeck: Harvard Law and Columbia Libraries have Reinbeck's *Die Natur* of March 19, 1714 in quarto, title page, blank verso; Vorrede, pages 3-6; Part I, 7-14; Part II, 42-88. Lieberwirth (page 108) lists a prior Latin version, *De Natura Coniugii et Improbanda Concubinatu,* Berlin, 1714, but I have seen no trace of it.

Harvard Law Library has the *Gedoppelter Anhang,* quarto, title page with text on verso (= page 90), 90-108. Harvard Law and Columbia have the *Nochmaliger Beweis,* title page with blank verso, text 111-156, and four page index. My microfilm from Jena includes a second edition of *Die Natur, Andere Aufflage* on the title page, printed by Rüdiger, Berlin, 1715; a *Gedoppelter Anhang* which is a different printing from the Harvard copy, though maintaining the same page numbers; and the *Nochmaliger Beweis* in the same edition as the copies at Harvard and Columbia, printed by Johan Andreas Rüdiger at Berlin.

Zierold: My microfilm copies are from Halle and Jena. No printer or place is given.

Antoninus' *Confutatio:* I have microfilms of two editions. Both have the same wording on the title page, blank verso and text 3-40, but the type and layout are different throughout. They may be differentiated by the ornament on top of Sig. A2, floral in one, circles between curlicues in the other; Jena has both editions, Halle and Harvard have the editions with the circles.

Von der Kebs Ehe: The German version was printed as item IX (although "6" on the title page) in the collection *Herrn Christian Thomasens . . . Ausserlesener und dazu gehöriger Schrifften Zweyter Theil* ("Thomasius' Selected Writings, and Related Writings, Second Part"), published by Renger at Frankfurt and Leipzig, 1714, pages 437-521, my photocopy from Halle University. In this version Kiechel's name has disappeared. Wherever in the 1713 Latin text there was a third person reference to *Dn. Praeses,* presumably Kiechel's reference to Thomasius, in the 1714 German text it is changed to first person; for example, *Dn. Praeses* on page 7 (1713) becomes *ich,* "I," on page 446 in 1714, and *Dn. Praeses* on page 20 (1713) becomes *von mir,* "by myself," on page 461 in 1714. Antoninus' *Wiederlegung,* item 7 on title page but X in the text, is on pages 522-610; his *Anhang,* 8 on the title page and XI in the text, is on pages 610-675. This collection is called "Second Part" with reference to a 1705 publication at Halle *Auserlesene und in Deutsch noch nie Gedruckte Schrifften* ("Selected Writings Not Hitherto Printed in German").

Grammlich: My microfilm of the November 14, 1714 *Defensio* is from Jena; title page, verso with dedications to four patrons continued on pages 3-4; text, pages 5-24. My microfilms of his 1716 *Tractatus* are from Jena and Harvard;

title page, blank verso; preface July 10, 1716 at Stuttgart, pages 3-4; part I titled as in 1714, [5]-46; part II now titled *Defensio Praemissa Examinis De Concubinatu opposita Marci Pauli Antonini Philosophi Tribocci Confutationi*, "Defense of the Preceding Examination of *De Concubinatu,* Against the Confutation of Marcus Paulus Antoninus, Alsatian Philosopher," pages [47]-72. The title page describes Grammlich now as "Seren. Duci Wirtemb. A Concionibus Aulicis," that is, of the palace preachers to His Serene Highness the Duke of Würtemberg. How Grammlich served the then reigning Duke (see note 187 below) is between him and his God.

163. One of these other books was the anonymous *Doctoris Theologi ad Generosissimum Dynastam Epistolica Disquisitio Instar alicujus Prophylactici, luxurianti seculo, inprimis incestae, (Jac. III, 17.) Sapientiae, abusuique incrustatae sententiae, De Licito Concubinatu Opponenda* (plus 66 more words), "Epistolary Disquisition of a Doctor of Theology to a Most Highborn Prince to Serve as a Kind of Prophylactic to this Age Rank with Especially Impure (James iii, 17) Wisdom and the Abuse of Shallow Axioms, To Oppose the Permission of Concubinage," etc., published by Gatfrey at "Freystadt," which Lieberwirth interprets as Helmstedt, 1714; title page with blank verso, [3]-104. I have microfilm copies from Jena and Halle. The latter bears a handwritten ascription of the work to Johan Deger, which I have not found elsewhere.

Another of these publications was *Ad Quaestionem: An Concubinatus Sit Tolerabilior Polygamia? Occasione Schediasmat. Inaugur. Jurid. De Concubinatu, Halae Edit. MDCXIII. Breviter et Distincte Respondere Voluit Ac Debuit Joh. Gottlob Stoltze, D. Lübben, Verlegts George Voss* ("To the Question: Whether Concubinage Is More to Be Tolerated Than Polygamy? On the Occasion of the Inaugural Juridical Schediasma on Concubinage published at Halle, 1713, Dr. Johan Gottlob Stoltze Has Wanted and Has Been Obliged to Reply Briefly and Distinctly, published at Lübben by Georg

Voss, 1715"). My microfilms are from Halle and Jena; title page with dedication on verso, text [3]-19, 1. The pamphlet is dated January 12, 1715 at *Luccaviae in Lusat. infer.,* = Luckau, in Lower Lausitz. Stoltze also dealt with the Willenberg controversy, of which more anon.

Lieberwirth, page 109, records a pseudonymous Germanus Constantus, *Neuen Moralischen Traktat von der Liebe gegen die Personen Andere Geschlechts* ("New Moral Treatise on Love towards Persons of the Other Sex"), Leipzig, 1717, against Thomasius and Antoninus. I have not located a copy.

The microfilms of books I requested from the University of Jena, and list as from there herein (based on information from Dr. Günther Steiger) reached me indirectly through the Zentral Antiquariat der Deutsche Demokratisches Republik, through the help of the Deutsche Staatsbibliothek of Berlin.

164. Thomasius' writings on plural marriage continued in print for many years. His 1685 Dissertations were reprinted 1714, 1715, 1721, 1733, 1739 and 1749. His 1713 *De Concubinatu* was reprinted 1717, 1724, 1732, 1741 and 1748. These dissertations also appeared in editions of his collected works.

His *Fundamenta* was published in 1705, 1708, 1713 and 1718. His *Institutionum Jurisprudentiae Divinae Libri Tres* appeared 1688, 1694, 1702, 1710, 1717 and 1730.

165. The story of the Willenberg-Weickhmann controversy is here reconstructed entirely from the books discussed herein, laboriously hunted down in many distant libraries. Also helpful were items in the *Unschuldige Nachrichten,* of which there is a file at Harvard-Andover Theological Seminary, passim; Zedler's *Lexicon,* particularly the article on Weickhmann, also articles on Willenberg, Schelwig, "Polygamia," and the other names in the story; Johan Georg Schelhorn, *Amoenitates Literariae,* ("Literary Beauties"), volumes 8 and 9; and Johan George Walch, *Historische und Theologische Einlei-*

tung (see note 161), pages 104-111. Willenberg was married once, had no children.

166. This discussion is in Liber II, Caput v of Willenberg's *Sicilimenta Juris Gentium Prudentiae, ex Libris Hugonis Grotii De Jure Belli et Pacis aliorumq; Virorum celeberrimorum Scriptis collecta Et ad meliorem Studiosae Juventutis captum in Quaestiones redacta,* "Gleanings from the Law of Nations Collected from Hugo Grotius' De Jure Belli et Pacis, and the Writings of Other Famous Men, and Edited in Question Form for the Better Grasp of Studious Youth," printed by Johann Zacharias Stolle at Danzig, 1709; frontispiece, title page with blank verso, 5 unnumbered pages of dedication to Danzig authorities, 7 unnumbered pages preface, 716 pages of text, five unnumbered pages of Index Capitum, 3 unnumbered pages giving the names of the 26 youths who had participated as Respondents and Opponents in these questions and Emendanda, (copy at Philadelphia Divinity School library, courtesy of Rev. John E. Lamb). The 1711 edition (copy at Erlangen-Nürnberg) and 1712 edition (copy at Columbia Law Library) substitute "Usum" for "Captum" in the title; describe themselves as "Second enlarged and corrected edition following the first Danzig edition, to which is added a subject index," published by Johan Ludwig Gleditsch and Maurice Georg Weidmann, Leipzig, 5 pages preface, 7 pages dedication, 582 pages text, plus indexes. The discussion is enlarged with more citations given.

167. The *Schediasma* was printed by Johann Zacharias Stolle (Stollius), printer to the Danzig Senate and Athenaeum. All the copies I have seen, from the University of Göttingen, from Copenhagen Royal Library, Erlangen-Nürnberg and elsewhere, are the texts as they were reprinted by Weickhmann attached to his *Vindiciae,* title page, [36]-40.

168. My photocopies of the *Vindiciae* are from the universities of Göttingen and of Erlangen-Nürnberg; title page with blank verso, [3]-34 pages, plus the 1712 *Schediasma.*

169. My photocopies of the Willenberg *Praesidia* are from Göttingen, and from Dr. Paul Raabe, of the Herzog August Bibliothek, Wolfenbüttel. Weickhmann in *Justitia Causae,* page 5, alleged that there were two issues, one for Danzig, one elsewhere, differing in text in some details. Willenberg (*Iterata Praesidia,* page 9), said that it was the result only of a printer's mishandling of revisions and corrections. The *Praesidia* has title page with blank verso, [3]-40, and Errata.

170. The *Justitia Causae* by Weickhmann has title page plus blank verso, dedication and preface to Danzig city officials, dated December 10, 1713, x pages, text 1-317, plus xi, index and Emendanda. My photocopies are from the University of Erlangen-Nürnberg and from the Bibliothek des Kammergerichts, Berlin, via the Freie Universität there.

171. My photocopy of Willenberg's *Iterata Praesidia* is from the Mainz Stadtbibliothek; title page, blank verso, 1-94 pages. Hoppe's life is in Jugler, 4:178-187; there is a copy of his *Commentatio Succincta ad Institutiones Justinianeas* (originally 1693) in the 1728 edition (by Schrey and Conrad at Frankfurt-on-Oder) at Erlangen-Nürnberg. Even Zedler offers no dates for Schultze, whose dissertation he gives as "De Eo Quod Non Vetat Lex, Vetat Fieri Pudor in Matrimonio Constituendo." Schultze had been inspector at the Danzig Athenaeum.

172. My photocopies of Schelwig's *De Polygamia* are from Göttingen, and from the British Museum (although it is not in their printed catalogue). Schelwig mentions the 1712 Amyraut edition, but not Milton nor Velthusius-on-Milton. His life is in Ephraim Praetorius, *Athenae Gedanenses, etc.* ("The Learned of Danzig"), Leipzig, 1713, published by Johann Friedrich Gleditsch and Son, 235 pages plus indexes, which also has data on Calovius, Hoppe, Willenberg and others; copy at Erlangen-Nürnberg.

173. My microfilm copy of Schelwig's *Reliqua* is from Harvard Law Library, title page, blank verso, [3]-48 pages.

174. My microfilm copy of Willenberg's *On Polygamy Against Meletius* is from the Mainz Stadtbibliothek, title page with blank verso, [3]-32 pages.

175. Not one of all the libraries to which I have written reports having a copy of the *Weickhmanniana,* although it was known to Zedler and other contemporaries. Possibly it was a broadside.

176. My microfilm copies of the *Kurtzer Beweis* are from the libraries of Halle and Göttingen. Cölln then adjoined Berlin on the Spree. The original English pamphlet may have had rather a different title. I have combed catalogues and card files by author, topic, place and date, and have consulted experts on that period but have not yet identified that original. The pamphlet has title page, blank verso, [3]-16 pages.

177. My microfilm copies of the *Declaration* are from the Royal Library of Copenhagen and the University of Jena, title page, blank verso, five unnumbered pages.

178. My photocopy of Lucius Verus is from the Biblioteka Narodowa, Warszawa, thanks to Dr. Alidia Gryczowa; title page, i, 23 unnumbered pages. I date it early because it does not mention the Petricov or Szembek decrees.

179. The text of the decrees is printed in Wernsdorff (see below).

180. I find a copy of the supposedly non-existent first edition of the Freudenhöfer pamphlet, printed at "Freystadt, 1715" at the University of Halle library, which also has the second edition ("Freystadt, 1715") of which I also have microfilm copies from the University of Heidelberg and Herzog August

183. My microfilm copy of J. A. E., *Unpartheysche Gedancken* is from Heidelberg University; title page with blank verso, ii, 1-28 pages.

184. My photocopy of Wernsdorff is from the University of Jena, and there is a copy of the pamphlet at New York Public Library. It was reprinted in Gottlieb Wernsdorff, *Disputationes Academicae* ("Academic Disputations"), edited by Christopher Heinrich Zeibich, published by Johann Joachim Ahlfeld, Wittenberg, 1736, volume I, 294-350, copy at General Theological Seminary, New York. Am-Ende, in his sketch of Leyser's life, regarded Wernsdorff (1668-1729) as the author.

185. My microfilm copy of Weickhmann's *Apologie, Anderer Theil* is from the University of Chicago, where I first found it and where it first dawned on me that it might be possible to locate and collect the materials needed to reconstruct this comedy. The book has title page with blank verso, xviii, 496, 65, xv pages.

186. My microfilm copies of the J. A. E. *Continuation* are from Heidelberg University, and from the Bibliothek des Kammergerichts, Berlin, through the aid of the Freie Universität, Berlin; title page with blank verso, ii, 1-52 pages. J. A. E. passes over the material repeated by Weickhmann from *Justitia Causae;* but he takes the occasion to answer Wernsdorff. He makes one comment (page 32) on how Leyser toyed with his opponents in *Polygamia Triumphatrix* as a cat plays with a mouse; almost admiring. J. A. E. says that he would reveal his identity if Weickhmann would publicly discontinue his *verfahrens*—which may mean either, simply, "proceedings," or, not so simply, "legal proceedings."

187. Among the publications which carry on the discussion may be listed:

Gustav Georg Zeltner, theologian of Altorf, published

Bibliothek, Wolfenbüttel. The second edition is disting from the rare first edition by the addition of the p "Zweyte und correctere Auflage" ("Second and More Co Edition") on the title page. That description refers to printing, not to a revised text. Both have title page blank verso, [3]-15 pages.

I find the attribution of Freudenhöfer to Thomasius early as 1728 in Johan G. Schelhorn, *Amoenitates Litera* ("Literary Beauties"), Frankfurt and Leipzig, at Daniel B tholomaeus', volume 8, page 389-390, linked to the 16 episode when copies of Thomasius' *Monats Gespräc* ("Monthly Discussions") were burned by the hangman Denmark in the course of one of his controversies with Masiu and others. At that time (1691) at "Freyburg," Thomasiu published under the name Attila Friedrich Frommhold *Rechts gegründeter Bericht, wie sich ein Ehrliebender Scribent zu verhalten habe, wann eine auswärtige Herrschafft seine sonst Approbirte Schrifften durch den Hencker verbrennen zu lassen von einigen passionirten verleitet worden* ("Report of a Legal Argument, How an Honor-Loving Writer Acted with Restraint When a Foreign Government Was Misled by Some Hotheads to Have His Otherwise Approved Writings Burned by the Hangman")—copy at Halle University; my thanks to Director J. Dietze and his staff for much help.

181. My microfilm copies of "Wiernowsky" are from Dr. Karol Lewicki of the Uniwersytet Jagiellonski, Krakow; and from Göttingen and Heidelberg; title page with blank verso, [3]-14 pages. William Ignatius Schütz, flourished 1660-1689, was assessor at the Imperial Supreme Court (Kammergericht) at Speyer; author of *Manuale Pacificum,* Gotha, 1689; he speculated that women may be men's equals in intellect (Zedler).

182. My microfilm copy of Weickhmann's *Apologiae Pars Prior* is from the University Library, Erlangen-Nürnberg; title page, ix, 3-345, xxiii.

Meletema Theologicum de Typo Polygamiae in N. Test. Abolito, "Theological Dissertation of Typological Polygamy Abolished under the New Testament," August, 1720, reported in the *Unschuldige Nachrichten,* 1720, pages 161-162.

Antonius van den Heuvel on June 27, 1721 submitted for his doctorate a *Dissertatio Juridica Inauguralis de Concubinatu,* at Leyden, a bare outline of an "Inaugural Juridical Dissertation on Concubinage," 14 pages plus five pages of verses in Dutch and Latin (New York Public Library).

In 1723 was published the book by Lütke discussed above, discussed in *Unschuldige Nachrichten,* 1724, 1061-1063. At Helmstedt in 1724 Polycarp Leyser (another of that name) as *praeses,* with Ludolph Paul Müller, held a disputation *De Limitibus Qui Jurisconsultis a Theologis Ponuntur,* "On the Limits Set by Theologians on Jurists," aiming to circumscribe Thomasius and his adherents in their comments on concubinage; reported in *Unschuldige Nachrichten,* 1724, page 593.

In 1728 Johan Michael Lorenzius published a *Dissertatio de Polygamia in Vetere Foedere Expressa Lege Prohibita* ("Dissertation on Polygamy Prohibited by Express Law in the Old Testament"), listed in Schott's edition of Lipen's Bibliography (see note 147). In 1735 there was another printing of the 1712/1717 Amyraut.

Another scion of the Leyser clan, Augustin Leyser, adverted to this theme several times in his voluminous works. In March 1736 Carolus Ferdinandus Zschochius was his respondent in a disputation for highest law honors *De Concubinatu Individuo,* "On Individual Concubinage," a brief outline after Thomasius, printed by Eichsfeld at Wittenberg in 28 pages; copy at New York Public Library. On December 13, 1736 Augustin Leyser was *praeses,* Albinus Ernestus Ulricus of Dresden, respondent, in a *Disputatio Iuridica de Polygamia, von der Viel-Weiberey,* printed by Eichsfeld at Wittenberg, where the disputation was held, [3]-26 pages; also following Thomasius, challenging the death penalty in bigamy; my microfilm copy from Copenhagen Royal Library.

In September 1739 Sigismund Jacob Baumgarten was

praeses, Benjamin Christophorus Hermann of Grüneberg respondent and author of a *Dissertatio Theologica de Polygamia Simultanea Illegitima, inprimis etiam ex numero hominum utriusque sexus in tellure fere aequali* ("Theological Dissertation of Simultaneous Polygamy as Illegitimate, Especially Since the Number of Persons on Earth of Both Sexes Is About Equal"), printed at Halle by Johan Christ. Grunert; focussing on Daphnaeus Arcuarius; with appendixes by Baumgarten and by Johan Gottlob Krüger; in which theology is mixed with statistics and algebra, 34, vi pages. My microfilm is from the Royal Library, Copenhagen; there is also a copy at Swift Library, University of Chicago.

In 1742 Delany's *Reflections* were published in German at Danzig, leading to the book by the Prémontvals, 1751-1752, and its German version in 1753-1754 (see note 132 above). Am-Ende and Clugius on Leyser, 1748, and the articles in Zedler's *Lexicon* belong in this sequence.

In the *Pastoral Sammlungen* ("Pastoral Collections") published at Frankfurt and Leipzig by Wolfgang Ludwig Spring's Heirs and Johan Gottlieb Garbe, 1750-1752, appeared a series of articles recapitulating these issues. In the Fünfter Theil, Part Five, 1750, pages 1-260, appeared Johann Philip Mehrling's *Abhandlung von der Sündlichkeit der Polygamie und des Concubinats zu allen Zeiten und allen Personen, welche jemals darin gelebet haben, oder noch leben,* "Discussion of the Sinfulness of Polygamy and Concubinage for all Times and All People Who Have Ever Lived Therein or Still Do." Mehrling was a Lutheran pastor.

In the Achter Theil, Part Eight, 1751, pages 157-359, there are animadversions by several critics dissenting from Mehrling not in principle but in details, and his answers.

In 1752 there appeared *Beytrag zu Johann Philip Fresenii Pastoral-Sammlungen,* Frankfurt and Leipzig, published by Johan Gottlieb Garbe ("Supplement to Fresenius' Pastoral Collections"). Part I, pages 1-228, *Gedancken von der Vielweiberey besonders der Patriarchen,* "Thoughts on Polygamy, Especially of the Patriarchs," were the questions of a doubter sent to Mehrling, the doubter's name not given. On pages 229-592 is printed Mehrling's *Umständliche Prüfung der Gedancken von der Vielweiberey,* "Detailed Examination of Those Thoughts on Polygamy."

The foregoing *Pastoral-Sammlungen* are at the Harvard-Andover Theological Library. The University of Pennsylvania has a 1756 printing by Johann Gottlieb Garbe, at Frankfurt, of the *Beytrag* volume, with the initial title *Die Viel Weiberey nach den Wichtigsten Gründen Behauptet und durch Unumstössliche Beweise Entkräftet* ("Polygamy Affirmed on the Most Important Grounds Refuted by Indisputable Demonstrations"), pagination as in the *Beytrag,* 1-228, 229-592.

On February 7, 1758 at Leyden, Jacob van der Lely delivered a *Specimen Juridicum Inaugurale de Concubinis,* 52 pages, plus 18 pages of verses, published by Johannes Le Mair; on July 9, 1761 at Harderwyck, Johannes Winter presented his *Dissertatio Juridica Inauguralis de Concubinis,* 20 pages; both at New York Public Library.

Probably more such publications could be found, and also instances where practice went beyond theoretical discussion, as in the following cases.

The Case of Eberhard Ludwig, Duke of Würtemberg: Eberhard Ludwig (1676-1733) was married in 1697 Johanna Elizabeth von Baden; and in 1707 bigamously to Christian Wilhelmine von Grävenitz, with the pastoral benediction of (Lutheran) Phäler von Tübingen. Eberhard Ludwig declared that as reigning sovereign in Würtemberg he was accountable only to God. For twenty-five years the situation troubled local politics in Würtemberg, but it seems to have attracted little or no attention elsewhere. It is not mentioned in any of the Thomasius or Willenberg literature. A kinsman of Duke Eberhard Ludwig, Leopold Eberhard, was involved in similar matrimonial complexities, with even less attention. See Eduard Vehse, *Geschichte der Deutschen Höfe seit der Reformation,* ("History of the German Courts Since the Reformation"), Hamburg, Hoffman und Campe, 1853, volume 25.

The Case of Frederick William II, 1744-1797, who was

King of Prussia 1768-1797. In 1765 he married Elizabeth of Brunswick-Wolfenbüttel, marriage dissolved in 1769. In 1769 he married Frederica Louisa of Hesse-Darmstadt (1751-1805), with whom he had seven children. He had a liaison with Wilhelmina Enke (1733-1820) with whom he had five children, covering the fact by marrying her to his valet. "With the connivance of his court preachers he contracted, during his wife's lifetime, two morganatic marriages: in 1787 with Julie von Voss (1766-1789) whom he made Gräfin Ingelheim; and in 1790 with Countess Sophia Juliana Dörhoff 1768-1834)"—so the Encyclopedia Britannica, 1968.

188. There is a vast literature on Mormon polygamy. Recent studies include: Thomas F. O'Dea, *The Mormons,* University of Chicago Press, 1957; Leonard J. Arrington, *Great Basin Kingdom, An Economic History of the Latter Day Saints,* 1830-1900, Harvard University Press, 1958; Kimball Young, *Isn't One Wife Enough?,* Henry Holt & Co., 1954.

The polygamous community of Short Creek, Arizona, was subjected to police raiding on July 26, 1953; see the *New York Times,* July 27, 28, 29; August 2, 3, 8, 14, 19, 29; September 24, November 20, December 1 and 27, 1953. For other instances of religiously sanctioned polygamy continuing in Utah, see the *New York Times* of December 27, 1965 and following days.

The abandonment of plural marriage by the main body of Latter Day Saints was partly under the duress of a long series of prosecutions by federal government authorities. See: Ray J. Davis, "The Polygamous Prelude," in *American Journal of Legal History,* 1962, volume 6, 1-27, for a summary of these cases. While the practical thrust of these prosecutions was in favor of a woman's right to equal status, the dicta of the courts, up to and including the United States Supreme Court, tended primarily to assert the dogmas of the dominant Christian denominations against the dogmas of smaller and localized Mormon sect, and left a checkered record of interpretation as regards constitutional rights, not only on religious freedom. In the case of *Cleveland vs. United States,* 329 US 14, 1946, the Supreme Court upheld the conviction of Fundamentalist Mormons under a prosecution brought under the Mann Act, although that Act was passed against prostitution-by-compulsion, not against religiously sanctioned bigamy. The Court majority quoted an earlier decision, Mormon Church vs. United States, 1889-1890, (136 US 1, 49), written by Justice Joseph P. Bradley, saying of polygamy "It is contrary to the spirit of Christianity and of the civilization which Christianity has produced in the Western World." Justice Frank Murphy submitted an exceptional dissenting opinion in the *Cleveland* case, exceptional in that he began to make an inquiry into the cultural, social and ideological aspects of plural marriage, quite limited in scope, but still the beginning of a questioning attitude rather than accepting the dogmas of a majority sect as if they were the law of the land.

189. For example, see Alexander Spoehr's studies in Field Museum of Natural History, Chicago, Anthropological Series, 1942, volume 33, page 92.

190. Compare: Montague Slater, *The Trial of Jomo Kenyatta,* Secker & Warburg, London, 1955, page 160. Jomo Kenyatta, (later to be the first president of independent Kenya, but in 1952 put on trial for alleged complicity in the Mau Mau movement) being cross-examined by Deputy Public Prosecutor Somerhough,

"Q. Do you practice polygamy?"

"A. Yes, but I do not call it polygamy."

For a description of traditional plural marriage among the Ibo of Nigeria in the middle of the nineteenth century, see the novel *Things Fall Apart,* 1958, by Chinua Achebe. A detailed account is given by Jomo Kenyatta, *Facing Mount Kenya. The Tribal Life of the Gikuyu,* with an introduction by B. Malinowski (with whom Kenyatta was studying anthropology), London, Secker and Warburg, 1938.

A woman's point of view, quite hostile, may be seen in

Rebecca Hourwich Reyher, *Zulu Woman,* Columbia University Press, 1948 (a somewhat fictionalized biography of Christina Sibiya, born 1900, divorced wife of Zulu king Solomon, 1893-1933), and in Rebecca Hourwich Reyher, *The Fon and His Hundred Wives,* Doubleday & Co., New York, 1952.

Recent studies which are grounded in serious sociological method and statistical analysis, which also distinguish among variant customs in different areas, include:

Arthur Phillips, editor, *Survey of African Marriage and Family Life,* published for the International African Institute by Oxford University Press, 1953, xli, 462 pages; a study growing out of the problems of British missionaries.

Jacques Binet, *Le Mariage en Afrique Noire* ("Marriage in Black Africa"), published by Les Editions du Cerf, Paris, 1959, 176 pages; a study growing out of the problems of Roman Catholic (French) missionaries.

Remi Clignet, *Many Wives, Many Powers. Authority and Power in Polygynous Families,* Northwestern University Press, Evanston, Illinois, 1970, 380 pages.

191. Among the adherents of the Jewish synagogue, the patriarchal-Biblical tradition of plural marriage had considerably but not completely faded away in practice by the time Judea and Galilee became Roman provinces, and was further inhibited by Roman civil law. It may possibly have been encouraged during the era of the rise of Islam. In Jewish religious law, the formal abolition of polygamy is associated with a synod led by Rabbi Gershom Ben Yehudah (960-1040), whose zone of activity was mainly in the Rhine valley, but whose ban was quickly and generally accepted as binding everywhere.

192. Angie Elizabeth Brooks, of Liberia, President of the 24th General Assembly of the United Nations, in a signed statement, *New York Times,* January 30, 1970, described the status of the Fon's wives at the time of the United Nations inquiry as being involuntary slavery.

In Langston Hughes, *An African Treasury,* Crown Publishers, New York, 1960, which has other materials on African plural marriage, there is a short story, *Anticipation,* by Mabel Dove-Danquah of Ghana, telling how Nana Adaku II, an Omanhene, celebrating the twentieth anniversary of his accession to the stool, aged 55, bored with his forty wives, pays the bride price for a girl who attracts him, only to discover that he had already married her two years previously.

193. Compare the attitude of Rev. David H. Barrett, of the Anglican church, associated with church mission activity in Nairobi, quoted in the *New York Times,* May 31, 1971, "For 150 years the Western churches have waged an all-out effort to get rid of polygamy and found it unchangeable. Now it's time for Africans to produce an African Christian marriage pattern."

Plural marriage as a customary institution figures in contemporary novels by African authors; for example, T. M. Aluko, *One Man, One Wife* (1959) and his *Kinsman and Foreman* (1966) referring to 1950; Nkem Kwanko, *Danda* (1964) referring to 1949; Khadambi Asalache, *A Calabash of Life* (1967) referring to Kenya of the past but seen through present day eyes; and it is the main theme in *The Polygamist,* by Ndabaningi Sithole (1972) referring to recent Rhodesia. Ideological aspects are discussed by John S. Mbiti, *African Religions and Philosophy,* Praeger Publishers, New York, 1964, pages 127, 142-145.

In the August 7, 1971 issue of the New York Amsterdam News, the most important newspaper in the United States serving primarily the Black (to use the term currently popular) community, a member of its editorial board, Carlos Russell, addressing himself to the problems of family structure in the development of "Black nationhood" in the United States, in an article headed *Is Polygamy the Answer?* asserted: "My position, as of now, is that the new nation will have to move towards the institutionalization of polygamy (one man with two or more wives) as the basis for its familial structure." He argues the validity of the African tradition; that, with the excess mortality among males, "It would seem to follow that the present societal norm of one male to one woman would not guarantee the survival of our people"; and that tens of thousands of "minority" children now in government shelters and foster homes "would be naturally taken care of" in polygamous families. Mr. Russell called for the beginning of a dialogue. Only one answer was forthcoming, *Monogamy vs polygamy,* in the issue of November 6, 1971, rejecting polygamy as an outmoded form based on an outmoded economic system; it was signed by a woman, Connie Carter.

In *Ebony,* a popular monthly with nationwide circulation, issue of March 1972, vol. XXVII, no. 5, an article by Jacquelyne J. Jackson, Ph.D., (associate professor of medical sociology, Duke University Medical Center, Durham, N.C.), considering various remedies to the imbalance of men and women, "Where Are the Black Men?" included these suggestions:

"Another solution to the sex-ratio problem might be the continuing development of alternative family forms, including that of polygyny (marriage of one male to two or more females), a system appropriate in the absence of a sufficient supply of males. Polygyny, of course, requires males who can adequately *support* several families. And, at the present time, few black males are economically equipped to participate in such an arrangement. Moreover, such a system is not an acceptable solution for most black females. Nevertheless, as some observers have indicated in private conversations, with the writer, the legitimacy of polygyny could well benefit some females who are involved in 'playing polygyny' but who legally are denied any of the benefits to which they might otherwise be entitled.

"On a recent visit to Kampala, Uganda, the vice-chancellor of Makerere University noted, in defense of polygyny, that the women participating as spouses had a legal status of wife, not that of mistress or concubine. Thus, not only were the children not "illegitimate" but both the women and their children had legal protection under the law which he regarded as a more civilized system than that existing in the United States. He may have a point worth further investigation. In any case, it is quite clear that there is not one absolute system of marriage and family which must be adhered to at any cost and under any circumstances. Such is true even for white Americans."

INDEX

This is a *selective* index. To avoid excessive length, which would defeat its utility, it is restricted mainly to names significant in this history as actors, as authors, or as authorities to whom these appealed; or where some particular notice or cross-reference is desirable. Names included in the text for completeness whose significance does not go beyond the immediate context are omitted from this index (contributors of verses to seventeenth century dissertations, sundry relatives and miscellaneous associates).

Bibliography: since so much of the book is bibliographical, it is impractical to repeat titles of books, names of publishers and printers, and places of publication, in the index or in a separate tabulation.